War, Prosperity and Depression

The U.S. Economy 1917–45

War, Prosperity and Depression

The U.S. Economy 1917–45

PETER FEARON

University Press of Kansas

© Peter Fearon 1987

First published in the United Kingdom 1987 by Philip Allan Publishers Limited
First published in the United States of America 1987 by the University Press of Kansas
(Lawrence, Kansas 66045), which was organized by the Kansas Board of Regents and is
operated and funded by Emporia State University, Fort Hays State University, Kansas State
University, Pittsburg State University, the University of Kansas, and Wichita State University

Library of Congress Cataloging-in-Publication Data
Fearon, Peter.
  War, prosperity, and depression.

  Bibliography: p.
  Includes index.
  1. United States — Economic conditions — 1918–1945
I. Title.
HC106.2.F42 1987   330.973′091   87-21571
ISBN 0-7006-0348-4
ISBN 0-7006-0349-2 (pbk.)

Printed in the United Kingdom

10 9 8 7 6 5 4 3 2 1

Contents

Preface

The aim of this book is to describe and analyse one of the most fascinating periods of economic turmoil in American history. It is written in plain English and therefore does not require familiarity with professional jargon or a formal grasp of economics. Those who wish to pursue particular topics in a more detailed way, however, will find bibliographical guides at the end of each chapter.

The era from 1917 to 1945 includes the Great Depression, an event whose economic and social significance is only marginally less than that of the two world wars which encapsulate it. Beginning in 1929, America was transformed. A decade of expanding national wealth gave way to one of despair induced by mass unemployment, bread lines, bank failures, eviction and farm misery. Over half a century later, the memories of hard times remain vivid for those who lived through the 1930s.

The continuing flow of literature on the causes and consequences of this unprecedented economic collapse and the vigour of the debate on its causes is testimony to the intellectual challenge which it still presents. For some, the possibility that such a crisis could recur is ever present. During the 1980s, stock market speculation, bank insolvency, high levels of debt and farm foreclosures have intensified these fears. It is quite possible that a study of recent history could give a greater insight into today's economic problems.

The challenge of the Depression was met, as most people know, by the New Deal. However, many of the policies instituted to correct the serious economic imbalance proved inadequate, and some were even counterproductive. High levels of unemployment still prevailed as late as 1941, eight years after Franklin Delano Roosevelt's first inauguration. It was World War II, not Roosevelt's peacetime policies, which created full employment and farm prosperity.

The Depression and the New Deal lie at the heart of this volume. However, an understanding of both the causes of this economic catastrophe and the rationale behind governmental responses to it requires an analysis of the preceding decade. An investigation of the 1920s, of course, reveals in graphic detail both the strengths and the weaknesses of the American economy. At the end of World War I the

United States emerged not only as the world's foremost industrial power, but also as the greatest creditor nation. During the 1920s the performance of the US economy aroused international admiration. In addition, high levels of imports combined with liberal lending overseas to ensure the buoyancy of the international economy.

The chapters on the 1920s account for the prevailing prosperity; they also show that this largesse was not evenly distributed, either between or within the rural and urban sectors. The role played by money and banking is treated in a separate chapter, so as to introduce gradually this important but potentially confusing field. Thus the scene is set for a more complete grasp of the complex causes of the Depression.

All history enthusiasts expect a clear chronological account of the period under review. In addition to satisfying that demand, this book poses key questions and seeks to answer them. Which groups of Americans gained most from the prosperity of the twenties? How did the Depression begin? Why did it become so severe? Could it have been avoided? Were the New Deal policies effective? Can we judge historical events with the benefit of hindsight, or should we temper any criticism by recognising the difficulties that contemporary decision makers faced? Why did war deliver the economic security that the New Deal reforms could not? The list of questions on this period could go on. Historians do not merely describe events, they must also investigate and explain.

There are few, if any, books which examine the American economy between 1917 and 1945. Most authors concentrate on the period from the end of World War I to the Wall Street crash of 1929, or on the depression years up to Pearl Harbor. For economic historians, however, there is a neat unity in the time span I have chosen. By focusing on the period from the start of World War I through the end of World War II, the reader can more clearly follow the ebb and flow of the economy and will gain a deeper appreciation of the forces pushing a nation towards instability. Moreover, the changing role of government in economic matters and the adaptation of institutions to new circumstances are all better illustrated if war, prosperity, depression and recovery are woven together.

In attempting to interpret some highly technical literature in clear and simple form, I have decided to avoid the distraction of footnotes. Periodically, there are references in the text to authors whose work I have found particularly valuable and who have made important contributions to controversies. The bibliographies which follow each chapter are thorough and up-to-date. They are designed to enable the exploration of themes which, because of space limitations, could not be pursued in great detail. The social, as well as the economic, historian should find these citations of great value.

I should like to express my thanks to the British Academy for the generous provision of grants which enabled me to undertake research in the United States. My gratitude is also due to colleagues who surrendered their valuable time in order to read all or part of the book in manuscript. D. H. Aldcroft, I. G. Bradley, J. G. Clark, M. Hoskins, D. M. Katzman, S. B. Saul and T. Wilson all made valuable contributions and gave me much encouragement. I benefited enormously from the clerical skills of Gillian Austen, who, assisted by Margaret Christie, produced many drafts with speed and accuracy. The greatest debt, however, is owed to my wife, Tricia, who has read through many variations of this book with patience and skill. She has repeatedly asked the sort of question that occurs only to the intelligent non-specialist and has also done her best to transform my literary style into clear English. It is to her that this book is dedicated.

Peter Fearon
Leicester
July 1987

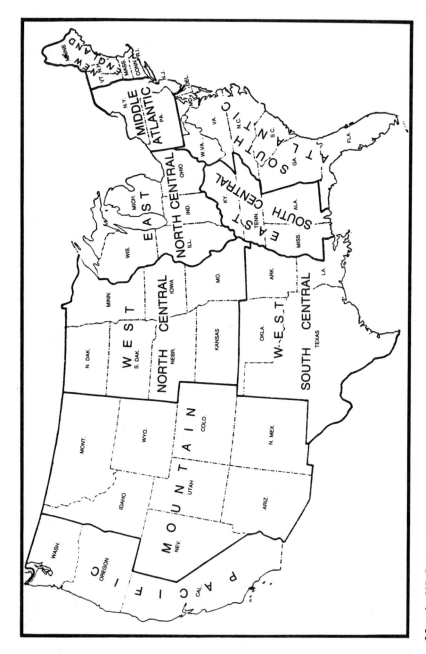

Map 1 US Geographic Divisions

x

PART I

World War I and the 1920s

1

War and 'Normalcy': 1914–29

In 1914, when Europe embarked upon its internecine struggle, the US was already the world's leading industrial power. From the middle of the nineteenth century, the expansion of her manufacturing sector had transformed her economy to such an extent that the US accounted for nearly 56 per cent of world manufacturing output, followed by Germany with 16 per cent and Britain with 14 per cent. This growth had been made possible by a combination of exceptionally favourable circumstances which encouraged the exploitation of America's abundant national resources. A rapid rise in population had created a mass market, especially in the cities where the influx of rural Americans, attracted by the economic and social challenge of urban life, was augmented by the millions of European immigrants of working age who were flooding into the country.

Manufacturing and services provided new jobs for the growing population. Between 1900 and 1914, the employed farm labour force was static in number, while non-farm labour expanded from 16 million to 25 million. Native Americans and the foreign-born formed not just an industrially motivated workforce, but also a body of avid consumers. Relatively high per capita incomes acted as a powerful stimulus to industrial expansion; the tastes and the purchasing power of urban consumers dictated what industry should produce. Visiting Europeans were quick to notice the lead which the US possessed in the mass production and consumer durable industries.

Concomitant with the growth of manufacturing industry was the rise to preeminence of big business. Beginning in the 1870s, firms were buffeted by the powerful forces of falling prices and increasing competition, from which no one was isolated as the railroad system expanded. Companies with high fixed costs were particularly vulnerable to commercial assault. Self-preservation drove many to seek means of minimising competition; the implementation of pooling arrangements, for example, become common. Many firms, however, became convinced that the greatest guarantee of security was an increase in size, which could most easily be achieved through merger.

3

The advantage of the large unit was that, by the implementation of mass production methods and vertical integration, it could manufacture at a lower unit cost. As companies increased in size and grew less numerous, however, their attitudes to competition changed. It was soon realised that if a few large corporations waged a price war it could mean ruin for them all. In industries where oligopoly prevailed, therefore, the cut and thrust of competition was often replaced by collusion.

The decline of the family firm in favour of the large corporation created a need for professional managers. Fortunately, the railroads, which had been the largest businesses in the world during the nineteenth century, had produced a distinct managerial class. These professional managers employed techniques which were far more sophisticated than any in Europe; many large corporations used work study teams, for example, as an aid to greater efficiency. Management was wedded to the idea of efficiency and the means of achieving it, pioneered by Frederick W. Taylor, the father of scientific management. Indeed, management science had reached such a degree of acceptance that it was taught in the most prestigious universities.

Big business was advantageously placed to expoit the new technology which became available during this period. US industrial success was made possible, in part, by great advances in production techniques which improved the efficiency of labour. High productivity was essential if workers were to receive high wages and their output was to be sold in quantity at home and overseas. The determination to reduce costs led to the manufacture and use of specialised machinery, based upon the existing expertise in standardisation and interchangeable parts. This was the lineage of Henry Ford's continuous assembly line.

Industrial enterprises were not spread evenly across the US; some states had a far greater commitment to manufacturing than had others (Figure 1.1). In general, industry was concentrated in the East North Central and Middle Atlantic states. Large areas, for example the South and the Mountain states, made little contribution to manufacturing growth except by the release of their surplus population to the cities.

A more cost effective and efficient system of distribution was needed to make the increasing number and diversity of goods readily available. Innovations in retailing were a natural consequence of changing consumer tastes strongly influenced by urban expansion. The growth of mail order houses and big department stores was the result of the revolution in mass retailing which came to fruition in American cities and which enabled consumers to benefit greatly from the wider range of merchandise and the lower prices at which it was sold.

As we have seen, the period of rapid industrialisation after 1870 had not been tranquil. Industry had experienced a period of price competition which was so intense that many survivors came to regard it as destabilising. They came to the conclusion that co-operation with rivals was not only desirable but possible where oligopoly existed. The growth of oligopoly power, however, caused resentment against the big corporations, evident not only among workers but also among

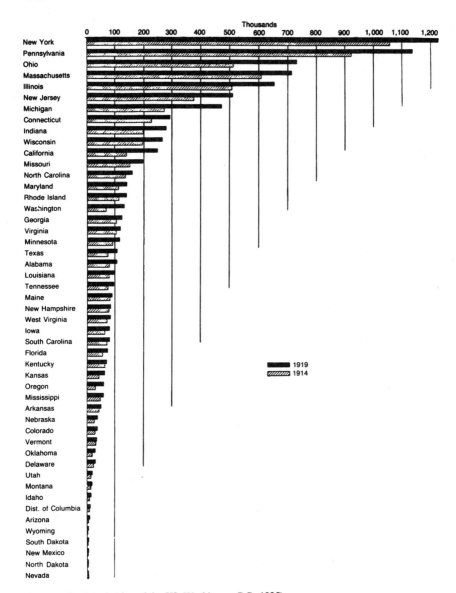

Source: Statistical Atlas of the US (Washington DC, 1925).

Figure 1.1 Average Number of Wage Earners, by States, 1919 and 1914

farmers, small businesses and political reformers. From the 1880s until war pressures were too fierce to withstand, there was a strong anti-monopoly movement in the US, spearheaded by the Populist and Progressive movements. With equal vehemence, the farmers opposed the powerful banking houses which had provided financial services for big business and the railroads. Farm feelings ran high against eastern money and industrial interests whose collusion, it was believed, resulted in cheap finance for large corporations but discrimination against the small operator.

One response of smaller businesses, which were also searching for stability in a period of rapid economic change, was to form trade associations. Members of these trade associations could exchange useful information, fight organised labour together, curtail competition which might be considered unfair and organise pressure groups to lobby politicians. Several hundreds of groupings were in existence before the war and were held by their supporters to be a sensible American middle way between cut-throat competition, which was anarchical, and monopoly, which was equally undesirable. Even commercially minded farmers used this device: by 1913, 3,099 agricultural marketing and purchasing co-operatives had been formed.

Unlike Britain, but like France and Germany, the US had a large agricultural sector. In 1914, 33 per cent of Amercia's population lived on 6.4 million farms, and agriculture supplied not only the cities with fresh food but also many manufacturing industries, such as food processing, cotton textiles and cigarettes, with raw materials. While France and Germany were agriculturally self-sufficient, the US, alone amongst leading industrial nations, had a farm surplus so large that it accounted for nearly half the value of all exports. Foreign markets were vital to the wellbeing of many American farmers. To the flow of agricultural products overseas we can add exports of machinery and manufactured goods. Imports of certain raw materials (for example, rubber and silk) and even manufactures were, however, essential, for even the US was not totally self-sufficient. Nevertheless, the value of exports exceeded imports and was sufficiently large to offset losses on invisible trade.

Throughout much of the preceding century, as domestic savings had been insufficient to finance economic growth, America had borrowed from Europe, especially Britain, so that in 1914 she was the world's leading debtor nation. From the turn of the century, however, US finance houses had themselves been engaged in overseas investment; by 1914, US foreign holdings had reached roughly half the value of the $7.2bn which had been lent to her. One advantage of the export of US capital was that before 1914, investment banks, such as the House of Morgan, had acquired considerable expertise in handling international transactions to add to their formidable domestic experience of financing mergers and underwriting share issues.

In 1914 the US was a vigorous, high wage economy, capable of either taking European inventions, such as the automobile, and adapting them to the American market or exploiting to the full the ideas of her own people. The new world, for example, saw the first ever powered flight which the Wright Brothers achieved in 1903. By the outbreak of the war, however, the age of the ruthless, individualistic entrepreneur, which had been a feature of the late nineteenth century, was being replaced by one in which corporate organisation and associational activities were becoming increasingly important (Hawley, 1979).

The United States during World War I

Even though the US did not enter the war until April 1917, the economy was affected by it from the beginning. The initial impact was one of uncertainty; exports to and imports from the old world shrank and domestic financial markets reacted sharply to the increased international anxiety. There was great concern in the markets which dealt with cotton and tobacco as these were commodities which were heavily dependent upon overseas trade. Once it was clear that the conflict would not be over by Christmas 1914, demands from Europe for munitions, raw materials and foodstuffs rose rapidly. Unlike 1941, the economy had no pool of unemployed to call on; indeed, hostilities had substantially reduced the flow of immigrants from Europe on which industry had come to depend.

Although the US officially adopted a neutral stance, the nation as a whole was more sympathetic to the Allied cause than to the German. Britain and France wanted to buy some of America's industrial and agricultural abundance and could do this, before the US entered the war, by paying in gold. As their limited gold reserves diminished, additional financial resources had to be found. US investments of Allied nationals were confiscated and sold; and in addition, money was borrowed from private American citizens. Britain and France used the banking house of J. P. Morgan to arrange their loans and co-ordinate their purchases. About $2bn was borrowed before April 1917, to which can be added approximately $3bn realised by the sale of investments. Most of this $5bn was spent in the US and acted as a great stimulus to the economy which more than made up for the loss of exports to Germany.

There were other pressures to which the economy had to respond. Substitutes had to be produced to replace lost imports. The inability to purchase German dyestuffs on which the US had been dependent in 1914 led to the growth of a new domestic industry. With European shipping diverted, ocean routes previously dominated by Britain and Germany were taken over by the US and also by Japan. Once the war was over this trade did not revert to old-world carriers, as Britain learned to her cost. The war led to a rapid growth of the US merchant fleet, built in order to exploit these opportunities. Indeed, the hostilities forced America to trade directly with many primary producing countries, whereas before 1914 these imports had often come by way of Europe.

In order to produce the goods demanded at home and abroad more workers were needed. The manufacturing labour force rose from 8.2 million in 1914, to 9.6 million in 1916 and to 10.2 million in 1918. This was in spite of the fact that immigration was substantiallly reduced and that eventually an army of four million was raised. The growth was achieved by a shift of workers from agriculture to industry and, as in Europe, by the employment of women in jobs traditionally the preserve of males. In addition, migration played a key role in allocating labour. Northern industrialists wanted workers, and the region where labour was most obviously in surplus was the South, where the prevailing wages were the lowest in the country. Between 1910 and 1920, about 650,000 whites and 550,000 blacks left the South with the bulk of the migration occurring after 1915. These migrants were not always refugees from the farm. About half were urban dwellers, many with experience in mining or in the steel industry. So desperate was the need for labour that recruiters travelled to the southern states and their success caused an increase in southern wage rates which, however, proved to be temporary (Wright, 1986). Blacks, of course, were attracted not only by the relatively high rates of pay in the North, but also by the less racially oppressive atmosphere.

Labour shortages in industry affected wages. Average annual earnings for manufacturing workers rose steadily from $580 in 1914, to $980 in 1918, before reaching a peak of $1,358 in 1920. Even though consumer prices had increased by 50 per cent by 1918 and had practically doubled by 1920, these workers made considerable gains, the more so as their hours of work were reduced. Especially fortunate were the unskilled who, because of an erosion of pay differentials, moved closer to the remuneration of the skilled. Nevertheless, not all non-farm employees saw their trades expand or their pay rise faster than inflation. Between 1916 and 1918 the volume of construction contracted by 40 per cent. The industry employed 1.3 million workers in 1914 but only 0.93 million in 1918. Some professional groups also experienced declining living standards. Teachers' pay, for example, was fixed for long periods and did not follow rapid changes in the cost of living. On the whole, however, there was a sharp decline in wealth inequality during World War I as disadvantaged groups made relatively greater gains.

Between 1914 and 1919 the physical volume of manufacturing output rose by 26 per cent, the most rapid rate of increase coming in the first two years. Output then dipped during 1919, and recovered in 1920, before falling to its 1913 level in 1921. The basis of this expansion was the growth of the manufacturing workforce, for although productivity did rise during the war years, it did not do so spectacularly. Increased manufacturing investment, though substantial, was not enough to produce war goods without price rises and, especially during the 1917–18 period, a substantial shift of resources from civilian to military use. Indeed, during this crucial period after the US entered the war, most of the gains in production were at the expense of the civilian economy (Clark, 1931; Soule, 1947). If we put the performance of the manufacturing sector between 1914 and 1919 into historical perspective it is far from outstanding. During the period 1899–1919 the physical volume of output grew erratically, rising by 22 per cent between 1899 and 1904, by 30 per cent between 1904 and 1909, and by 6 per cent between 1909 and 1914. These fluctuations reflect the economic conditions during which measurements were taken, but nevertheless we can note that the level of growth achieved from 1914 to 1919 was less than that for 1904 to 1909, a period of peace.

If we consider those manufacturing industries which grew most spectacularly during the war, the motor industry stands above the rest. The volume of output in this industry had quadrupled by 1919; associated industries, such as rubber goods with a near threefold increase and petroleum refining which doubled, also benefited (Figure 1.2). Moreover, these three industries increased their efficiency

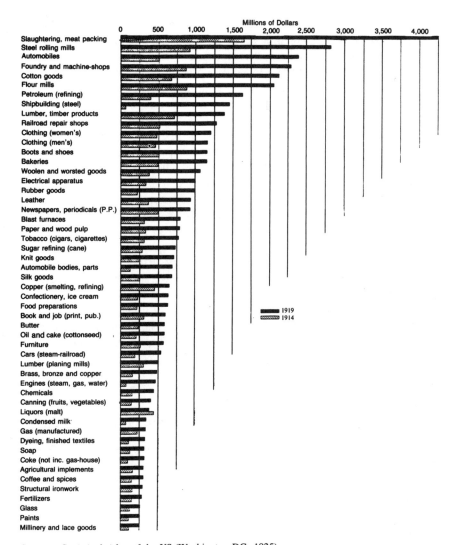

Source: *Statistical Atlas of the US* (Washington DC, 1925).

Figure 1.2 Value of Products for Leading Industries, 1919 and 1914

and were amongst the most successful at absorbing inflationary pressures (Mills, 1932). Passenger car sales, which had tripled between 1914 and 1917, declined susbtantially during the following year as a result of government restrictions. By the end of the war there was a pent-up demand for automobiles which the manufacturers were able to exploit during the 1920s.

War dramatically improved the income of the American farmer who had, in any case, been favoured with good times since the last years of the nineteenth .

century. The Allies wanted food and raw materials and naturally turned to the US as provider. There was little scope for increasing the number of farms by 1914, or for raising productivity, as the tractor age was in its infancy. Agricultural output, in spite of great attempts to increase it, remained fairly constant between 1914 and 1920; one result of this was that farm prices rose faster than non-farm prices to the great satisfaction of producers. The average net income that each farm received from its farming operations rose from $649 in 1914 to $1,370 in 1918. Not all this diverse group had an equal share of the benefits: the producers of grains, tobacco and hogs in particular were most fortunate. The rise in agricultural prices led to a rapid growth in land values which, in turn, encouraged the farmer to borrow. It also guaranteed a loan since land was the farmer's collateral. Some farmers sold out and even at historically high prices there was always someone willing to buy the land, so great was rural optimism. Total farm mortgage debt had been $4.7mn in 1914; it rose to $6.5mn in 1918 and $8.4mn in 1920 before the post-war depression set in (Chapter 2). War pressures had also led to a doubling of farm workers' wages by 1918.

Inflation affected both belligerents and non-belligerents during the war, and in the immediate post-war years. An indication of how the demands of war affected the prices of some key US commodities can be seen in Table 1.1. It is noticeable that the price of wheat and wool began to rise from the moment that war commenced in Europe. Prices continued to rise until 1920 when, except for anthracite coal, a sharp fall took place which was most pronounced in agricultural com-

Table 1.1 Wholesale Prices of Selected Commodities, 1913–23 ($ per unit)

	Wheat	Cotton, raw	Wool	Coal, anthracite	Steel rails	Brick
	Bu.	lb	lb	ton	100 lb	1,000
1913	0.81	0.13	0.56	5.3	30.0	6.6
1914	0.94	0.12	0.59	5.3	30.0	5.5
1915	1.29	0.10	0.71	5.6	33.3	6.1
1916	1.33	0.15	0.85	5.9	40.0	8.0
1917	2.30	0.24	1.57	6.9	56.0	8.9
1918	2.12	0.32	1.82	8.3	49.3	11.9
1919	2.42	0.33	1.78	9.5	53.8	16.0
1920	2.46	0.34	1.60	10.5	45.7	21.9
1921	1.33	0.15	0.83	10.6	40.7	15.2
1922	1.21	0.21	1.24	10.9	43.0	17.3
1923	1.11	0.29	1.38	11.4	43.0	19.8

Source: Historical Statistics of US Colonial Times to 1970, 2 vols (Washington DC, 1975), Series E123, 126, 127, 129, 130, 134.

modities. The rate of inflation was at its most rapid before the US entered the war, after which its pace moderated, a tribute, perhaps, to price controls.

That prices rose when there was an almost insatiable international demand for all that US farms and factories could produce is not surprising. Price rises could easily be passed on to the Allies but, of course, American citizens had to pay these prices too. Wage increases were necessary, therefore, to maintain, let alone increase, living standards. There were other inflationary pressures. The gold which flooded into the country as part payment for exports infiltrated both circulation and the money supply, which had increased, by April 1917, by 45 per cent. Friedman and Schwartz (1963) maintain that this expanding money supply was the primary cause of the 65 per cent rise in wholesale prices. After US entry into the war, the methods of financing Allied war purchases were changed. The US government now extended credits which amounted to £7.3bn by the end of the war; a further $2.2bn was added in the post-war period. At the same time as she directly aided her European allies, the US also had to finance her own war effort. Income tax was raised as were taxes on profits, estates and a whole range of goods and services. In spite of these efforts a large budget deficit was unavoidable. The federal budget moved from a small surplus in 1916 to a deficit of $853mn, the largest since the Civil War, in 1917; the following year's deficit was $9bn and that of 1919 over $13bn. The national debt, which for decades had hovered round the $1bn mark, had, by 1919, reached $25bn. In spite of increased revenues, only 27 per cent of war expenditure was covered by taxes, the rest was borrowed. During 1917 and 1918, the Treasury, assisted by a powerful advertising campaign, persuaded the public to purchase $17bn worth of bonds issued as four Liberty Loans; the 1919 Victory Loan raised an additional $4.5bn. The purchase of war bonds became a symbol of patriotism; those who failed to lend their money to the government could, if the news became public, be subject to abuse.

America's central bank, the Federal Reserve, had been established in 1913 and amongst its objectives were: the maintenance of the gold standard, the curbing of speculation, the provision of sufficient credit for legitimate business, and the stabilisation of interest rates. During the war, these aspirations were of secondary importance to the task of helping the Treasury finance the military machine. The Federal Reserve supplied member banks with ample reserves so that the Treasury was able to borrow what it needed at low rates of interest. The Fed also implored banks to buy government securities or lend, on favourable terms, to any person or institution willing to borrow in order to purchase them. All this was highly inflationary and resulted in a sharp increase in the money supply. The Federal Reserve's expansionary credit policies continued in 1919, as did inflation.

In every war government control over resources increases, and this conflict was no exception. Even before the US became directly involved, there was a growing lobby for industrial mobilisation as a precautionary measure in case America was drawn into the battle. In August 1916 a Council of National Defence was formed. It spawned a number of special committees which investigated the economic and logistical problems which would confront the country if a large army had to be raised and sent to Europe. In addition, the military capacity of industry was assessed and the possibility of governmental controls over the economy debated. The Council of National Defence and its committees brought many businessmen to Washington DC where they stayed for the duration of the war. They were 'dollar-a-year men', released by their companies to work for the government for a token fee. The federal government did not have a large civil service and lacked the expertise necessary to organise the economy for a modern war. Business executives were, therefore, welcomed with open arms.

Military orders inevitably favour large companies — they are in the best position to promise speedy delivery on tanks, trucks and munitions. The crusade against monopoly which the government had waged before the war was, therefore, soon abandoned. It is interesting to note that Franklin Roosevelt performed a similar U-turn once World War II began. Working with a spirit of patriotic fervour, which was also financially advantageous, business stressed co-operation rather than competition — an attitude which was consistent with pre-war ideals. Now, however, the majority believed that co-operation extended not only to fellow producers but to the government and to trade unions which supported the war. The government itself looked favourably on any device that would ensure stability; a new concept of the public interest enabled, even encouraged, firms to collude. There was a near unanimous view in Washington that war and the vigorous pursuit of anti-trust ideas were incompatible.

Thus we see that before America's war began, businessmen who were supporters of the trade association movement and those who had been plucked from the desks of large corporations had moved into very influential positions. These were individuals to whom unfettered competition was abhorrent; when the government became the largest single employer of labour their ascendancy was already assured. Indeed the war abolished competition. Any business which could produce what the government wanted would get a guaranteed sale, and a guaranteed profit. For several years industry, labour and the government were locked together in an economy which provided full employment, high profits and rising output.

Even before April 1917, it was clear that the best method of allocating scarce resources was to adopt a modified version of the war socialist economy which was already in operation in Europe. The free market could not deliver goods at the right price or in the desired quantities. Food supplies were a serious problem as agricultural output in Europe continued to decline and as the German submarine campaign hampered shipments. The US government wanted to encourage a rise in production, eliminate waste so that more would be available to send to Europe, shift farmers from less important to more essential crops, control speculation and make distribution more efficient. It was also realised that if food purchases by all the Allies could be co-ordinated, this would obviously give buyers a far greater control over prices than if there was a free-for-all. The government moved quickly in this direction because at a time of escalating farm prices, policies to moderate their increases assumed a new importance. In August 1917 the Lever Food Control Act gave President Wilson the power to control not only food but also fuel and fertilizer supplies. To translate these powers into action the US Food Administration was created, headed by an energetic organiser who had already made his fortune as a mining engineer — Herbert Hoover.

The Food Administration did not introduce direct price control on foodstuffs but went about its complex task by using a variety of techniques. Consumers were subjected to an advertising campaign which urged them, for example, to cut down on meat and wheat consumption, to grow vegetables, and to consider the harmful effects of wasteful habits and of hoarding. This appealed to Hoover because people were voluntarily becoming involved in the war effort to their own satisfaction and to the nation's profit. In the battle to achieve greater efficiency, many agreements were made with both farm and business organisations. The Food Administration was also a regulatory agency, with power to license and to control operators. Using its authority to buy and sell produce, a guaranteed price was offered to wheat growers through the newly created US Grain Corporation. An attempt was made to stimulate the production of hogs by fixing their price in relation to that of corn, their principal feedstuff. Food prices continued to rise under Hoover's agency, but he emerged from the war with great credit. The publicity drives had made him widely known as a tireless worker with strong humanitarian principles. Hoover himself was impressed by the success of voluntarism during the war; people had responded to challenge and to the opportunity to help themselves.

In 1917 and 1918 there was a proliferation of regulatory agencies. The US Fuel Administration fixed coal prices, the Emergency Fleet Corporation built ships, and the US Housing Corporation constructed housing for defence workers. Washington even became directly involved in labour issues, not surprising when we consider that it was the country's major employer, and welcomed the support of the American Federation of Labour for the war effort. Sam Gompers, the President of AFL, won concessions which increased the power and the prestige of affiliated unions, whilst those labour organisations which opposed the war, for example the Industrial Workers of the World (IWW), faced increasing isolation and harassment. Key AFL officials were given positions on important committees; firms working on government contracts were obliged to recognise unions and accept collective bargaining. The National War Labor Board (April 1918) was established to adjudicate on industrial disputes. Union leaders in the US were not more successful in preventing all strikes than were those in Europe, but full employment, their identification with a national cause, and employer tolerance led to a steady expansion in membership during the war. AFL membership was approximately two million in 1914; it rose to 2.8 million in 1918 and by 1920 had topped the 4 million mark. This was an expansion that could not have taken place without the war.

The industrial counterpart to the Food Administration was the War Industries Board (WIB), which achieved a new prominence when the financier Bernard

Baruch assumed its chairmanship in the spring of 1918. The WIB had wide-ranging powers to set priorities and even to fix prices; it could also commandeer plants if such action were deemed necessary. In order to increase output and efficiency, raw material supplies were directed from low to high priority areas. A drive to force standardisation upon industry was a success; for example, varieties of coloured typewriter ribbon and of ploughs were just two of the many commodities that were compulsorily reduced in number. Price fixing was forced upon the steel companies (see Table 1.1) and some raw material producers. As a further aid to industry, the War Finance Corporation was established to provide capital where it was in short supply. The all-embracing nature of state control can be seen when we add to our list of regulatory bodies the US Railroad Administration, which was formed to run the nation's railway system when private industry proved to be unequal to that task. We can note, however, that the leaders of private business liaised with public agencies, not the government, and business received the credit for the economic management of the war bureaucracy.

The US finished the war with few idle resources in the economy. Victory was won at the cost of 50,000 dead — a great loss, but small indeed compared with the horrendous casualties suffered by the European powers. The nation's wealth increased. GNP (in 1958 prices) rose from $126bn in 1914 to $152bn in 1918 and low pay groups benefited most as the demand for their services increased relatively faster than it did for other groups. Family incomes had risen as households with more than one wage earner became more common. Women moved from low pay jobs to employment where pay was higher and work more regular, though their remuneration was less than for males. As in Europe, women were obliged to abandon these occupations when peacetime conditions returned. The war, however, also generated a great deal of social tension and led to a rise in xenophobia and a fear of political radicalism. There was deep suspicion of Americans whose allegiances were suspect; indeed, some states forbade the teaching of German in schools. This was a time when 100 per cent Americans alone were acceptable; German-Americans, or, as they were called, 'hyphenated Americans' were not. The migration of blacks to northern cities in response to labour shortages led to racial tension which erupted, periodically, into violence. Bloody race riots in East St Louis (1917) and Chicago (1919) were just two of several outbursts which illustrate the passions which the Ku Klux Klan viciously exploited during the 1920s. The Soviet Revolution of 1917 also had a profound effect on the American people. Their reaction to it assumed paranoiac proportions in the immediate post-war years. Socialists who, of course, had been amongst the most vociferous anti-war groups, were placed in the general category — Reds — of those who could only do the state harm. In this era of intolerance, the Eighteenth Amendment to the Constitution ushered in prohibition, an attempt to impose a new morality on the country which in the end proved a lucrative source of income for organised crime.

High incomes, therefore, did not lead to social stability. Industry, however, was strong. Four years of high profits and high levels of investment left firms in an excellent position to embrace the peace. Even machinery installed specifically for war output can be adapted for peacetime use with a minimum of effort. Unusual concessions had been made to organised labour, but these could always be rescinded. Most importantly, many captains of industry had worked with, and even encouraged, a system of co-operation between firms and government, the scale of which had never been witnessed before. Indeed, some were eager to continue with it into the post-war world, but the call of private industry quickly removed the dollar-a-year men from Washington. They had, however, seen the nation cope effectively with crisis using direct government action. It will come as no surprise to realise that when the next crisis, the Great Depression, loomed large, many of the institutions of 1917–18 were reinstated, to a small degree by Hoover, but on a wider scale by Roosevelt. Many of the men who had played a prominent role in the wary economy re-emerged to head the new regulatory agencies designed to wage another war, this time against the depression.

Internationally, the most important event was the transformation of the US from debtor to the world's leading creditor nation. Foreign governments had cashed in the dollar holdings of their citizens and had borrowed extensively from the US; once the war was over, the payment of these war debts had to be undertaken by economies seriously weakened by four years of costly carnage. The British, for example, found that their income from overseas investment and from shipping services, high before 1914, was much reduced after 1918. Could they and the French and the Germans pay their debts?

The problems of readjustment after a major war are formidable. By late 1918 approximately nine million Americans, that is, 25 per cent of the civilian labour force, were engaged in producing goods, many of which would not be required in peace. Furthermore, over four million men in the armed forces had to be demobilised. There were no specific plans to deal with the transfer of resources back to private industry, but there was a widespread desire to return to peacetime conditions as soon as possible. Many war contracts were cancelled as soon as the Armistice was declared, although it was not possible to halt immediately all work which was in progress. Controls, however, were dismantled quickly, indeed too quickly. The WIB began to remove price controls, most of which had disappeared by the end of 1918; other regulations, for example, on fuel and raw materials, were also abandoned. With great rapidity those in uniform were discharged and many returned to their peacetime occupations, to which they were legally entitled.

Post-War Boom and Bust

During the winter of 1918–19, industry displayed great uncertainty. Many basic industries cut back on production as war orders declined. Unemployment loomed as a serious problem for a while, but women and the elderly left their jobs to accommodate returning soldiers, although not always willingly. After some months of decline, the economy began to pick up in the spring of 1919 and embarked upon a vigorous boom which lasted until January 1920. During this industrial expansion, wholesale prices, which had been rising since 1914 though held in check by price controls, rose by a further 50 per cent, as did industrial production. There was also intense speculative activity in commodities and land, much of it using borrowed money.

Many consumers avidly purchased goods which they had been unable to obtain during the war; automobile sales increased, as did residential construction. For several years the level of personal savings had been exceptionally high and now people had the opportunity to spend the rewards of substantial wartime earnings. Moreover, full employment ensured a high demand for goods. Business, anxious to take advantage of rising prices, invested heavily in capital equipment, which they had been unable to purchase during the war, and in factory space; in addition, the stock of inventories rose. The level of consumer demand was also kept buoyant by high levels of exports and by the Federal Reserve. During the war Fed policy was to assist the Treasury which wanted to borrow at low rates of interest. This need continued after the war; not until the floating of the Victory Loan was completed in 1919 did the Federal Reserve begin to put into reverse its easy money policy.

There were, however, other forces which gradually came to exert a restraining influence upon economic expansion. Federal expenditures had reached a peak in December 1918, as did the budget deficit, but then began a steep decline. With reduced expenditure and raised taxes, the deficit, which was helping to keep the economy buoyant, was transformed into a surplus in late 1919; the federal budget remained in surplus throughout the 1920s. A significant portion of the market for American goods lay overseas, especially in war-devastated Europe. The economies of the old world were in such a parlous state that they were unable to export to the US and therefore could not pay for the foodstuffs and capital goods which they urgently needed. To help them, and the American economy, the US government negotiated post-war relief loans which, together with private loans, gave European nations the necessary dollars. During 1920, however, total American lending declined, adversely hitting exports.

Although industry tried to increase output, it failed to do so. In part the explanation for this is that the change from a war economy to a peace economy entailed a great deal of dislocation. Output, too, was held down by the chaos caused by serious strikes in the railroads, the steel industry, bituminous coal mining, and other sectors where workers tried to consolidate wartime gains and to prevent an erosion of their real incomes. Rising prices affected many groups: consumers began to curtail expenditure; speculators, who had borrowed large sums from banks, wondered when the collapse would come, especially as a drop in prices would increase debts in real terms. Moreover, as the cost of credit rose, both speculators and legitimate investors began to take stock of the situation as did housebuilders and mortgage seekers. In particular, commodity dealers became apprehensive about the possibility of ruinous inflation. In other words, the economy was in an increasingly precarious position as 1920 approached.

The downturn began in January 1920, slowly at first and then gathering momentum, until a trough was reached in mid-1921. By that time industrial production had fallen by 35 per cent, wholesale prices had halved, and unemployment, which had been 1.4 per cent of the civilian labour force in 1919 had risen to 11.7 per cent in 1921. The latter figure represented a jobless total of between four and six million. Moreover, many of those in work were forced to accept severe wage reductions. As the depression was an international phenomenon, both exports and imports contracted.

This post-war slump was unusually severe: how can it be explained? We have portrayed an economy that was delicately poised in 1919. There were supply constraints as well as widespread anxiety over rising prices and the level of speculation. One destabilising influence was the level of government expenditure which contracted sharply during 1919 and ended the year as a deflationary force. However, both Friedman and Schwartz (1963) and Pilgrim (1974) isolate monetary factors as the harbinger of depression. The Federal Reserve, freed from its task of supporting the Treasury, began to tighten credit, and to exhort banks, as it was later to do in 1929, not to lend for speculative purposes. Interest rates were raised just prior to the downturn in the economy, but more significantly, they were sharply increased in January 1920 and again in June, when the economy was already in serious trouble. There can be little doubt that the actions of the Federal Reserve made the ensuing recession a good deal worse. The restriction in credit hit business generally but especially the construction industry and also automobile sales, which depended upon the ability of consumers to borrow cheaply. In addition, commodity dealers and speculators panicked when faced with the rising cost of borrowing and quickly unloaded their stocks, causing massive price falls.

During the depression, nominal GNP fell by 30 per cent but, because of the drop in prices which was especially precipitous, real GNP contracted by only 12 per cent. The economic squeeze was severe; business rapidly reduced its debt and also saw costs decline as wages and raw material prices fell. As there were many consumer wants still unsatisfied, industry was in a position to stage a recovery as soon as the price falls had run their course, credit provision had returned to normal, inventories had been liquidated and speculation brought to a halt. Indeed, this happened quickly and the expansion of output between 1921 and 1924 was extraordinarily rapid.

Another favourable set of circumstances, especially if compared with 1929–33, can be seen in banking. The number of bank failures which had averaged just over 50 per year during the period 1916–19, rose to 167 in 1920 and 505 during the following year. As the latter figure was exceeded six times between 1922 and 1929 it must be kept in perspective. Compared with the paralysis of the banking sector after 1929 the events of 1920–1 were modest and did not exert an unduly depressing effect upon the economy. Indeed, the post-war depression was dominated by short run factors. Both business and consumers quickly adjusted to the new price level and soon the demand for housing, motor cars, furniture, electricity and other consumer durables began to reassert itself.

The brevity of the slump owed nothing to policy initiatives — quite the reverse. Federal expenditures, reduced in 1921, were cut again in 1922 to generate an even larger deflationary budget surplus. As for monetary policy, the Fed had not only raised interest rates, but had kept them high throughout the crisis. Friedman and Schwartz blame the Federal Reserve for the severity of the depression, a theme to which they return in their explanation of the more dramatic collapse after 1929. Why was monetary policy so perverse? In the first place the Fed thought that it had a primary responsibility to curb inflation and to reduce speculation, so that order could be restored to financial markets. To do this, a tight monetary policy was needed. Moreover, the Federal Reserve did not appreciate that if interest rates were kept high after the boom had broken, this would generate a severe deflation; once the economy turned down, the correct policy was to reduce interest rates. The authorities, however, did not look upon monetary policy as an active counter-cyclical tool. They perceived a role for it that was far more modest: to prevent financial panics and to provide credit for genuine investment.

On the other hand, Herbert Hoover, who had been appointed Secretary of Commerce in 1920, was not inactive. He persuaded President Harding to convene the President's Conference on Unemployment which met in September 1921. To Hoover unemployment was an irritating example of waste, the eradication of which should not be left entirely to natural recovery forces; the pwoer of government could be used to help both the unemployed and the economy. The Conference did not suggest that national government should usurp local responsibility in reducing the numbers of jobless, but it could advise, encourage and even collect data so that communities would be better able to cope with their misfortune. There was support for public works funded by the government; indeed it was suggested that Washington should accumulate a fund which could be used to finance work projects in the future. The primary function of central government, however, was seen as that of an instructive catalyst and the Conference was an interesting illustration of Hoover's philosophy of helping people help themselves (Wilson, 1975). The economy recovered before the policy recommendations of the Conference could be put into effect, but it spawned a number of committees which analysed economic change during the 1920s. Some of their findings appeared in *Recent Economic Changes in the United States*, a two-volume work published in 1929.

'Normalcy'

1921 marked the end of the war-induced boom—bust. The previous year President Harding, who had a talent for alliteration, if for little else, had called for 'Not heroism but healing, not nostrums but normalcy'. If 'normalcy' meant a return to 1914 it was clearly an impossibility for the US, as it was for all nations affected by the conflict. Not only was America now the world's leading creditor nation but the relative strength of her economy had increased. Oligopolies and trade associations had received a boost from the war and an increase in public approbation. Although the power of government was severely pruned after 1918, it is interesting to note that the federal budget was stabilised at a level far higher than before 1914; the same was true for the number of federal employees. Politically, America could attempt to erase the effect of war from the national psyche; the economic effects could not be expunged.

Table 1.2 Business Cycle Turning Points, 1918—38

Peak	Trough
August 1918	April 1919
January 1920	September 1921
May 1923	July 1924
October 1926	December 1927
June 1929	March 1933
May 1937	May 1938

Source: A.F. Burns and W.C. Mitchell (1946), *Measuring Business Cycles*, p. 78.

The 1920s have been dubbed both 'prosperity decade' and the 'New Era'. It was a period of rapidly increasing wealth, great stability and buoyant optimism, which made the depression which began in 1929 all the more shattering. If we look at the fluctuations of the economy during the inter-war years (Table 1.2) five business cycles can be isolated: 1919—21, 1921—4, 1924—7, 1927—30, and 1933—8. The exact monthly turning points are often a matter of dispute, but the picture which emerges is of an economy growing from a low point in 1921 to a peak in 1929, with two interruptions, which proved to be minor, in 1924 and 1927. During this period economic growth was most rapid between 1921—3 and 1928—9. The expansion took place within a framework of exceptional price stability; indeed, during the late 1920s prices actually declined in spite of great economic activity. Moreover, levels of unemployment were relatively low. Table 1.3 shows the rapid growth of GNP, a measure of the nation's wealth between 1919 and 1930. In addition, Figure 1.3 illustrates the fluctuations in industrial production during the 1920s and 1930s. This graph shows how vigorously the economy recovered after 1921, the sharp recession of 1924 and also the downturn which occurred through most of 1927. It is also evident from this figure that in 1924 and 1927 durable manufactures suffered a more serious decline than did non-durables. The volatility of durable goods manfacture is displayed particularly dramatically in the years after 1929.

The rise in GNP was dominated by the growth in consumption expenditure;

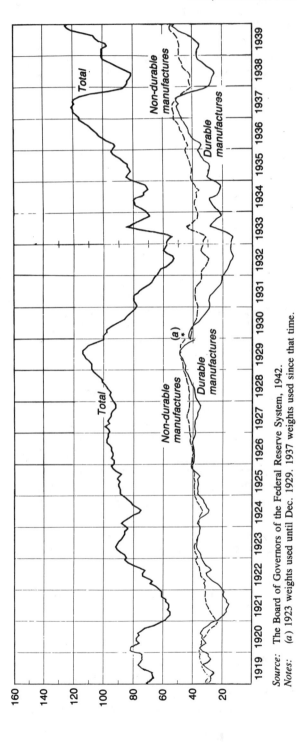

Source: The Board of Governors of the Federal Reserve System, 1942.
Notes: (a) 1923 weights used until Dec. 1929. 1937 weights used since that time.

Figure 1.3   Index of Industrial Production by Major Divisions (adjusted for seasonal variation, 1935–1939 average for total = 100)

Table 1.3 Gross National Product and its Components, 1919–30 ($ billion)

Year	GNP	Consumption expenditures	Gross private domestic investment	Net exports of goods and services	Govt purchases of goods and services
1919	80.0	53.3	12.4	4.9	9.5
1920	89.7	62.8	17.5	3.5	5.9
1921	74.5	58.3	7.8	2.1	6.3
1922	74.4	57.4	10.1	1.0	6.0
1923	86.6	63.9	15.7	0.8	6.2
1924	88.0	67.8	12.2	1.4	6.7
1925	91.9	67.3	16.2	1.1	7.3
1926	98.3	73.1	17.0	0.8	7.3
1927	96.7	72.7	15.1	1.1	7.9
1928	98.7	75.0	14.1	1.4	8.2
1929	104.6	78.8	16.2	1.2	8.5
1930	91.2	70.8	10.3	1.0	9.2

Source: J.A. Swanson and S.H. Williamson, 'Estimates of national product and income for the United States economy', *Explorations in Economic History*, 10 (1972–3).

consumer durable spending was especially buoyant. Note too the rising level of investment which to a great extent was dependent upon a construction boom. High investment levels demonstrate the optimism of investors. As this was an age of high company profits and plentiful credit, investment was never held back for a want of funds. However, as R.A. Gordon (1961) has observed, more than 80 per cent of the increase in GNP between 1919 and 1929 was in the flow of consumer goods. GNP growth in the 1920s, although faster than that experienced by Britain, Germany and France, was nevertheless lower than the figure reached in the US during the two decades 1889–1909.

The national wealth was distributed (in fact maldistributed, as we shall see later) among a population which grew from 106 million in 1920 to 123 million in 1930. The Census of 1920 was the first to record that the proportion of the population classified as urban, 51 per cent, was greater than the rural population. The census definition of urban, however, was a settlement of more than 2,500 inhabitants, not a very useful indicator of city growth. A different statistic will suffice: in 1910 there were 60 cities with more than 100,000 inhabitants, 68 in 1920, and by 1930 there were 92. A large part of the increased population gravitated to urban centres, particularly large metropolitan districts where the concentration of people was considerably greater by 1930. By that year 56 per cent of the population were classified as urban. There was also a marked growth in smaller satellite communities which were located on the periphery of big cities. They owed their existence to the spread of automobile ownership, improved public transport and the spread of electricity.

The End of Free Immigration

Perhaps the most dramatic socio-economic event of the post-war years was the introduction of legislation to halt the free flow of immigration from Europe. In the past there had been violent outbursts by nativists directed against those immigrant groups which seemed, at the time, to pose the greatest threat to established values: the Irish, the Chinese, the Japanese and the Italians all experienced hostility during the nineteenth century. Objections against free immigration became more widespread after 1890 when the origins of European immigrants changed from the north of the continent (old immigration) to the south and east (new immigration). Could people coming from Italy, Greece, Poland and Russia be as easily assimilated as the British and the Scandinavians? By adopting spurious eugenic theories, many writers attacked the new immigrants as racially inferior; their swelling numbers could only lead to race suicide, the destruction of the Anglo-Saxon stock. Organised labour also joined the chorus of those who called for immigration controls, if not for an outright ban. Unions believed that a reduction in flow would lead, eventually, to an increase in the wages of their members. Not surprisingly, however, business interests agreed that any restriction on free immigration would strangle industry by cutting off a valuable supply of labour, and politicians representing urban centres, where the foreign-born congregated, added their voices in opposition to the imposition of controls.

In spite of the growing concern, little was done to halt immigration which, in any case, ceased to be a problem during the war as numbers were reduced. A compulsory literacy test was introduced in 1917 but, as most immigrants could successfully complete it, it had little impact upon numbers. In both 1913 and 1914 just over one million immigrants arrived in the US; in 1918 the figure was 31,000 and during the following year only 25,000. By that time, however, attitudes to foreigners were far more hostile than they had been before 1914. The years 1920 to 1924 in particular mark a period of intolerance, insecurity and paranoia in American history. New immigrants were identified with crime, inferior living standards, drunkenness and political extremism, especially communism. The large numbers of Catholics and Jews amongst the new arrivals added fuel to the flames of bigotry. The foreign-born were also identified with the bitter and disruptive strikes of 1919–20; foreigners were believed to be part of a great conspiracy to undermine the American way of life. In such an atmosphere rumour fed upon rumour. In July 1921, for example, the Federal Reserve Board sent a circular to the Directors of the Reserve Banks claiming that communists were spreading panic and starting runs upon banks for sinister purposes. However, an exhaustive inquiry into the run on the Boston Five Cents Bank, which bank officials suspected was communist inspired, revealed that the rush of depositors to withdraw their savings was based upon understandable fears for their money, not a Red plot. The Ku Klux Klan, which attracted an alarming level of support during this period, appealed not only to those who hated blacks, but also to people whose hatred extended to Jews, Catholics and organised labour. Unfortunately there were frequent opportunities to terrorise those who did not conform to the Klan's interpretation of American values.

In 1921, 650,000 immigrants arrived from Europe at a time of high unemployment. Now business could not object to controls on the grounds that labour would be in short supply, and even those who hesitated to join the more vociferous anti-immigrant campaigns felt that the time had come for legislation. Congress decided to limit European immigration to 358,000 annually, a figure clearly below the numbers wishing to come. Those fortunate enough to be accepted were chosen according to a formula which allowed each European nation 3 per cent of the foreign-born persons of that nationality who lived in the US in 1910. There were, however, no restrictions on the movements of Canadians or Mexicans. In 1924 more restrictive legislation was introduced although unemployment had fallen from its very high 1921 level; social fears aroused by immigration were clearly greater than the possible economic cost of fewer foreign workers. The Johnson-Reed Act set the number of European immigrants at 2 per cent of the number of foreign-born of each nationality who were resident in the US in 1890. Since this was before the influx of people from southern and eastern Europe, it had the desired effect of severely restricting immigration from these groups. In 1924 also, immigration from Asia, which had been restricted for some time, was banned. In 1927 the National Origins Act limited European immigration to 154,000 each year and gave each country a quota based upon the 1920 census. The US had moved therefore from an annual inflow from Europe which had averaged 930,000 in the five years before 1914 to an average figure of less than 160,000 between 1925 and 1929.

The economic impact of changes in immigration flows is hard to assess. The foreign-born in the US made a significant contribution to the labour force which was greater than their absolute numbers would suggest. The age and sex profile of immigrants was different from that of native Americans as the former group had more males of working age and fewer young or elderly dependents. During the late nineteenth century, when the foreign-born were one-seventh of the total population, they comprised one-fifth of the workforce. Moreover, the immigrant labour force not only stimulated the demand for housing; it also had a restraining influence upon wages which would have risen more rapidly without it. There was a danger, therefore, that when American industry expanded during the 1920s it would have encountered a labour supply bottleneck. The fact that it did not was due, on the one hand, to rapid increases in productivity and to migration, both of which will be examined in future chapters.

Employment

We have established that there was a rising population in this period but, after 1921, no unemployment crisis. How were these newcomers absorbed into the labour force? Table 1.4 gives a picture of the distribution of employment during

Table 1.4 Distribution of the Employed Labour Force, 1920–30 (millions)

Year	Total non-agricultural	Mining	Construction	Manufac-turing	Transport & public utilities	Wholesale /retail trade	Finance, insurance & real estate	Services	Govt employment	Farm labour force
1920	27.4	1.2	0.9	10.7	4.3	4.0	0.9	3.1	2.4	10.4
1921	24.5	0.9	1.0	8.2	3.9	4.0	1.0	3.1	2.4	10.4
1922	26.6	0.9	1.3	9.1	3.9	4.7	1.0	3.2	2.5	10.6
1923	29.2	1.2	1.4	10.3	4.2	5.2	1.1	3.2	2.5	10.6
1924	28.6	1.1	1.6	9.7	4.1	5.0	1.2	3.3	2.6	10.6
1925	29.8	1.1	1.7	9.9	4.0	5.7	1.3	3.3	2.8	10.7
1926	30.6	1.2	1.8	10.2	4.0	5.9	1.3	3.4	2.9	10.7
1927	30.5	1.1	1.8	10.0	4.0	5.9	1.4	3.4	2.9	10.5
1928	30.5	1.0	1.7	10.0	3.9	6.0	1.5	3.4	3.0	10.5
1929	31.3	1.0	1.5	10.7	3.9	6.1	1.5	3.4	3.0	10.5
1930	29.4	1.0	1.4	9.6	3.7	5.8	1.5	3.4	3.1	10.3

Source: Historical Statistics of US, Colonial Times to 1970, 2 vols (Washington DC, 1975), Series D127–139.

the 1920s. These figures, however, refer only to paid employees in the non-farm sector; they do not include proprietors, the self-employed, or unpaid family workers, so may not be strictly comparable with other labour force data. Nevertheless, the trends in all other series will be the same as those in our table. The importance of the manufacturing sector as an employer is immediately clear, but the number of workers in this sector was the same in 1929 as it had been in 1920; there was no net job creation in manufacturing as a whole. This statement should, however, be interpreted with caution; it does not mean that the composition of the manufacturing workforce was exactly the same in 1929 as it was in 1919. Some industries had expanded during the decade but others had contracted, and this is shown in changes in employment. Those manufacturing industries which gained the most wage earners between 1919 and·1929 include: electrical machinery and supplies, which includes the manufacture of radio equipment (55 per cent), bakery products (42 per cent), furniture (38 per cent), petroleum refining (37 per cent), chemicals (36 per cent) and motor vehicles and parts (30 per cent). At the same time the number of workers in railroad repair shops decreased, as did those employed as shipbuilders, shoemakers and boilermakers. The bulk of the new jobs which absorbed the expanding labour force was created in the wholesale and retail trade, in finance and related services, in construction, and in government employment. Many of these occupations were white-collar, required relatively high levels of education or a facility for dealing with members of the public, and were located in big cities.

Although the manufacturing labour force was static between 1919 and 1929, output rose by over 60 per cent. The 1920s were a decade of great productivity growth in manufacturing and in other sectors of the economy also. Indeed, this was a time of US economic dominance. During the late 1920s, US manufacturing output accounted for just over 40 per cent of the world total. More particularly, America, with only 6 per cent of the world's population, produced 57 per cent of the total international output of machinery. This was an era, too, where, in the domestic market, consumer durables, with the automobile to the fore, construction, and the growth of public utilities, achieved a new prominence. Company profits were high, as was speculation, credit was cheap, workers were placid and consumers dedicated to material acquisition. Indeed the combination of rapid economic expansion, full employment and price stability was as close to economic paradise as seemed possible. The US had an overseas role too. As a major importer of raw materials and semi-manufactured goods, she was linked to many primary producing nations. As the world's leading capital exporter, she had ties with both advanced industrial and agricultural nations. Germany looked to America for international funds to finance war debt repayments; for Latin America the US investor was vital if living standards were to remain intact.

The 'New Era' was not perfect, however. The largest group which did not regard it with unrestrained enthusiasm was that of farmers. Affluent during the war, but disgruntled in peace, millions of Americans were tied to the farm in the decade of the city. Their problems will be analysed in the next chapter.

Bibliography

The changing industrial structure of the United States and the concomitant rise of a new managerial class is described and analysed in the excellent volumes written by A.D. Chandler, E.W. Hawley and R.H. Wiebe. In spite of its age, G. Soule's work remains one of the best sources for the war and post-war years though it should be supplemented by M. Friedman and A.J. Schwartz for a more rigorous treatment of price movements and monetary policy. Those interested in the social impact of World War I should consult D.M. Kennedy and M.W. Greenwald; J. Higham's book contains a particularly interesting study of immigration. As a general introduction to the 1920s, however, it is difficult to better W. Leuchtenburg.

Aldcroft, D.H. (1977) *From Versailles to Wall Street, 1919–1929*, Allan Lane.

Chandler, A.D. (1977) *The Visible Hand: The Managerial Revolution in American Business*, Belknap Press.

Clark, J.M. (1931) *The Costs of the World War to the American People*, Yale University Press.

Cuff, R.D. (1973) *The War Industries Board: Business–Government Relations during World War I*, John Hopkins University Press.

Friedman, M. and Schwartz, A. (1963) *A Monetary History of the United States, 1867–1960*, NBER.

Gilbert, C. (1970) *American Financing of World War I*, Greenwood Press.

Gordon, R.A. (1961) *Business Fluctuations*, 2nd edn, Harper.

Greenwald, M.W. (1980) *Women, War and Work*, Greenwood Press.

Hall, T.G. (1973) 'Wilson and the food crisis: agricultural pace control during World War I', *Agricultural History*, 47.

Hall, T.G. (1977) 'Government controls: How to understand the experience of World War I', in T.H. Peterson (ed.) *Farmers, Bureaucrats and Middlemen: Historical Perspectives on American Agriculture*, National Archives, Washington DC.

Hawley, E.W. (1979) *The Great War and the Search for a Modern Order*, St. Martins Press.

Higham, J. (1969) *Strangers in the Land*, Atheneum.

Hughes, J.R.T. (1974) *The Governmental Habit: Economic Controls from Colonial Times to the Present*.

Kennedy, D.M. (1980) *Over Here: The First World War and American Society*, Oxford University Press.

Koistinen, P.A.C. (1967) 'The "Industrial–Military Complex" in Historical Perspective: World War I', *Business History Review*, 41.

Leuchtenburg, W.E. (1958) *Perils of Prosperity, 1914–1932*, University of Chicago Press.

Mills, F.C. (1932) *Economic Tendencies in the United States*, NBER, New York.

Mullendore, W.C. (1941) *History of the United States Food Administration, 1917–1919*, Stanford University Press.

Nelson, K.L. (1971) *The Impact of War on American Life: The Twentieth Century Experience*, Holt, Rinehart & Winston.

Noggle, B. (1974) *Into the Twenties: The United States from Armistice to Normalcy*, University of Illinois Press.

Pilgrim, J.D. (1974) 'The upper turning point of 1920: a reappraisal', *Explorations in Economic History*, XI.

Potter, J. (1974) *The American Economy Between the World Wars*, Macmillan.

Rockoff, H. (1981) 'Price and wage controls on four wartime periods', *Journal of Economic History*, June.

Rudwick, E. (1964) *Race Riot in East St Louis: July 2, 1917*, University of Illinois Press.

Schlesinger Jr., A.M. (1957) *The Crisis of the Old Order: 1919–1933*, Houghton Mifflin.
Shannon, D.A. (1965) *Between the Wars: America 1919–1941*, Houghton Mifflin.
Soule, G. (1947) *Prosperity Decade: From War to Depression 1917–1929*, Rinehart.
Tuttle Jr., W.M. (1977) *Race Riot: Chicago in the Red Summer of 1919*, Atheneum.
Wiebe, R.H. *The Search for Order, 1877–1920*, Hill and Wang.
Williamson, J.G. and Lindert, P. (1980) *American Inequality: A Macroeconomic History*, Academic Press.
Wilson, J.H. (1975) *Herbert Hoover: Forgotten Progressive*, Little, Brown.
Wilson, T. (1948) *Fluctuations in Income and Employment*, Macmillan.
Wright, G. (1986) *Old South, New South: Revolutions in the Southern Economy since the Civil War*, Basic Books.

2

Agriculture and Migration During the 1920s

During the 1920s, the US was a manufacturing giant with a large agricultural sector which accounted for 40 per cent of the value of all exports. However, the farm was losing out to the city. Table 2.1 shows that the farm population was steadily declining both absolutely and relatively to the urban population. Even during the years of war-induced prosperity, the number of farm dwellers fell, as high non-agricultural incomes encouraged migration. In 1920 the urban population (at 51 per cent of the total) exceeded the rural for the first time. The significance of that is, however, misleading. The figure for the farm population in Table 2.1 is, in fact, only 30 per cent of the total for that year. The reason for this discrepancy is that the Census defined as 'rural' any settlement of less than 2,500 inhabitants; therefore virtually all farmers were rural dwellers although not all rural people were farmers. Some occupations, for example coalmining and even cotton textile manufacture, were classified as rural if they were located in settlements of less than 2,500 people. The farmers used the banks, stores, schools and other services in small towns and villages. Indeed, the fortunes of farmers and non-farm rural Americans were closely linked.

The number of farms increased during the war and continued to do so until 1921; it then declined but by the end of the decade had begun to increase again. The figures for average farm size show a similar trend. Averages, however, are often deceptive and there was an enormous difference in the size of American farms. In 1925 there were over 2.4 million farms with less than 50 acres and over 3.8 million with less than 100 acres. Many of these very small units were engaged in a desperate struggle to provide an income for the families who occupied them. In many cases only half the cash income of a small farm came from farming. The remainder was earned by the operator and members of his family working elsewhere. In 1930, 720,000 farmers worked for more than a hundred days away from their farms. Since about 50 per cent of the country's farms produced 90 per cent of the produce that was marketed, the remainder sought to provide as much of their own food as possible; any marketable surplus was a welcome bonus.

28

Table 2.1 The Farm Sector, 1914−30

Year	Farm population		Number of farms ('000)	Average acreage per farm acres	Index of gross farm output (1929=100)
	Total ('000)	Per cent of total pop.			
1914	32,320	32.8	6,447	141	88
1915	32,440	32.4	6,458	142 ‧	92
1916	32,530	32.0	6,463	143	83
1917	32,430	31.5	6,478	144	91
1918	31,950	30.6	6,488	145	87
1919	31,200	29.7	6,506	146	87
1920	31,974	30.1	6,454	149	87
1921	32,123	29.7	6,511	146	83
1922	32,109	29.3	6,500	145	88
1923	31,490	28.2	6,492	144	93
1924	31,177	27.5	6,480	144	91
1925	31,190	27.0	6,372	145	96
1926	30,979	26.5	6,462	145	96
1927	30,530	25.7	6,485	147	99
1928	30,548	25.4	6,470	149	98
1929	30,580	25.2	6,512	150	100
1930	30,529	24.9	6,295	157	95

Source: Columns 1−4: *Historical Statistics of US, Colonial Times to 1970*, 2 vols (Washington DC, 1975) Series K 1, 2, 4, 7; Column 5: J. Kendrick, *Productivity Trends in the US* (NBER, Princeton University Press, 1961), Table B−11.

Some small farms were very profitable, especially those engaged in truck farming (market gardening). Most, however, were very badly managed and located on infertile soil, resulting in desperately low incomes for their operators. There was massive underemployment in agriculture. In general, the larger farms were the most commercially oriented and the most businesslike in their approach to production and marketing and their use of labour. Indeed, if the most productive agricultural methods had been more widespread, about a quarter of the farms which existed in 1920 could have produced all the food and raw materials that the country required.

The US was not a nation of farm owners, for less than one half of the 6.4 million farms in 1920 were fully owned. There were several distinct classes of farm operators: full owners owned and operated the farms on which they lived, some of which were free from mortgage debt (see below); a second group comprised the 657,000 part owners who owned some land but who also farmed or sub-let rented land; the remainder fell into a third group who farmed only rented land. In this last category were over 2.6 million tenants. The growth of tenancy (by over 200,000 during the 1920s) was viewed with alarm. It challenged the view that the 'agricultural ladder' from day labourer to tenancy to ownership could only be ascended. Absolutely, there were more white tenants (two million) than black, but as blacks accounted for only 12 per cent of the total population they were relatively heavily represented in the ranks of tenants. The vast majority of black farmers lived in the South where half of them were tied to a tenancy arrangement known as share-cropping.

Croppers must be distinguished from cash tenants who owned their own tools and work stock, paid all the expenses of the farm and a specified cash rent. These tenants were entrepreneurs; they were decision makers who had full responsibility for running the farm and were relatively numerous in northern states such as Iowa and Illinois (Map 2.1). Share-croppers were almost exclusively confined to the South and the most common form of contract was the '50 per cent' arrangement. The cropper owned no work stock or any tools; these were provided by the landlord as was the land, a cabin, fuel and half the fertiliser used. The cropper also received small advances of cash or supplies on credit. In exchange, the cropper gave his landlord half the crop at the end of the season. With the money he received for the remaining half, any debts owing to the landlord were settled. The cropper was closely supervised by the landlord throughout the growing season. In other words, the landlord was the sole entrepreneur and the cropper contributed nothing to farm enterprise. Nor had he any long-term commitment to the farm. A high proportion of croppers left at the end of the season and moved to another land owner. In many ways the croppers were indistinguishable from the three million hired workers who sought work on the land.

Between 1915 and 1919 there was enormous pressure upon the agricultural sector to produce more but, unlike manufacturing industry, output stagnated in the face of unprecedented demand. Why were farmers so unresponsive to rising prices? What governs the level of farm output? In the case of crops, the amount of land available and how much is planted are important variables. By 1914 there was only a limited amount of land not being farmed in the US but there had occurred a compensating shift of emphasis — from pasture to crops is one example — where such a change was deemed possible. The increase in demand took place before mechanisation had made a significant impact upon agriculture; labour shortages, therefore, were often a restraint on the amount produced. The most important influence upon output, however, is beyond the farmer's control. Storms, flood or drought can have a devastating effect upon the harvest, as can pests such as the boll weevil, which wreaked havoc with the cotton crop. In the long run, agricultural research can conquer pests and plant diseases. But the weather did (1917 and 1918 were poor harvest years), and still does, have the final say on how much is harvested. As a result, output and prices can fluctuate erratically.

The farmer, therefore, cannot easily emulate the factory owner by rapidly increasing output, nor can he follow business practice by cutting output in a depression. In 1920–1 factories everywhere discharged workers and reduced the production of goods. An individual farmer, however, who decided to market less would face ruin. It would require massive co-operation on the part of farmers to achieve cutbacks, something which is impossible to envisage. As a result,

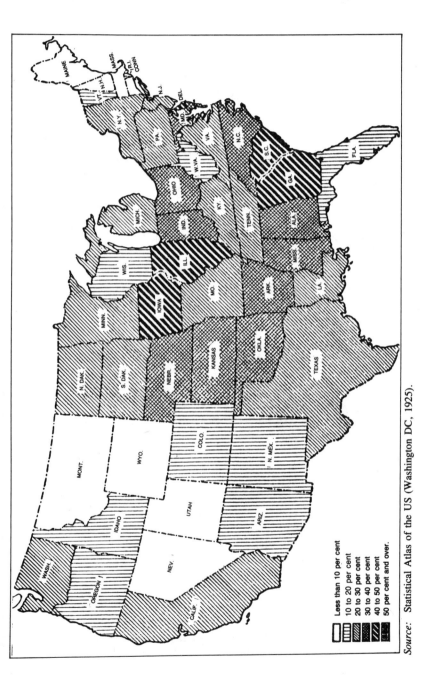

Less than 10 per cent
10 to 20 per cent
20 to 30 per cent
30 to 40 per cent
40 to 50 per cent
50 per cent and over.

Source: Statistical Atlas of the US (Washington DC, 1925).

Map 2.1 Per Cent of all Farmland Operated by Tenants, by States, 1920

agricultural prices fell more than the prices of manufactured goods during 1920—1 and again in 1929—33.

Agriculture in the 1920s was a very diverse industry, covering a huge geographic area with vastly different soils and weather systems. The variety of crops grown was enormous: potatoes, peaches, oranges, cotton, corn, wheat, rice, tobacco and sugar form in no way an exhaustive list. Each crop had its own production and marketing problems. Add to this the truism that some farmers are more efficient than others, and one appreciates that sweeping statements run the risk of gross oversimplification. However, as each crop cannot be examined individually, generalisations are unavoidable.

The most commonly accepted measure of changing farm fortunes during the 1920s was the parity ratio which is presented in Table 2.2. Its fluctuations were watched with interest by farm pressure groups, farmers and politicians with large rural constituencies. The parity ratio is the relationship between two price indices. The index of prices received by farmers is a measure of the changes in the average prices that farmers obtain for their agricultural commodities. The prices-paid index measures the changes in the average prices of items purchased by farmers (for example manufactured goods), but also includes payment of taxes and hired labour.

Table 2.2   Indices of Prices Received and Paid by Farmers and the Parity Ratio, 1914—30 (1910—14 = 100)

Year	Prices received by farmers for all farm products	Prices paid by farmers including interest, taxes and wage rates	Parity ratio
1914	101	103	98
1915	99	105	94
1916	119	116	103
1917	178	148	120
1918	206	173	119
1919	217	197	110
1920	211	214	99
1921	124	155	80
1922	131	151	87
1923	142	159	89
1924	143	160	89
1925	156	164	95
1926	145	160	91
1927	140	159	88
1928	148	162	91
1929	148	160	92
1930	125	151	83

Source: Historical Statistics of US, Colonial Times to 1957 (Washington DC, 1961), Series K129, 137, 138.

The base period for both indices is 1910–14. The parity ratio is calculated by dividing the prices-received index by the prices-paid index and multiplying the result by 100. This ratio, therefore, measures the purchasing power of products sold by farmers in terms of the goods that they buy, compared with their purchasing power during the base period. If it rises above 100, then the farmers' average purchasing power, per unit of farm commodities, is higher than it was in 1910–14; if below, purchasing power is less than in the base period. Since farmers considered as normal the price relationship which existed between 1910–14, a parity ratio of less than 100 was regarded as a clear sign of agricultural misfortune.

Table 2.2 shows that during the war the prices of agricultural commodities rose more rapidly than the cost of goods which the farmer bought. The terms of trade for the farmer reached a peak of 120 in 1917 and even by 1919 had only fallen to 110. During the 1920–1 slump, however, agricultural prices fell much more steeply than non-agricultural prices, and the parity ratio hit a low of 80 in 1921. Farmers, therefore, experienced a rapid reversal of fortune within a few years. Farm prices consequently staged a recovery after 1921 and finally stabilised at a level which was 45 per cent higher than the pre-war base. Unfortunately, the farmer's input prices stabilised at more than 60 per cent above 1914 levels. The result was that the farmer's terms of trade remained below the pre-war level throughout the rest of the decade and the farm community interpreted this failure as a clear indication that its economic relationship with the non-agricultural world was out of balance. The ability to quantify misfortune gave farmers a strong sense of grievance.

The parity ratio is a commonly used statistical series. We need, therefore, to be sure what it measures and how it should be used. It is important to remember that the indices which make up the ratio measure prices only; they take no account of changes in quality. This is reasonable for farm products because the wheat or hogs sold in 1929 were of identical quality to those marketed in 1919. The same cannot be said for manufactured goods. The automobile which the farmer purchased in 1929 was much superior to the vehicle manufactured in 1919; the same was true of other consumer durables. This was a gain for the farmer which cannot be included in the parity ratio. Another problem is the choice of a base period which avoids distortions. 1910–14 was a period when fortune favoured the farmer. Since the late nineteenth century farm prices had increased and agriculture had embarked upon a golden age. Not only were prices high but for several years before 1914 they were unusually stable. On the other hand urban wages, during a period of heavy immigration, were relatively low. The base period for the parity ratio therefore relates to a time when agriculture was very prosperous; it is little wonder that farmers strove to return to it.

The farmers' purchasing power depends not only upon the price of the commodities which they sell but also upon the quantity. High prices and low quantities do not always bring about prosperity. For farmers whose crops were seriously depleted by flood or drought, high prices were irrelevant. The parity ratio can-

not measure quantity any more than it can distinguish between profitable or unprofitable crops.

Finally, taxes are included in the prices-paid index; indeed, the level of taxation caused much rural agitation during the 1920s. It would be wrong to assume,
however, that a rise in taxes automatically meant a drop in farm living standards.
Like other sectors of the community farmers benefited from the taxes which they
paid. New schools and new roads, for example, added more to the quality of
rural life than if individual farmers had spent tax money independently. The parity
ratio itself, therefore, is an insufficient indicator of changing farm fortunes.

Difficulties abound in comparing rural and urban expenditure patterns. Food
and fuel on the farm is far cheaper than that purchased in the city. It was also
possible for many farm families to supplement their income by working in non-
agricultural occupations for a considerable part of the year. Nevertheless, average
farm income was always lower than that elsewhere; 6.5 million farms produced
only 9 per cent of the national income during the late 1920s. The figure for
manufacturing was 21 per cent, for finance, insurance and real estate 16 per cent,
and for services 12 per cent. While agriculture contributed progressively less to
the national economy during the 1920s, the total farm population fell only slightly.
Although there may have been many non-pecuniary advantages to farm life, the
rapid increase in national wealth was being generated elsewhere.

Farm income estimates are a more illuminating indication of changing
agricultural fortunes. The net income which farmers received just from farming,
expressed as an average for each farm, was $1,395 in 1919 but fell to $517 in
1921. From this low point it rose steadily and, between 1926 and 1929, averaged
$918 annually. This figure was below the level attained between 1917 and 1920,
but it was higher than in the years before 1914. Table 2.3 gives details of the
cash income gained from selling crops and livestock, and its pattern is similar.
From a trough in 1921, total cash receipts grew steadily and by the late 1920s
were substantially greater than the annual average of 1910–14 ($6bn). If income
growth alone is considered, farming as a whole seemed a fairly buoyant industry.

Nevertheless, many farmers viewed the agricultural situation in the 1920s with
a jaundiced eye. They were convinced that prosperity was synonymous with urban
life. It is, of course, a gross oversimplification to say that all farmers were gloomy.
The fruit and vegetable industry was one sector which experienced rapid expansion during this period. Capitalising on high urban incomes and dietary changes
which gave less emphasis to grains and the potato, truck farmers (market
gardeners) found a valuable market. Those near to the New York and Philadelphia
metropolitan districts were helped by the expansion of a highway system which
enabled perishables to be grown further away from their markets, and also by
the growth of the canning industry. These small, highly productive, farms
demonstrate that not all small units were unprofitable. Unfortunately, the southern
states, where small farms were disproportionately numerous and incomes lowest,
were unable to take full advantage of this changing demand, as the region possessed
few large urban markets.

Table 2.3 Cash Receipts from Marketing Farm Produce,
1918–29 ($ billion)

Year	Total	Crops	Livestock and livestock products
1918	13.5	7.0	6.5
1919	14.5	7.6	6.9
1920	12.6	6.6	6.0
1921	8.1	4.1	4.0
1922	8.6	4.3	4.3
1923	9.5	4.9	4.6
1924	10.2	5.4	4.8
1925	11.0	5.5	5.5
1926	10.6	4.9	5.7
1927	10.7	5.1	5.6
1928	11.0	5.0	6.0
1929	11.3	5.1	6.2

Source: Historical Statistics of US, Colonial Times to 1970, 2
vols (Washington DC, 1975), Series K265–7.

While changing consumer tastes assisted one group of farmers, they disadvantaged a large group: wheat growers. During the late 1920s the per capita consumption of cereals had fallen to 230 lb compared with an estimated 350 lb at the start of the century. During the same period, meat consumption remained stable, while dairy products and fresh fruit showed substantial gains. These shifts were to be expected as incomes rose and the population became increasingly urbanised. The change was not good news for wheat farmers who faced a continual erosion of the domestic market. In addition, exports, which had been a lucrative source of income up to 1920, fell sharply for the rest of the decade as European farms recovered from the effects of war and other producers such as Canada, Argentina, and Australia sold their surpluses on the world market. Wheat, which had fetched $2.40 per bushel in 1919 and 1920, averaged half that price for the remainder of the decade.

It was difficult for wheat growers to adjust production to take account of changing demand. Even if a wheat grower in western Kansas knew that there was a demand for cauliflowers in Kansas City, there was little he could do to satisfy it. His land, his machinery, his expertise and the weather gave him an advantage in wheat production which he was reluctant to forego. Moreover he, like farmers all over the country, was an optimist: the next harvest must bring better prices. When wheat prices fell to less than $1 per bushel during the bad years of 1921–3, the acreage planted with winter wheat in Kansas was larger than when the price was over $2 per bushel. As a rule, a fall in the price of agricultural commodities tends to encourage farmers to produce more, not less.

Apart from the elements, there were other serious impediments to any substantial change of land use. Often the innate conservatism of farmers was to blame, sometimes the shortage of finance, sometimes tradition and custom, sometimes ignorance and occasionally the fear that if the new methods failed it would be impossible to revert to the old. Farms are not manufacturing enterprises. They do not have the flexibility to change or to curtail ouput when prices fall. Moreover, surpluses from one year remain to depress prices in the next. Even when it was clear that a cotton surplus must be dealt with if prices were to recover, voluntary acreage reduction schemes, which anticipated New Deal agriculture strategy, never worked (Fite, 1948).

The millions of people in agriculture, plus those rural dwellers who did business with farmers, made up a formidable political force. However, the commercial farmers most systematically lobbied congressmen and joined farm pressure groups. A number of senators formed a bipartisan body, the Farm Bloc, in 1921 in order to oppose legislation unfavourable to farmers and promote that which was advantageous. They espoused tariff protection which even the growers of export-oriented crops such as wheat and cotton wanted. In 1919 farmers had been confident as to the future of exports. European farming was in disarray and Russia, the former granary of the continent, no longer engaged in international trade. Their confidence was sadly misplaced. The value of agricultural exports fell sharply in 1920–1 and remained depressed until the end of the decade, while the export of non-agricultural goods rose rapidly. Wheat farmers, therefore, wanted tariff protection from Canada and Argentina; cotton producers feared the import of cheap, high-grade cotton. Farmers felt that manufacturing interests had done well from protection, and they too should benefit. Substantial protection, however, was not forthcoming until the Hawley–Smoot tariff in 1930. It was to prove a Pyrrhic victory.

Other pressure groups existed outside Congress, such as the Farm Bureau and the National Grange. These expressions of farm 'self-help' supported the translation of McNary–Haugen bills into law. These measures were designed to raise the domestic prices of some key agricultural commodities while at the same time avoiding the stumbling block of high export prices. In its final form, the plan envisaged a federal export agency which would purchase sufficient quantities of a crop, say cotton or wheat, to raise the US price to 100 per cent parity and to hold it there with the aid of tariffs. As this new domestic price would be above the price of cotton and wheat in world markets, any surplus would be exported for what it could fetch and the loss in export sales would be paid by an equalisation fee, or tax, on sellers. The McNary–Haugen proposals were debated in Congress five times between 1924 and 1928, and passed twice, but on each occasion were vetoed by President Coolidge. It is unlikely that this extremely cumbersome formula would have worked. By protecting the domestic market it would have encouraged retaliation by foreign governments and antagonised both business and consumers. Rather than addressing the key issue of reducing the output of particular crops, it would have encouraged producers to maximise production to take advantage of higher prices. Moreover, not all farmers would have gained, for only certain 'primary' crops were included in the scheme.

Many commercially oriented farmers, following the example of business and its trade associations, joined co-operative marketing associations. The hope was that these organisations would improve the quality of products, reduce costs, stabilise prices, finance advertising compaigns and exert more control over freight, storage and marketing costs. Such associations had been active before 1914 and grew during the twenties, attracting the support of such luminaries as Herbert Hoover. Only a few were successful, the most notable being the California Fruit Growers Exchange. Others fell by the wayside for various reasons: farmers were a difficult group to organise, organisational skills were absent in some cases and the large purchasers of agricultural commodities (such as the meatpackers and the millers) formed associations which became more powerful than those organised by farmers.

In order to help farmers help themselves, the Capper−Volstead Act (1922) exempted farm co-operatives from the restrictions of the anti-trust laws. In response to complaints about the cost of credit, the Agricultural Credits Act (1923) created 12 federal credit banks which advanced funds to farmers at modest rates. As all farmers needed credit, any reduction in its cost was welcomed. Finally, in 1929, President Hoover established the Federal Farm Board, one aim of which was to stimulate further the development of co-operatives, in which the new President had great faith. In addition, a fund was created to be used for the purchase and storage of surplus crops in the belief that by holding surpluses off the market temporary price falls could be avoided. The Federal Farm Board, as we shall see, proved hopelessly unequal to this task when prices dropped precipitously in 1930.

Enormous structural problems afflicted the US farm sector. These were exacerbated by the adherence of many people to poor farming techniques which led to soil destruction and erosion. Encouraged by high wartime prices, wheat farming had spread into submarginal areas which proved no longer economically viable in peacetime. Added to this, farming still continued to be carried out in areas where it could be justified in the pioneering days, but not in a period of commercial agriculture. Small farms on poor land were a sure recipe for poverty. Misery was compounded by the fact that farm families tended to have more children than urban families. The result was a strain on education which, though improving during the 1920s with the advent of the school bus and therefore school consolidation, was inferior to that in most cities. This placed some rural migrants at a disadvantage in the urban job market. Rural diet, in areas of farm poverty, was so deficient that health standards were appallingly low. Families on small farms were particularly disadvantaged, since they had less space to grow their own food. The poorest rural counties in the country were found in the southern Appalachians and in the Piedmont region. In fact, over two-thirds of all the farms producing less than $1,000 worth of products in 1929 were located in the South.

For farmers, 1929 was a reasonably good year, but in the country as a whole

28 per cent of farms produced less than $600 worth of products, including the milk, eggs, vegetables and other produce used by the family. If part-time farmers are deducted from this total about one million farm families remain with a gross agricultural income — often their only income — of less than $600. For these families net income was a paltry $100—$300. Not surprisingly, they contributed only 3 per cent, when measured by value, of all farm products sold or traded.

There were, of course, many examples of farm prosperity. Among the most prosperous were a group of Iowan farmers, 96 per cent of whom owned automobiles, 94 per cent telephones and 80 per cent washing machines. These were high figures even by urban standards. However, only 19 per cent of these farm houses had bathrooms and inside lavatories, significantly below urban levels. Farmers generally were avid purchasers of automobiles, their isolation giving them a greater incentive for ownership than city dwellers. By 1930, there were over 4.1 million automobiles on American farms, to which we can add 900,000 trucks and 920,000 tractors. The use of tractors raised farm productivity, especially in grain production, but machinery was even being used in the cotton fields by 1930. The automobile gave the farm family much greater freedom. Neighbours could be visited, and it was possible to drive to the city to go to the cinema, or to shop in department stores where the range of goods was much greater. The city, moreover, often had cheaper credit than the local bank. Unfortunately, these new shopping patterns led to the decay of many rural communities whose stores had less to offer than those in the metropolis. Even small country banks, whose isolation had ensured a monopoly, went out of business under the strain of new competition. In all, 5,000 banks failed during the 1920s, the vast majority being located in rural centres in the grain producing states (see Chapter 4).

The acquisition of consumer durables and expensive capital equipment gives the impression of an affluent farm sector. This view is confirmed by Holt's (1977) study of income growth and distribution during the 1920s. Following a sharp contraction of nearly a third in 1920—1, per capita income of the farm population, as a whole, rose significantly. Holt calculates that it increased at a rate twice that of non-farm income between 1921 and 1929. Only the richest 7 per cent of the entire non-farm population increased its income by a greater amount than the farm population during the 1920s.

If this is so, why was there so much agitation amongst farmers about a squeeze on living standards? An examination of Table 2.4 provides an explanation for farm discontent. A consequence of the steep rise in farm income to 1919 was a rapid increase in land values which, by 1920, were 70 per cent above 1914 levels. A speculative boom in land developed; farmers who sold out made a big capital gain and those who bought also anticipated a capital gain. Astronomically high prices did not deter purchasers. The most marginal land rose fastest in value and farmers were even prepared to take on second mortgages in order to purchase. Credit could be readily obtained since land, now considered a prize possession, was offered as collateral. The anticipation was that, given the agricultural chaos in Europe, land values would continue to rise. A look at the volume of transfers shows few foreclosures before 1920 but an increasing number of voluntary sales. The result was that aggregate mortgage debt nearly doubled between 1914 and 1920. Nevertheless, the rise in mortgage debt and in the value of farm property rose together until 1920 (Table 2.4). Mortgage debt was not evenly distributed; indeed, seven states were responsible for more than half the value of all farm mortgages (Figure 2.1).

If the expectations of good times on the farm were not fulfilled, the result could be disaster not only for many borrowers but also for lenders. Farm aspirations received a severe jolt during the depression of 1920−1, but after this farm income staged a spectacular recovery from the very low level to which it had fallen. It rose steeply to 1925, by which time pre-war levels had been reached, and then stabilised for the remainder of the decade. The value of farm property, however, declined steadily from its 1920 peak until 1929, by which time it had reached the level which had prevailed prior to wartime speculation. On the other hand, mortgage debt rose after 1920, in spite of falling property values and, although there was a slight decline from the high levels reached by 1924, the 1929 figure was considerably above that of 1920. This increase occurred because farmers had to substitute long-term mortgages for the short-term debts which they had

Table 2.4 Indicators of Agricultural Change, 1914−30

Year	Realised gross farm income ($m.)	Total mortgage debt ($)	Index of value of farm property (1967=100)	Volume of transfers /000 farms Voluntary	Foreclosures and assignments
1914	7.8	4.7	28	28.0	3.3
1915	8.1	5.0	28	28.3	3.5
1916	9.7	5.3	30	33.0	3.8
1917	13.4	5.8	33	36.7	3.7
1918	16.5	6.5	36	37.0	3.1
1919	17.9	7.1	39	48.8	3.2
1920	15.9	8.4	48	43.4	4.0
1921	10.6	10.2	44	26.3	6.6
1922	11.1	10.7	39	24.4	11.7
1923	12.2	10.8	37	26.1	14.6
1924	12.8	10.7	36	25.5	16.7
1925	13.7	9.9	35	29.6	17.4
1926	13.3	9.7	34	28.3	18.2
1927	13.3	9.7	33	26.3	17.6
1928	13.6	9.8	22	23.5	14.8
1929	13.9	9.8	32	23.7	15.7
1930	11.5	9.6	31	19.0	18.7

Sources: Cols 1−3: *Historical Statistics of US, Colonial Times to 1970*, 2 vols (Washington DC, 1975) Series K264, 364, 16; Cols 5, 6: H. D. Guither, *Heritage of Plenty* (Danville, Ill., 1972), p. 109.

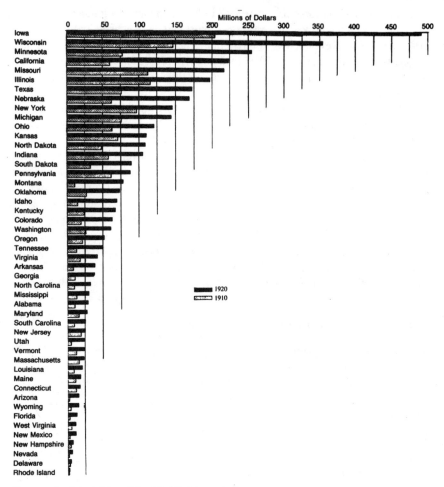

Source: Statistical Atlas of the US (Washington DC, 1925).

Figure 2.1   Mortgage Debt on Owner-operated Farms, by States, 1920 and 1910

accumulated, particularly between the years 1919—22. These mortgages were taken out at the new lower levels of farm values (Black and Boddy, 1940).

The expectations of those who had gone into debt to buy land when its price was high were unrealised, but the debt had to be repaid; many farmers were unable to do this, as is evidenced by the increasing number of foreclosures. The farms foreclosed were either let to tenants or sold to buyers who took out mortgages in order to purchase. By 1930, although the average debt per farm was only $200 higher than in 1920, the average net value of farm property was $2,750 less (Black and Boddy, 1940). The problem for many was that money had been rashly lent, and foolishly borrowed on land which would only be profitable if wartime price levels had prevailed. Farmers were victims of their own optimism (Johnson, 1973–4). Those deeply in debt found that income levels never exceeded farm operating costs by enough for the debt to be repaid, while at the same time maintaining living standards.

A look at Kansas, America's premier wheat state, illustrates graphically some of the problems facing farmers. During the five years preceding 1914 the average annual area sown to wheat in Kansas was seven million acres, but the average between 1918 and 1922 was 11.5 million acres. Once the post-war boom broke and prices fell, the acreage set aside for wheat cultivation declined but began to rise again in 1925; each successive year to 1931 established a new peak. To cultivate these farms, the 31,000 tractors used in 1925 increased to 66,000 in 1930 and the number of combines rose from 6,400 to 24,000. The level of debt increased, credit for these purchases coming from both local merchants and banks; the percentage of farms mortgaged increased noticeably between 1925 and 1930. The result was that the output of wheat steadily expanded. The crop proved to be the largest in the history of the state, even though the price of wheat that year had fallen to half that of 1928 and one quarter of the wartime peak. Wheat farmers needed to be rescued from their own enthusiasm. Too many acres were ploughed up and planted, often in those cyclically arid counties which would later become part of the dustbowl.

In conclusion, it is clear that agricultural income grew at a satisfactory rate during the 1920s and many farmers could improve their living standards considerably. As the wealth of the country increased, farmers who were able to respond to changing tastes benefited from buoyant demand. There were, nevertheless, problems particularly for the operators of small units who were never able to provide themselves with an adequate standard of living. Unfortunately they were so numerous that they distort the perception of total agricultural wealth. Much of the agricultural discontent of the 1920s, however, was the result of land speculation, based on an excessive optimism which increased the debts of a significant number of farmers to levels which became unsupportable. For them the rising level of income was poor compensation for the capital gains which never materialised. Moreover, farmers in debt would be in a perilous position if farm prices declined.

Migration

Migration enabled the total farm population, whose fecundity during the twenties was still high, to decline by about one million. Table 2.5 charts the pattern of this movement as people left farms for villages, towns and especially for cities. Once mass unemployment, a feature of the 1920–1 depression, subsided, the flow of people was such that the farm population experienced a net loss of over six million. The peak of this movement occurred between 1922 and 1926, but every year saw substantial flight away from the land. The American people have

Table 2.5 Migration to and from Farms, 1921–30 (000s)

Years	To farms	From farms	Net movement
1921	560	−896	−336
1922	759	−1323	−564
1923	1115	−2252	−1137
1924	1355	−2162	−807
1925	1581	−2068	−487
1926	1336	−2038	−702
1927	1427	−2334	−907
1928	1705	−2162	−457
1929	1698	−2120	−422
1930	1604	−2081	−477

Source: Historical Statistics of US, Colonial Times to 1970, 2 vols
(Washington DC, 1975), Series C78–80.

always been highly mobile. Indeed, each census taken between 1870 and 1930 has shown 25 per cent of the native-born population resident in a state other than the one in which they were born. Put another way, migration was such that, in 1930, 23 per cent of the total population — 22 million native whites and three million native blacks — were residing outside the state in which they had been born. From the earliest times the population had moved steadily westward and, during the last decades of the nineteenth century, had become urbanised at a rapid rate.

The scale of the movement depicted in Table 2.5 is impressive because it represents an annual average of between 3 and 6 per cent of the farm population. As a whole, the migratory pattern is more complex than an easily understood translation from farm to city. Table 2.5 also shows that a considerable number of people were moving to farms; the net migration figure of six million is the difference between the number of people leaving farms and the number arriving on them. The picture which emerges is of a two-way flow, and not simply farm dwellers seeking non-farm jobs. Indeed, it has been estimated that between 1920 and 1930 there were about 19 million moves from farms to towns or cities and some 13 million moves from towns or cities to farms. In other words, 32 million moves when the farm population numbered approximately 30 million. This does not mean that 32 million people moved; clearly, many individuals were highly mobile and migrated between town and country regularly. We can note, however, that a very large turnover of population was required to achieve a net loss of six million farm residents.

What sort of people migrated? In general, those who left the farm were young; migrants over 45 years old were rare. The study by Thornthwaite (1934) shows that the age limit for males migrating to Detroit during the 1920s was approximately 45 years. In contrast, during the preceding decade, there had been a net movement into Detroit of males up to the age of 65 years. The migratory pattern of the 1920s was also replicated in San Francisco and Cleveland. Not only were migrants relatively young but a disproportionate number of females left for a new life in urban America. The sons of farm owners, on the other hand, were more likely to remain on the land than the offspring of tenants or croppers. Not surprisingly, the sick and infirm had little incentive to move to the city.

Those moving to farms included many who were considered past their prime for urban jobs. There was a net emigration from Detroit, and some other cities, of men over 45 years of age. New Era factories provided work for the young, not for those in middle age or older. Other migrants to the farm included those returning to claim their inheritance, those returning so that younger brothers could have a chance of urban employment, and some who wished to retire in their birthplace. There was also a great deal of seasonal migration. Agriculture had fluctuating needs for labour; city dwellers could move to the countryside at harvest time when work was plentiful. There were also armies of migratory workers who followed the harvest, moving enormous distances across the country. These were hired labour; a farm family would welcome the return of urban relatives which would release them from the need to hire. Industrial labour could also be seasonal. Automobile manufacturing and construction experienced marked seasonal peaks and troughs in hiring. Unemployment in a city with no dole payment or other welfare benefit was a miserable prospect. Under such circumstances a move back to the family farm is understandable.

Migrants generally moved relatively short distances, often to an adjacent state, though a significant number moved further afield. All states experienced outward and inward migration but the greatest net gainers were the sunshine paradises of California and Florida and the industrial giants of Michigan and New York. The states which lost most people were Georgia, Pennsylvania, South Carolina and Kentucky. The overall pattern of migration in the 1920s was not the westward movement which had previously prevailed. Instead there was a migration of people from the interior to states on the Pacific coast, those surrounding the Great Lakes and those on the North Atlantic coast. The four centres of greatest attraction were New York, Los Angeles, Chicago and Detroit. Between 1920 and 1930 the counties which comprise these metropolitan areas gained 4.5 million migrants. Among those states losing population were many which had ploughed up grassland for wheat during World War I and southern states where poverty was endemic. The southern states provided a disproportionate number of migrants, scarcely surprising as unskilled wages during the 1920s were lower than in the decade before 1914 (Wright, 1986). Some 60 per cent of the total flow came from this region and only two states in it, North Carolina and Florida, gained population during the 1920s. The north-eastern quadrant of the country proved the most attractive to migrants. By 1930 this region contained more than three million southerners and 1.6 million people who had been born west of the Mississippi river.

Large-scale migration of blacks from the South to big northern cities had begun during World War I and continued during the 1920s. Black migration differed from that of whites in at least two respects. First, few blacks moved to the far West whereas the Pacific coast proved very attractive to whites. Secondly, migrating blacks favoured large urban centres and ignored villages and towns. By 1930 nearly 90 per cent of the black population of the North lived in cities; in contrast, only 32 per cent of those who lived in the South were urban dwellers. Such was the mobility of blacks after 1916, that by 1930 one out of every four had migrated from their home state. Some blacks made the long journey from the deep South to the North; for others the move was to an adjacent state. By 1930, 72,000 blacks had moved into North Carolina from South Carolina but 47,000 had moved out of North Carolina to Virginia and Maryland. Black migrants moved northwards in fairly straight lines as the previous example shows. Thus blacks travelled from Mississippi through Arkansas and Missouri on their way to Illinois and Michigan. In the Midwest, they followed the railway routes, their principal means of transport. By 1930, Chicago, Cleveland, Detroit, New York, Philadelphia, Washington DC and Baltimore all had black populations which had been growing strongly for over a decade and which were developing sizeable ghettos. Like whites, many blacks maintained strong family ties by migrating frequently to and from their place of origin.

Why did so many people leave the farm? Most were attracted by the greater economic opportunities which were available to urban residents. On average, non-farm wages were always higher than the returns from farming so a move to an industrial job, even one within the same state, was financially rewarding. Poor hill farmers in North Carolina moved to the growing cotton textile industry in that state, attracted by pecuniary rewards. There were also marked regional differences in remuneration to which migrants responded. in 1929, for example, an unskilled labourer in manufacturing industry in Arkansas earned 26 cents per hour but in Illinois the rate was 50 cents; for the same type of work a resident of South Carolina could expect 20 cents per hour but moving north the rate increased: North Carolina 24 cents, Virginia 28 cents, Pennsylvania 42 cents and New York State 54 cents. Not only were there more non-agricultural jobs in the North but the rate of pay was far higher. It is hardly surprising that this was so attractive to many working in agriculture, even though the cost of living in the city was far higher than on the farm.

Most rural migrants had few skills to offer city employers but they had youth on their side and a capacity for sustained work. Unemployment during the 1920s was low, but the net expansion in jobs during this decade was in service, not in manufacturing (see Table 1.4). A significant proportion of these were white-collar occupations, from which many southerners were barred either by colour or inferior education. The expansion of factory employment during the 1920s occurred in the consumer durable sector. Here, the use of assembly lines called for unskilled operatives who could be trained quickly and, of most importance, who were willing to work under pressure. In addition, the reduction of immigration from Europe provided an opportunity for the native-born to move into jobs which had previously been the preserve of new arrivals. Native Americans had one important skill which most Europeans lacked: fluency in English. Many of these jobs, however, were the dirty, unsocial tasks into which the immigrant is forced in any society. Blacks in particular found this a route to industrial work. In addition, black Americans dominated domestic service, a growth sector during the 1920s which gave employment to nearly two million at the end of the decade. It was especially important as it provided earnings for women when their husbands experienced short-time working or unemployment.

Migrants were pulled to the city by relatively high wages and pushed there by the poor returns from farming. The reasons for moving, however, were not always pecuniary. People left both poor farms in the Appalachian region and rich farming states such as Iowa because the natural rate of population increase was so high. There were not enough farms to absorb all rural youth. Moreover, the disadvantages of farm life included very long hours at certain times of the year, loneliness, even when eased by automobile ownership, restricted opportunities to acquire a good education and the lack of modern facilities in farm homes, as so few had electricity or piped water. Tenancy was on the increase and the possibility of farm ownership, often the reward for years of deprivation, was becoming more remote. In fact, the growth of population meant that fewer labourers could become tenants. City life, on the other hand, was thought to be glamorous, lively and exciting. The increasing use of automobiles not only made migration physically easier but also prepared rural people for it. They could visit the metropolis and see for themselves the wide range of choice available to consumers. Farmers had welcomed the automobile, believing it would transform rural life and make it so attractive to young people that the city would be less tempting. In fact it had the opposite effect.

Blacks had special reasons for leaving the South, but whether these incentives proved more powerful than monetary gain is open to debate (Higgs, 1976). By migrating to northern cities they escaped not only the boll weevil and acute poverty but also the Jim Crow laws, rural America's system of 'apartheid', which denied them not only the franchise but freedom in other spheres. Eating places, centres of entertainment and education were all segregated. Indeed, there were few if any occasions on which whites and blacks could meet as equals. This of course was insignificant compared with the terror of lynchings. In 1919, 76 blacks were lynched; during the 1920s as a whole, 291 blacks suffered this fate. Blacks did not escape discrimination when they moved to the big northern cities; after all, the ghetto was a form of *de facto* segregation. The restrictions on them, however, were so light compared with the repression of the South that even periodic race riots were no deterrent to black migrants.

In addition to the movement off the farm, there was movement between cities. In part this can be attributed to the pull of more attractive jobs, in part to the push of unemployment, or, indeed, the urge to move somewhere else. The Northeast, the traditional home of the cotton textile industry, was threatened by the increasing use of manmade fibres and, more particularly, by the gravitation of the industry .to the southern states. Textile jobs in the Carolinas, Georgia and

Alabama expanded but the New England states faced contraction. As a result northern cities which had depended for their prosperity upon cotton textiles fell upon hard times. Between 1920 and 1930, for example, four Massachusetts industrial cities, Fall River, Lawrence, Lowell and New Bedford, experienced migration losses amounting to about 20 per cent of their 1920 population. Many northern coal communities, prosperous during the war and in the immediate post-war years, could not compete with cheaper non-union southern fields when market conditions changed. They too lost people.

This redistribution of population had significant economic benefits. It moved many people from low productivity, low wage occupations to relatively high productivity, higher wage jobs. Even though the driving force behind migration was not always economic, people did move to higher wage areas or occupations. They provided a steady source of labour when the flow from Europe was reduced. The urban market for manufactured goods increased, to the benefit of big business. The housing market was also stimulated as new arrivals sought accommodation. By absorbing the expanding farm population the cities acted as a safety valve for the countryside. Many migrants did not, however, increase their real incomes as urban living costs were high. Their housing, because of severe overcrowding, was often inferior to that which they had left. All found that the choice of jobs available to them within a radius of a few miles of home was much greater than in rural regions. The risk of unemployment, however, was always present for the city dweller. In the short term, unemployment could be weathered but in the long term it made many Americans see the advantages of farm life.

Bibliography

Both agriculture and migration attracted a great deal of contemporary attention during this decade as there was a growing concern about the position of the farmer vis-à-vis the city dweller. Some of the works published during the interwar period (for example, C. Goodrich, *et al.*, E.L. Kirkpatrick, and J.H. Kolb and E. de S. Brunner) still make interesting reading, though, unfortunately, not all libraries have copies. The best modern works on farm issues during this period are by M.K. Benedict and J.H. Shideler; however, important regional problems are analysed in T. Saloutos and J.D. Hicks, G.C. Fite (1984) and G. Wright. For an interesting approach to migration, read J.G. Clark, *et al.*

Benedict, M.K. (1953) *Farm Policies of the United States, 1790—1950*, Twentieth Century Fund.
Black, J.D. and Boddy, N. (1940) 'The agricultural situation, March 1940', *The Review of Economic Statistics*, May, XXII.
Clark, J.G., *et al.* (1977) *Three Generations in Twentieth Century America*, Dorsey Press.
Engberg, R.C. (1927) *Industrial Prosperity and the Farmer*, Macmillan.
Fite, G.C. (1948) 'Voluntary attempts to reduce cotton acreage in the South', *Journal of Southern History*, 14.
Fite, G.C. (1984) *Cotton Fields No More: Southern Agriculture, 1865—1980*, University Press of Kentucky.

Goodrich, C., *et al.* (1935) *Migration and Planes of Living, 1920–1934*, University of Pennsylvania Press.

Guither, H.D. (1972) *Heritage of Plenty*, University of Illinois Press.

Higgs, R. (1976) 'The boll weevil, the cotton economy and black migration, 1910–1930', *Agricultural History*, 50.

Holt, C.F. (1977) 'Who benefited from the prosperity of the twenties?', *Explorations in Economic History*, 14.

Johnson, G.L. and Quance, C.L. (1972) *The Overproduction Trap in U.S. Agriculture: A Study of Resource Allocation from World War I to the Late 1960s*, Johns Hopkins Press.

Johnson, H.T. (1973/4) 'Postwar optimism and the rural financial crisis of the 1920s', *Explorations in Economic History*, 11.

King, C.L. (ed.) (1975) *Farm Relief*, Ayer Publishing. First published in 1929.

Kirkpatrick, E.L. (1971) *The Farmer's Standard of Living*, Ayer Publishing. First published in 1929.

Kolb, J.H. and Brunner, E. de S. (1933) 'Rural life', in *Recent Social Trends in the United States*, McGraw-Hill.

Nourse, E.G. (1924) *American Agriculture and the European Market*, McGraw-Hill.

Nourse, E.G. (1929) 'Agriculture', in *Recent Economic Changes in the United States*, McGraw-Hill.

Peterson, G.M. (1933) 'Wealth, income and living', *Journal of Farm Economics*, July, XV.

Report of the National Resources Committee (1938) *The Problems of a Changing Population*, Washington DC, May.

Saloutos, T. and Hicks, J.D. (1951) *Agricultural Discontent in the Middle West 1900–1939*, University of Wisconsin Press.

Schwartz, H. (1945) *Seasonal Farm Labor in the United States*, Columbia University Press.

Shideler, J.H. (1957) *Farm Crisis 1919–1923*, University of California Press.

Tang, A.M. (1958) *Economic Development in the Southern Piedmont, 1860–1950: Its Impact on Agriculture*, University of North Carolina Press.

Täuber, C. and Täuber, I.B. (1959) *The Changing Population of the United States*, John Wiley.

Taylor, C.C., *et al.* (1972) *Rural Life in the United States*, Greenwood Press, Westport, Conn. First published in 1949.

Thompson, W.S. and Whelpton, P.K. (1969) *Population Trends in the United States*, Kraus Rep. Co. First published in 1933.

Thornthwaite, C.W. (1934) *Internal Migration in the United States*, H. Milford.

Tindall, G.B. (1967) *The Emergence of the New South, 1913–1945*, Baton Rouge.

Truesdell, L.E. (1978) *Farm Population of the United States*, Louisiana State University Press.

Vance, R.B. (1929) *Human Factors in Cotton Culture*, Chapel Hill.

Vance, R.B. (1971) *All These People: The Nation's Human Resources in the South*, Russell and Russell. First published in 1945.

Wright, G. (1986) *Old South, New South: Revolutions in the Southern Economy since the Civil War*, Basic Books.

3

The Economy During the 1920s

The 1920s was an era of vigorous economic expansion, interrupted by a serious depression in 1920–1 and two minor recessions in 1924 and 1927. The increase in national wealth was so great that it earned this period the appellation 'prosperity decade'. Superficially at least, this seems deserved. Labour experienced rising real wages, reduced hours of work and relatively full employment at a time when trade unionism was in decline. The population embarked upon a spending spree which led to a dramatic rise in the ownership of consumer durables, with the automobile to the fore, and to a house-building boom. Wherever electricity spread, business and the public benefited. The manufacturing sector's consumption of electricity doubled during the decade and residential use tripled. Industry enjoyed high profits, substantial productivity advances, industrial harmony and public trust. New jobs were created in the expanding white-collar occupations and in the service sector, which was developing rapidly as wealth, plus additional leisure, created a growing market. On the international front, the US was the world's leading creditor nation, second only to Great Britain in international trade, and had a large balance of payments surplus. Not surprisingly, many Americans during the 1920s exuded optimism and an economic euphoria which manifested itself in speculation in property and in the stock market.

Absolutely, economic performance was good; in relative terms it was even better. Great Britain had high unemployment, relatively low productivity growth and labour unrest. The British economy was retarded by the weight of the old staple industries such as cotton textiles, coal, shipbuilding and iron and steel, in contrast to the striking advance of the consumer durables sector in America. Britain had been at the centre of the world economy before 1914 but now, with a weakened balance of payments, she was unable to resume her position as the leading international lender. Wistful British politicians and political commentators debated how the country could get back to the halcyon days which existed before 1914; in the US, minds concentrated upon the present and the future. Britain seemed to display a lack of vigour when compared with the US, a condition which was worsened, as many North Americans believed, by national welfare policies.

48

US newspapers reported the despair of unemployed British families existing on dole payments and contrasted their lot with American citizens who had no such public benefits to erode their initiative. That US unemployment levels were less serious seemed to follow naturally from these observations.

The German economy was in an equally sorry plight. Rampant hyper-inflation was only brought to a halt in 1924 with the aid of American intervention and thereafter the German economy was sustained by massive flows of American money. From 1924 to 1929 German unemployment was high, agriculture was depressed and a substantial reparations bill had to be paid. Indeed, Europe as a whole did not get back to 1913 levels of output until 1925. Recovery from the effects of 'the war to end all wars' was a depressingly lengthy process for the Old World.

During 'prosperity decade', the occupants of the White House were the Republican presidents Warren Harding (1920–3) and Calvin Coolidge (1923–9). Both were distinctly non-interventionist by nature, as was the Secretary of the Treasury, Andrew Mellon. These three stressed the limits of government power; they believed that state intervention could destabilise the economy and hold back expansion. Harding and Coolidge listened to the supporters of business, especially the two most powerful lobbyists, the National Association of Manufacturers (NAM) and the US Chamber of Commerce. These pressure groups believed that it was the duty of the government to reduce to a minimum the burdens on business. The federal government obliged; taxation on the wealthy was cut in the belief that the benefits would trickle down to enrich the masses. Positive aid, too, was tried: additional tariff protection was given to industry. War experience had blunted the anti-trust crusade and Congress now legislated in favour of big business; in addition, the courts used their powers to prevent trade unions from exercising their strength to the full during strikes. The result was that business grew larger and unions smaller. Neither Harding nor Coolidge displayed any enthusiasm for federal leadership in social reform, preferring to leave such matters to the states or the localities who, it was thought, were in a better position to assess the needs of their fellows and minister to them.

Harding, Coolidge and Mellon were part of a group, becoming old-fashioned by the 1920s, who felt that the least government was the best government. Mellon even saw great benefits in depressions: they cleansed the economic system, sending the weak to oblivion and enabling the survivors to rise strong and reinvigorated. He counselled against any government intervention during economic crises, believing that action, however well motivated, would have a deleterious long-term effect by merely postponing the inevitable. Thus we see a very pro-business administration in Washington whose ethos can be summarised in Calvin Coolidge's aphorism 'the business of America is business; he who builds a factory builds a temple'.

Not all politicians or businessmen were dedicated to the cause of political nonintervention. Considerable numbers of industrialists who had served the government during World War I had been impressed by the advantages gained from governmental guidance. Congress, for its part, enacted several regulatory statutes during the 1920s. The Transportation Act (1920), for example, gave the Interstate Commerce Commission authority to set minimum prices; the Federal Radio Act (1927) set up the Federal Radio Commission to allocate frequencies for broadcasting. Thus the regulatory trend established before 1914 continued, though only in specialised areas.

There was also a growing conviction, shared by the Secretary of Commerce, Herbert Hoover, that economic booms and slumps were not acts of God over which there was no control. Hoover and his acolytes believed that economic performance could be improved and stabilised if sufficient information were gathered to enable informed decisions to be made. This view stemmed in part from the wartime experience when data gathering on a large scale was undertaken for the first time. There were high hopes that Amercia was close to developing a new, superior form of capitalism which other nations would envy, but, because of their class or nationalistic rivalries, could not emulate (Barber, 1985).

The Department of Commerce became an assiduous collector and disseminator of business information. Where it could not gather statistics itself, it supported and co-operated with trade associations which were themselves enthusiastic accumulators of data. Indeed, the trade associations had an important role in the new economic model. Individual firms operating independently were potentially unstable, but as part of a wider grouping, they benefited from the additional information, the collective will and the improved managerial standards which stemmed, or were supposed to stem, from associationalism and which gave greater control over economic fluctuations. Business decisions could be planned more sensibly in a manner similar to the deliberations of major corporations. The big corporations did not need the protection of trade associations, but thousands of small companies felt that the oligopolistic advantages enjoyed by their larger competitors could be extended if they joined forces with fellow producers. The advantages of such collusion, as we have seen, were clear before 1914: stabilisation of output, cost reduction, and more effective political lobbying were just some of them. Their experience of the war economy, and indeed the serious price falls of 1920–1, convinced even more proprietors that stability was far more likely under the umbrella of collective action. For these reasons, trade associations grew from about 700 in 1919 to over 2,000 by 1929.

Associations appealed to Hoover as examples of management using its collective intelligence to help itself. They were the acme of industrial voluntarism. The federal government played its part by providing information and advice; Hoover's department strove to educate management to eliminate waste and to use the most up-to-date production methods. Hoover, the engineer, felt that efficiency was the way to dampen the swings of the trade cycle. If depression did strike, however, he was a supporter of counter-cyclical public works to lessen the impact upon jobs.

Another important part of the Hoover strategy, as Barber explains, was high wages. Efficient industries could increase output, but what if the products could not be sold? High wages would eradicate the danger of over-production. Moreover, high wages would also lead to a contented workforce, one which would willingly co-operate with management initiatives and avoid the costly conflicts so apparent in Europe. Labour, now without the distraction of alcohol which was banned by prohibition, and no longer influenced by troublesome unions, could form a harmonious liaison with the employers, a striking illustration of the American way. To counter the argument that high wages would penalise labour by pricing workers out of jobs, immigration controls were imposed, in order to cut off a cheap labour supply. To satisfy business worries that high wages would adversely affect costs, tariffs were increased, while at the same time a contradictory export campaign was pursued.

This new capitalism was not to everyone's taste. For some it was redolent of excessive government intervention, for others it was a pale substitute for the only guarantee of stability: planning. Those who shared Mellon's economic Darwinism felt that any interference in the free workings of the economic system was doomed to failure. To the energetic Secretary of Commerce and 'under-secretary of everything else', however, this was the new era of advancing wealth without the instability of past decades. The age of the technocrat had dawned and America was to display its advantages to the world.

Manufacturing Industry

Some of the principal factors relating to manufacturing during the 1920s have already been considered in Chapter 1. During this decade the population of the US rose by 16 per cent while the number of wage earners employed in manufacturing industry declined slightly. Nevertheless, because of rapidly increasing productivity, output increased considerably. Manufacturing growth was concentrated into two sharp bursts: 1921–3, when the economy rebounded vigorously from the post-war depression, and 1928–9. During the intervening years other sectors played a leading role in the growth of the economy.

Although the manufacturing labour force seems unchanged in the period under consideration, closer analysis reveals that workers were leaving declining industries while other industries expanded their workforce. Machinery, automobiles, textiles and iron and steel gained numerically while transport equipment producers, together with rubber, leather and chemical manufacturers, lost labour. There was also a geographic reorganisation of the workforce. The New England, Mid-Atlantic and West North Central states saw their manufacturing wage earners decline while those in the rest of the country increased. Thus Massachusetts had 714,000 manufacturing wage earners in 1919 but only 557,000 in 1929, while in New Jersey 509,000 wage earners declined to 442,000. In contrast, Michigan, the home of the automobile industry, experienced a rise from 471,000 to 530,000, and North Carolina a similar rise from 158,000 to 210,000, as the cotton textile industry gained further ground and cigarette sales grew. Thus some states which had been industrially powerful during the nineteenth century were losing ground to newcomers. In general, however, the northern states monopolised the production of both producer and consumer durables during the 1920s.

Another noticeable feature of this decade is that, in spite of increasing output, the number of firms in the manufacturing sector declined. The 214,000 establishments in 1919 fell to 196,000 in 1921; in 1929 the figure was 211,000. Clearly, the amount that the average firm could produce increased during the 1920s. A reason for the reduction was the strong merger movement which was evident not only in manufacturing industry but also in finance, in banking, and in utilities.

Manufacturing industry at this time was dominated by the production of durable goods. Between 1922 and 1929 the output of durables rose at about 6 per cent per annum while non-durables grew at less than 3 per cent per annum. Both producer and consumer durables formed a larger proportion of GNP during the twenties than in any period before 1914. However, as Gordon (1961) stresses, the growth of the manufacturing sector accounted for only 15 per cent of the increase in national income. Other industries, such as construction, public utilities and especially the service and the financial sectors, played a more significant role. Indeed, a rise of some four million in the non-agricultural labour force took place outside manufacturing.

The striking feature of manufacturing is the formidable growth of productivity after 1920. Table 3.1 shows the contraction of this sector during 1920−1, when employment fell by 25 per cent, and the vigorous growth which followed. The recession of 1924 is visible, but that of 1927 does not show up in these data. Figures for investment, the key to productivity expansion, are shown in Table 3.2. The importance of the construction industry (see below) is immediately apparent. It is also clear that the level of expenditure on producer durables remain-

Table 3.1 Indexes of Manufacturing Productivity, 1920−9 (1929 = 100)

Year	Output	Persons engaged	Output per person	Man-hours	Output per man-hour
1920	66.0	100.1	65.9	107.3	61.5
1921	53.5	77.4	69.1	75.4	71.0
1922	68.1	84.7	80.4	84.7	80.4
1923	76.9	96.2	79.9	99.3	77.4
1924	73.4	90.2	81.4	89.2	82.3
1925	81.9	92.7	88.3	93.4	87.7
1926	86.2	94.7	91.0	96.4	89.4
1927	87.1	93.5	93.0	95.2	91.5
1928	90.1	93.8	93.2	94.2	95.5
1929	100.0	100.0	100.0	100.0	100.0

Source: J. Kendrick, *Productivity Trends in the US* (NBER, Princeton University Press, 1961), Table D-11.

Table 3.2   Gross Private Domestic Investment, 1919–29
($ billion)

Year	Gross private new construction	Gross private producer durables	Gross private domestic investment
1919	4.4	3.9	12.4
1920	5.4	4.8	17.5
1921	4.8	3.0	7.8
1922	6.3	3.2	10.1
1923	8.1	4.6	15.7
1924	8.9	4.3	12.2
1925	9.8	4.7	16.2
1926	10.5	5.1	17.0
1927	10.0	4.7	15.1
1928	9.5	5.0	14.1
1929	8.9	5.6	16.2

Source: J.A. Swanson and S.H. Williamson (1972–3),
'Estimates of national product and income for the
United States economy', *Explorations in Economic
History*, 10 (1972–3), Table A-2.

ed high throughout, though its most rapid advances were at the beginning and the end of the decade. How can this relatively high level of investment be explained?

In the first place, there was a strong incentive to invest since it was financially rewarding and the resulting profits provided the funds for further investment. Moreover, if the amount of self-finance was ever insufficient, there was ample funding to be had from the banking sector or, indeed, from the flourishing stock exchange. High profits also contributed to the general feeling of business optimism which was evident during this period and without which no investment boom can take place.

Business received a further stimulus from the high level of demand for its products. Consumption expenditure did not collapse during the depression of 1920–1 and its buoyancy during the 1920s was even more impressive than that of investment. Consumers were keen to acquire new items; they were even prepared to go into debt to buy automobiles and new homes. The growth in the range of products flooding onto the market was extensive and was accompanied by massive advertising campaigns and professional marketing. As demand rose, industry responded by producing more goods.

Changing technology also played a key role in productivity improvement. US industry had a long established tradition of using interchangeable parts and an emphasis upon standardised products, which had increased during the war years. These techniques were avidly adopted by the new consumer durable industries.

Much of the recently introduced machinery, though sophisticated, could be used by unskilled and semi-skilled workers. The spread of electricity enabled companies to use machinery which was far more efficient and flexible than that powered by either steam or water. The use of special tools, many of them automatic and made from new non-ferrous metals (for example, tungsten carbide), which increased their speed and cutting power, became more widespread (Rezneck, 1951). The machinery industry displayed one of the fastest rates of expansion during the twenties. If we aggregate the wage earners in the various groups which comprise this industry there were more workers than in any other manufacturing industry. There were over 10,000 machinery firms employing 860,000 in 1925 and 1.1 million in 1929. The growth of output in electrical machinery was especially rapid after 1920, but all branches embarked upon a programme of technological improvement. They satisfied an expanding home market as well as providing 35 per cent of the world's exports of machinery. This industry was at the cutting edge of the productivity drive of the 1920s.

During the late nineteenth century, the heavy industries, which were dominated by large corporations, pioneered mass production techniques. These were exploited, for example, by the iron and steel companies where large masses of materials were handled in a continuous sequence and where demand was relatively uniform. The new consumer durable industries were also able to use mass production techniques which, with special-purpose machinery and a cost-conscious management, enabled firms to make large profits without increasing prices. These factors, plus new management techniques and a lack of opposition to change from the labour force, provided an effective means of responding to an expanding market. High profits, rising stock prices and little legal opposition to increasing size helped to bring about a strong merger movement during the 1920s. The big corporations were able to use increasingly sophisticated office equipment: the use of the telephone, the teletype and more effective means of keeping business records meant that head office could be located in Chicago or New York, and plant or raw materials supplies, hundreds of miles away, could be controlled. One incentive to increase size was the belief that growth would lead to more influence upon the level of sales. It also meant that the unit costs of advertising, marketing, scientific research and works study were all reduced. Management could be more effectively trained and more efficiently used in large rather than in small units. Moreover, the big corporations could afford the latest capital equipment and the scale of their production enabled them to use it more efficiently. By 1930, the 200 largest corporations in manufacturing and in transport produced more than 56 per cent of the goods and services in these sectors (Cochran, 1951).

As a result of growing investment and increasingly professional management, output per man hour and per unit of labour input displayed a steep rise throughout the decade (Table 3.1). However, we must not consider productivity advances as a mere arithmetical exercise. What were the results of the increases which have been described?

One result was that in spite of the enormous growth of consumer demand, the level of wholesale prices remained remarkably stable after 1922. This is not the pattern of price behaviour we would expect in the course of a vigorous boom. An inflationary spiral would have been more typical. As manufacturing productivity was very much higher than in other sectors of the economy, the goods which were produced, many of which could be described as luxuries, were placed within the reach of many ordinary families. However, we must realise that, given the surge of productivity improvement, there was ample scope for considerable price reduction, not just price stability.

Another beneficiary from productivity growth was labour, through reduced hours of work and increased wages. The position of the labour force will be discussed later but it should be noted that the financial gains of the workforce were extremely modest if compared with the productivity growth. The vast bulk of the productivity gains, therefore, went not to the consumer, nor to labour, but to shareholders or other owners in the form of profit. Such a distribution meant that income became progressively skewed in favour of the owners of capital. Profits increased the attraction of share ownership and were a powerful force encouraging mergers. Moreover, highly profitable firms were no longer dependent upon the banking sector for finance; as a result banks had to seek other ways of using depositors' funds to earn money. Finally, US exports could compete successfully with goods produced by workers whose wages were lower than those in America because American productivity levels were always higher.

The industry which best illustrates the rise to prominence of consumer durables and which became so big that it influenced the whole economy, is automobile manufacture. By 1929 motor vehicle producers ranked seventh in the league of manufacturing wage earners and first if assessed by the value of their product (Table 3.3). Workers in the motor vehicle bodies and parts sector were the eighth most competitive amongst the number of wage earners and ranked ninth when the value of its products was considered. Together these two industries employed 447,000 wage earners, fractionally less than the leading employer, foundry and machine shop products (454,000) and above the second ranked cotton goods industry (425,000). Factory sales of automobiles rose from 1.9 million in 1920 to 4.4 million in 1929. During the 1920s the US manufactured approximately 85 per cent of the world's passenger cars, a dominance made all the more striking when we consider that just two companies, Ford and General Motors, together accounted for 65 per cent of US sales. Ford dominated the automobile profit league between 1920 and 1926, General Motors thereafter.

The influence of the automobile industry was pervasive. It provided one of the chief markets for the steel industry and for the manufacturers of glass and tyres. In addition, motorists were regular purchasers of petrol. The technology of these anci¹liary industries, and many more, was revolutionised by the demands of the motor car. To satisfy the needs of motorists, a highway construction boom was undertaken; to finance it, many states went deep into debt. New jobs were created in automobile repair shops, in showrooms and in petrol stations. The holiday

Table 3.3 Relative Importance of Leading Manufacturing Industries, 1929

Industry	Number of establishments	Wage earners		Value of products	Value added by manufacture
		Av. for year	Rank	Rank	Rank
Foundry and machine shop products not elsewhere classified	8,605	454,441	1	4	1
Cotton goods	1,281	424,916	2	11	13
Lumber and timber products not elsewhere classified	12,915	419,084	3	12	6
Iron and steel: steel works and rolling mills	486	394,574	4	3	2
Car and general constr. and repairs, steam railroad repair shops	1,851	368,681	5	13	12
Electrical machinery and supplies	1,802	328,722	6	6	4
Motor vehicles, not incl. motor cycles	244	226,116	7	1	5
Motor vehicle bodies and parts	1,154	221,332	8	9	11
Knit goods	1,888	208,488	9	23	19
Boots and shoes, other than rubber	1,341	205,640	10	19	18

Source: 15th Census of US Manufactures, 1929

business expanded as motorists took to the road; the growth of Florida and California was, in part, a response to increasing leisure time and the growing income of motorists. The suburban real estate boom would not have been possible without the expansion of motor vehicle ownership, nor would the new shopping plazas or chain stores, located on the fringes of cities to attract rural as well as urban customers from a wide area. In 1919, General Motors, with the foundation of its Acceptance Corporation, pioneered the development of modern consumer credit. By the mid-1920s over 70 per cent of motor car sales were financed by hire purchase, which was vital as they were relatively expensive. There seemed to be scarcely any part of the economy which was not influenced by the passenger car, the truck, the bus or the tractor.

The pioneer who brought the car to the people was Henry Ford. His use of

the continuous assembly line led to a tremendous reduction in the man-hours required to produce a single vehicle. That vehicle, the model T, was so standardised that it was available only in black. Its price, however, was progressively
reduced, from $950 to $290 in 1924, which respresented three months' wages
for the best-paid factory worker. Ford continued to improve his capital equipment, introducing new purpose-built machinery and reorganising the factory lay-
out in order to improve efficiency. The majority of jobs in automobile plants were
for unskilled workers. Indeed, as early as 1923, Henry Ford had claimed that
80 per cent of all automobile jobs took no more than a week to learn. The emphasis when hiring labour was not on the level of skill but on the dexterity, speed,
stamina and ability to concentrate on repetitive tasks. The need was for young
workers, which fits in with the migratory patterns identified for Detroit in Chapter
2.

The attraction of automobile jobs was their relatively high pay: Ford's rate
of $7 per day as a minimum, established in 1929, was a striking example. A
survey taken of 100 families of Ford employees who earned $1,700 in 1930 found
that 47 owned an automobile (a lower level of ownership than we might have
expected, given the national figures) 36 owned a radio, 5 an electric sewing
machine, 19 an electric vacuum cleaner, 49 an electric washing machine and 98
an electric iron. Furthermore, 59 families had hire purchase commitments, mostly
for furniture, electrical goods and automobiles. These families were very comfortably off by the standards of the unskilled but it is interesting to note the penetration of consumer durables and the willingness to go into debt in order to acquire
them. There was, however, no guarantee that labour would be employed con-
sistently throughout the year. Indeed, the industry was prone to wide seasonal
variations in output which led to considerable job insecurity. During the 1920s,
the seasonal range of output for the automobile industry was such that December,
the low point, was 33 per cent below average and May, the peak, 24 per cent
above it. Workers were frequently laid off, and as their training occupied only
a few days it cost very little for employers to take on new workers with no
experience.

Eventually Ford, after producing 15 million model Ts, succumbed to the strategy
pioneered by General Motors, namely, annual model changes and built-in
obsolescence. In 1927 Ford closed down his plants, throwing tens of thousands
out of work, and tooled up for the Model A which appeared in the following
year. By that time, however, General Motors had assumed the leadership of the
industry.

Henry Ford, of course, was an anachronism — a nineteenth-century entrepreneur
in the age of the technocrat. The vision of the future in American industry was
created by General Motors, which pioneered the multi-divisional structure under
the guidance of Pierre du Pont and Alfred P. Sloan. The management structure
which General Motors evolved during the 1920s did not rely upon a centralised
organisation but upon separate divisions whose functions were defined according to the particular segment of the market which each served. There were,

therefore, five different divisions for particular classes of motor cars, ranging from the most expensive — Cadillac, to the cheapest — Chevrolet. A general office was staffed by executives who, freed from the burden of discharging daily operating duties, formulated policy with the aid of data collected and prepared by skilled staff. The corporation attempted to match production with demand, with each division submitting forecasts of the resources which it would require for each month's production. Forecasting techniques became extremely sophisticated; allowances were made for expansion and contraction in the economy caused either by the trade cycle or by seasonal fluctuations. Statistics on market share and sales were collected regularly to monitor the accuracy of predictions. As Alfred Chandler has shown, the General Motors model, with its general office and autonomous integrated divisions, was gradually adopted by other major corporations.

In spite of high levels of demand, automobile output fluctuated. 1921, 1924 and 1927 saw production decline, but 1928 and the first half of 1929 was a time of exceptional growth for cars and for trucks. During these years nearly 17 per cent of the total value of fully and semi-manufactured goods was accounted for by automotive products. In addition to the home market, a flourishing export trade was built up. Between 1927 and 1929, 30 per cent of all commercial vehicles and 10 per cent of passenger cars were exported. Furthermore, by the end of the decade American manufacturers had established over 60 auto assembly plants overseas. America had taken to the automobile avidly, but it was impossible for the expansion which began in 1928 to continue indefinitely. No one could have envisaged, however, the contraction which actually took place.

The output of durable goods expanded by 40 per cent between November 1927 and June 1929, yet both consumer and producer durables were prone to great cyclical swings. In previous depressions, for example, automobile output and machinery production contracted severely. Nor was the growing dependence upon exports reassuring, as a drop in the income of overseas purchasers or the erection of tariff barriers could seriously hinder sales. In 1929 there was still scope for additional sales of both automobiles and of a wide range of electrical goods. Not everyone who wanted these goods possessed them and many more could not afford them. In spite of the rapid electrification of the country, only 10 per cent of farms had electricity in 1930, compared with 85 per cent of non-farm dwellings. The purchase of consumer durables, however, required buoyant incomes and the confidence to go into debt. In this context the distribution of income during the twenties, an issue which we will analyse later, is important.

In any investigation of the depression it is understandable that the manufacturing sector should be probed for weaknesses. In doing so, we should not overlook its strengths. The tremendous growth of output in 1928—9 was accomplished without pressure on wages or other costs. There was no sign of inflation and there was no shortage of capital. Furthermore, the crises of 1924 and 1927 had been weathered. Manufacturing industry could satisfy industrial and consumer demand, seemingly without difficulty. Indeed, the growing stock market speculation was, in a sense, a tribute to the productive power and the profitability of American industry.

Construction

Table 3.2 reveals the importance of the building sector for the overall level of investment during the 1920s. At its peak, in 1926, the value of new construction was double that of producer durables and represented over 60 per cent of gross private domestic investment. In 1926 also, residential building accounted for just over 40 per cent of the value of total new construction. We should note, however, that residential construction was not only important but was also unstable; a long building cycle, with peaks 15 to 20 years apart, is noticeable from the middle of the nineteenth century until 1933. The building cycle was characterised by its great amplitude; there was often a marked difference between the peak and the trough. A downturn in building usually coincided with a major depression in the economy, but not always; for example, no slump accompanied the trough in the cycle which occurred in 1909.

During the 1920s the US experienced a building boom, the details of which are presented in Table 3.4. After a brief flurry of activity which was halted by

Table 3.4 Expenditure for New Construction, 1918–30 ($ million)

Year	Total new construction	Private non-farm residential building	Private non-residential building	Public construction
1918	5.1	0.5	2.4	0.7
1919	6.4	1.4	3.0	0.9
1920	6.7	1.2	4.2	1.2
1921	6.4	2.0	2.8	1.5
1922	8.0	3.2	3.2	1.7
1923	9.7	4.2	3.9	1.6
1924	10.8	4.8	4.1	1.9
1925	11.9	5.2	4.6	2.1
1926	12.6	5.2	5.3	2.1
1927	12.4	4.8	5.2	2.4
1928	12.0	4.5	5.0	2.5
1929	11.2	3.4	5.3	2.5
1930	9.0	1.9	4.3	2.8

Source: *Historical Statistics of US, Colonial Times to 1970,* 2 vols (Washington DC, 1970), Series N70–7. These figures have been rounded up.

the 1920—1 depression, the construction industry embarked upon a period of spectacular growth. Until 1926, residential building was the driving force, but, as that declined, non-residential and public construction helped to keep the aggregate level of activity high. The decline of residential building from its peak in 1926 to 1929 is noticeable. Nevertheless, during the latter year the value of new house building, expressed in constant dollars, was greater than in any year between 1881, when these data were first collected, and 1923.

How can this construction boom be explained? Clearly, the one and a half million people who were added to the population each year needed housing, and extensive migration greatly added to demand both in the cities and in suburbia. Moreover, a backlog had been created during World War I, when little construction took place. To this we can add the stimulation of expanding incomes and stable building costs. Furthermore, the tastes of house purchasers changed during the 1920s, in part due to the influence of the automobile. Car ownership enabled suburban development to take place, but, in addition, there were significant improvements in public transport during the decade. Smaller families increased the demand for more compact houses or apartments. A rising interest in leisure activities persuaded many that locations outside cities were far more desirable than the confines of the metropolis.

Many of the new houses, of course, were beyond the reach of even those with average incomes. Such people often purchased older property, sometimes the home of those who moved to the periphery of the city. Most families, however, continued to live in rented accommodation, though the proportion of homes in this category fell from 59 per cent in 1920 to 54 per cent in 1930. A high proportion of single migrants to the city followed tradition and lived in hotels, rooming houses, or became lodgers. If the latter, they provided an important addition to the often deficient income of the families whose home they shared.

Home ownership necessitates a high level of debt. During the late nineteenth century, US savings were insufficient for all domestic needs and imports of capital were required to help finance economic expansion. During the 1920s, however, savings were so ample that all domestic calls upon them could be met and, in addition, an extensive amount of overseas lending undertaken. Not only were savings relatively high but the growth of specialist institutions mobilised these funds and made them available for mortgage borrowers all over the country. In this context the savings and loan associations were especially important, but mutual savings banks, commercial banks and life insurance companies also provided home finance. Residential non-farm mortgage debt rose from less than $8 bn in 1919 to $27 bn in 1929. Credit was plentiful for mortgage seekers and the confidence which prevailed during the decade encouraged a relatively high level of debt. However, many prospective home owners were forced to borrow on a short-term basis; they found these loans very difficult to renew after 1929. Enthusiasm in this field often spilled over into speculation, which was especially evident in Florida during the mid-1920s.

The boom was accompanied by an improvement in building techniques. Trade associations in the building industry financed research in order to advance technology. New materials, better paints and quick-drying cement were among the improvements which resulted. Sound building standards became more widely accepted and the construction companies, by using new electric or air pressure tools, were able to increase the efficiency of their workforce. In addition, a higher proportion of building became subject to zoning regulation than had been the case previously.

Non-residential building was influenced by the high level of company profits. Corporations could easily finance new office buildings or erect department or chain stores; indeed, the growth of commercial buildings was more spectacular than that of industrial. Public utilities, especially electric light and power and telephones, also made an important contribution to the growth of private non-residential construction. The expansion of automobile ownership changed shopping habits. Rural dwellers in particular were prepared to drive long distances to large urban centres. Retail store construction, often on the outskirts of cities, was welcomed by everyone except, perhaps, small-town shopkeepers.

The most important element in public construction was road building. The Federal Highway Act (1916) obliged all states which did not already have a highway department to establish one. The Federal Bureau of Public Roads was then able to co-operate with the state departments in building a co-ordinated system of highways. In addition, several regional planning bodies were established during the 1920s in order to stimulate co-operation in road building. Nevertheless, in spite of these great efforts, the percentage of roads surfaced in some states, mainly rural, was very low at the end of the decade. The improving road system, however, was conducive to greater mobility, the development of bus and truck operations, and increased automobile ownership.

An assessment of the construction industry at the end of the decade is not easy. The decline in residential construction after 1926 does not coincide with a rise in housing costs, or a fall in income, or a drop in economic activity. Nor does it indicate that all Americans were adequately housed. Demand was declining among those who could afford to buy, given the prevailing distribution of income. It is clear, however, that if the building sector as a whole collapsed it could have serious repercussions on the entire economy. The industry was a major employer and high levels of unemployment would swiftly follow its decline. We should note also the links between construction and many other industries which benefited from the boom and would be smitten by the slump. Lumber, structural steel, cement, brick, clay products, plumbing, heating equipment, paint, glass and furniture are just a few among those which would feel a chill blast. Many of the bulky commodities used in building were transported by rail; a fall in freight revenues would lead to unemployment for many railway workers. An adverse change in business conditions would also lead to a decline in non-residential building, as company profits were reduced and expectations dimmed. Finally, the high level of mortgage debt held by individuals could assume intolerable proportions if prices fell and increased the real burden. Difficulties over repayment would coincide with a reluctance to purchase new housing. Unfortunately for the construction industry, the decision to postpone the purchase of a home is an easy one to take.

Jobs and Income

Table 3.5 shows the growth of the labour force during the 1920s and the estimates of unemployemnt which were calculated by Stanley Lebergott. Although the federal government collected data on an impressive scale during and after World War I, at no stage did it embark upon a systematic attempt to measure national unemployment. The censuses of 1890, 1900 and 1910 attempted to record the numbers of those who were without jobs on the census dates but the results were considered to have little value since publication took so long. Indeed, so dissatisfied were officials with this method of compilation that the 1910 figures were never published. President Harding's unemployment conference in 1921 had to make do with 'guesstimates' of the numbers of the unemployed, which ranged from four to six million.

Both Germany and Great Britain had unemployment insurance schemes which made possible a national count of those without work who had contributed to the scheme. No similar programmes existed in the US and observers had therefore to rely upon a variety of estimates covering particular industries, localities or

Table 3.5 The Labour Force and Unemployment, 1920–30
(thousands of persons 14 years old and over)

		Unemployed		
Year	Civilian labour force	Total	% of civilian labour force	% of non-farm employees
1920	41,340	2,132	5.2	8.6
1921	41,979	4,918	11.7	19.5
1922	42,496	2,859	6.7	11.4
1923	43,444	1,049	2.4	4.1
1924	44,235	2,190	5.0	8.3
1925	45,196	1,453	3.2	5.4
1926	45,629	801	1.8	2.9
1927	46,375	1,519	3.3	5.4
1928	47,105	1,982	4.2	6.9
1929	47,757	1,550	3.2	5.3
1930	48,523	4,340	8.9	14.2

Source: *Historical Statistics of US, Colonial Times to 1970*, 2 vols (Washington DC, 1975), Series D4, 8–10.

groups of workers. The figures produced by Lebergott are the most acceptable but they are estimates, and are not derived from a systematic recording of the jobless. A range of alternative calculations, and some of their deficiencies, can be found in a short article by Smiley (1983).

Table 3.5 shows a rising labour force which, after 1921, did not face a major unemployment crisis. The growth in total employment between 1920 and 1929 was the result of an increase of approximately 50 per cent in service jobs. We have seen that jobs in domestic service, public service and finance expanded, while agriculture, mining and manufacturing contributed practically nothing to the net growth. Given the increase in service jobs, it is not surprising that the number of females employed rose from 8.3 million in 1920 to 10.6 million in 1930. During the same period the percentage of the female labour force that was married rose from 23 to 29 per cent. The number of homes with two wage earners, therefore, increased during the 1920s. In contrast, during the 1930s, the labour force rose by six million but, in spite of the New Deal, 14.6 per cent of the civilian labour force were unemployed in 1940, as were 21.3 per cent of non-farm employees. The 1920s, therefore, appear as a triumph of relatively full employment.

This interpretation has been challenged by Bernstein (1960), who views the period as one of severe insecurity and widespread unemployment in many industries and areas. There is no doubt that many industries were relatively depressed at this time. Shipbuilding, footwear, the railways and cotton textiles in New England were hard hit. Another staple industry — coalmining — experienced severe regional problems. In 1918 petroleum, natural gas and hydro-electric power supplied 18 per cent of US energy needs; by 1927 the figure was 36 per cent. The coal industry as a whole had substantial surplus capacity but the economic squeeze was felt most severely in the high-cost union fields of the North, which could not compete with operators in West Virginia or Tennessee, where the costs of coal extraction and wages were lower. The average number of men working daily in US coal mines was 862,536 in 1923 but only 654,494 in 1929. In the more depressed fields, wages had been cut during this period, the two-day week had become common, and so had widespread poverty.

A number of investigations highlight the problems faced by workers during 'prosperity decade'. A study of Philadelphia undertaken in April 1929, before the depression began to bite, showed that 10.4 per cent of wage earners were out of work. The Lynds' classic study of Middletown (Muncie, Indiana) in 1924 found that workers and their families faced higher levels of unemployment than Lebergott's figures would suggest. Other studies also found unemployment to be a worrying problem (Keyssar, 1986; Stricker, 1983; Worcester, 1929). Many workers viewed the 1920s as an era of job uncertainty; they were anxious about the pace of technological advance which could render them jobless even if skilled, and frustrated by the seasonal fluctuations in many trades. The remorseless march of machinery was identified by many as a source of misfortune. Calculations by F.C. Mills (1932) demonstrated that manufacturing employment had become more unstable. Between 1923 and 1929 one worker in twenty was forced to seek employment in a new manufacturing or non-manufacturing industry, more than double the separation rate for 1899—1914. A large number of industries, the most obvious being construction, were highly seasonal, but we have noted that automobile manufacturing exhibited this characteristic also. Out of work, with no unemployment benefit and often little savings, the jobless faced a harsh reality. There are few studies of the relative difficulty with which the unemployed found new employment during the 1920s. Investigations by Lubin (1929) and Myers (1929) revealed that, of the groups which they studied, the majority had to wait for three or four months before re-employment, and most then earned less than in their previous jobs.

The evidence available is not sufficient to back Bernstein's assertion that the 1920s was a bleak period for jobs. We do need, however, to look beyond the aggregate statistics and remember that the labour market was volatile for certain groups and that even short periods without work could result in grave financial hardship. Moreover, few workers had any security of employment; the unskilled particularly were liable to instant dismissal when business conditions altered. They also faced competition for jobs from new arrivals from rural America.

Organised Labour

During the 1920s, unionism experienced a decline after a substantial growth during the war and post-war period. Union membership, which had just exceeded five million in 1920, fell sharply for two years and then rose steadily to reach 3.4 million in 1929. Unions failed to win key strikes in 1919 and 1920, where victory was essential if wartime gains were to be consolidated. These failures were exacerbated by the 1920—1 depression; unemployment rose, wages were cut, and employers who previously had recognised unions were able to withdraw that recognition once recovery began.

After 1921, unions faced strong employers who were hostile to the labour movement and fought against it positively, by using injunctions against strike action. Many of these injunctions were based on the 'yellow dog contract', where an employee promised to refrain from striking, or even joining a union, as part of his or her conditions of employment. Failure to keep this 'oath' led to the use of the legal process by employers, a course of action made all the more easy by the relatively anti-union stance taken by the courts in their interpretation of the law. Unions were also kept at bay, especially in the new consumer goods industries, by a combination of high rates of pay and a vigorous weeding out of any workers who attempted to organise their fellows. The automobile companies were amongst the most prominent anti-union employers. Management praised the open shop, or the 'American Plan' as it became known, and confidently asserted their right to run their businesses without outside interference.

In an age of high profit, many firms were able to provide what they saw as substitutes for trade unionism. Company unions, or worker representatives on works councils, were presented as a more modern way of dealing with, or better still, avoiding, industrial disputes. Welfare capitalism was developed to keep the workforce contented. Company sports facilities, company housing, company catering, pension plans, house magazines, profit sharing agreements and other devices were used to persuade the workforce that their loyalties lay with their firm and not with a trade union (Brandes, 1970). Furthermore, workers dependent upon their employers for housing or pensions would not court dismissal. Employers could congratulate themselves that this was an era of industrial peace, in sharp contrast to the years between 1916 and 1921 when the number of strikes was high.

The union cause was not helped by the AFL. Union leaders had never made any attempt to form a political alliance with the Republican or the Democrat parties. Unlike organised labour in Britain, they did not found their own political party. Instead, the AFL was more concerned with quashing any political initiative which might be tinged with socialism. Conservative and craft-conscious, the AFL did not try to organise workers in the new consumer goods industries or in the expanding service sector. As membership in the traditional strongholds such as coalmining, metals and machinery, textiles and transport fell, the centres of employment growth were relatively unorganised. The drift of the cotton textile industry to the southern states meant a migration from a highly unionised region to one where trade unions had made little impact. Many local unions were moribund during the twenties and some were in the hands of organised crime or small-scale crooks, whereas business rose in the public esteem. The union movement seemed an anachronism, occasionally tainted in the public's mind with socialism, unable to keep its own house in order and becoming increasingly irrelevant to the New Era.

Earnings and the Distribution of Income

What happened to wages and hours of work during the 'prosperity decade'? At first glance, wage rises seem to have been impressive. Lebergott calculates that, after a deduction for unemployment, the average annual real earnings for all employees rose from $639 in 1922 to $793 in 1929. Another calculation by the US Bureau of Labor Statistics shows that average weekly earnings in manufacturing rose from $21.28 in 1922 to $24.76 in 1929. However, there are serious problems in analysing the wage patterns of the 1920s. First, there is the issue of a base year: 1920 and 1921 are not suitable because wages were significantly reduced during those years. The use of 1922 and 1923, on the other hand, leaves too short a period for a meaningful trend to be established for the rest of the decade. More fundamentally, workers in various occupations had vastly different employment and unemployment experiences. There were also regional rigidities in the labour market. As Wright shows, while northern industrial wages rose, unskilled wages in the South were lower during the 1920s than they had been in the decade before 1914. Generalisation about earnings can disguise these extremes, and the substantial gains of a few can obscure a lack of progress or a decline for the remainder.

Both Bernstein and Sticker view the 1920s as a period of very modest gain for many workers, especially if they were unskilled. Table 3.6 shows the changes in manufacturing wages in a number of industries, and attempts to distinguish between the remuneration of those who were skilled and those who were not.

Table 3.6 Earnings and Hours of Production Workers in 25 Manufacturing Industries, 1920–30

	Unskilled male			Skilled and semi-skilled male		
Year	Average hourly earnings	Average weekly hours	Average weekly earnings	Average hourly earnings	Average weekly hours	Average weekly earnings
1920[a]	$0.53	49.2	$26.06	$0.69	49.4	$34.10
1921	0.44	46.5	20.28	0.60	45.9	27.36
1922[a]	0.40	50.5	20.30	0.57	49.8	28.11
1923	0.44	50.3	22.28	0.62	49.9	30.81
1924	0.46	48.9	22.41	0.64	47.5	30.55
1925	0.46	50.3	22.93	0.64	48.6	31.29
1926	0.46	50.2	23.21	0.65	48.5	31.61
1927	0.47	49.9	23.54	0.66	48.1	31.51
1928	0.47	50.4	23.89	0.66	48.5	31.94
1929	0.49	50.2	24.40	0.67	48.8	32.60
1930	0.48	45.9	21.90	0.66	44.0	29.17

Source: *Historical Statistics of US, Colonial Times to 1970*, 2 vols (Washington DC, 1975), series D839–44.

Notes: (a) Average of 6 months, July–December.

One can see immediately the decline in weekly earnings for all workers during 1920–1. We should remember that as there was no unemployment benefit, the large number of jobless had no earnings for the duration of their unemployment. Between 1923 and 1929 the average working week declined slightly for the skilled and semi-skilled but not for the unskilled. The absolute increase in average weekly earnings is about the same for both groups, though the unskilled, starting from a lower base, did relatively better. However, one of the costs of being unskilled is a greater degree of job insecurity. If, as seems likely, the unskilled on average spent more months without work each year than the other groups, annual earnings for a large number would be significantly reduced. White-collar workers, on the other hand, had a far higher degree of job security than all manufacturing workers.

The wage increases, however measured, were very small if related to increases in productivity. Many studies of the distribution of income during the 1920s have shown that a disproportionate share went to a tiny percentage of the total population. The Brookings Institution (Lever *et al.*, 1934) showed that 21 per cent of the 27.5 million families in the US during 1919 received only 4.5 per cent of the national income. At the other extreme, 0.1 per cent of the families at the top of the wealth scale received as much as 42 per cent of the families at the bottom. This study estimated that a family income of $2,000 was, in 1929, just sufficient to cover basic necessities; 60 per cent of families were below this level. The wealthy, of course, saved a high proportion of their income. It is not surprising, therefore, that in 1929, 80 per cent of US families contributed only 2 per cent of the nation's total savings; the wealthiest 10 per cent, on the other hand, contribued 86 per cent.

US income has always been distributed in favour of the relatively affluent, but what is noticeable is that during the 1920s this maldistribution became more pronounced. In 1922, the top 1 per cent of income recipients received 12 per cent of all personal income; by 1928 they received 13.7 per cent (Lampman, 1960). Williamson and Lindert 1980 identified the period 1914−20 as one during which the differentials between rich and poor became less pronounced. Unskilled labour made relative gains compared with the wages of the skilled and the professional classes. During the 1920s, however, this trend was reversed and at the end of the decade the gap between the traditionally high-paid and low-paid jobs was as great as it had been in 1916. In other words, these groups were as far apart as they had ever been. Holt's calculations show that the disposable per capita income of the top 1 per cent of wealth holders in the non-farm population grew by 63 per cent between 1923 and 1929; the income of the lowest 93 per cent contracted by 4 per cent. The wealthy few also benefited from the enormous growth in capital gains during the stock market boom; not so the bulk of the population.

The prosperity of the 1920s was real: the houses, automobiles, consumer goods and roads were visible, even if stock market profits were not. This growing wealth was not, however, equitably distributed. Bernstein's view that the 1920s were 'golden . . . only for a privileged section of the American population' is still valid. We note that the consumer boom of this era was sustained by a very narrow section of the population. The wealthy were the major consumers, who provided the savings which were translated into investment and hence into further productivity increases. The affluent, too, speculated on the stock market and benefited from increasing capital gains until the catastrophic collapse of October 1929. A growing proportion of the nation's wealth, during the 1920s, was going to those who were savers rather than spenders, who used the stock market as the barometer of their economic fortunes, and whose spending on consumer durables and housing could not continue indefinitely.

Bibliography

A clear introduction to the economy during the 1920s has been written by J. Potter. This work can be supplemented by W.J. Barber's excellent monograph which analyses the economic ideas and policies of this decade. Few will be disappointed by I. Bernstein's highly readable account of the social implications of economic change, or by R.S. and H.L. Lynd's in-depth study of Muncie, Indiana. Those who wish to read more on the automobile industry could begin with the work of J.B. Rae.

Aldcroft, D.H. (1977) *From Versailles to Wall Street*, Allan Lane.

Barber, W.J. (1985) *From New Era to New Deal: Herbert Hoover, the Economists and the American Economic Policy, 1921–1933*, Cambridge University Press.

Bernstein, I. (1960) *The Lean Years: A History of the American Worker, 1920–1933*, Little, Brown.

Brandes, S.D. (1970) *American Welfare Capitalism, 1880–1940*, University of Chicago Press.

Brody, D. (1960) *Steelworkers in America: The Non-Union Era*, Harvard University Press.

Brody, D. (1965) *Labor in Crisis: The Steel Strike of 1919*, Lippincott.

Brunner, K. and Meltzer, A.H. (1968) What did we learn from the monetary experience of the United States in the Great Depression?', *The Canadian Journal of Economics*, 1.

Burgess, W.R. (1983) *The Reserve Banks and the Money Market*, Garland Publishing. First published in 1946.

Clarke, S.V.O. (1967) *Central Bank Cooperation: 1924–31*, Federal Reserve Bank of New York.

Cochran, T.C. (1951) 'Business organization', in H. Williamson (ed.) *The Growth of the American Economy*, Prentice-Hall.

Copeland, M.T. (1929) 'Marketing' in *Recent Economic Changes in the United States*, McGraw Hill.

Costigliola, F.C. (1976) 'The United States and the construction of Germany', *Business History Review*, 50.

Costigliola, F.C. (1985) *Awkward Dominion: American Political, Economic and Cultural Relations with Europe, 1919–33*, Cornell University Press.

Falkus, M.E. (1971) 'United States economic policy and the "Dollar Gap" of the 1920s', *Economic History Review*, 24.

Fearon, P. (1979) *The Origins and Nature of the Great Slump, 1929–32*, MacMillan, London.

Fischer, G.C. (1968) *American Banking Structure* (New York, 1968) Columbia University Press.

Friedman, M. and Schwartz, A.J. (1963) *A Monetary History of the United States, 1867–1960*, NBER, Princeton.

Gordon, D.M., Edwards, R. and Reich, M. (1982) *Segmented Work, Divided Workers: The Historical Transformation of Labor in the United States*, Cambridge University Press.

Gordon, R.A. (1961) *Business Fluctuations*, 2nd Ed., Harper, London.

Hawley, E.W. (1979) *The Great War and the Search for a Modern Order: A History of the American People and their Institutions, 1917–1933*, St. Martin's Press.

Hogan, M.J. (1977) *Informal Entente: The Private Structure of Co-operation in Anglo-American Economic Diplomacy 1918–28*, University of Missouri Press.

Holt, C.F. (1977) 'Who benefited from the prosperity of the twenties?', *Explorations in Economic History*, 14, No. 3.

Keller, R.R. (1973) 'Factor income distribution in the United States during the 1920s: a re-examination of fact and theory', *Journal of Economic History*, 33, March.

Keller, R.R. (1982) 'Supply-side economic policies during the Coolidge–Mellon era', *Journal of Economic Issues*, XVI, No. 3.

Keyssar, A. (1986) *Out of Work: The First Century of Unemployment in Massachusetts*, Cambridge University Press.

Kocka, J. (1980) *White Collar Workers in America 1890–1940*, Sage Publications, London.

Krooss, H.E. and Blyn, M.R. (1971) *A History of Financial Intermediaries*, Random House.

Laidler, H.W. (1931) *Concentration of Control in American Industry*, NBER, New York.

Lampman, R. (1960) *Changes in the Share of Wealth Held by Top Wealth Holders, 1922–53*, NBER, New York.

Lary, H.B. (1943) *The United States in the World Economy*, US Dept. of Commerce, Washington DC.

League of Nations (1943) *Relief Deliveries and Relief Loans, 1919–1923*, Geneva.

League of Nations (1943) *Europe's Overseas Needs and How They Were Met, 1919–20*, Geneva.

Lebergott, S. (1964) *Manpower in Economic Growth: The American Record Since 1800*, McGraw Hill, New York.

Lebergott, S. (1976) *The American Economy: Income, Wealth, and Want*, Princeton University Press.

Lever, M. *et al.* (1934) *America's Capacity to Consume*, Brookings Institution.

Lewis, C. (1938) *America's Stake in International Investment*, Brookings Institution.

Lubin, I. (1929) *The Absorption of the Unemployed by American Industry*, Brookings Institution Pamphlet Series, Vol. 1, No. 3, July, Washington DC.

Lynd, R.S. and Lynd, H.L. (1929) *Middletown*, Harcourt Brace.

Mills, F.C. (1932) *Economic Tendencies in the United States*, NBER, New York.

Mintz, I. (1951) *Deterioration in the Quality of Foreign Bonds Issued in the United States*, NBER, New York.

Monthly Labor Review (1930) 'Standard of living of employees of Ford Motor Co. in Detroit', *MLR*, 30, June.

Moulton, H.G. and Pasvolsky, L. (1932) *War Debts and World Prosperity*, Brookings Institution.

Myers, R.J. (1929) 'Occupational readjustments of displaced skilled workmen', *Journal of Political Economy*, 37.

Nelson, R.L. (1959) *Merger Movements in American Industry, 1895–1956*, Princeton University Press.

Palyi, M. (1972) *The Twilight of Gold, 1914–1936: Myths and Realities*, University of Chicago Press.

Parrini, C.P. (1969) *Heir to Empire: United States Economic Diplomacy, 1916–1923*, University of Pittsburgh Press.

Potter, J. (1974) *The American Economy Between the World Wars*, Macmillan, London.

Rae, J.B. (1959) *American Automobile Manufacturers: The First Forty Years*, Chilton Co., Philadelphia.

Rezneck, S. (1951) 'Mass production and the use of energy', in H. Williamson (ed.) *The Growth of the American Economy*, Prentice-Hall.

Rothbard, M.N. (1963) *America's Great Depression*, Van Nostrand.

Schumpeter, J.A. (1946) 'The decade of the twenties', *American Economic Review*, 36, May.

Silverman, D.P. (1982) *Reconstructing Europe after the Great War*, Harvard University Press.

Smiley, G. (1983) 'Recent unemployment rate estimates for the 1920s and 1930s', *Journal of Economic History*, 43.

Stricker, F. (1983) 'Affluence for whom? — Another look at prosperity and the working classes in the 1920s', *Labor History*, 24, Winter.

Studenski, P. and Krooss, H.E. (1952) *Financial History of the United States*, McGraw Hill, New York.

United Nations (1949) *International Capital Movements during the Interwar Period*, New York.

Vatter, H.G. (1967) 'Has there been a twentieth-century consumer durables revolution?', *Journal of Economic History*, 27.

Wanniski, J. (1978) *The Way the World Works*, Basic Books.

White, E.N. (1983) *The Regulation and Reform of the American Banking System, 1900–1929*, Princeton University Press.

Wicker, E.R. (1966) *Federal Reserve Monetary Policy, 1917–1933*, New York.

Wik, R.M. (1973) *Henry Ford and Grass Roots America*, University of Michigan Press.

Williamson, J.G. and Lindert, P.H. (1980) *American Inequality: A Macroeconomic History*, Academic Press.

Wilson, J.H. (1972) *The Twenties: The Critical Issues*, Little, Brown.

Woolf, A.G. (1984) 'Electricity, productivity and labor saving: American manufacturing, 1900–1920', *Exploration in Economic History*, 21.

Worcester, D.L.W. (1929) *The Standard of Living*, National Conference of Social Work, USA.

Wright, G. (1986) *Old South, New South*, Basic Books.

4

Banking and Finance During the 1920s

The Structure of Banking

After years of bitter debate, the US founded a central bank, the Federal Reserve, in December 1913. The establishment of such an institution came relatively late compared with the industrially advanced European nations. There was, however, a long established hostility to central banking in America. Opponents feared a concentration of economic power which could be manipulated either by the federal government, or by powerful financial interests in Wall Street. It required the shock of multiple bank failures during the depression of 1907 to moderate the vehemence of critics. The Federal Reserve was, however, the result of a compromise between opposing factions and therefore differed significantly in its structure from the central banks in Europe. Instead of a single institution, the US established 12 regional bodies, each of which acted as a central bank. A Federal Reserve Board, located in Washington DC, was set up to supervise the system. The supporters of this form of central banking felt that not only would it avoid the evils which might emanate from concentration, but it would also recognise the diverse needs of different parts of the country for credit. In addition, the fact that each state had its own banking regulations, and that the structure of commercial banking differed from, for example, Britain, militated against a unified central bank. Few bankers wanted a powerful Federal Reserve, nor did they see any reason to alter fundamentally the structure of US banking. All that was needed, they believed, was more careful supervision and some gentle guidance.

Amongst the aims of the Federal Reserve were the prevention of financial panics, of bank failures and of speculation; in addition the legitimate credit needs of both agriculture and business were to be satisfied and the gold standard supported. No sooner had the Fed been established than it was involved in assisting the Treasury, in a subordinate role, in its efforts to finance the war economy. The effects of war-induced dislocation did not disappear until 1921. It was only after this date that the Fed was able to operate within the framework of normal peacetime conditions.

71

The US banking system differed from that of Britain in that not every commercial bank was a member of the Federal Reserve. National banks, which had a charter from the federal government laying down minimum capital requirements, were compelled to join. State banks, which received their charter from individual states, could become members if they were able to meet minimum capital requirements, but were under no obligation to do so. The result was that some state banks did join the system, but many did not. Apart from exclusion on the grounds of size, state banks resented the examination and the regulation which membership required. Many felt that some of the advantages of membership could be provided by correspondent banks — large institutions which acted as bankers and financial advisers to the small. Thus in 1921 only 9,779 of the 29,018 commercial banks were members of the Reserve, while the majority, 19,239, were not. In 1929, the 23,695 banks were divided between 8,522 members and 15,173 non-members. In general, the big banks joined the Reserve and, not surprisingly, the small ones remained outside. This division is clearly visible if we examine bank deposits. In 1920 the deposits of member banks amounted to $23 bn, while those of non-members were $9.6 bn. In 1929 the figures were $38 bn and $13 bn respectively.

Though bank deposits grew during the 1920s, the number of commercial banks declined. The highly volatile nature of commercial banking is depicted in Table 4.1 which shows that while many new banks were established between 1921 and 1929, each year saw a net decline. The major reason for this reduction was bank failure. During the years 1921–9, 776 national banks, 229 state member banks, and 4,416 non-member banks were suspended. During the worst year, 1926, there were 924 failures, but even in the best year, 1922, 343 banks suffered the same fate. This was an extraordinarily high rate of failure during a decade of economic stability. Both relatively and absolutely, the failure rate among non-member banks was greatest, but even the backing of the Fed was no guarantee of security. Bank failures were not evenly distributed; there were very few in the New England states. Indeed, nearly 90 per cent of all failures occurred in rural areas in the South, the Midwest and the West. These banks were very small, many having a capital of less than $100,000, and were often heavily committed to real estate loans. The reasons why such banks were in difficulties are manifold. Small banks were often inefficient, were less profitable, and usually tied to the fortunes of a single commodity or locality. The decades before 1914 had seen a tremendous increase in the number of banks so that by the 1920s many areas were clearly 'overbanked'. Moreover, many institutions faced the sort of problems which were outlined in Chapter 2. Farmers were unable to repay the mortgage debts which they had taken out before land values fell in 1921. Rural business, including banks, suffered when the automobile enabled people to trade over a wider area, thus breaking old monopolies.

Another reason for the decline in the number of banks was the popularity of

Table 4.1 Changes in the Number of Incorporated Commercial Banks, 1921–9

	1921	1922	1923	1924	1925	1926	1927	1928	1929
INCREASE IN NO. OF BANKS:									
TOTAL	638	585	583	525	509	525	455	324	316
New banks	472	409	458	383	403	345	296	252	235
Conversions from private banks	60	46	49	27	22	14	18	15	9
Reopenings of suspended banks	93	118	68	108	81	160	127	53	69
Unclassified	13	12	8	7	3	6	14	4	3
DECREASE IN NO. OF BANKS:									
TOTAL	826	783	1,007	1,197	1,010	1,468	1,267	1,089	1,324
Suspensions	461	343	623	738	579	924	636	479	628
Consolidations and absorptions	305	394	329	373	363	462	567	534	636
Voluntary liquidations	48	35	51	80	59	75	57	71	57
Conversions to private banks	—	1	1	2	2	4	2	2	1
Unclassified	12	10	3	4	7	3	5	3	2
NUMBER AT END OF YEAR	29,018	28,820	28,396	27,724	27,223	26,280	25,468	24,703	23,695

Source: Board of Governors of Federal Reserve, *Banking and Monetary Statistics 1914–41* (Washington DC, 1943) Table 14.

mergers, a movement which paralleled that in industry. During the 1920s consolidation among banks, especially those in large cities, became increasingly common. This was a reflection both of the urge to diversify into different kinds of banking business and the attempt to attract large accounts. One result of bank mergers was the rise of banking giants in the major metropolises of New York, Chicago and Boston. Indeed, mergers led to a growing concentration of banking resources in such cities (Krooss and Blyn, 1971). Another by-product was a rapid increase in branch banking, especially by national banks. The McFadden Act (1927) had made it easier for national banks to form branches but only where state law permitted. As 22 states forbade branching, its growth must be put into perspective: in 1929 only 764 banks operated a total of 3,522 branches. The typical bank in 1929 was an independent unit, not part of a group, chain or branch enterprise.

This was in very sharp contrast with Britain where then, as now, a few banks with many branches provided financial services for the bulk of the population. A powerful case could be, and inded was, made for a similar system in the US. Supporters of branching contrasted the high failure rates in the US unit system with the lack of failures in Britain, and with the single failure which had occurred in Canada. Their catalogue of criticisms was extensive. Small unit banks were no longer profitable since the country's economic structure had become more sophisticated. The transformation of shopping habits, the growth of alternative sources of credit and the need of some borrowers for larger sums than small banks could provide, progressively undermined the viability of many institutions. Small banks could not attract or retain first-rate staff; they were frequently the victims of embezzlement. Branch or multiple banking enabled institutions to diversify their assets and their liabilities, to withstand losses, to transfer funds from areas of surplus to those of shortage, and, through economies of scale, to lower their costs. Furthermore, multiples, not influenced by personal friendship or prejudice, could make more informed judgements and offer better advice on investment. Branching advocates also felt that multiples were much more competitive than small banks and were the only means by which the growing power of big city financial institutions could be countered. This was a formidable case which castigated the US banking system as fundamentally unsound and inefficient.

The supporters of unit banking were unmoved. Had not this system enabled the US to emerge as the world's most powerful financial nation? If business needed to borrow large sums from banks, why not engage the services of several small units rather than one large institution? Nor were unit bank supporters impressed by the statistics of failure rates. They argued that the cause of failure lay in agriculture, not banking: stabilize agriculture and bank failures would disappear. Moreover, the effects of failure had been much exaggerated. Losses to depositors were very low: $47 per depositor, or less than 1 per cent of total deposits. In addition, it could not be assumed that the lack of failure in British banking would be repeated in the US.

More positively, unit banks were held up for public praise as institutions which appreciated the needs of borrowers, since the banks were part of the local community. They would not neglect the small saver in favour of the large, nor ignore new business. Moreover, many small units did not stand entirely alone: they had valuable links with city correspondent banks from which they received up-to-date advice. The correspondent banks were also willing to assist the small bank in satisfying a large customer. In addition, there was a powerful emotional case which proved to be very popular. The growth of multiples, and the consequent demise of unit banks, it was argued, would lead to an unhealthy and un-American concentration of financial power. The independence of the banking sector would be destroyed and a few powerful institutions, heavily involved also in investment banking, insurance and other areas, would become so powerful that they would be able to dictate even to the Federal Reserve.

The US banking system was unstable in the 1920s and in spite of the case made in favour of unit banking, there seems little doubt that more branching, though not a cure for all ills, would have minimized many problems. Multiple banking would have led to greater efficiency and better protection for investors. With so many banks standing in isolation, and closely tied to the prosperity of their local communities, it is clear that in the event of a severe depression failures would increase. Could the banking system have been strengthened? Stabilisation was one of the responsibilities of the Federal Reserve, and in this it failed. In its defence the Fed could argue that as the majority of failed banks were not members, the blame for their demise must be laid elsewhere. Moreover, any structural changes proposed for US banking had to recognise the powers of individual states which had enormous control over the form which financial institutions took within their boundaries.

Because business profits were so high during the 1920s, corporations reduced their bank borrowing. If self-finance was inadequate, the attractions of the stock market beckoned. Farmers, too, were less active borrowers, partly because the federal government provided some credit but mainly because declining land values undermined credit-worthiness. During the same period, however, bank deposits increased, but a major part of this growth, especially in the larger national institutions, was in time deposits on which banks had to pay interest. Big banks, therefore, were able to attract the idle balances of business and wealthy individuals, but at a price. Banks still lent to small enterprises and to the wholesale and retail trade, but these commercial loans were not sufficiently profitable; other more lucrative areas were developed. City banks moved into real estate, stock market and consumer lending; they also undertook more foreign business. So profitable was the stock market, it seemed natural for commercial banks to move into investment banking. The largest formed subsidiaries which underwrote and sold new issues, and indeed, performed all the duties of investment banks. This was a particularly rewarding area during the late 1920s but it tied many commercial banks to the vagaries of the volatile stock market. With an increasing proportion of loans advanced for the purchase of stocks, of property and consumer goods, many banks became heavily dependent upon the continuation of prosperity.

Monetary Policy

Early in the period of 'normalcy' there was a marked disagreement among Federal
Reserve banks concerning their role. Some regional banks, for example, wished
to pursue an active strategy, others merely wanted to respond to economic events.
Banks often acted independently, unilaterally raising discount rates, or purchasing and selling government securities. In aggregate, therefore, monetary policy
lacked cohesion. The Federal Reserve Board did not have the power to impose
coherence, but the New York Bank, because of its size, its domestic and international experience, and the character of its governor, Benjamin Strong, emerged
as a leader. Strong urged that the open market operations of each be co-ordinated,
since their collective action would be an effective addition to monetary policy.
In 1922, a committee was formed to supervise the sales and the purchase of government securities. This was just one example of the New York Bank exercising
its power and expertise.

There was a growing faith in the efficacy of monetary policy during the 1920s.
The distinguished economist, Irving Fisher, for example, was convinced that
cyclical fluctuations could be eradicated if prices were kept stable. By controlling the money supply the Reserve could ensure, so Fisher believed, that changes
in the aggregate price level would be minimised and that, as a result, the trade
cycle would be laid to rest. The view of the Fed, however, was that price stability
was the result, not the cause, of business stability. It was the latter, therefore,
which attracted the attention of Reserve bankers, and they attached great importance to policies with that aim.

In 1924 and in 1927, when the economy moved into recession, the Fed adopted
liberal credit policies. Government securities were purchased and discount rates
were lowered. As a result, member banks could extend credit. These easy money
policies, coinciding with an economic downturn, were of great benefit to industry
and commerce, and as neither recession became serious, it would appear that
Reserve policies were highly successful (Brunner and Meltzer, 1968). International, rather than domestic, considerations, however, were the primary motive
for action. The US was the only belligerent nation to stay on the gold standard
during the war and in the post-war years of turmoil. The Fed, and Strong in particular, were anxious to ensure that those European countries which had abandoned the gold standard during, or shortly after, the war should return to it. In
order to encourage them to do so, credit was extended to foreign central banks
and US interest rates were kept low to reduce inward gold movements. If Europe
lost gold, a return to the gold standard would be delayed. It was important that
the US avoided tight money policies which would have acted as a magnet, attracting gold from all over the world.

The most important reason for the era of easy money between 1924 and 1928,
therefore, was this desire to encourage the readoption of the international gold
standard. Although the Reserve's defenders have asserted that monetary policy
was used during the 1920s with imagination and success (Burgess, 1946; Fried-

man and Schwartz, 1963), the domestic gains were probably largely fortuitous. Easy money coincided with buoyant demand for housing and consumer goods, but was not itself responsible for this buoyancy. Moreover, the art of central banking was not sufficiently developed for the implementation of an effective counter-cyclical monetary policy (Wicker, 1966).

Though the aims of the Federal Reserve were superficially straightforward, they sometimes led to inconsistency or debate. For example, enthusiastic support for the gold standard abroad was contradicted by management of it at home. The massive influx of gold into the US which had occurred during the war and post-war years was sterilised. Under gold standard rules one would expect a sharp rise in prices, but the gold stock was not allowed to exert inflationary pressure since this would not be consistent with the aim of internal stability. This policy was maintained even after Britain returned to gold in 1925. One effect, however, was that the gold held by the US was not redistributed and other nations, whose currencies were once again linked to gold, were prevented from acquiring the precious metal which they desperately needed. Another problem was stock market speculation, which the Fed recognised as harmful. Bankers debated whether or not to raise interest rates steeply in order to combat speculation, even though this ran the risk of destabilising business. In this context there was unease that the monetary expansion of 1927 had added to stock market excesses. The problem was how to distinguish between credit which would be used for legitimate purposes and that which would be used for speculation. The last years of the decade saw the Reserve impaled upon the horns of a dilemma as bankers struggled to discover a means of controlling Wall Street mania without destroying prosperity.

If the potential areas of instability during the 1920s include speculation, an over-emphasis upon consumer durables and a relatively high level of debt, to what extent can these 'excesses' be due to an over-expansion of credit? One school of thought depicts the 1920s as a period of disguised inflation: in other words, given the great advances in productivity, prices should have fallen but were prevented from doing so by expansionary monetary policies (Palyi, 1972; Rothbard, 1963). There is little, if any, justification for this view. The growth in the money supply between 1920 and 1929 was, as the following measures show, modest. In 1929, M_1 (currency held by the public plus demand [current account] deposits) was only 10 per cent above its 1920 level. The rise in M_2 (M_1 plus time [deposit account] deposits) was, at just less than 40 per cent, greater because of the expansion in time deposits which took place during the 1920s. Given the concomitant rise in real GNP, these figures do not indicate excessive monetary expansion. Nor can they explain, moreover, the phenomenal growth in the Dow-Jones index of stock prices which rose from 106 in the third quarter of 1926 to 354 in the third quarter of 1929. It is also apparent that the massive growth of credit to finance brokers' loans during the most frenetic period of bull market activity did not come from the banking system (see Chapter 6).

The 1920s was a period of learning by doing for the Federal Reserve as it emerged from the shadow of the Treasury. Reserve banks came to realise the benefits that arose from the co-operation which was essential for the implementation of open market operations. We can note, too, the growing confidence in the ability of monetary policy to offset the worst effects of booms and slumps, a far cry from the system of *laissez-faire* espoused by traditionalists. The Fed was also prepared to play an international role, urging the readoption of the gold standard and keeping US interest rates relatively low for that purpose. The decade ended, however, with the problem of stock market speculation emerging as a dangerous destabilising force.

Fiscal Policy

In 1918 taxes on individual incomes, on companies and on excess profits were high; the budget, however, was in deficit. The rapidity with which the war economy was dismantled quickly altered this state of affairs. Increased taxes and drastically reduced expenditure transformed the deficit which, for the fiscal year ending 30 June 1919, was $13.4 bn into a surplus of $291,000 12 months later. This deflationary fiscal policy exerted a powerful influence upon the economy and was a leading contributory factor in the slump of 1920–1 (Chapter 1).

The pattern of federal finances for the New Era is clear. In each year between 1920 and 1930 the federal budget was in surplus. Budget expenditures were stabilised at just less than half the level they had been in 1920, though this was over four times greater than before World War I. Total public debt, which had risen from $1.2 bn in 1915 to $25.5 bn in 1919, was steadily reduced; by 1929 the figure was $16.9 bn.

In 1921, when the administration of President Harding assumed power, government expenditure had fallen sharply from its 1919 peak but budget receipts were still relatively high. There was ample scope to respond to pressure groups, such as the National Association of Manufacturers, and to cut taxes. The President, and his Secretary of the Treasury, Andrew Mellon, were enthusiastic supporters of a lessening of the tax burden on business and a reduction of the public debt. They sought a minimum domestic role for the federal government which, they thought, would maximise the freedom of business to create wealth from which all would benefit. The Treasury, however, faced a problem. If a reduction in public debt was held to be of paramount importance then taxes would have to be kept high. If taxes were cut, not only would the opportunity for debt reduction be limited, but a decision would have to be made on who should benefit — the wealthy or the less well-off.

Mellon attached most importance to a reduction in tax rates on upper income groups. Such a policy, he argued, would persuade the wealthy to switch from investment in tax-free securities or foreign bonds to investment in productive industry. The reward for the nation would be a flowering of entrepreneurial spirit which would lead to more jobs and hence more taxpayers. Federal income taxes were steadily reduced in 1924, 1926 and 1928, with the wealthy benefiting most.

The maximum marginal rate of personal income tax, which had risen because of the war, was 77 per cent in 1919; by 1928 it was 25 per cent. These tax reductions did not result in a fall in revenue and were accompanied by a rise in national wealth. The budget surpluses which materialised each year were not only the basis for reducing tax rates, but also enabled the Treasury to engage in debt reduction. By the late 1920s, Mellon's fiscal strategy was clearly identified in the public mind with the growing prosperity.

Although there were substantial expenditure reductions between 1918 and 1922, especially on defence, revenues remained sufficiently high to spend in areas which gave support to business. The growing sums given to Hoover's Department of Commerce come into this category. Another and unavoidable increase in public spending was created by the need to finance the benefits of war veterans.

In the 1970s and 1980s supporters of tax reduction programmes looked back to. the 1920s and identified the 'prosperity decade' with the Mellon tax cuts (Wanniski, 1978). To what extent was fiscal policy responsible for the 1920s prosperity? The economy was growing strongly: in fact, before the tax cuts and the enormous rises in productivity, stable prices, high profits and mounting optimism were not induced by fiscal policy. Rather, we could argue with Keller (1982) that the rapidly growing economy enabled Mellon to reduce the public debt, cut taxes and still maintain a budget surplus. Furthermore, the benefits of tax reductions did not trickle down to the majority of the population as the growing maldistribution of income testifies. With the redistribution of the tax burden, the wealthy had more money to spend and also more with which to speculate. Federal fiscal policies in the 1920s did not generate economic growth; on the contrary, the experiment was made possible by a prosperous economy.

Capital Flows and the Balance of Payments

As we have seen, one of the most important effects of World War I was the transformation of the US from the world's leading debtor nation to its most important creditor. Before America entered the war in April 1917, the Allies paid for vital US imports partly in gold, partly by mobilising and selling US securities held by British citizens, and partly by raising private loans in the New York market. The burden of meeting these financial requirements fell mainly upon Britain who acted as banker to the Allies. Between April 1914 and the entry of America into the war, approximately $3.2 bn was raised in the US. In addition, the Allied governments raised loans from private individuals in countries other than the US; for example, France floated loans in London.

By April 1917, the resources of the Allies to finance dollar purchases were close to exhaustion but the participation of the US in the war meant that government loans became available. The Liberty Loan Acts empowered the Secretary of the Treasury to lend up to $10 bn; by the time of the Armistice roughly $7 bn had been advanced to the Allies. During this period loans were also made by

Table 4.2   Net Inter-Allied Indebtedness at the Armistice ($mn)

Borrowing country	From US	From Great Britain	From France	TOTAL
Belgium	172	422	535	1,129
France	1,970	1,683	—	3,653
Great Britain	3,696	—	—	3,696
Greece	—	90	155	245
Italy	1,031	1,855	75	2,961
Serbia (Yugoslavia)	11	92	297	400
Portugal	—	61	—	61
Romania	—	78	220	298
Russia	187	2,472	955	3.614
TOTAL	7,067	6,753	2,237	16,057

Source: H.G. Moulton and L. Pasvolsky, *War Debts and World Prosperity* (Washington DC, 1932), p. 426.

Britain and France to other Allied powers. Table 4.2 shows the extent of inter-
governmental debt among the Allies at the end of the war. War debts were,
however, even more complex than this table implies since they involved, as
creditor or debtor, 28 countries. Germany was the leading debtor nation and the
US, which received payment from 16 countries, the leading creditor. Six nations,
however, were particularly heavily involved: Germany, the US, France, Britain,
Italy, and Belgium.

We must add to war debts another category of inter-governmental lending: post-
war reconstruction and relief loans. When the war finished, Europe was in disarray. Agricultural output was far lower than before the war, capital equipment
had been worn down and not replaced, and transport systems were severely
disrupted. The continent as a whole was in desperate need of food, raw materials
and manufactured goods but had no foreign exchange with which to purchase
them. Indeed, during 1919 and 1920, continental Europe imported about $17.5 bn
worth of goods but could only send overseas exports worth $5 bn. Part of this
import surplus was financed by the returns from shipping services, by remittances
from emigrants, and by the expenditure in Europe of the American and British
armies. Of major importance, however, were loans for reconstruction and relief,
the bulk of which — nearly 80 per cent — were provided by the US.

America, with its large agricultural surplus and shipping space, was the only
nation which could satisfy the needs of Europe after the war. Moreover, the US
possessed the administrative structure necessary for sucessful relief work. The
US Grain Corporation was already buying and selling almost all important food
crops. Wheat, which could not be sold at home or abroad for cash, could therefore

be easily sent to European governments on credit. As the US Food Administration still maintained export controls, relief suplies to the Old World could be ensured. To control the distribution of supplies a new agency, the American Relief Administration (February 1919), was established, with Herbert Hoover at its head. America was thus able to avert the threat of famine, especially in Central Europe. US farmers, of course, gained from this exchange which kept US grain prices relatively high. It is noticeable that Britain, seeking to buy wheat in the cheapest markets, redirected its purchases to countries other than the US after 1918. The relief-receiving countries did not have this flexibility. The post-Armistice and relief loans added a further $3 bn to the amount borrowed from the US.

The third category of inter-governmental war debt — reparations — did not directly affect the US. Reparations were the payments which the victorious Allies exacted from vanquished Germany. After much argument, the Reparations Commission announced, in 1921, that the sum which the German nation would have to pay was 132 billion gold marks, plus a variable payment equal to 26 per cent of her exports. The total debt would be discharged over 42 years. It was a sum which the French regarded as too low but which J.M. Keynes, in his polemic *The Economic Consequences of the Peace*, considered beyond Germany's ability to pay. This dispute need not concern us, but what is important was that France and Britain were the principal beneficiaries from reparations; the United States did not claim a share. Both Britain and France, however, were heavily in debt to the US and therefore needed these payments if they were to repay their own war debts. The Europeans favoured a reduction of all war debts and reparations, a request which fell on deaf ears in Washington. The Americans refused to accept that there was a connection between the level of reparations and the repayment by Britain and France of the sums borrowed to pursue the war.

Those who favoured a revision of war debts claimed that these transactions were not merely commercial. The European armies had suffered severe losses compared with America, and therefore the debts should be regarded as part of that war effort. Moreover, the loans had been spent almost entirely in the US and had therefore helped to boost American business. If all war debts were cancelled, or significantly reduced, no single country would have to make a sacrifice. Moreover, once free of oppressive debts, the European economies would be able to expand and provide additional outlets for US exports.

A powerful group opposed revision. They pointed out that the loans were a legally binding agreement; failure to repay would undermine the fabric of international credit. Moreover, many Americans felt that the European Allies had been vengeful towards Germany in the peace negotiations and had been financially extravagant in their economic policies after 1918. As a result, the Allies attracted little sympathy when they claimed that war debts were a crippling burden. No international conference was called to discuss the problem of indebtedness since the Americans knew that the only reason for calling one would be to plead for a reduction in all debts. This refusal to accept that war debts and reparations were closely related was, as events were later to show, extremely short-sighted. Britain began annual payments of her war debt to the US on a schedule which was not due for termination until 1984; for France the final payment was due in 1987.

In January 1923, the Reparations Commission declared Germany in default with her payments. French and Belgian troops invaded the Ruhr and the German policy of passive resistance led to a complete collapse of the mark in a vortex of hyper-inflation. To find a way out of this impasse, a committee was formed under the chairmanship of Charles Dawes, a Chicago banker, and, in 1924, it produced the Dawes Plan. The aim of this plan was to restore confidence in Germany, by stabilising her currency and fixing reparation payments at a level which would make regular payment possible. Annual payments were reduced and an Agent General for Reparations (S. Parker Gilbert, a US lawyer) was given the role of supervising the delicate task of transferring German marks into currencies acceptable to her creditors. Most important, an international loan was raised to help Germany make the adjustment from hyper-inflation to normality.

It is interesting to note that although the US refused to recognise officially that all international debts were closely connected, the importance of US officials in reparations-related issues is testimony to their concern. In 1929 another American, Owen Young, established a new system of reparations payments. The Young Plan, however, was soon made irrelevant by the disintegration of the world economy. Between 1924 and 1929 Germany paid in full the reparations laid down by the Dawes Plan, and Britain and France continued to repay their debts to the US. Germany's ability to pay, however, was ensured by the large sums she was able to borrow from US citizens.

Thus far we have been concerned with international lending between governments, but during the 1920s, especially after 1924, private capital flows became important. Indeed, during these years the US became the world's leading international lender, taking over the role that Britain had occupied before 1914. It was during the 1920s that New York rose to prominence as an international money market. Between 1925 and 1929 inclusive, $5.1 bn of foreign dollar loans were floated in the US (Lewis, 1938). The chief recipients of US loans were Germany, which became the largest international borrower during the 1920s, Canada, Italy, Australia, Chile, Argentina, Brazil and Columbia. American money paid for highways, public utilities, sanitation works, ports, harbours, and a wide variety of other construction projects.

The reasons for this massive flow of capital overseas are not difficult to find. The growth of income, especially as it was skewed in favour of the wealthy, resulted in savings so ample that a domestic boom was financed and considerable overseas lending took place at the same time. The Federal Reserve kept domestic interest rates relatively low in order to encourage other countries to readopt the gold standard. As a result, the returns from overseas loans became more attractive. As the number of countries on the gold standard increased, American investors became even more optimistic, believing that financial stability was assured. They interpreted the Dawes Plan as a vote of confidence in Germany and lent so avidly that the Agent General for Reparations became alarmed. His warnings went unheeded. Indeed, the banks and finance houses which received generous commissions for underwriting loans were anxious that the enthusiasm of the public should not be dented. The euphoria which was noticeable in the stock market boom was also present in the overseas securities market. As Cleona Lewis observed, 'foreign bonds were a gamble and in the late 1920s the country was in a gambling mood'.

There were, nevertheless, obvious benefits from these capital flows. They satisfied the tremendous international demand for dollars which gave a variety of nations the means to purchase US goods or repay debt. American construction companies, for example, gained from the many public building projects which US investors financed in Central and South America. Many countries needed to build up their economies after 1918 but had very low levels of foreign exchange. The flow of dollars enabled them to buy essential imports which would otherwise have been denied to them. Being in debt was not necessarily a serious handicap: after all, the US itself had been the world's major debtor nation before 1914. It was, however, essential that the level of debt be kept in line with a realistic assessment of the ability to service it.

Unfortunately, capital flows had attendant risks. Enthusiasm to lend rode roughshod over common sense. High-pressure salesmanship urged borrowers to take more and left lenders unaware of possible repayment problems. Intense competition among financial institutions for this lucrative business led not only to corruption but also to a false optimism that US funds would always be available. The question of servicing difficulties was often dismissed. Indeed, some countries with such problems were able to negotiate new loans. It was felt that if the US economy were to move into recession, the reduced opportunity for domestic investment would mean that more funds would be available for foreigners, not less. Mintz (1951) has produced evidence to show that, as the 1920s progressed, the judgement of financiers worsened.

Borrowers, too, were foolish. All foreign debts had to be serviced in foreign exchange, in this case dollars, gold or currencies which could be converted into gold. In other words, debtor countries had to export goods or services to obtain the means to meet their obligations. Often foreign money was sunk into ventures which made no contribution towards repayment. Between 1924 and 1929, Germany borrowed twice as much as was needed to discharge her formidable reparations obligations. Much of the borrowed money was used to finance an increase in German living standards as libraries, swimming pools and other municipal schemes attracted foreign funds. Such investment did not produce exports. Rashness was also evident in Latin American loans. Many economies were dependent upon one or two exports: Brazil and Columbia relied upon coffee, Chile on nitrate and copper. International commodity prices are notoriously fickle: a price fall in these primary products would make debt repayment difficult, if not impossible. That the balance of payments of a borrower was precarious was, however, no barrier to acquiring American money.

Private capital flows, which expanded so dramatically during the 1920s, were a source of great instability. Borrowers and lenders had entered an unreal world in which the possibility of disaster had been dismissed. Many countries came to rely upon this flow of American money and their economies would face serious problems of readjustment if its flow was stemmed.

It is not surprising that the US dominated international trade during the 1920s. At the end of the decade she was, with 15.6 per cent of world trade, the world's leading exporter. The US share of world imports, at 12.2 per cent, placed her second behind Britain. Exports were, however, on average only 5 per cent of GNP during the late 1920s and imports just 4.4 per cent. The demand for imports, which were primarily raw materials and semi-manufactured goods, was kept buoyant by the expansion in manufacturing output. In 1922 Congress passed the Fordney—McCumber Act which raised the average tariff in the US to a new peak. This action by the world's leading creditor nation — which not only had a healthy balance of payments surplus, but also a large gold stock — was economically inexcusable, though politically popular. If foreigners could not sell their goods in the US, how could they obtain the dollars which they needed to buy US exports and to repay their debts? Falkus (1971) argues that this legislation was, in fact, a red herring. It was American self-sufficiency which prevented more imports from penetrating US markets rather than tariff barriers. Nevertheless, the erection of tariff barriers during the 1920s showed a blatant disregard for the problems of borrowers.

The attempts, spearheaded by the Federal Reserve, to encourage the readoption of the international gold standard also contained the seeds of instability. Readoption was patchy as nations returned to gold at different times with different exchange rates (Fearon, 1979). At one extreme Britain returned to gold, in 1925, at the exchange rate which had prevailed in 1914. As a result sterling was overvalued and this had a depressing effect upon the British economy and upon exports. The French franc, on the other hand, which was formally tied to gold in 1928, was undervalued: the French economy boomed, exports expanded and the nation's gold reserve increased spectacularly. Indeed, at the end of the decade, the US and France had between them the bulk of the world's gold. Other countries were therefore obliged to defend the convertibility of their currency with slender gold reserves. The US sterilised its large gold stock in order to prevent inflation; the French pursued the same policy. The US during the 1920s wanted to increase trade barriers, maintain a balance of payments surplus, keep its gold stock intact, and have price stability. At the same time, international debts were to be repaid; this was only possible with a high level of capital flows from the United States.

Our analysis of the 1920s shows that the American economy, in spite of apparent strength, had many weaknesses, though their nature is only fully apparent with the benefit of hindsight. The vigorous expansion in manufacturing industry was heavily dependent upon the growth of producer and consumer durables, both of which are prone to sharp cyclical fluctuations. Residential construction, another key ingredient of 1920s prosperity, reached a peak in 1926 and had declined considerably by 1929. The distribution of income became progressively less egalitarian as the decade progressed and as a result the consumer boom was becoming increasingly dependent upon the expenditures of a relatively small cohort of wealthy people. There were undoubted weaknesses in the structure of commercial banking which was dominated by small independent units, many of which were tied to agrarian markets. Speculation in real estate and especially on the stock market had assumed disturbing proportions by 1929; control of this speculation was proving elusive. The popular gambling spirit was also displayed in overseas lending. Finally, the public had gone into debt on a large scale to finance purchases of homes, consumer durables and shares. A serious depression would create difficulties over repayment especially if accompanied by sharp price falls which would increase the real burden of debt.

Bibliography

Additional information on the structure of the financial sector is available in H.E. Krooss and M.R. Blyn; it can be supplemented by the more specialist work of E.N. White. For a thorough analysis of monetary policy and the role of the Federal Reserve, the publications of M. Friedman and A.J. Schwartz and of E.R. Wicker, though technical, are invaluable. A short introduction to US international economic relations can be found in P. Fearon; D.H. Aldcroft, F.C. Costigliola (1985) and D.P. Silverman provide more detailed, though manageable, accounts on this topic.

Aldcroft, D.H. (1977) *From Versailles to Wall Street*, Allan Lane.
Brunner, K. and Meltzer, A.H. (1968) 'What did we learn from the monetary experience of the United States in the Great Depression?', *The Canadian Journal of Economics*, 1.
Burgess, W.R. (1983) *The Reserve Banks and the Money Market*, Garland Publishing, New York. First published in 1946.
Clarke, S.V.O. (1967) *Central Bank Cooperation: 1924—31*, Federal Reserve Bank of New York.
Costigliola, F.C. (1976) 'The United States and the reconstruction of Germany', *Business History Review*, 50.
Costigliola, F.C. (1985) *Awkward Dominion: American Political, Economic and Cultural Relations with Europe, 1919—33*, Cornell University Press.
Falkus, M.E. (1971) 'United States economic policy and the "Dollar Gap" of the 1920s', *Economic History Review*, 24.
Fearon, P. (1979) *The Origins and Nature of the Great Slump, 1929—32*, Macmillan.
Fischer, G.C. (1968) *American Banking Structure*, Columbia University Press.
Friedman, M. and Schwartz, A.J. (1963) *A Monetary History of the United States, 1867—1960*, NBER, Princeton.
Hogan, M.J. (1977) *Informal Entente: The Private Structure of Co-operation in Anglo-American Economic Diplomacy 1918—28*, University of Missouri Press.
Keller, R.R. (1982) 'Supply-side economic policies during the Coolidge—Mellon era', *Journal of Economic Issues*, XVI, No. 3.
Krooss, H.E. and Blyn, M.R. (1971) *A History of Financial Intermediaries*, Random House.
Lary, H.B. (1943) *The United States in the World Economy*, US Dept of Commerce, Washington DC.

League of Nations (1943) *Relief Deliveries and Relief Loans, 1919–1923*, Geneva.
League of Nations (1943) *Europe's Overseas Needs and How They Were Met, 1919–20*, Geneva.
Lewis, C. (1938) *America's Stake in International Investment*, Brookings Institution, Washington DC.
Mintz, I. (1951) *Deterioration in the Quality of Foreign Bonds Issued in the United States*, NBER, New York.
Moulton, H.G. and Pasvolsky, L. (1932) *War Debts and World Prosperity*, Brookings Institution, New York.
Palyi, M. (1972) *The Twilight of Gold 1914–1936: Myths and Realities*, University of Chicago Press.
Parrini, C.P. (1969) *Heir to Empire: United States Economic Diplomacy, 1916–1923*, University of Pittsburgh Press.
Rothbard, M.N. (1963) *America's Great Depression*, Van Nostrand.
Silverman, D.P. (1982) *Reconstructing Europe after the Great War*, Harvard University Press.
Studenski, P. and Krooss, H.E. *Financial History of the United States*, McGraw-Hill.
United Nations (1949) *International Capital Movements during the Interwar Period*, New York.
Wanniski, J. (1978) *The Way the World Works*, Basic Books, New York.
White, E.N. (1983) *The Regulation and Reform of the American Banking System, 1900–1929*, Princeton University Press.
Wicker, E.R. (1966) *Federal Reserve Monetary Policy 1917–1933*, Random House.

PART II
The Great Depression, 1929–33

5

Industry and Agriculture, 1929—33

The depression which began in 1929 came as a shock to the business community, to politicians, and to economic commentators. There were few, if any, who could have predicted the scale of the collapse. In the United States money income fell by 53 per cent between 1929 and 1933; because of a sharp decline in prices the fall in real income was less, but, at 35 per cent, still substantial. As Friedman and Schwartz observe, as early as 1931 money income was lower than it had been in any year since 1917 and real per capita income in 1933 was reduced to the level of 1908, which was itself a depression year. The scale of the problem is depicted in Table 5.1 which shows the path of GNP in real and in money terms, from 1928 to 1941. Using constant 1929 dollars, we can see the extent of the collapse in GNP to 1933 and its steady rise to 1937 when it had just surpassed its previous peak. The price falls which accompanied the depression were so severe that, if GNP is measured in current prices, its 1937 level was below that of 1929 and, indeed, did not rise above its 1920s peak until 1941. It is not surprising that the 1930s earned the sobriquet 'depression decade'.

The only previous depression which realistically compares with that of 1929—33 is the post-war crisis of 1920—1. The main characteristics of 1920—1 were its brevity and its severity: prices, employment and wages fell sharply. Particularly striking was the fall in prices. Between 1920 and 1922 wholesale prices fell for 21 months consecutively, leading to a total fall of 45 per cent; between 1929 and 1933 the fall was less — 38 per cent — and spread over 44 months. We should remember, however, that the price contraction which started in 1920 came after five years of inflation, in contrast to the years of stability before 1929. The price adjustments which followed 1929 proved, therefore, a greater shock than those of 1920—1.

The downswing which began in 1929 lasted for 43 months. The 'Great Depression' has the dubious distinction of being the second longest economic contraction since the Civil War, second only to that which began in 1873 and continued for 65 months. The length of a depression, however, can give only a limited indication of its impact; the amplitude and the international ramifications of 1929—33 give those years a special importance.

Table 5.1   GNP at Constant (1929) and Current Prices

	GNP 1929 prices ($bn)	GNP current prices ($bn)
1928	98.5	98.7
1929	104.4	104.6
1930	95.1	91.2
1931	89.5	78.5
1932	76.4	58.6
1933	74.2	56.1
1934	80.8	65.5
1935	91.4	76.5
1936	100.9	83.1
1937	109.1	91.2
1938	103.2	85.4
1939	111.0	91.2
1940	121.0	100.5
1941	131.7	124.7

Sources: Col. 1: J. Kendrick, *Productivity Trends in the US* (NBER, Princeton University Press, 1961), Table A-11a; Col. 2: J.A. Swanson and J.H. Williamson, 'Estimates of national product and income for the United States economy', *Explorations in Economic History*, 10 (1972–3).

Once the economy began its descent in the middle of 1929, the path to the depths reached in March 1933 was not uniformly precipitous. There were three partial revivals, periods when Hoover could be justified in believing that the worst was over and recovery was in sight. There was an upturn evident during the early months of 1930 when international lending revived and the automobile industry, along with steel and heavy construction, showed signs of life; by late 1930, however, conditions had deteriorated again. During the first half of 1931 another burst of activity generated hope. This was more widely based than its predecessor and owed its existence to growth in the textile, tyre, shoe and leather industries; it came to a grinding halt during the second half of the year. Finally, there was a marked and more general revival during the summer and autumn of 1932, but later in the year this too was seen to be another false dawn, and a fresh contraction produced a final low point in the spring of 1933.

As Table 5.2 shows, there was a marked fall in the output of the major European industrial nations as well, though the greater severity of the depression in North America should be noted. As national economies disintegrated, so did the machinery of international economic and financial co-operation which had been painstakingly constructed after 1918. The anxiety to correct balance of payment deficits caused by diminishing exports led to the introduction of controls on imports such as tariffs — and here the US played a significant role in 1930 with the

Table 5.2 Indices of Total Industrial Production, 1925–35 (1929 = 100)

	1925	1926	1927	1928	1929	1930	1931	1932	1933	1934	1935
Belgium	77	81	90	97	100	93	83	73	77	79	88
France	80	88	84	94	100	99	85	74	83	79	77
Germany[a]	79	76	95	100	100	86	72	59	68	83	96
Italy	88	92	87	99	100	93	84	77	83	85	99
Netherlands	NA	79	87	94	100	109	101	90	90	93	95
Austria	87	86	93	100	100	91	78	66	68	75	82
Denmark	92	89	86	93	100	108	101	94	107	118	126
Ireland	NA	95	96	97	100	100	101	104	113	121	128
Norway	91	82	84	94	100	103	82	92	94	97	108
Sweden	74	80	85	88	100	102	97	89	93	111	125
UK	87	75	95	94	100	94	86	89	95	105	114
Canada	70	80	85	94	100	91	78	68	69	82	90
US	81	88	85	90	100	83	69	55	63	69	79

Notes: (a) The figures for Germany are for the territory which is now West Germany.

Source: Calculated from *Industrial Statistics 1900–57* (Paris, OEEC, 1958), Table 2.

Hawley–Smoot tariff — or of quotas or competitive devaluations. As export earnings fell, those nations who were in debt faced serious problems and as a result lenders became apprehensive as to the security of foreign loans. The turmoil which followed the international *sauve qui peut* of 1931 led to the abandonment of the gold standard by many nations including Great Britain, followed by the US in 1933.

In an analysis of the Great Depression a number of questions need to be asked. Why did the depression occur? Why in 1929? Why were the periods of recovery not sustained? Were domestic or international events the most important? Which enterprises were most affected? Which regions, occupations, and ethnic groups were hardest hit? What, if anything, was done to alleviate the slump? Why was it so long lasting and so severe? This is certainly not an exhaustive list, but it is important to investigate both what happened and why it happened. The first step must be to examine, in some detail, the events of 1929–33.

Industry in Depression

The contraction of manufacturing output during the depression was savage. By 1932 it had fallen to almost half its 1929 level while, in contrast, agricultural output remained static. During the boom of the late 1920s the manufacturing sector was the chief generator of expanding income. Indeed, taken as a whole, 1929 was an exceptionally good year, with the largest production figures ever recorded. After a June peak, however, output declined in automobiles and in the closely linked iron, steel and rubber industries. The collapse in the motor vehicle sector was especially pronounced; during the first half of 1929 growth had been very rapid but by the end of the year reduction in automobile output was the greatest in the entire manufacturing sector. Optimists gained some satisfaction from noting that the situation in late 1929 seemed no worse than in late 1927 and actually improved in early 1930. The predictions of the pessimists were, unfortunately, to be more accurate in the long run.

The variations in industrial performance manifested during 1929 were to continue through to 1933. The durable goods industries, which include iron and steel, coke, lumber, cement and goods manufactured from these materials such as automobiles, locomotives and ships, were more seriously affected than non-durables, examples of which are textiles, leather, food, tobacco and paper. Throughout most of the 1920s these two industrial groups had been of roughly equal importance, though the output of durable goods fell much more rapidly than that of non-durables during the recessions of 1920−1, 1924 and 1927. Events after 1929 were no exception to this rule: while maufacturing output as a whole fell by nearly 50 per cent, the decline in durable goods was between 70 and 80 per cent, whereas the production of leather and shoes, tobacco and food products fell only by 10 to 20 per cent. The purchase of durable goods can be postponed relatively easily: some are items of luxury, others are capital goods subject to a sensitive derived demand. They rise fastest in expansion but fall furthest in depression, which explains why the greatest ever cyclical falls took place in the 1930s in pig iron and steel ingots and in orders for passenger and freight cars. Furthermore, contrary to precedent, these durable goods industries remained at or near their low point even when the trough was reached: the upturn which one might have expected in the final stages of the depression did not materialise.

Marked differences between durable and non-durable groups can also be seen in employment and pay rolls. The former measures the number of wage earners but does not reflect short-time working; the latter is simply the amount paid out in wages and therefore does take account of the changes in the volume of employment and of wage rates. During the worst years of the depression the number of manufacturing wage earners fell by 40 per cent, while the decline in employment in the durable goods industries was around 55 per cent; in the non-durable goods sector a more modest fall of 30 per cent was recorded. Factory pay rolls in the manufacturing sector were reduced by about 60 per cent in the three years after 1929 — a higher figure than the 40 per cent reduction in the number of employees, since pay rolls reflect the incidence of both short-time working and reduced wage rates. The pay roll decline was very unequal in different branches of the economy: for banks and brokerage houses it was a mere 15 per cent; for durable goods industries the wage bill fell by 75 per cent as compared with 50 per cent in other manufacturing industries. It is easy to see that the depression was at its most acute in the production of goods whose purchase could most easily be deferred. Even the unemployed had to buy food, and a certain amount of clothing; they purchased petrol but not new motor cars, houses or furniture. These items would not figure in the shopping lists of the nation until the worst of hard times had passed.

Not only were there marked variations in the output of different industrial groups, but the price falls which were noticeable after the middle of 1929, most conspicuously in agricultural products but also in manufactured goods, developed in a similarly unequal manner. From 1929 until the first quarter of 1933 the average wholesale prices of raw materials declined by 50 per cent, semi-finished goods by 40 per cent, and finished commodities by 30 per cent. If we look more closely at some commodity groups, we see that farm prices fell by 65 per cent and retail food prices by 43 per cent; on the other hand house furnishings, chemicals, fuel and lighting suffered a decline of less than 30 per cent. Wholesale prices, which had more than doubled between 1913 and 1920, had, by early 1933, fallen to 14 per cent below their 1913 level. If all prices had fallen by exactly the same amount the economy would not have been faced with such a serious problem of readjustment, but these marked differences complicated the prospects of recovery.

The discrepancies between price falls can be explained in a number of ways. Raw material prices were heavily influenced by agriculture, a sector in which there was no control over output. Industrial prices, on the other hand, reflected the greater degree of flexibility in manufacturing: when factories cut back or ceased production the stocks of manufactured goods, unlike those in agriculture, were limited, as were price reductions. Wholesale prices fell by more than general retail prices because the indexes which measure retail prices encompass a wide range of manufactured goods and services including rents which could be fixed for long periods, public transport fares which are never very flexible, and utility bills which are also subject to infrequent adjustment. Furthermore, the retail trade is more localised and much less competitive than the volatile international markets on which wholesale prices are largely determined. The price changes which came after the collapse of the 1920s boom were not limited to the United States, but were part of a world-wide phenomenon (Table 5.3). The problems caused by

Table 5.3 Percentage Decline in Wholesale and Retail Prices from Average 1929 Levels until March 1933

	Wholesale prices	Retail prices
Belgium	40.8	16.8
Canada	32.6	21.3
Denmark	18.0	9.2
France	37.8	5.9
Germany	33.6	24.2
Italy	37.0	17.3
Japan	19.3	20.5
Sweden	25.0	10.0
UK	28.5	16.5
US	36.8	28.2

Source: League of Nations, *World Economic Survey 1923–33* (Geneva, 1933).

the diversity of deflationary pressures in domestic economies were multiplied manifold when applied to the international economy, especially when the fixed exchange rates of the 1920s were shattered by competitive devaluations.

The collapse of the economy made dramatic inroads into company profits. Corporate earnings which, in 1929, had constituted nearly 10 per cent of GNP were negative in 1931 and remained in the red during the following year. The trough for corporate profits came in 1932; by 1933 there was a noticeable recovery which was maintained in 1934. In spite of the fact that profits fell steeply, dividends were still paid (although they too declined) as businesses distributed more than they earned in post-tax profits. This in turn led to an erosion of corporate assets and, inevitably, serious implications for both working capital and creditworthiness (Moulton *et al.*, 1940).

Aggregate figures, though a valuable guide, do not tell us all we need to know about company performance. Not all companies were profitable in 1929, nor did they all show losses in 1932. Fabricant's (1935) analysis reveals that even in 1932 the very large corporations were, on balance, still making profits. It appears that in the depths of the depression rates of earnings were positively linked with size; in other words, in all industrial groups during 1932, small companies were relatively worse off, on average, than large, and this was also true within the same industry.

Given their problems, the failure rate of small businesses was lower than might have been expected. Roos (1971) suggests that this was probably due to the greater flexibility of small firms which could cut wages and trim overhead expenses with greater ease than could the large corporations. It is possible that small businesses were more likely to shed labour than the large, as they lacked the resources to hoard workers. If that is so, it would go far to explain the staggering unemployment of the depression. Although the industrial giants dominated output, just over 50 per cent of manufacturing employees worked for businesses employing less than 300 workers, whereas only 10 per cent were attached to companies with a workforce of over 10,000. The role of small businesses in the American economy during the 1930s deserves closer investigation than it has received so far.

Of all the constituent parts of GNP, none experienced a greater fall than investment where the unprecedented decline is seen by some writers as the key to understanding the depression's severity. Measured in current prices, gross private domestic investment had reached $16.2bn in 1929; by 1932 the figure was less than $1bn. This fall came about because of a virtual halt in building activity and a paralysis in the producer durable sector. Investment decisions are heavily influenced by recent past performance and expectations of future profits. The outlook during 1932 and 1933 in particular was so gloomy that even if funds had been available for new plant and equipment, the incentive to use them for this purpose was lacking. The plant and machinery purchased during the 1920s and still *in situ* was under-utilised; machines could easily be kept in production for longer periods than would have been tolerated in times of prosperity.

Finally, we need to understand that the spatial impact of the depression was highly variable. Factory employment held up best in the South Atlantic states and in the West North Central region. Unfortunately, these areas had relatively fewer manufacturing workers than the mid-Atlantic and New England states where, both absolutely and relatively, the decline in employment was extremely severe. Most seriously affected was the East North Central region, encompassing the major manufacturing states of Illinois, Indiana, Michigan, Ohio and Wisconsin, where the production of durable goods was of particular importance. Here, in the manufacturing heartland of America, the suffering from unemployment was seen to be most acute. States which experienced a relatively weak decline in their manufacturing industries were those in which non-durables such as shoes, textiles, tobacco and food products were relatively important.

Industry: Some Case Studies

Industrial performance during the depression varied widely as can be shown by an investigation of automobile maufacturing, cotton textiles, and construction. It is not possible to undertake an analysis of a large number of industries, though L.V. Chandler (1970) does provide a useful list showing the decline in real output between 1929 and 1933. Amongst the least affected, with the percentage decline in parentheses, were footwear (3.4), textiles and products (6.4), cigarettes (6.6) and gasoline production (7.4). Those industries which contracted most included machinery (61.6), cement (63.1), automobiles (65.0), common and face bricks (83.3) and locomotives (86.4).

The Motor Vehicle Industry

The purchase and repair of motor cars accounted for expenditures of roughly $4bn annually between 1925 and 1929, a figure on a par with that of residential construction. Moreover, the automobile industry used 85 per cent of the petrol consumed in the United States, 83 per cent of the crude rubber, 60 per cent of the plate glass, 50 per cent of the lubricants, 30 per cent of the nickel, and 26 per cent of the lead. It was also the largest purchaser of carbon, alloy steel and malleable iron. The industry had achieved a record output in 1929, in spite of the fact that during the last quarter of that year demand declined. Total production of motor vehicles in 1929 was 23 per cent greater than that achieved in 1928, which in turn was 28 per cent higher than that of 1927 — an expansion of such proportions that some form of cutback in production was inevitable. The drop in output between 1929 and 1933 was, however, unlike anything which the industry had anticipated or previously experienced (Table 5.4).

Production for the first five months of 1930, although lower than the record level established in 1929, was not very different from that of 1928. However, from the early summer of 1930 a long decline set in. Some 4.5 million passenger vehicles were manufactured in 1929, but only 2.8 million in the following year.

Table 5.4   Motor Vehicle Industry (1929 = 100)

	Average no. of wage earners	Total wages paid	Production	Value of products
1927	83	84	63	77
1929	100	100	100	100
1931	64	48	43	42
1933	54	34	35	30
1935	87	74	74	64

Source: *Report on Motor Vehicle Industry* (FTC, Washington DC, 1940) 76th Congress, 1st Sess., House Document No. 468.

The fall continued in 1931, interrupting a cycle which had been evident since 1916. From that date output had advanced in a three-year sequence — two of growth followed by one of decline. 1932 was even worse, with only 1.1 million passenger cars emerging from factories whose workforce had practically halved over three years. In addition, a world-wide drop in purchasing power reinforced by quotas, devaluation and higher tariff barriers combined to drive exports from a peak of 635,207 units in 1929 to a mere 65,492 in 1932.

The record 1929 output had been achieved because of a rise in the proportion of relatively cheap cars — those costing less than $1,000 — and this became an established trend in the worst of the depression years. The low-price market was dominated by the 'Big Three' producers — Ford, General Motors, and Chrysler. By 1933 they had increased their share of the passenger car and truck market to 84 per cent, from the 1929 figure of 74 per cent. One of the results of the depression, therefore, was a greater concentration in the automobile market as many of the smaller producers had either been taken over or liquidated. During this period the relative positions of the 'Big Three' corporations changed: before 1927 Ford dominated passenger car sales, but by 1929 its share of the market had fallen to 31 per cent compared with General Motors' 32 per cent and Chrysler's 8 per cent. In 1933 the figures for each of these companies were 21 per cent, 41 per cent and 25 per cent respectively. General Motors, therefore, emerged from these troubled years in a relatively strong position.

Falling sales hit profits. Even General Motors slipped into the red in 1932, while Ford's losses were far greater. All manufacturers wanted to grab a larger share of a rapidly declining market, and in attempting to do this they resorted to price cutting, as well as wage cuts and lay-offs. More positively, big firms like Ford cut the commission given to dealers, increased their advertising, built new models and diversified into specialist commercial vehicles such as furniture vans, dust carts, coal trucks and the like, which had previously been the preserve of small independent producers who now reeled under the threat of this new competition. The big firms, however, were able to weather the hardships of the depression more easily than the small mainly because they dominated the sales of low-price vehicles.

The difficulties faced by the automobile manufacturers illustrate neatly the stranglehold of the slump. It was not that purchasers defaulted on hire purchase agreements, or that travel was seriously curtailed in these troubled years; indeed, Americans continued to drive their atuomobiles for leisure or for job search and covered much the same distances in the early 1930s as in the late 1920s. These drivers did not, however, buy new automobiles at the same rate as in the past, but kept their vehicles on the road longer. Indeed, the replacement parts and accessories business became an important source of revenue for the manufacturers, as well as a much needed source of trade for repair shops. As the average life of the automobile had increased from about five years in 1913 to about eight in the 1930s, and as the stock of automobiles in 1930 was fairly new, reflecting the relatively high sales of recent years, customers could wait for better times before returning to the showroom.

In the fight to stay in business the room for manoeuvre was limited. During the post-war depression of 1920–1 manufacturers had cut prices vigorously and watched the market stage a rapid recovery. By 1930 similar price reductions were not possible, in spite of desperate cost cutting inside each plant. The crisis of 1920 came after years of inflation, but that of 1930 arrived when the average retail price of an automobile was not only relatively low but had also been declining for several years. According to the National Automobile Chamber of Commerce, the average retail price of passenger cars at the factory was $953 in 1927, $876 in 1928, and $824 in 1929. Moreover, the vehicle of 1929 was far more sophisticated and costly to manufacture than the primitive open car of 1920 and the already efficient motor industry could not produce at a price low enough to attract reluctant purchasers who, in any case, had a tempting range of cheap used vehicles from which to choose. Nor did the manufacturer have complete control of his costs. One of the basic raw materials used by the car makers — steel — showed an unusual price resilience in the depression. The big automobile manufacturers, working at 30 per cent of capacity, did what they could to preserve their market position in the face of such difficulties, but sales continued to fall. Given the geographical concentration of the motor vehicle industry, one can understand how the state of Michigan and, in particular, the city of Detroit, were so hard hit. Moreover, as the industry accounted for over half the entire domestic consumption of rubber, plate glass, upholstery leather and malleable iron, and more than a quarter of aluminium, lead and nickel consumption, as well as over 10 per cent of the output of steel, hard wood timber, copper and tin, the misery which followed in the wake of its collapse permeated large sections of the country.

The Cotton Textile Industry

In 1929 the cotton goods industry ranked second amongst manufacturing groups in terms of the number of wage earners, and was by far the most important branch of the textile industry, even though its relative importance had declined since World War I. Although a large number of states produced cotton goods, manufacturing was concentrated in New England and in the South Eastern region; for some time, however, the latter area had been growing at the expense of the former. Whereas the South produced about 50 per cent by value of all cotton goods in 1923, this figure had risen to about 70 per cent some ten years later. Unlike the automobile industry, cotton manufacture was composed of a large number of relatively small units and was subject to intense, even vicious, competition which led to periodic overstocking. Moreover, the industry was a victim as well as a beneficiary of changing styles, customs and fashions, and also of economic conditions. The ease with which new competitors could enter the market when demand expanded was one of the factors which explains why the rate of profit on invested capital in cotton textiles was lower in the 1920s than in many other manufacturing industries.

Even before the depression began to bite, the cotton textiles industry had faced serious problems of overcapacity, especially in New England, as silk and rayon made inroads into the 'fine' cottons which were the speciality of its mills, and as the coarser fabrics, principally woven in the South, gained from growing industrial demand. Moreover, the expanding capital stock of the southern mills became progressively more efficient than that of their northern rivals; using relatively cheap labour and unhindered by restrictive labour legislation, the South was able to reap great cost advantages. It would be wrong, therefore, to suggest that all the problems which the industry experienced between 1929 and 1933 were the product of the depression, since the northern section had been in decline for some time. Indeed, unemployment and short-time working had been worrying features of northern mill towns since the collapse of war-induced prosperity.

The industry was clearly not uniformly prosperous in 1929, but we should note that cotton textiles did have an advantage over many other manufacturing concerns, suffering far less fluctuation in output from boom to slump than did capital goods or durable goods industries. It was further helped by the low prices for raw cotton which prevailed during the worst years of the slump, making its products exceptionally cheap.

An analysis of the cotton textile industry requires a careful separation of the forces already evident before 1929 from those caused by the contraction of economic activity after that date. The industry reached an employment peak of 472,000 in 1923, for example, a figure which had dropped to 425,000 by 1929. A further fall to 330,000 was evident in 1931 but the 1933 returns showed an increase in the labour force to 379,000. A census taken in 1932 would no doubt have identified that year as the trough, but the recovery in 1933, helped by increasing demand as well as shorter working hours, was rapid. As in other industries, the decline in the production of cotton goods was not evenly spread across all producing states. The South emerged from the depression with some hope, but New England cotton producing centres faced even more formidable problems than had been the case during the steady decline of the 1920s. The depression, therefore, accelerated changes which were already inevitable, as can be seen from the fact that the New England mills employed 195,000 workers in 1923, a figure which had been reduced to just over 90,000 by 1933. During the same period southern mills increased their workforce from 220,000 to 257,000 or, put another way, the South's share in the volume of employment was 46 per cent in 1923, 60 per cent in 1929, and 68 per cent in 1933. The net result was that Massachusetts, which had 70,788 wage earners in its textile mills in 1929, had only 45,418 in 1933, whereas Alabama, Georgia and South Carolina increased their workforce. The declining volume of employment was, therefore, concentrated in New England, a high-wage region. One result of the labour shakeout was to reduce the already low average weekly earnings in the industry.

Earnings rose more in manufacturing as a whole during the 1920s than they did in cotton textiles, but between 1929 and 1932 cotton showed the greatest resilience. Pay rolls fell less in cotton than the manufacturing average, principally because there was less short-time work in the mills; employment, too, fell less than it did in manufacturing as a whole. The regional shifts of the industry, combined with the decline in earnings during the worst depression years, had the effect of reducing wage differentials since average hourly earnings fell more in the troubled North than in the less affected southern states. Nevertheless, at a time when price cutting was endemic, southern mills could still produce cloth more cheaply than their competitors. Though the industry as a whole fared better than did the producers of consumer durables, for people had to buy clothing, there were still serious social problems in textile communities in 1933. Many mills were forced to close in relatively isolated settlements in New England where they were often the main source of employment. The stranded textile workers shared a fate similar to that of many desolated coalmining communities. Even in larger centres such as Fall River, New Bedford and Lowell, there was little or no chance of alternative employment, and the disappearance of long established industry not only undermined local confidence but also seriously affected city budgets as property tax receipts fell substantially.

The Construction Industry

The collapse of investment, in which construction played a major role, was an important feature of the depression. The building of new homes and business premises had been a central element of the buoyant economy of the 1920s, but the construction sector, by peaking in 1926, had anticipated the general economic decline by several years. Once the depression took hold, the slide was of spectacular proportions. The industry was, of course, a major employer, having in 1930 just over 2.4 million wage and salaried workers. It was, however, a victim of the seasons and even in good years the months December through March brought enforced idleness in most states.

The decline between 1929 and 1933 was staggering. Total expenditure on new construction (in constant 1929 dollars) fell from $11.2bn to $3.7bn. In 1929, 509,000 new housing units were started (compared with 937,000 in 1926) plummeting to a paltry 93,000 in 1933. House building had been declining steadily for several years before the onset of the depression, but aggregate construction had been maintained at a high level by the buoyancy of non-residential activity. After 1929, there was a collapse in the industry of such magnitude that expenditure on new private construction during the late 1930s was only a third of the amount recorded for the late 1920s.

The drop in the value of residential construction of about one third between 1926 and 1929 was substantial; yet during the latter year output was still high compared with the early 1920s. Indeed, the economy expanded during the first half of the 1920s when new construction increased, and continued to expand during the last few years of the decade, although the industry was then in decline. The fact that builders produced fewer dwellings in the late 1920s cannot be explained by a fall in per capita income, nor by a rise in housing costs: incomes rose and costs were stable; nor were all Americans adequately housed. The most likely explanation is that the demand for housing declined as a result of demographic factors and a growing maldistribution of income. The shortages of the 1920s — brought about by war-induced neglect, by immigration, and an increasingly mobile population — were largely satisfied by the end of the decade. Once the depression began to bite, the decline in the industry accelerated. Falling incomes, dismal expectations, reduced migration, postponed marriages and births, a rise in real interest rates, the drop in the creditworthiness of potential borrowers, the fact that building costs did not fall as rapidly as the general price level, and the numerous vacant houses and apartments account for the depressed housing market. Even when a revival did take place in residential building it was feeble. The failure of this important industry to expand more vigorously during the 1930s is one reason why economic recovery was so disappointing.

Construction probably suffered more than any other sector of the economy during the depression. No other industry showed a decline in production, from peak to trough, of more than 70 per cent. During the first quarter of 1933 the construction industry was able to find employment for only about 25 per cent of the workers attached to it. Although this figure is influenced by winter conditions, during the whole of 1932 only 34 per cent of the industry's workforce was employed and many men, both skilled and unskilled, faced destitution.

The collapse in construction affected not only those directly involved in it, but also many industries whose prosperity was heavily dependent upon building activity. Structural steel, brick making and lumber suffered badly, as did the transport sector which carried these bulky materials. The glass industry, whose principal customers were in construction and automobiles, found the demand for plate and window glass dramatically reduced. Not surprisingly, 1932 was the worst year in the history of furniture manufacturing. An industry of small establishments, furniture making was already experiencing difficulties in 1929 when numerous firms failed to make a profit; by 1932 operations were only 30 per cent of capacity and about a quarter of manufacturers went out of business. This posed particular difficulties for states such as New York, Illinois, Michigan, Indiana and North Carolina where over half the nation's wage earners in furniture making were located. Nor should we forget that furniture retailing was equally unremunerative. The links between construction and other leading industries emphasise its powerful influence upon the economy.

Our examination of automobiles, cotton textiles, and construction has shown that the impact of the economic crisis differed from industry to industry and between regions. In the sectors examined, the producers of consumer goods with a relatively short life, such as cheap cotton fabrics, fared best, though even workers in sheltered industries did not emerge unscathed. For example, the footwear industry, which had always been one of the most depression-proof, saw both employment and output fall relatively little between 1929 and 1933. However, pay rolls were not stable: in 1932 they were nearly 40 per cent lower than in 1929. Similarly, in meat packing, output fell by just a few percentage points between 1929 and 1932 while employment declined by around 13 per cent, and pay rolls by a much steeper 37 per cent. The cigarette industry proved to be virtually depression-proof, with employment and output moving down only slightly before continuing the growth established during the 1920s, so that by 1937 cigarette output was one third above its 1929 level. Cigar producers were not so fortunate and here the decline in output and employment which had been evident since 1914 was intensified by the slump; as a result, cigar making became one of the most depressed occupations of the thirties. A combination of food processing and tobacco manufacture helped mitigate the worst aspects of the industrial depression in a few southern states such as Virginia and North Carolina, and to alleviate, slightly, the impact of desperately low raw cotton and tobacco prices. The labour force in the traditional industrial states, however, found little to soften the blow of the slump.

The manufacturing and construction industries bore the brunt of the depression's attack upon the non-agricultural sector. Automobiles and housing had kept the economy buoyant during the 1920s, but they brought a host of associated enterprises down with them in the long fall between 1929 and 1933. Their contraction had grave implications for rapid recovery, which would be difficult to engineer unless dominant sectors such as these could be expanded and thus pull the rest of the economy towards full employment.

Farms and Farmers

The collapse of agricultural prices after 1929 was dramatic and soon embraced virtually all farmers. Those who were more efficient or farmed good soil could stave off disaster for a while, but in the end they too were dragged down. A few examples will illustrate the farmers' plight: cotton which sold for around 17¢ per lb in 1929 realised under 6¢ per lb in 1931; corn plummeted from 60¢ per bushel in 1930 to 32¢ per bushel the following year, and wheat fell from 67¢ per bushel to 39¢ per bushel during the same period. Table 5.5 spells out farm misfortunes: what is immediately apparent is the dramatic fall in the parity ratio to its trough in 1932. The parity ratio fell steeply between 1929 and 1932 because the prices paid by farmers did not fall as steeply as did agricultural prices. While manufacturing concerns were laying off workers and reducing output, aggregate agricultural output remained buoyant.

Table 5.5 The Parity Ratio, 1928–32 (1910–14 = 100)

Year	Prices received by farmers	Prices paid by farmers	Parity ratio
1928	148	162	91
1929	148	160	92
1930	125	151	83
1931	87	130	67
1932	65	112	58
1933	70	109	64

Source: *Historical Statistics of US, Colonial Times to 1970*, 2 vols (Washington DC, 1975), Series K129, 137, 138.

As the depression worsened farm people were forced to cut their consumption of manufactured goods, which inevitably intensified unemployment in the cities. Small towns and villages, in which a high proportion of the American population lived, owed their livelihood to the farmers who came to buy goods or to use services: they, also, were hit by the decline in farm income. Farmers were soon in a desperate plight. The average net farm income in 1929 was $945; it had fallen to $304 by 1932. Faced with such a sharp reduction of purchasing power, farmers curtailed expenditure: for example, consumption of fertiliser and lime halved between 1929 and 1933. Farm labourers also felt the onslaught of the depression as wage rates tumbled. The daily wage (without food or accommodation) fell from $2.30 in 1929 to $1.15 in 1933; by the latter year, US farmers had reduced their expenditure on labour by half. Where possible, farm workers were replaced with unpaid family help. Further economies meant that taxes went unpaid and machinery and property fell into a state of disrepair. As the steep decline in the parity ratio shows, however, farm costs did not fall as rapidly as farm receipts.

One could pay tribute to the American farmer for maintaining output under such adverse conditions if the result had not been so disastrous. In spite of the precipitous fall in prices, the cotton crop of 1931 came close to an all-time record. The following year saw no significant reduction in acreage, despite the fact that stocks of cotton were ominously high. Similarly, as wheat prices tumbled between 1929 and 1931, production increased. Stocks of wheat were three times greater than those which had prevailed during the late 1920s.

There appeared to be little that farmers could do to reduce output. Diversification seemed out of the question, especially as virtually all crops had dropped in price. Attempts to persuade farmers to restrict voluntarily their acreage of wheat and cotton went unheeded. A suggestion from the Federal Farm Board, that part of the cotton crop should be ploughed up, is indicative of the general desperation — although the idea was ridiculed by farm organisations. Senator Huey Long of Louisiana proposed a 'cotton holiday' and sought an agreement between cotton producing states not to plant in 1932. This, he believed, would raise prices and reduce stocks. It was not possible, however, to get the co-operation of all cotton producers. Moreover, groups such as cotton ginners, textile manufacturers and transport interests were opposed to a scheme which would have been extremely difficult to enforce and which would also have priced the US out of international markets (Fite, 1985). Desperate remedies were proposed, therefore, but action never matched rhetoric.

The decline in farm income and the growth of stocks, or carry-over, were only part of the agricultural problem. Many farmers were in debt, a burden which had been considerably worsened in real terms by deflation. Operators who had used their crop as collateral for loans found themselves in great difficulty when its realised value turned out to be a fraction of its estimated value. An even worse situation confronted those who lost their entire crop through drought. Farmers' inability to pay debts put an intolerable strain upon local banks, many of which failed. Those who wished to raise new loans in order to tide them over a difficult situation found that declining property values further undermined their creditworthiness. Most lending institutions were no longer willing to extend credit, for they realised the difficulties which farmers were facing and naturally questioned their ability to repay.

The depression led to a disintegration in the rural credit relationships which were essential to all levels of operation. Many large landlords, for example, could themselves no longer obtain credit. As a result, they were unable to extend much needed loans to their tenants. The debt problem was so serious that some owners found themselves reduced to the level of tenants or croppers. Insurance companies and commercial banks held more than one third of the $9.8bn farm mortgage debt in 1929, much of it short-term and falling due for repayment. Many farmers were unable to meet the payments and, since the creditors were unwilling to renew loans, this inevitably led to foreclosure. Almost one million farms were repossessed between 1930 and 1934, and their former owners were reduced to the ranks of tenants, wage labourers, or even homeless unemployed.

Foreclosure sales aroused great passion in many rural communities as families, many of them long-time residents, were faced with eviction. Farms which had been efficiently managed had become the victims of a capricious collapse in prices, and it seemed grossly unjust that such people should lose their homes and their livelihood. In some areas the fear of violence at forced farm sales was so great that they were banned by state law.

Farmers' anger and frustration grew to fever pitch as the crisis deepened. In parts of the country politically radical movements sprang up. The Farm Holiday Movement, which gained ground in the Midwest, was an attempt by farmers to raise prices by preventing perishable goods reaching markets. Milk delivery trucks, for example, were waylaid and their contents destroyed. Such outbreaks were scattered and ineffective, and prices continued to decline.

To add to farm misery, a drought in 1930 caused grave problems. Livestock died, or had to be sold off cheaply, because of a lack of feedstuff. Crops failed, leaving farmers even deeper in debt. Small operators who grew much of their own food watched it shrivel and die; as a result their already poor diets deteriorated further. Although the drought had a devastating impact upon many farm families, it was not sufficiently widespread to reduce the output of crops, such as cotton, which were grossly in surplus. The level of distress was such, however, that the Red Cross had to mount a major relief operation in order to combat its worst effects.

As the agricultural scene in the early 1930s was one of widespread misery, it is perhaps surprising that the number of farms steadily increased: 6,546,000 in 1930, 6,608,000 in 1931, and 6,687,000 in 1932 rising to a peak of 6,814,000 in 1935. One of the main factors influencing this increase was a change in the traditional pattern of migration from rural to urban areas. In modern times the land had always been a net exporter of people, but after 1929 the lack of opportunities in the urban sector discouraged migration to such an extent that, in 1933, there was a net movement of population towards the farm. Many city dwellers facing the bleak prospect of urban unemployment took part in a back-to-the-land movement in an attempt to grow enough food to support themselves. This movement, illustrated in Table 5.6, was to empty farmhouses on land which had been abandoned because it was relatively infertile; these new farmers were self-sufficient

Table 5.6   Estimated Movement of Farm Population ('000s)

Year	Farm population 1 April	Migration to farms	Migration from farms	Net migration
1928	30,548	1,705	−2,162	−457
1929	30,580	1,698	−2,120	−422
1930	30,529	1,604	−2,081	−477
1931	30,845	1,985	−2,046	−61
1932	31,388	1,918	−1,762	156
1933	32,393	1,826	−1,219	607

Source: *Historical Statistics of the US, Colonial Times to 1970* (Washington DC, 1975), Series C78–80.

rather than market-oriented producers. The back-to-the-land movement was especially noticeable in the New England states and was even welcomed, mistakenly, by some as a solution to the problem of urban unemployment and poverty. The curtailment of migration threw an extra burden on farm families and their communities, which only the reappearance of urban jobs could begin to ameliorate.

During the election campaign of 1928, Hoover had promised that the farm problem would be a priority for his administration were he elected. He believed that the difficulties which many farmers faced could be resolved by better marketing arrangements which would permit a more controlled distribution of crops. Further essentials were greater co-operation between farmers and an improvement in the quality of the information given to them. A firm believer in the co-operative associations which had proved popular during the 1920s, he wished to see them extended. Hoover's vision for agriculture was one of sturdy independence. He was not in favour of federal price controls or subsidies, but was prepared to admit that the farm sector had suffered more from the vagaries of international markets than had manufacturing industry.

Hoover therefore supported the Agricultural Marketing Act (1929) which sought to prevent speculation, minimise waste and maximise stability by promoting co-operative marketing associations. This Act also created the Federal Farm Board, which was authorised to offer loans to co-operatives in order to make them more effective and more attractive to farmers. In addition, stabilisation corporations were set up to buy and therefore to control surpluses, using funds allocated by the Board.

Such an emphasis on farmer co-operatives was sound but the results would only be noticeable in the long term. No sooner had this policy been accepted, however, than the agricultural situation radically changed. In 1930 farmers required immediate assistance, not promises of benefits in the distant future.

In response to falling prices, the Cotton Stabilization Corporation and the Grain Stabilization Corporation were created in 1930. Both were modelled on agencies which had been established during World War I to prevent price fluctuations. The Corporations began to buy cotton and wheat in an attempt to support prices, resulting in the accumulation of massive surpluses. In June 1931 price supports were abandoned. The problem was far more serious than the Federal Farm Board had imagined and the continuing purchase of wheat and cotton was quite beyond its relatively slender resources. It had become clear, however, that price support policies which did not include a measure of output control were doomed to failure. For a while prices were raised above the levels which would have prevailed without support, but they remained very low. Once this policy was jettisoned, however, the Board had no practical alternative to offer.

An additional string to Hoover's bow was tariff protection. In 1930 he signed the Hawley–Smoot tariff bill which raised US import duties to record levels. It invited, and received, immediate retaliation. The precise effect of this legislation on agriculture is impossible to compute; between 1930 and 1933 there was a steep decline in farm exports, but the decrease in value was of greater significance than the reduction in volume. The general view was, however, that Hawley–Smoot did very little, if anything, to help the US farmer.

Hoover's farm policies had led to the accumulation of enormous stocks purchased at relatively high prices. As Fausold (1977) has pointed out, the President was ill equipped to make the dramatic intervention in agriculture which was required. His philosophy of voluntarism, co-operation and individualism might have been successful if there had been no major depression; once a crisis occurred, however, Hoover demonstrated far less flexibility, imagination and compassion than his successor.

During the 1920s, farm pressure groups had become more politically aware and more skilful in presenting their case. They had, of course, failed to persuade Coolidge to sign the McNary–Haugen bills (Chapter 2), but had gained valuable experience in enlisting support for this and other legislation. Farm interests accepted the Agricultural Marketing Act with no enthusiasm. Even in 1929, many agricultural leaders argued that the prevailing prices were unacceptably low for commercial operators and that the Act did not aim to bring about an immediate rise. Once prices dropped further, however, farm groups were galvanised into action.

The initial response of farm advocates was to support plans which had achieved popularity during the 1920s: for example, guaranteed prices to cover costs of production or the removal of surpluses from the domestic market prior to dumping overseas. However, although American farmers had always believed that it was essential that they produce as much as possible, an increasing number accepted that the surpluses must be curtailed. While the Domestic Allotment Plan, which proposed price incentives to persuade farmers to reduce their crops, was not greeted with universal approval, some farm leaders, Henry Wallace among them, did give it their support and acreage reduction became the keystone of New Deal farm strategy.

By 1932 most farmers and their organisations were convinced that intervention by the federal government was essential if farm living standards were to improve. They also believed that the nation as a whole could not become prosperous unless the farm sector was also prosperous. Even urban dwellers were prepared to accept that the depression could not be conquered unless farm purchasing power was substantially raised. It was to Roosevelt that the farmers looked for action.

In 1930, 24 per cent of the non-agricultural labour force worked in the manufacturing sector and 5 per cent in construction. A high proportion of Americans, therefore, suffered a sharp reduction in income from a combination of unemployment, wage cuts and short-time working. Other parts of the economy were also affected by this economic crisis. Employment in transportation and public utilities, for example, declined from 6.1 million in 1929 to 4.7 million in 1932, and in the wholesale and retail trade from 3.9 to 2.8 million. The problem in agriculture, on the other hand, was not unemployment but extremely low income for the 25 per cent of the population who lived on farms. As domestic consumption fell, even more labour was discarded and fewer agricultural products were sold. In 1932 a desperate people looked for a political leader who could break the vicious downward spiral of prices and incomes.

Bibliography

An excellent account of the collapse of the economy between 1929 and 1933 can be found in L.V. Chandler (1970) *America's Greatest Depression, 1929–1941* (Harper and Row, New York) which presents in tabular form the movements of key economic variables during these tumultuous years. To accompany this volume, readers should consult A.U. Romasco. Agricultural problems and policies are presented in the encyclopedic work of M.R. Benedict, though a less detailed, but still valuable, presentation can be found in H.D. Guither. The serious problems facing cotton growers are deftly analysed in G.C. Fite.

Industry

Brookings Institute (1936) *The Recovery Problem in the United States*, Washington DC.
Campbell, B.D. (1966) *Population Change and Building Cycles*, University of Illinois Press.
Epstein, R.C. (1934) *Industrial Profits in the United States*, NBER, New York.
Fabricant, S. (1935) *Profits, Losses and Business Assets, 1929–34*, NBER Bulletin No. 43, April 11.
Gilman, G. (1956) *Human Relations in the Industrial South East: A Study of the Textile Industry*, University of North Carolina Press.
Gordon, R.A. (1949) 'Business cycles in the interwar period: the "quantitative historical" approach', *American Economic Review*, XXXIX, No. 2, May.
Harrison, R.E.W. and Thompson, C.O. (1936) *Review of the American Machinery Industries*, US Dept of Commerce, Domestic Commerce Series No. 93, Washington DC.
Hickman, B.G. (1973) 'What became of the building cycle?' in P. Davis and M. Reder (eds) *Economic Growth: Essays in Honor of Moses Abramovitz*, Academic Press.
Katz, H. (1977) *The Decline of Competition in the Automobile Industry 1920–40*, Arno Press, New York.
Kennedy, E.D. (1941) *The Automobile Industry*, Reynal and Hitchcock.
Matthews, R.C.O. (1959) *The Trade Cycle*, Cambridge University Press.
Mitchell, W.C. and Burns, A.F. (1936) *Production During the American Business Cycle of 1929–1933*, NBER Bulletin No. 61, Nov 9.
Moulton, H.G. *et al.* (1940) *Capital Expansion, Employment and Economic Stability*, Brookings Institution, Washington DC.
Nevins, A. and Hill, F.E. (1957) *Ford: Expansion and Challenge 1915–1933*, Scribner.
Roos, C.F. (1971) *NRA Economic Planning*, Da Capo Press, New York.
Sloan, A.P. (1963) *My Years with General Motors*, Doubleday.
Thomas, R.P. (1977) *An Analysis of the Pattern of Growth in the Automobile Industry*, Arno Press, New York.
Wagoner, H.D. (1968) *The US Machine Tool Industry from 1900–1950*, MIT Press.

Agriculture

Alston, L.J. (1983) 'Farm foreclosures in the United States in the interwar period', *Journal of Economic History*, XLII.

Benedict, M.R. (1953) *Farm Policies of the United States, 1790–1950*, The Twentieth Century Fund, New York.

Fausold, M.L. (1977) 'President Hoover's farm policies, 1929–1933' *Agricultural History*, 51.

Fite, G.C. (1981) *American Farmers: The New Minority*, Indiana University Press.

Fite, G.C. (1984) *Cotton Fields No More: Southern Agriculture, 1865–1980*, University of Kentucky Press.

Goodrich, G., Allin, B.W. and Hayes, M. (1935) *Migration and Places of Living, 1920–1934*, University of Pennsylvania Press.

Guither, H.D. (1971) *Heritage of Plenty: A Guide to the Economic History and Development of US Agriculture*, University of Illinois Press.

Hamilton, D.E. (1982) 'Herbert Hoover and the Great Drought of 1930', *Journal of American History*, 68.

Romasco, A.U. (1965) *The Poverty of Abundance: Hoover, the Nation, the Depression*, Oxford University Press.

Shover, B.L. (1965) *Cornbelt Rebellion: The Farmers' Holiday Association*, University of Illinois Press.

Snyder, R.E. (1984) *Cotton Crisis*, University of North Carolina Press.

Thornthwaite, C.W. *et al.* (1934) *Internal Migration in the United States*, University of Pennsylvania Press.

Woodruff, N.E. (1985) *As Rare as Rain: Federal Relief in the Great Southern Drought of 1930–31*, University of Illinois Press.

Worster, D. (1979) *The Dust Bowl: The Southern Plains in the 1930s*, Oxford University Press.

6

Banking, Money and Taxes

Banking and Finance

The banking and financial sector was not immune to the ravages of the depression: just as businesses went bankrupt, so banks closed their doors to depositors. Bank failures were, of course, not uncommon in the United States: there were 29,087 commercial banks in 1920, a figure which had been reduced to 24,505 by 1929, though the aggregate level of deposits — \$36 bn — was the same for both years (Chapter 4). A combination of merger (White, 1985) and liquidation had substantially reduced bank numbers, even during the relatively prosperous twenties. Far worse was to come with the waves of bank failures which had reduced the financial system to a state of paralysis by the time Roosevelt took the presidential oath. Table 6.1 shows the extent of the banking catastrophe and it is immediately clear that smaller banks experienced a far greater mortality rate than did the larger member banks. It is also evident that this financial haemorrhage was effectively stemmed in 1933, and from that point on, even during the recession of 1937−8, losses were relatively slight. The US was not the only advanced country which experienced depression-induced bank failure: banks collapsed in many European countries, in particular Austria and Germany, although not in Britain.

Bank insolvency was not evenly distributed during the period 1929 to 1933; it came in clusters. The first crisis, in late 1930, was not as significant as those which followed, and recent research has shown that it arose principally from the failure of a major southern investment banking company which dragged down in its wake banks in a dozen states (Wicker, 1980). These failed institutions had much in common with those which had disappeared during the late 1920s: they were already in a very weak position when the depression began, and were unable to withstand the effect of a sharp decrease in agricultural income. This crisis can be viewed, therefore, as a continuum of previous experience rather than as a watershed in the economy (Stauffer, 1987; Wicker, 1982; White, 1984). The 1930 round of bank failures did, however, include the collapse of the Bank of United

Table 6.1   Commercial Bank Suspensions: Number and Deposits, 1929–41

| | Number | | | | | Deposits ($mn) | | | | | Estimated losses borne by depositors ($mn) |
| | | Member banks | | Non-member banks | | | Member banks[b] | | Non-member banks[b] | | |
Year	Total	National	State	State	Private	Total	National	State	State	Private	
1929	659	64	17	547	31	230,643	41.6	16.5	164.8	7.7	77
1930	1,350	161	27	1,104	58	837,096	170.4	202.4	449.0	15.2	237
1931	2,293	409	107	1,697	80	1,690,232	439.1	294.0	936.0	21.1	391
1932	1,453	276	55	1,085	37	706,188	214.2	55.1	429.1	7.8	168
1933[a]	4,000	1,101	174	2,616	109	3,596,698	1,610.5	783.4	1,189.5	13.3	540
1934	57	4	—	43	13	36,937	0.04	—	35.5	1.4	10
1935	34	4	—	30	—	10,015	5.3	—	4.7	—	4
1936	44	1	—	42	1	11,306	0.5	—	10.7	0.07	4
1937	59	4	2	52	1	19,723	7.4	1.7	10.5	0.09	5
1938	54	1	1	50	2	10,532	0.03	0.2	9.7	0.5	5
1939	42	4	3	34	1	34,998	1.3	24.6	9.7	0.01	18
1940	22	1	—	21	—	5,943	0.3	—	5.7	—	14
1941	8	4	—	4	—	3,726	3.1	—	0.58	—	2

Notes: (a) Figures for 1933 not strictly comparable with other years.
          (b) Figures have been rounded.

Source: Board of Governors of Federal Reserve System, *Banking and Monetary Statistics 1914–41* (1943), Table 66.

States, the largest commercial bank ever to have failed up to that time. Many small savers, seduced by the grand title of this New York institution, lost their deposits. By early 1931 stability had been restored, but not for long; from March to June a relapse set in, and from August to December, in response to events in Europe, the situation worsened considerably. Fearful of losing their savings, many depositors chose to withdraw their money and keep it at home where they judged it would be safer than in their local bank. Indeed, as prices fell, the real value of the cash that they held actually increased.

By the spring of 1932 the tide of failure had abated, only to reappear in November when a state-wide banking holiday was declared in Nevada. In February 1933, because of extraordinary pressure on Detroit banks, the Governor of Michigan proclaimed a banking holiday in that state. By the end of the month ten states had general restrictions on deposit withdrawals and a further nineteen had more limited restrictions, imposed either under statutes or by independent action (Kennedy, 1973). Once one state had closed its banks, others came under pressure, and one of Roosevelt's first actions as President was to close all the nation's banks so that a solution to the problem could be sought. By this time public confidence in the banking system was at an all-time low and the regard in which many bankers were held was no higher. Other financial institutions also came under severe pressure: several prestigious investment banking houses were only just pulled from the brink of disaster (Carosso, 1970) and building and loan associations collapsed because of falling property values and mortgage defaults.

Panic gripped American depositors. As the depression worsened, their faith in financial institutions, which even in good times had been viewed with some suspicion, evaporated; the lines of depositors outside banks could not be ignored and savers knew that at a certain point their bank would be unable to pay out. The sensible course of action was to join the rush for withdrawals; this had the effect of making closure more likely and of spreading the panic. A bank's closure did not automatically result in a total loss to the depositor; there was the possibility of a merger or consolidation with a stronger bank as happened during the 1920s, but this occurred in a relatively small proportion of stricken institutions between 1930 and 1933 (White, 1985). Even a liquidated bank might eventually repay its debts in full, but the unfortunate depositors had no access to their savings until the receiver's task had been completed, and this was often a slow process. Frozen cash could not be spent and the local economy was further weakened. Even worse, a closed bank in a small community made it virtually impossible for local farmers or businessmen to obtain essential credit.

Why did so many banks fail? What was done to prevent such failures? Did the failures affect the economy as a whole, and if so, how? We can begin to answer these questions by pointing out that the safest area for banks was the mid-Atlantic region, whereas the vast majority of those which closed their doors were small units situated in rural areas, with the states of Nevada, Arkansas, North Carolina and Mississippi losing the largest proportion. These institutions were affected by the serious fall in the prices of crops, livestock and land which prevented borrowers from repaying their debts. Once this happened the banks were forced to sell their assets, many of which — especially real estate and securities — were fast becoming worthless. In this severe depression fewer people made deposits and more needed to live on their savings — indeed, aggregate personal saving in the United States was negative during 1932 and 1933. There was, of course, still a demand for credit, but at a much reduced level; farmers in particular still had to borrow. The banks, however, were more interested in liquidity than lending. As stories of bank failure became more common 'a contagion of fear', to use Friedman and Schwartz's apt phrase, swept the country. Queues of anxious depositors meant that withdrawals exceeded deposits and the banks had to close. The public took to hoarding currency, that is, they preferred to keep it out of the banking system rather than move their savings from one bank to another.

Although most failed banks were located in rural areas, as the depression developed many large banks in major cities were unable to remain solvent: indeed, some studies have shown that it would be wrong to assume that big banks were always sound (Gambs, 1977; Muchmore, 1970). Sometimes their misfortunes were closely related to those of the small institutions which used them as bankers; the withdrawal of funds from correspondent banks could, and did, bring those bodies down. Other big banks crumbled under the pressure of industrial collapse, such as those in Chicago and Detroit; many, however, survived because bank holidays gave them a breathing space. Banks are the most important financial intermediaries; they have greater assets than non-bank institutions, but more particularly, they alone have the power to create and destroy money. Savings and loan associations cannot lend more than the total of their deposits; commercial banks are not so constrained and lend more than is deposited. If, however, depositors withdraw large sums of money from the banking system the reverse situation occurs: the stock of money is reduced.

Given the structure of American banking, it is not surprising that the depression should have had such devastating results. Since there was a long-established opposition to branch banking, the single office independent unit was the most common. Unit banking had its defenders even when the system was collapsing like a stack of cards, but its disadvantages were great (Chapter 4). There was a need for regionally diversified branch banking, clearly shown when many unit banks were unable to withstand the movement of deposits out of depressed agricultural regions (Chandler, 1971); the tragedy was that such failed banks had a far more depressing effect upon the local economy than failed businesses. Although Gambs feels that the degree of branching bore little relation to the number of failures, there is a strong body of opinion supporting the view that unit banking could not withstand a mild shock, let alone a severe crisis.

The fact that the banking system was riddled with weaknesses does not explain why the failures were concentrated in particular periods rather than evenly distributed between 1929 and 1933. We have already seen that the 1930 crisis was really a continuation of the pressures which were all too evident during the

1920s, but the 1931 failures were of a different dimension. A new bank crisis in March helped stifle a recovery in the economy which was underway, though by then public anxiety had already been aroused by unfavourable events overseas. A number of Latin American countries had recently left the gold standard, as had Australia, while Europe was showing clear signs of political and economic instability. In May the Kreditanstalt, Austria's largest commercial bank, failed and soon banks in Hungary and Germany were forced to close their doors. American banks were enmeshed in the economies of the Old World because of the extensive private lending which had been undertaken by US citizens, who now doubted the ability of the debtor nations to repay their loans. American investors wanted to withdraw their funds where possible, and few wanted to lend. Their actions put such pressure on debtor nations that default seemed likely, and it was to prevent this catastrophe that in July, President Hoover proposed a year-long moratorium on inter-government debts which would, it was hoped, give Germany in particular a breathing space and at the same time enable her to pay all private overseas debts. The Hoover Moratorium was an inadequate solution, and Germany decided to freeze all foreign funds which were, in fact, mostly American. The fear spread to Britain which, by September, was unable to support the then exchange rate of £1 = $4.86: sterling was devalued and the gold standard abandoned. Speculators then turned to what they felt was the next weakest currency — the dollar.

In 1931 there was a massive outflow of gold from the United States, as many foreign Central Banks withdrew their deposits. To stem this overseas flow the Federal Reserve raised its discount rates. The gold drain came to a halt, but the banking system underwent a severe squeeze; although it could be argued that the policy of the Federal Reserve had been the correct one to deal with the outflow of gold, it was disastrous with respect to the preservation of the banking sytem: The banks were desperate for liquidity; what they wanted was cheap credit and lots of it. Low interest rates and open market operations (that is, the purchase of government securities which would increase bank reserves), were among the most positive actions that the Reserve could have taken to institute an easy money policy; this would have enabled the banks to cope more easily with withdrawals and, therefore, would have reduced the risk of failure. Unfortunately, the policy which emerged was a tight money policy, the very opposite of what was required to save the banking system.

Once the storm of the 1931 crisis had abated, the economy began to show marked signs of recovery. Indeed, between April and August 1932 the Federal Reserve bought $1 bn worth of securities in an open market operation which made monetary policy relatively liberal. There was widespread hope that the worst was over and that the United States, in common with other industrial nations, was fully on the path to recovery. These hopes were destroyed during the winter of 1932–3, a particularly distressing period in American history. Hoover had lost the presidential election in November, but Roosevelt was not to assume office until the following March. The nation, therefore, had no leadership for four crucial months as Hoover and Roosevelt were unable to reconcile their differences. This 'lame duck' period was one of great uncertainty and much speculation. Would the policies of the new administration be inflationary? Would the budget go into further imbalance? Would the new President abandon the gold standard and devalue the dollar? So strong were the doubts that once again the dollar came under speculative pressure while at home depositors hastened to the banks in order to remove their savings. The Federal Reserve responded, as it had in the previous crisis, with a tight money policy designed to protect the dollar from international speculation. Unfortunately, as in 1931, this policy put so much pressure on a banking system already battered to virtual insensibility that there was little option other than to close it down. In both 1931, and in 1932−3, therefore, tight money policies were adopted when the banks needed as much cheap credit as the Federal Reserve could provide. The Reserve had the powers to institute a liberal monetary policy and, as Chandler (1971) points out, it is quite possible that many of the banks which succumbed could have been kept open if alternative policies had been pursued.

To those long accustomed to bank stability, the United States experience is startling. Was it not possible to prevent all, or at least some, of the failures? If it was, who was responsible for the disaster? Surely the Federal Reserve System, which had been established in part as a response to bank crises, had an important role to play in minimising such failures by acting as lender of last resort to the commercial banks at times of stress?

At this point we should reiterate certain facts about the Federal Reserve System. Firstly, not all banks had joined the Fed — indeed, small banks could not meet the minimum capital requirements for membership (Chapter 4). As Table 6.1 shows, the majority of the banks which were suspended between 1929 and 1933 were not members of the system. They were part of a body of some 15,500 small unit institutions dependent entirely upon their own resources. It is hardly surprising that as incomes, employment and agricultural prices collapsed, so did the banks. Another difficulty was that the Federal Reserve was not a unified central bank, being made up of 12 constituent parts. During the 1920s the powerful Federal Reserve Bank of New York, under its governor Benjamin Strong, had emerged as a clear and authoritative leader; its international experience, its domestic dominance and the powerful personality of Strong meant that Reserve policies followed New York's lead. Strong died in 1928 and in the crucial years that followed there was no one of his stature to provide the positive sense of direction which the Federal Reserve needed.

On the other hand, many of the bankers who met in order to determine policy were men of experience. They were convinced that the Federal Reserve had been successful in containing the recessions of 1924 and 1927 by the use of vigorous open market operations; why were the same policies not pursued with similar determination between 1929 and 1933? Why was monetary policy so inept? Friedman and Schwartz (1963) claim that the Fed had the powers to deal with the banking panic, and, by repeating its policies of 1924 and 1927, could have done so. That it did not was due to the death of Strong; with his demise the New York Reserve Bank, which was bigger, more sophisticated and more expert than the others, lost influence. Under Strong, New York would have pressed for vigorous open market operations, and unlike those who did advocate this course between 1930 and 1933, he would have been able to overcome objections to it. Elmus Wicker (1966) is, however, kinder in his assessment of the role of the Fed, believing that the events of 1924 and 1927 did not provide relevant blueprints for policy during the early 1930s. Where Friedman and Schwartz see inconsistency, he sees consistency; where they castigate, he discovers genuine confusion coupled with disillusion as to the effect that Federal Reserve policy could have upon the economy. According to Wicker, the counter-cyclical policies of 1924 and 1927 were not introduced primarily to provide succour for the domestic economy; what most influenced the Federal Reserve were international considerations. Policies, which included open market purchases, were designed to maintain or encourage the international adoption of the gold standard by discouraging a movement of specie to the United States. They had, however, as a fortunate by-product, an expansionary effect upon the domestic economy. When the Reserve took positive action to preserve foreign confidence in the dollar in 1931 and again in early 1933, its policies, though consistent with those of 1924 and 1927, now had an adverse effect upon financial institutions.

Others have emphasised a further element of confusion within the Federal Reserve (Brunner and Meltzer, 1980; Chandler, 1971). The governors of the Federal Reserve Banks did not distinguish between nominal and real interest rates, though this was a period of severe deflation in which real values differed markedly from nominal values. Thus the officers of the system thought that the policy which they were pursuing after the Wall Street crash was one of easy money — perhaps even too easy — and that open market purchases aimed at reducing already historically very low interest rates would be pointless. Their use of nominal interest rates, which were low, as an indicator of monetary ease, instead of real rates, which were relatively high, gave the wrong message. They believed that monetary policy was easy and, as the depression worsened, felt that there was nothing more that they could do to lessen the remorseless disintegration of the economy. Furthermore, there was, at this time, a commonly held view amongst US central bankers that the country had too many banks and that the liquidation of a number of them was not a matter for concern. Their desire to save banks in the early stages of the depression, therefore, was not strong, but as the financial crisis deepened the economics of purgation had fewer staunch adherents.

President Hoover, typically, urged voluntarism upon the bankers, and in response to his promptings, a number of private banks agreed to form, on 4 October 1931, the National Credit Corporation with a capital of $500 mn. Its aim was to restore public confidence in the commercial banking system by creating a body which could lend to individual banks in distress (Kennedy, 1973; Olson,

1977). It was not a success, and within a short time commercial bankers and central bankers made a plea for federal government intervention, a course of action that Hoover had been hoping to avoid.

In January 1932 Hoover reluctantly established the Reconstruction Finance Corporation to lend to both member and non-member banks, to other financial institutions, and to the beleaguered railroads. Modelled on a World War I federal agency, the War Finance Corporation, the RFC, had a capital of $500 mn provided by the government and the authority to borrow $1.5 bn, a figure that was raised to $3.3 bn in July. Its chairman was Eugene Meyer, who was also governor of the Federal Reserve Board. He and several members of the RFC executive had also seen public service in the WFC itself. During 1932, the RFC lent approximately $950 mn to 5,582 banks and its foundation coincided with a distinct drop in bank instability; it was unable, however, to prevent the failure of the banking system during early 1933.

It is difficult to calculate the impact of the RFC. The additional liquidity which it gave to the banking system coincided with large-scale open market operations by the Federal Reserve between April and August 1932, which were also of considerable help to the financial community. The RFC, moreover, was conservative in its lending policies, which led to a disbursement of relatively small sums at high interest rates so that the agency would not directly compete with private lenders. More important, perhaps, than the supply of funds was the restricted demand for them. Any bank borrowing from the RFC could be considered by a depositor to be in trouble; the banks, therefore, were anxious for confidentiality in these transactions. From August 1932, however, on the instruction of Congress, the RFC was obliged to make public the names of banks to which it had made loans during the previous month; in January 1933 all loans given before the preceding August were made public. As a result, banks borrowing from the RFC openly paraded their weakness, the very thing that they wished to avoid. The estbalishment of the RFC was a clear sign that voluntarism had failed and for the first time in peace, the federal government intervened directly in the workings of the economy (Olson, 1977; Nash, 1979). Had the RFC been established in early 1931 and had it pursued a generous lending policy, it might have been more successful, but in any event it was no substitute for more vigorous Federal Reserve action (Chandler, 1971).

More federal intervention to aid the financial sector was evident in 1932. Hoover pressed for the passage of the Glass–Steagall Act (February 1932) which enabled the Federal Reserve banks to adopt a more liberal lending policy. In July the Home Loan Bank Bill set up 12 federal Home Loan Banks which helped building and loan associations and other institutions heavily involved in the home mortgage business. Rather like the RFC, a telling criticism of the Home Loan Banks was the sluggish manner in which they lent relatively small sums of money to combat a serious problem. We can see, however, that the federal government was not inactive during the crisis, and by 1932 its approach had changed from one of exhortation and voluntarism to direct intervention. Unfortunately, by then the situation had deteriorated to such an extent that federal action was at best a short-term palliative, but in the long term a failure. As we have seen, the Federal Reserve did have the power to ameliorate the banking crisis, if not to prevent it altogether, but a lack of leadership and vision meant that its internal squabbles could not be satisfactorily resolved; as a result the vital easy money policies, such as reduced discount rates, open market operations and the lowering of member bank reserve requirements, were not pursued systematically. Furthermore, institutional weaknesses made the banking system particularly vulnerable, with too many small unit banks and no deposit insurance schemes which would have reassured the public.

The striking difference between the liquidation of banks and that of businesses, according to monetarists, is their effect upon the money supply. Just as banks can expand the supply of money through lending more than is deposited with them, their demise and the public's preference for hoarding money has precisely the opposite effect. As Friedman and Schwartz have demonstrated, between 1929 and the banking holiday of 1933, the stock of money in the US fell by one third, the most dramatic decline ever; they and their disciples hold the view that the severity of the depression was caused by this sharp drop in the money stock. This phenomenon, and the failure of the Federal Reserve to prevent it, will occupy a prominent position in our analysis of the causes of the depression in Chapter 9.

The Stock Market

One aspect of the 1920s boom which caught the imagination of the public was the behaviour of securities markets, especially the Wall Street Stock Exchange in New York. During the 1920s stock prices increased at twice the rate of industrial production and soared to dizzy heights during the period of rapid economic expansion which took place in 1928–9 (Wigmore, 1985). The rewards for investors were great. An index of stock prices (1935–9 = 100) calculated for the month of June shows a spectacular progression: 56 in 1921, 77 in 1924, 103 in 1926, 153 in 1928, and 201 in 1929. The fortunate stock holders received not only dividend payments, but also substantial capital gains from a highly liquid asset which seemed only to increase in value. For the most part, the owners of stocks were wealthy and the behaviour of the stock market helps to explain why the share of national wealth enjoyed by this relatively small group increased during the 1920s.

Although stock prices were rising throughout the 1920s, we should not conclude that it was solely the attention of speculators which had forced them to improbable heights (Sirkin, 1975). Indeed, the number of speculators was small, probably less than one million even when the stock market boom was at its most vigorous (Galbraith, 1952). A combination of factors including a prosperous economy, a maldistribution of income, high rates of profit, a plentiful supply of credit and, above all, investor confidence helped to push up the value of stocks which had been underpriced in the early 1920s. The growth of speculation caused some concern amongst officials of the Federal Reserve, who became convinced that if the speculative bubble should burst it would have a serious effect upon the economy. The Fed, therefore, decided to take action, and exhorted member banks not to lend money for speculative purposes. More positively, it embarked upon a tight money policy from the middle of 1928, raising discount rates and selling government bonds. The hope was that as borrowing became more expensive, speculation would become less profitable and would eventually fade away. A tight money policy can affect legitimate demands for credit; the Fed, however, believed that its actions would curtail stock market excesses without damaging business interests.

Fixed firmly in the public eye is the Wall Street Crash of October 1929 which in popular myth is often cited as the cause of the depression. It was a collapse which took virtually all investors by surprise, even though it was clear by September that stock prices were behaving in an erratic manner. Prices had fluctuated in the recent past, but after a period of uncertainty had resumed their upward trend; indeed, their rise during the first nine months of 1929 was very steep (Wigmore, 1985). By September, however, share prices had reached their zenith and at that time a considerable revision of future earnings was taking place. There was a growing apprehension about the economy, as automobile and steel output had passed their peak; some investors were concerned about the amount of speculation, believing that it would ultimately bring the market down. It has been suggested that stock holders reacted adversely to the debate in the Senate which showed that the US was embarking upon a new wave of tariff protection (Wanniski, 1978), though this, if it mattered at all, was probably of very marginal significance. In October the wobble in the market turned into a slide — not a smooth slide for prices did fluctuate — but on 24 October, Black Thursday, 12,894,560 shares were traded, more than double the previous record as panic selling took hold. After a short pause, 28 October saw 9,213,000 shares traded; the following day was even worse, with a record 16,410,000 transactions. After more tortuous wriggles the market reached its 1929 low on 13 November. An index of share prices (1935−9 = 100) which reached a peak of 237 in September had fallen to 160 in November. The market then rallied and struggled to 191 in April 1930. Its collapse from this low point to 46 in March 1933 was extraordinarily steep.

The strategy of the Federal Reserve had been cruelly destroyed. By raising interest rates the Fed had produced the opposite effect to that intended because at the higher rates it had become more profitable for institutions or individuals to lend to the market. Many share deals were financed by credit, with the investor making a down payment and borrowing the rest from his broker, using the shares as collateral. This was known as 'buying on the margin', and the purchaser was confident that the gain made from owning the share would be more than enough to cover both the capital cost and interest charges on the broker's loan. The brokers in turn borrowed money which they advanced to their clients. As long as share prices rose everyone was happy, but if shares failed to make the expected gains, some purchasers would be unable to repay the brokers' loans. If the price fall was very steep, the broker would also find himself in difficulty, as the shares which were used as collateral now had to be sold on a rapidly falling market. This seemed a distant scenario before October 1929. So buoyant was the market that investors were prepared to borrow at relatively high interest rates, and Table 6.2 shows a dramatic rise in loans to brokers between 1927 and 1929.

Table 6.2   Brokers' Loans by Groups of Lenders ($mn)

	Total	New York city banks	Outside banks	Others
June 1927	3,570	1,130	970	1,470
June 1928	4,900	1,080	960	2,840
June 1929	7,070	1,360	665	5,054
June 1930	3,795	1,885	480	1,430
June 1931	1,600	1,065	155	380
June 1932	335	260	20	55
June 1933	890	720	70	100

Source: Board of Governors of Federal Reserve System,
Banking and Monetary Statistics, p. 494, Table 139.

This table also shows that the new funds flooding in to finance the purchase of stock were not coming from the banking system, but from sources outside it. These outside sources included some major corporations such as Bethlehem Steel, Standard Oil, Chrysler, and Anaconda Copper which found lending to brokers a lucrative use for their profits; foreign banking houses or individuals with surplus funds also lent to the market. Money which before 1928 would have gone in the form of loans overseas was directed to the stock market, a change which had serious implications for foreign borrowers. Indeed, as Kindleberger (1973) has observed, the danger posed to the market in 1929 was not on the level of prices and turnover but in the credit mechanism that supported it.

The action of the Federal Reserve in raising interest rates explains the willingness to switch funds to the market (Wicker), which in turn accounts for at least some of the rise in prices and trading. The fact that funds were available, however, did not cause speculation. We should not forget that the demand for loans was already exceptionally strong and that no one was forced to borrow. Reserve policy does not provide an explanation for the stock market crash unless we believe Friedman and Schwartz who maintain that the tight money policy was an important factor in retarding economic progress. This is an issue which will be analysed in some detail later. Too much emphasis on the events of 1929 is, however, unwise for even at their low point in November, stock prices were still at the same level as in mid-1928. Moreover, in early 1930 the market revived and politicians, businessmen and bankers all expressed confidence in the economy; unfortunately, the price increases were not sustained. Once it was clear, by mid-1930, that there would be no general revival in the economy, stock prices began to slide, and by the middle of 1932 they had fallen to about a quarter of their 1929 peak (Table 6.3). This decline was even more pronounced than that of manufacturing output or employment and the market remained relatively depressed for the rest of the decade. Those who had confidently expected an increase in capital gains experienced staggering capital losses.

Table 6.3 Index of Stock Prices, 1926–39 (1929 = 100)

Year	Total	Industrial	Public utility	Railroad
1926	52.5	52.8	42.6	67.9
1927	62.2	62.6	49.4	80.9
1928	78.8	81.5	63.5	87.2
1929	100.0	100.0	100.0	100.0
1930	78.5	74.2	91.5	84.8
1931	49.8	46.1	63.4	49.2
1932	25.5	24.5	33.7	17.9
1933	33.1	34.7	33.3	25.6
1934	38.0	42.8	29.4	28.2
1935	41.1	47.9	30.4	23.1
1936	58.3	67.2	44.5	34.7
1937	58.7	69.3	44.4	33.5
1938	43.8	52.5	31.2	17.7
1939	46.9	55.4	36.0	19.1

Source: Calculated from *Statistical Abstract of the US, 1940*, Table 338.

The problem of evaluating the role of the stock market in the depression involves an exercise in separating cause from effect. Did the crash help cause the depression, or did the stock market enthusiastically follow the economic collapse? It would be convenient if one could closely identify the Wall Street Crash with the decline in the real economy because it coincided with a steep fall in industrial output, but to do so slavishly would be to accept that the tail could wag the dog. The really pronounced drop in the market set in from the middle of 1930 when the economic recovery was not sustained. From this point, as we have seen, one of the most serious blows which affected the economy was bank failure, but the declining stock market cannot be blamed more than marginally for that. Similarly, gross private investment tumbled after 1930 but in this sphere the stock market had always played a minor role, financing only 6 per cent of investment in 1929. Ploughed back profits were the most important source of investment; the sums raised on Wall Street were often earmarked for financing mergers or acquisitions, so that the elimination of profits is the key to low levels of investment, not the declining market. We know too that only a minority of Americans owned stocks and that these people must have been concentrated amongst the most wealthy; could a reduction in their wealth bring about the dramatic fall in aggregate consumer spending so noticeable after 1929? (Green, 1971)

There is no agreement as to the impact of the stock market crash; for example, Friedman and Schwartz and one of their most severe critics, Temin (1976), are cautious in their appraisal. Mishkin (1978), however, emphasises the role played by the crash and the subsequent fall in stock prices, which sharply reduced the wealth of households which were already heavily in debt by 1929; as a result there was a steep reduction in expenditure as real debts increased. Kindleberger (1973; 1979) sees the stock market occupying an even more central role in a depression which he claims had international origins. The collapse of the market led to a credit crisis in New York which undermined commodity imports, leading to dramatic price falls; in addition, automobile sales, heavily dependent upon credit, were also affected (Field, 1984). Kindleberger believes that the link between the falling stock market and the economy was in its impact on credit and, through credit, on prices. Once deflation set in, banks were affected in the US and abroad, as were overseas trade and capital flows. Even if one does not accept the central role of the stock market as put forward by Kindleberger, it can be accepted that as share prices and dividend payments fell, so did the wealth and spending power of households, especially those which had helped to sustain the boom of the twenties. Moreover, we should remember that the stock market played a key role in the culture of the 1920s; its collapse would have adversely affected the expectations both of consumers, most of whom never owned shares, and of businessmen, as well as helping to destroy faith in financial institutions. Thus, although the role which the Wall Street Crash played in the depression is by no means clear, the fall of the market in mid-1930 strongly affected consumption patterns, the level of savings and the confidence which Americans had in their economy.

The Budget, the Deficit and Taxes

The actions of the monetary authorities in the US were independent and not under the control of the federal government. The economic policies of central government, therefore, were limited to fiscal policy: that is, the use of taxation and government expenditure to regulate aggregate economic activity. During a depression, when labour and capital are greatly under-utilised and the demand for goods depressed, a government can stimulate the economy by lowering taxes, by increasing expenditure, or by some combination of both policies. The additional money given to consumers would be spent on goods and services, thus encouraging business to produce more and in doing so employ more workers. Of course, we must not view the government of 1930 as being central to the economy as it might be considered in the 1980s. Americans in 1930 did not feel that Washington should (or could) guide the economy towards maximum employment and output. In a crisis the federal government would exhort the people and institutions to help themselves; it could advise or guide local communities in their attempts to cope with the effects of depression but the view was that, when the correct conditions prevailed, private business would raise the economy from the depths. The power of government was limited in another way too — federal expenditure was a very small proportion of GNP, only 2.5 per cent in 1929, whilst receipts were, in that year, only 3.7 per cent.

In this vast decentralised country the federal government was not the only taxing unit; the 48 state governments and over 180,000 minor political units had the power to levy taxes and to go into debt. State and local expenditures were greater than those of central government, amounting to 7.5 per cent of GNP in 1929 — the figure for receipts was about 7.3 per cent. However, if the economy as a whole was to be stimulated, this action had to come from Washington whose tax base and borrowing powers were more extensive than those of the states and the local units. Moreover, if the benefits from stimulation were to be felt over the entire nation, it was unrealistic to expect local units to take a lead, as the advantages to be gained might not be readily apparent to taxpayers and voters. Moreover, most state constitutions prohibited deficits; indeed, during the New Deal, budget surpluses at the state and local levels reduced the expansionary impact of federal deficits (Chapter 13).

It was widely felt during the 1920s that the federal budget should be balanced: that is, receipts should be sufficient to cover expenditures including the repayment of debt, and, between 1920 and 1930 inclusive, the federal budget was comfortably in surplus. Another commonly accepted view was that tax cuts were beneficial; indeed, those introduced by Andrew Mellon during the 1920s had coincided with a period of rapid economic expansion. In a depression, of course, budget balancing is at best difficult and usually impossible. The government has to estimate its receipts for some time ahead when preparing its expenditure plans, but once economic activity declines, receipts fall away. One of the most striking features of the business cycle of 1927−33 was the dramatic reduction in income tax receipts, which fell to one third of their cyclical peak, a steeper decline than that of GNP. In particular, the massive fall in taxes paid by corporations quickly undermined revenue estimates which proved far too optimistic. As a result, the first quarter of 1931 saw the beginning of a deficit problem that lasted through the decade.

Under such circumstances President Hoover's options were limited. Most economists, and virtually all the business community, were firm supporters of the balanced budget — a concept which had also great popular appeal. The average voter believed the government should balance its books — it was a simple exercise in good housekeeping. For the administration the problem, however, was complex. Economic intelligence was very poor at this time; there was an absence of accurate data on the movements of key economic variables; even the level of unemployment was a matter of vigorous debate. While the decision-making process was hampered by a lack of information, the periodic signs of recovery in the economy convinced Hoover that good times were about to return and gloomy budget forecasts would only serve to dampen the optimism of the industrialists. Hoover was not a *laissez-faire* politician; he was passionately concerned about social problems, particularly unemployment, and had been a strong supporter of public works programmes during the depression of 1920–1. Under his Presidency the expenditure of the federal government increased: the National Industrial Conference Board calculated that an additonal $1.2 bn over the 1929 figure was spent in 1932, attributable solely to the depression. The amount spent on public works, for example, rose from $201 mn in 1929 to $507 mn in 1932. Given the catastrophic fall in private construction, however, these sums were but a drop in the ocean, and the debate over the financing of public works illustrates the dilemma which faced the President.

While the benefits of public works had been extolled during the 1920s, the problem was one of financing them once the depression began and the budget moved into deficit. Hoover felt that there was very limited scope for paying out of current taxation, which would worsen the deficit, or for relying on borrowing, which would result in the government competing for scarce funds with private business. This led Hoover to support only self-liquidating schemes, that is, projects which would eventually pay for themselves. There was a vociferous group — the liquidationists — who felt that any government intervention would be harmful as it would prevent the natural fall of the economy from reaching a level from which sustained recovery could begin. The state therefore should stand aside and let events take their course. Hoover did not subscribe to this view, but neither did he see any merit in the gigantic public works projects advocated by pressure groups or by eminent politicians such as Senator Robert Wagner of New York. While the President was bombarded with pleas for more public works expenditure, he was also assailed by those who wanted more economy and who never tired of driving home their message: that budget deficits undermined business confidence and led, ultimately, to inflation. 1932 was a presidential election year, and during the campaign Hoover's opponent, Franklin Roosevelt, repeatedly attacked the deficits; the unfortuante Hover was criticised, not for inactivity, but for heading a spendthrift administration. Majority opinion favoured the orthodoxy of balanced budgets, and certainly a massive spending spree on the part of the government would have been impossible to justify either intellectually or politically.

At the same time, as the depression worsened, some gradually came round to the view that there was an alternative. The analogy with war became increasingly common; if high deficits are acceptable in war, why not in the fight against economic ruin? These voices did not carry sufficient weight to convince the administration, which placed heavy emphasis upon self-liquidating public works for which, it felt, government lending was permissible. Unfortunately, major self-liquidating projects, such as bridges or dams for which consumers can be charged a toll or a fee, cannot absorb the unemployed quickly, as a long period of planning and preparation is necessary before work can begin. This is one of the reasons why agencies such as the RFC were slow to lend: there were relatively few self-liquidating projects to hand which did not compete with private business. With limited finance, the impact of self-liquidating public works could not be great enough to absorb more than a small proportion of the unemployed, though one could argue, with some justification, that the policy could have been more expansive than it was.

As the budget moved, in the space of a few years, from a large surplus to a large deficit, it was clear that 1932 would be a year of fiscal crisis. In late 1931, therefore, the Hoover administration decided to raise taxes sharply, a strongly deflationary move and one quite at variance with the contemporary view that tax cuts were associated with economic advance. Why were taxes raised? As Stein observes, to say that taxes were increased in order to balance the budget is simplistic, as informed analysis did not take the budget literally: after all, surpluses could be run in other years to make up for depression deficits. Moreover, just what should go into the expenditure column in the budget was open to some debate; for example, included in the items of government expenditure was the $500 mn in capital stock for the RFC which could have been omitted on the grounds that, as a capital advance, it was theoretically recoverable. Similarly, some creative accounting could have erased other temporary depression expenditures, thus reducing the deficit and removing the pressure for a damaging tax increase. Stein's explanation places great emphasis upon the state of the economy in late 1931 when the decision to raise taxes was taken. Britain had just abandoned the gold standard and devalued sterling; as speculative pressures mounted on the dollar, gold flowed out of the United States, the banking system came under great pressure as depositors removed their savings, and the Federal Reserve raised interest rates — an action which, as we have seen, had savage repercussions on the banks. Hoover was anxious to prevent the dollar going the same way as sterling but at the same time he believed that it was vital to keep credit available for private business. He therefore came to the conclusion that financing a higher deficit by borrowing would harm business and the banking sector, because the government would absorb funds otherwise available for private investment, thus forcing up interest rates. The deficit, moreover, would have an adverse effect upon confidence, both at home and overseas, fuelling the fear of inflation which would in turn lead to a further gold outflow. The conditions of the time explain, if not excuse, the tax increase.

Therefore we see that fiscal policy became strongly deflationary during 1932. Federal spending had increased between 1929 and 1932, although by an amount sufficient to have only a minimal effect upon the worsening economy. Moreover, we should remember that much of the pressure for increased spending came from Congress which had been captured by the Democrats in 1930. However, while the administration's policy was to get as near as possible to a balanced budget, unavoidable deficits, which were expansionary, did occur. Indeed, E. Cary Brown's study of fiscal policy during the thirties found that if the spending of all branches of government was aggregated, the stimulating effect of fiscal policy was larger in 1931 than in any other year during the decade. If the federal budget alone is considered, the two-year period 1929–31 was one of greater fiscal stimulation than any similar term during the entire 1930s (Chapter 13). Unfortunately, the expansionary effect of fiscal policy, accidentally arrived at, was cut short by the large tax increase of 1932.

Bibliography

The most readable account of the banking crisis which engulfed the United States is by S.E. Kennedy. For a comprehensive account of the stock market, read R. Sobel. Those who wish to explore monetary policy more deeply can begin with L.V. Chandler (1971). Students of fiscal policy will find H. Stein clear and concise.

Brown, E. Cary (1956) 'Fiscal policy in the "thirties": a reappraisal', *American Economic Review*, 46.

Brunner, K. and Meltzer, A.H. (1980) 'What did we learn from the monetary experience of the United States in the Great Depression?', *Canadian Journal of Economics*, 1.

Carosso, V. (1970) *Investment Banking in America: A History*, Harvard University Press.

Chandler, L.V. (1950) *Benjamin Strong: Central Banker*, Brookings Institution, Washington DC.

Chandler, L.V. (1971) *American Monetary Policy 1928–1941*, Harper and Row.

Epstein, G. and Ferguson, T. (1984) 'Monetary policy, loan liquidation and industrial conflict. The Federal Reserve and the open market operations of 1932', *Journal of Economic History*, XLIV.

Field, A.J. (1984) 'A new interpretation of the onset of the Great Depression', *Journal of Economic History*, XLIV.

Firestone, S.M. (1960) *Federal Receipts and Expenditures during Business Cycles, 1879–1958*, NBER, Princeton.

Friedman, M. and Schwartz, A.J. (1963) *A Monetary History of the United States 1867–1960*, Princeton.

Galbraith, J.K. (1961) *The Great Crash, 1929*, Houghton Mifflin.

Gambs, C.M. (1977) 'Bank failures — a historical perspective', *Federal Reserve Bank of Kansas City Monthly Review*, June.

Gayer, A.D. (1938) *Public Works in Prosperity and Depression*, NBER, New York.

Green, G.D. (1971) 'The economic impact of the stock market boom and crash of 1929' in Federal Reserve Bank of Boston, *Consumer Spending and Monetary Policy: The Linkages*, Conference Series No. 5, June, Boston.

Kennedy, S.E. (1973) *The Banking Crisis of 1933*, University of Kentucky Press.

Kindleberger, C.P. (1973) *The World in Depression 1929–1939*, University of California Press.

Kindleberger, C.P. (1979) 'The international causes and consequences of the great crash', *Journal of Portfolio Management*, 6.

Mishkin, F.S. (1978) 'The household balance sheet and the great depression', *Journal of Economic History*, XXXVIII.

Muchmore, L. (1970) 'The banking crisis of 1933: some Iowa evidence', *Journal of Economic History*, XXX.

National Industrial Conference Board (1933) *Federal Finances 1923–1932*, New York.

O'Hara, M. and Easley, D. (1979) 'The postal savings system in the depression', *Journal of Economic History*, XXXIX, pp. 741–53.

Olson, J.S. (1977) *Herbert Hoover and the Reconstruction Finance Corporation, 1931–1933*, University of Iowa Press.

Rasche, R.H. (1972) 'Impact of the Stock Market on Private Demand', *American Economic Review*, LXII, May.

Sammelson, P.A. (1979) 'Myths and realities about the crash and the depression', *Journal of Portfolio Management*, 6.

Sirkin, G. (1975) 'The stock market of 1929 revisited: a note', *Business History Review*, XLIX.

Sobel, R. (1965) *The Big Board: A History of the New York Stock Market*, Macmillan.

Stauffer, R.F. (1981) 'The Bank failures of 1930–31: a comment', *Journal of Money Credit and Banking*, 13.

Stein, H. (1969) *The Fiscal Revolution in America*, University of Chicago Press.

Temin, P. (1976) *Did Monetary Forces Cause the Great Depression?* W.W. Norton.

Thomas, R.G. (1935) 'Bank failures — causes and remedies', *Journal of Business*, 8.

Upham, C.B. and Lamke, E. (1934) *Closed and Distressed Banks*, Brookings Institution, Washington DC.

Wanniski, J. (1978) *The Way the World Works*, Basic Books.

White, E.N. (1985) 'The merger movement in banking, 1919–1933', *Journal of Economic History*, XLV.

Wicker, E.R. (1966) *Federal Reserve Monetary Policy 1917–1933*, Random House.

Wicker, E.R. (1980) 'A reconsideration of the causes of the banking panic of 1930', *Journal of Economic History*, XL.

Wicker, E.R. (1982) 'Interest rate and expenditure effects of the banking panic of 1930', *Explorations in Economic History*, 19.

Wicker, E.R. (1984) 'A reinterpretation of the banking crisis of 1930', *Journal of Economic History*, XLIV.

Wigmore, B.A. (1985) *The Crash and its Aftermath: A History of Securities Markets in the United States 1929–33*, Greenwood Press.

7

Foreign Trade and Capital Flows

The Overseas Account

The depression was worldwide and not confined within the boundaries of the United States. Through exports, imports and capital flows, America was enmeshed in the international economy and it is clear that if her economy collapsed, her trading partners would inevitably be affected. Table 7.1 shows the dominance of the United States in international trade during this period, ranking second only to Britain as an importer (though if raw materials alone were included she would be first) and leading as an exporter.

By purchasing a large volume of imports the United States provided dollars for the primary producing countries who used them to pay off their debts, or to purchase goods either from the US or, indeed, from any other nation. Thus many economies depended upon their exports, especially of foodstuffs and raw materials, for supplies of much needed dollars. Between 1929 and 1932, however, world trade collapsed: in 1930 the total value of international trade, measured in gold dollars, was 19 per cent less than in 1929. There was a further fall of 28 per cent in 1931 and of 33 per cent in 1932. Overall, between 1929 and 1932 world trade contracted by 61 per cent. There was also a substantial decline of about 27 per cent in the volume of goods traded during the same period. The smaller reduction in quantity compared with value can be explained by the fact that although the volume of manufactured goods traded dropped by 40 per cent, the decrease in foodstuffs, 11 per cent, and raw materials, 18 per cent, was much less. It is clear that imports joined exports in a downward spiral as incomes were progressively reduced (Table 7.2) and as all nations desperately attempted to balance their international payments by cutting imports and expanding or at least maintaining the level of their exports.

The problem facing US exporters can be illustrated by looking at a few key commodities. The 3,982 million bales of cotton exported in 1929 were valued at $771mn but the 4,803 million bales sent overseas in 1932 at a mere $345mn. Petroleum-based exports were valued at $962mn in 1929 but at only $209mn in

Table 7.1 Percentage Shares of World Trade

Country	1929		1932	
	Imports	Exports	Imports	Exports
US	12.90	15.61	9.58	12.39
UK	15.19	10.74	16.43	10.06
Germany	9.00	9.72	7.98	10.70
France	6.41	5.95	8.44	6.08

Source: League of Nations, *World Economic Survey 1932–3*
(Geneva, 1933), p. 218.

Table 7.2 Percentage Decline in Import and Export Dollar Values since
1932

Country	Imports			Exports		
	1930	1931	1932	1930	1931	1932
US	28	52	69	27	54	69
UK	14	34	58	22	50	64
Germany	23	50	65	11	29	58
France	10	27	49	15	39	61
Chile	14	56	87	42	64	84
Peru	33	62	78	28	58	67
Brazil	38	65	75	31	48	61
Argentina	25	57	74	43	53	64
Australia	35	72	74	29	47	55

Source: League of Nations *World Economic Survey 1932–3* (Geneva, 1933), p. 214.

1932; during the same period exports of automobiles and parts declined from
$541mn to a paltry $76mn. The pattern for exports was that agricultural products, such as raw cotton maintained or even increased their volume but fell steeply
in price, while the decline in the value of manufactured products was, in the main,
a result of the smaller quantities traded; manufacturing prices are more resistant
to sharp change than those in agriculture. In 1929 finished manufactures accounted
for just over half the value of all US exports and their contraction dealt a serious
blow to the US economy.

   Import prices showed an even more pronounced reduction than those of exports,
tumbling to a level which was below even that of the late 1890s. This deflation
did not, however, lead to an increase in the volume of imports entering the United
States because consumption was determined by the overall economic situation,
not by price. Some 66 per cent of US total imports during the inter-war years
was made up of crude materials, crude foodstuffs and semi-manufactures. They

· were imports for the manufacturing sector: a decline in industrial production meant a commensurate decline in imports.

Between 1929 and 1932, the value of exports dropped from $7.0 bn to $2.5 bn; the fall in imports was similarly steep, from $5.9 bn to $2.0 bn. A reduction in invisible earnings was also evident, especially after 1931 when defaults on overseas loans adversely affected interest payments. The balance of payments, however, remained in the black although the amount of the surplus was reduced. The US was able to maintain her large gold stock; although she experienced significant gold losses on two occasions, neither crisis was due to balance of payments disequilibrium. In late 1931 overseas holders of dollars switched to gold because they feared a possible devaluation in the wake of Britain's abandonment of the gold standard. In early 1933, uncertainty over Roosevelt's resolve to maintain the exchange rate led to a similar lack of confidence in the dollar. The influx of gold during this period was sufficient, however, to ensure that the net loss was quite small.

As the incomes of overseas countries fell rapidly after 1929, these countries did not buy American goods on the same scale as before the depression. Unfortunately, the actions of the United States made an already desperate situation worse, for in June 1930 President Hoover signed the Hawley−Smoot bill which raised American protective tariff levels sharply to an all-time high. It was impossible to justify this action on the grounds of national security or even by using the popular infant industry argument. There were vigorous protests from many foreign governments and, in a rare display of unity, 1,028 American economists made a public protest against the tariff in *The New York Times*. Hawley−Smoot led to immediate retaliation: Canada, Cuba, Mexico, and France were among the first countries to raise tariffs and were followed by many others, so that by 1932 there had been extensive world-wide tariff increases. The American action led to a great degree of bitterness and resentment among many nations, who viewed it as an example of destructive economic insularity on the part of a powerful creditor country. There is a great deal of justification for this view.

As the protectionist spirit took hold, exports were limited not only by tariffs but also by quotas, foreign exchange control, clearing agreements and licensing systems. In additon, trade was distorted by barter arrangements, as countries strove to conserve scarce gold and foreign exchange. In August 1931, for example, the Brazilian government agreed with the American Grain Stabilization Corporation and the Bush Terminal Corporation of New York to exchange 1,275,000 sacks of coffee for 25 million bushels of wheat over an 18-month period. With agreements such as this, trade became increasingly bilateral — the practice of buying in the cheapest market and selling in the dearest was cast aside, as countries became more concerned about their trading balance with individual nations rather than their overall position. The picture was further complicated by devaluations which gave some nations a competitive edge by cheapening their exports in terms of other currencies. The advantage was often short-lived as trade rivals quickly retaliated either by devaluing their own currencies, or by raising tariffs to keep out relatively cheap imports.

There are mixed views concerning the impact of the Hawley–Smoot legislation. Friedman and Schwartz and Temin do not allot it a significant role in their analyses. Kindleberger (1973) sees its significance as a demonstration that the US was unwilling to take responsibility for the international crisis. Lary (1943) is very cautious in his assessment of the importance of Hawley–Smoot in the reduction of imports and suggests that after 1930 the decline in domestic economic activity was more important than tariff increase. He points out that the fall in imports on which heavy duties had been imposed was not significantly greater than that for other commodities. Recently, however, writers have placed Hawley–Smoot at, or near, the centre of their analysis of the cause and the course of the depression. Wanniski (1978) links the long debate on tariff increases in Congress with the stock market's crumble and fall. Saint-Etienne (1984) views the passage of the Act as leading to the financial crisis which broke out on the continent of Europe during the following year, the devaluation of sterling, and subsequent speculative pressure on the dollar. He concludes that if the Federal Reserve had increased the money stock and Hoover had vetoed Hawley–Smoot there would have been no depression. Meltzer (1976; 1981) claims that Hawley–Smoot prevented American prices from falling even further and, as a result, the demand for US exports was curbed. He also believes that if the United States had not been on the gold standard and had adopted flexible exchange rates, the effect of the tariff upon output and prices would have been mitigated. Gordon and Wilcox (1981) emphasise the retaliation which followed Hawley–Smoot, which they feel was especially effective in cutting US food exports by 66 per cent between 1929 and 1932. As a result, farm income was depressed, which in turn put pressure on local banks; they failed in large numbers and in doing so reduced the money supply. Kindleberger, however, asserts that the retaliation against the tariff increase was directed towards American manufactures, not farm exports.

How much of the decline in foreign trade experienced by the United States was caused specifically by Hawley–Smoot is impossible to calculate, though we can say that it was an extremely damaging piece of legislation. During the 1920s exports to the United States had been a vital source of dollars: Europe, for example, was able to balance part of its trade deficit with the New World through its surpluses with primary producers, who were themselves dollar earners or in receipt of capital from the United States. Any deliberate action which helped to reduce the level of international trade, itself delicately poised in 1930, would have serious repercussions. There can be little doubt that Hawley–Smoot was a major jolt to world commerce at the very time when contracting income was about to usher in an era of declining exports and imports.

The flow of dollars to the rest of the world as payment for imports to the United States was not the only source of that currency. America, the world's largest international lender during the 1920s, had helped to keep the international economy afloat by private investment overseas, and it is to this phenomenon that we now turn.

Overseas Capital and International Debt

Cleona Lewis (1938) observed that during the 1920s American investors were attracted by the high yields of foreign bonds but chose to ignore the additional risks endemic in foreign lending. Speculation at home and abroad captured the imagination of the investing public and, too often, the rashness of the borrowers matched the exuberance of the lenders. The fact that the United States was able to finance a domestic boom and, at the same time, send money overseas, convinced foreigners that in the event of a recession there would be more savings for overseas investment, not less. American capital seemed to come from a bottomless well, but even before 1929 there were signs that the supply was erratic.

Towards the end of the 1920s, sections of informed opinion inside the US grew apprehensive about the level of international lending. It was realised that debtors might invest their dollars unwisely — using them to finance projects which would not assist repayment. Moreover, in the case of primary producers, export earnings could often be dependent upon the fortunes of a single commodity where a violent fall in price would make full repayment impossible. It was known that Germany, the world's leading borrower, had absorbed twice as much foreign money as was needed to discharge her formidable reparation obligations. The growing realisation that a debt crisis in Germany would have serious repercussions for US citizens and their banks led to another attempt to clear up the reparations issue. By 1929 Germany herself was disenchanted with the operation of the Dawes Plan which had placed vital parts of her economy in the hands of foreigners; moreover, the duration of the period over which reparations should be paid had still not been determined. The time seemed ripe for some debt adjustment.

A new committee of experts was appointed under the chairmanship of an American lawyer, Owen D. Young, who was instructed to keep war debts out of the discussion; the United States still clung to the delusion that war debts were an issue quite separate from reparations. In 1929 the Young Plan emerged, as a device to remove the issue from the political arena. Germany now assumed the responsibility for the transfer of the monies raised for reparations into gold or into foreign currencies acceptable to her creditors, a function previously discharged by the Agent General for Reparations. The management of the reparations account was entrusted to an independent institution created especially for this purpose — the Bank for International Settlements. The Young Plan established new payment schedules which, on average, were less onerous than those imposed under the Dawes Plan. Germany was to pay 1,708 million marks in 1930–1, from which point payments were calculated on a rising scale to 1965–6, when 2,429 million marks would be paid; from then the sums were to be progressively reduced until the debt was discharged in 1988. No sooner had the Young Plan been unveiled, however, than the economic deterioration in Germany and in the rest of the world made it irrelevant.

Even before 1929, overseas lending by the Untied States had reached a peak. In 1928 funds were diverted to the domestic market by the higher interest rates which, as we have seen, the Federal Reserve introduced in an unsuccessful attempt to curb stock market speculation. As a result, in 1929 net United States long-term investment abroad dropped to half the 1928 level. Once the stock market had crashed, and interest rates had fallen, the first half of 1930 saw a marked revival in overseas lending. This flow was not sustained and a decline set in which became especially pronounced in the last half of 1931. Indeed, from 1931 onwards repayment of the principal on foreign loans was considerably greater than new capital issues.

Why did US citizens become increasingly reluctant to lend overseas after the middle of 1930? Potential borrowers were desperate for American capital and were prepared to pay very high rates of interest to obtain it, but without success; by late 1930 the expectations of US investors had undergone a profound change. They had become more interested in the security of their investment and less in the yield. Coffee — on which Brazil and Colombia depended, sugar — the life blood of Cuba, wheat — on which Canada and the Argentine relied for the bulk of their export earnings, all fell dramatically in price, yet these countries had borrowed heavily from the United States. Obviously they, and others in a similar position, could not export enough to repay their debts and were unable to borrow more because American investors recognised the deep financial pit into which their economies had sunk. This anxiety turned to panic once the first defaults on overseas debt were announced and investors tried to repatriate their funds as quickly as possible.

In Europe the problem was Germany, whose economy had moved towards recession in 1928. The overseas investor was apprehensive not only about the economic decline which was readily apparent by 1930, but also about the electoral success of the Nazi party which vowed to halt reparation payments; the prospect of a customs union between Germany and Austria, which angered the French, gave further cause for concern. The economic conditions of Germany continued to worsen and, after the collapse of the Kreditanstalt bank in Austria, financial chaos spread to the world's major borrowers. In response to this crisis the Hoover Moratorium took effect in July 1931; this was an agreement to suspend all reparation and war debt payments (but not private debt payments) for one year. Intra-government debts were thereby suspended but not cancelled, leaving total liabilities unchanged. To make the position of the United States absolutely clear, a joint resolution was passed by Congress in December 1931, when certifying the Hoover Moratorium, which proclaimed that 'it was against the policy of Congress that any of the indebtedness of foreign countries to the United States should be cancelled or reduced'. Unfortunately, by the end of Hoover's 12-month breathing space, the economic situation had worsened, and yet another group of experts met at Lausanne in 1932 to examine the problem. In effect the Lausanne Agreement swept away the bulk of reparations obligations. Germany was asked to deposit government bonds with the Bank of International Settlements, but these bonds were not to be sold for a further three years. More to the point, when Hitler became Chancellor in 1933, Germany refused to recognise reparations.

Immediately after Lausanne, the British and French governments made small token payments of their war debts to the United States, and then ceased payment altogether. Both countries felt that they could not continue discharging their debts, the annual payments of which were not to end for Britain until 1984 and for France until 1987, without receiving reparations. In spite of all the energy expended, Lary has calculated that the average annual receipts from these war debts between 1916 and 1931 amounted to only 0.27 per cent of US national income. Private debt was similarly affected: by 1935, 77 per cent of outstanding Latin American loans were in default; for Chile, Columbia and Peru the figure was 100 per cent. Many European loans were in the same position; for example, in 1931 Germany had adopted exchange control, thus making it impossible for American citizens to withdraw their capital. The political response in the United States was self-righteous anger which found expression in the Johnson Act of 1934, prohibiting both public and private loans to the government of any nation which was in default to the United States. The Johnson Act signalled the end of the American lending which had been vital to the world economy during the 1920s; however, even without this piece of legislation it is probable that the public had become so disenchanted that practically all tempting offers from abroad would have been resisted. Nevertheless, the US was able to demonstrate publicly her belief that all the faults lay with the borrowers and none with the lenders.

For debtor nations the problems emanating from the reduction in American lending were formidable. With a decline in borrowed money and in export earnings, they were forced to use their reserves of gold and foreign currency. However, in 1929 the bulk of the world's gold was held by the United States and France; the debtors, therefore, could not rely upon their meagre reserves for long. As an alternative to long-term capital some tried to attract short-term funds. However, short-term capital — hot money — is highly volatile; it could, and did, leave in response to changing interest rates elsewhere. Moreover, interest rates raised in the frantic search for foreign funds only served to undermine fragile domestic economies, without succeeding in their original aim. Countries in trouble took steps to cut imports and, as a result, exported the depression; they also implemented deflationary policies designed to cheapen their exports further. In addition, they pursued only those economic strategies which they believed would prove attractive to the foreign investor whose capital they still sought.

Primary producing countries were faced with particularly serious problems as the prices of their exports fell very steeply and, indeed, much further than the prices of the manufactured goods which they imported. In other words, the terms of trade moved so sharply against them that even loans which appeared soundly based when undertaken in the 1920s were, by 1930, at risk. Many of these countries had, by the early 1930s, reduced their pre-depression level of imports by

60 per cent in a desperate attempt to balance their payments. Unfortunately for debtor nations, the United States cut her lending and imports at the same time and default was therefore inevitable.

In Europe those nations linked by reparations and war debts also faced intractable problems. By 1933 wholesale prices, measured in terms of gold, had fallen by 35 per cent and the burden of all debts, therefore, had risen substantially. As world trade had collapsed, it was impossible to earn the necessary foreign exchange or gold from exports. The 1931 devaluation of sterling meant that British debts to the US, which were payable in gold dollars, were increased, but her receipts, payable in sterling, were reduced. Germany, the most hard-hit European nation during the depression, was heavily in debt. The rise of the Nazis, the degeneration of the banking system, the sharp decline in her export earnings, and the domestic view that Germany should demonstrate that reparations were too great a burden to be borne by a declining economy − all combined to bring about default.

The refusal of the United States to admit publicly that reparations and war debts were inextricably linked was a great error. When that recognition did come in the form of the Hoover Moratorium it was too late; by 1931 all inter-governmental debts needed reducing, not merely postponing. The United States delivered a number of serious shocks to the international economy after 1928. Initially, because of the stock market boom, capital was diverted from its overseas channels. The tight money policy which the Federal Reserve had instituted to curb speculation spread to other countries, as they too had to raise interest rates, an action which undoubtedly affected their economies. After Wall Street crashed, the flow of capital diminished for, once agricultural and raw material prices had fallen, investors recognised the serious difficulties which were afflicting borrowing nations and which would affect their ability to repay. As the depression bit into the American economy her imports were reduced (by 68 per cent between 1929 and 1933), a situation made worse by the adoption of the Hawley−Smoot tariff, which encouraged the beggar-my-neighbour policies soon to become a common feature of the thirties. The supply of dollars to the rest of the world which resulted both from American overseas lending and from payment for her imports was drastically cut from $7.4 bn in 1929 to $2.4 bn in 1932. Debtors were forced, therefore, to adopt deflationary economic policies which accelerated the decline in income for all nations.

We should not lose sight of the fact that the movement of dollars during the 1920s was important for boosting US exports, and some part of their fall after 1925 can be explained by the evaporation of such capital flows. However, the decrease in exports influenced the US depression to only a limited extent; the fall in gross investment was substantially more important. From 1922 to 1929 inclusive, exports averaged 5.3 per cent of GNP annually; at their trough, in 1932, they accounted for 3.1 per cent (Lipsey, 1963). Foreign trade was not sufficiently important to explain more than a small part of the contraction in GNP between 1929 and 1933. Table 7.3 shows that exports and imports had a much greater

Table 7.3 Per Cent Ratios of Exports and Imports to National Income in 1928 and 1938

	Export ratios		Import ratios	
	1928	1938	1928	1938
US	6.3	4.6	5.0	3.2
UK	20.3	10.4	28.8	17.9
Canada	28.3	22.1	26.2	17.6
Germany	16.6	7.0	19.4	7.6
France	22.9	8.5	23.5	12.8
Belgium	56.1	33.1	57.4	35.3
Italy	12.1	8.0	18.4	8.6
Sweden	20.0	16.6	21.7	18.7

Source: K.W. Deutsch and A. Eckstein, 'National industrialisation and the declining share of the international economic sector 1890–1959', *World Politics*, 13 (1960–1), p. 274.

impact on the economies of every other great industrial nation. US self-sufficiency meant that imports were far smaller as a proportion of national income than in even the Fascist states of Italy and Germany which pursued a vigorous policy of autarky. America was thus protected from the worst effects of a trade contraction; unfortunately this was far from sufficient to prevent a devastating collapse in her economy.

Bibliography

The most succinct introduction to international economic relationships during these years can be found in P. Fearon, though C.P. Kindleberger's more detailed study presents complex arguments with great clarity. US foreign trade is described and analysed in H.B. Lary, and C. Lewis provides a thorough account of capital flows.

Clarke, S.V.O. (1967) *Central Bank Cooperation 1924–31*, Federal Reserve Bank of New York.

Fearon, P. (1979) *The Origins and Nature of the Great Slump 1929–1932*, Macmillan.

Fleisig, H.W. (1976a) 'War debts and the great depression', *American Economic Review*, Papers and Proceedings, LXVI.

Fleisig, H.W. (1976b) *Long-Term Capital Flows and the Great Depression: The Role of the United States, 1927–1933*, Arno Press.

Gordon, R.J. and Wilcox, J.A. (1981) 'Monetarist interpretations of the Great Depression: an evaluation and critique' in Brunner (ed.) *The Great Depression Revisited*, Martinus Nijhoff Publishing.

Jones Jr., J.M. (1982) *Tariff Retaliation: Repercussions of the Hawley–Smoot Bill* Garland Publishing. First published in 1934.

Kindleberger, CP. (1973) *The World in Depression 1929–1939*, University of California Press.

Lary, H.B. (1943) *The United States in the World Economy*, US Dept of Commerce, Washington DC.

Lewis, C. (1938) *America's Stake in International Investment*, Brookings Institution, Washington DC.

Lipsey, R.E. (1963) *Price and Quantitative Trends in the Foreign Trade of the United States*, NBER, Princeton.

Meltzer, A.H. (1981) 'Comments on "Monetarist interpretations of the depression"' in Brunner (ed.) *The Great Depression Revisited*.

Mintz, I. (1951) *Deterioration in the Quality of Foreign Bonds Issued in the United States*, NBER, New York.

Saint-Etienne, C. (1984) *The Great Depression 1929–1939: Lessons for the 1980s*, Hoover Institute Press.

United Nations (1949) *International Capital Movement during the Inter-War Period*, New York.

Wanniski, J. (1978) *The Way the World Works*, Basic Books.

8

People in Depression

The People

The most searing legacy of the depression was unemployment, which mounted steadily from the relatively low levels experienced between 1922 and 1929. The percentage of the civilian labour force without work rose from 3.2 in 1929 to 8.7 in 1930, and reached a peak of 24.9 in 1933. The estimates for unemployment amongst non-farm employees, which include the self-employed and unpaid family workers, are even higher (Table 8.1). These are horrifying figures: millions of American families were left without a bread-winner and faced the very real possibility of destitution. In Britain the decision to cut dole payments to the unemployed split the Labour Party in 1931; in the United States there was no such welfare system to provide a safety net for those out of work. Nor do the unemployment figures tell the whole story: by 1931 there was extensive part-time working and those lucky enough to retain employment for a three- or four-day week are classified as employed.

Unemployment never smites the working population with equal severity. We have already established that certain occupational groups were relatively hard hit: for example, those employed by the railroads or by durable goods manufacturers, while others who were lucky enough to work for insurance companies or the federal government fared far better. In deciding whom to fire companies rid themselves of their youngest and their oldest workers; since hiring fell to an all-time low, youngsters coming onto the labour force faced a bleak prospect. Skilled workers had the advantage of flexibility: at least they could apply for unskilled jobs, and even the most menial occupations attracted applicants who in normal times would have been regarded as over-qualified. Minority groups were disproportionately affected; blacks, as the most recent entrants to manufacturing industry, were ejected on the 'last hired, first fired' principle, while jobs such as domestic service and waiting-on-table, which previously had been monopolised by blacks, now attracted white competition. As whites did the hiring it is not surprising that black male and female unemployment was relatively much higher than that of whites.

Table 8.1 Unemployment, 1929–33 (000s)

		Percentage of	
Year	Total	Civilian labour force	Non-farm employees
1929	1,550	3.2	5.3
1930	4,340	8.9	14.2
1931	8,020	16.3	25.2
1932	12,060	24.1	36.3
1933	12,830	25.2	37.6

Source: *Historical Statistics of US, Colonial Times to 1970*, 2 vols (Washington DC, 1975) Series D8–10.

Unemployment was not a totally new experience for Americans, especially for those employed in industry. Even the most sophisticated manufacturing industries suffered from seasonal unemployment, as did construction. Moreover, the sharp increase in unemployment in 1921, to 11.7 per cent of the civilian labour force, illustrated that the economy was not immune from cyclical fluctuations. The recovery from the trough of 1921 was rapid, however, and by 1923 unemployment had declined to 2.4 per cent. In contrast, after 1929 there was no light at the end of the tunnel: unemployment seemed a permanent feature of life. Survival for the workless was especially difficult during the harsh winter months when additional expenditure on fuel, clothing and even food was unavoidable. Americans became discontented with an economic system which forced Iowa farmers to burn surplus corn for winter fuel at a time when mining communities throughout the land were in a desperate plight, enduring hunger as their coal could not be sold.

Hoover was convinced that the prompt wage reductions which had accompanied the 1920–1 depression had magnified its effect. Shortly after the Wall Street Crash, the President summoned a group of business and industrial leaders to Washington and implored them to avoid discharging workers and, above all, to maintain wage levels. Initially employers were willing to comply, but as economic conditions continued to worsen they began searching desperately for ways to cut costs. Inevitably, wages and salaries were progressively reduced from the beginning of 1931. An investigation undertaken by the National Industrial Conference Board in mid-1932 found that of the companies surveyed, 27 per cent had experienced a reduction in employment since 1929; 80 per cent of them, however, had reduced salaries and 75 per cent had imposed wage cuts. The extent of the decline in wages and salary scales differed from industry to industry: it was most marked in manufacturing, least in insurance. On average, salaries contracted by around 15 per cent and wages by about 11 per cent, and, as a rule, the greatest reductions were experienced by those who worked for smaller companies. Another investigation, by M. Ada Beney, shows that in 25 selected manufacturing industries the low point in average hourly earnings was reached in June 1933, by which time they had fallen nearly 24 per cent from their 1929 level. Average weekly money earnings, of course, were even more depressed because, in addition to the decline in wage rates, there was also a reduction in the number of hours worked during each week as firms tried to spread the work available amongst their employees. As a result, in February 1933 the average weekly earnings of the 25 selected manufacturing industries had fallen 43 per cent below 1929 levels. The many series on earnings are difficult, at first glance, to reconcile. Differences in the base period chosen, the number of industries surveyed, and the manner in which averages are calculated can create confusion. The overall conclusion is that earnings declined most steeply in those industries in which unemployment was highest.

An analysis of money earnings does not tell us the whole story, since this depression saw marked price falls which had a significant effect on real earnings. Table 8.2 shows that urban dwellers gained significantly from a fall in the price of essential goods. As lower income groups spend a high proportion of their income on food, rent, clothing and fuel, they must have especially benefited from price falls.

Table 8.2 Index of Cost of Goods Purchased by Wage Earners and Lower Salaried Workers in 33 Large Cities (1929 = 100)

Year	All items	Food	Clothing	Rent	Fuel, electricity, ice	Household furnishings	Miscellaneous
1928	100	98	102	103	100	100	99
1929	100	100	100	100	100	100	100
1930	97	95	98	96	98	96	100
1931	89	78	90	92	96	87	99
1932	80	65	79	83	91	75	97
1933	75	63	77	72	88	74	93
1934	78	71	83	67	89	82	93
1935	80	75	84	67	89	84	93

Source: Calculated from *Statistical Abstract of the US, 1940*, Table 357.

Indeed, those who were fortunate enough to retain their jobs, to suffer no loss in hours worked and to maintain their wages rates, would have noticed a considerable increase in their real income. Federal employees living in Washington DC are an example of a particularly favoured group. Their relative insulation from the worst effects of the depression is shown by a contemporary survey of their cost of living. Compared with a base period, which was the first six months of 1928 = 100, the cost of living for all federal employees had declined by March

1933 to 83. Those most favoured by price movements were the families of employees with salaries of less than $2,500, whose index had declined to 79; those least favoured were single individuals who lived and ate in hotels, whose index declined to 88. The people covered by these surveys were a small, very select group, with secure employment, and are used merely as an illustration to show that some can benefit from deflation.

For the bulk of the nation the picture was far from comforting. Table 8.3 shows that for production workers in manufacturing, average hourly earnings were maintained until 1931 but that hours worked per week declined steadily once the depression began. The combination of these two variables reduced average weekly earnings to very low levels in 1932 and 1933. The final column in Table 8.3 indicates that in spite of the effect of falling prices, real weekly wages did decline below their 1929 level, thus demonstrating that even those in employment had to reduce their expenditure. These figures, however, need to be interpreted with caution because they refer only to people in work and there was a substantial minority with no weekly earnings at all. In order to come to a clear conclusion about household purchasing power we would need to know for how many weeks during the year, on average, a worker might expect to find employment. Unfortunately, such detail is not available but it is reasonable to assume that, if any adjustment is made for unemployment, average annual real earnings declined substantially between 1929 and 1933.

Many contemporaries had expected that the fall in prices which inevitably accompanied inter-war depressions would have prevented the decline from becoming too steep and, indeed, would eventually have assisted recovery. Their reasoning was that the fall in retail prices would bring about a rise in real income, and that

Table 8.3 Earnings of Production Workers in Manufacturing, 1928–35

Year	Average hourly earnings	Average weekly hours	Average weekly earnings	Consumer price index (1929=100)	Real weekly earnings (1929 prices)
	1	2	3	4	5
1928	$0.56	44.4	$24.70	100.0	$24.70
1929	0.56	44.2	24.76	100.0	24.76
1930	0.55	42.1	23.00	97.5	23.60
1931	0.51	40.5	20.64	88.9	23.22
1932	0.44	38.3	16.89	79.2	21.32
1933	0.44	38.1	16.65	75.6	22.02
1934	0.53	34.6	18.20	78.2	23.27
1935	0.54	36.6	19.91	80.1	24.86

Source: Cols 1–3: *Historical Statistics of US, Colonial Times to 1970*, 2 vols (Washington DC, 1975) Series 802–04; Col. 4: calculated from *Historical Statistics*, Series E135.

once this was recognised by consumers they would begin to spend on the goods which had been reduced to bargain levels; such spending would help to generate a recovery. This did not happen, in part because real incomes actually declined; consumers may also have been confused by the complexitites of the price falls which we, for reasons of convenience, have expressed as an average. More importantly, however, there is a difference between a sudden once-and-for-all drop in prices and a gradually falling price level. The former persuades the consumer to go out and spend, while the latter brings about an unwillingness to buy, as no purchaser is very sure for how long the price fall will continue. As everyone wants to buy at the lowest price, the temptation is to hold off until the drop in prices has run its course. Falling prices, therefore, far from inducing a revival in the economy, caused a paralysis on the part of consumers and investors. In addition, deflation played havoc with business expectations and helped to reduce investment to the very low levels of 1932 and 1933; business suffered further as the fall in prices brought about a sharp increase in its level of real debt.

In the fight against mounting unemployment, few American workers could rely upon a trade union for protection from dismissal as the numbers organised in 1930 represented only 11.6 per cent of the non-agricultural workforce. Precisely how much protection a more widespread union membership could have given is unclear, but probably little. Some occupations which were relatively highly unionised, for example, construction, the railroads, metals and machinery, fared particularly badly in the depression, and in Europe, unions more powerful than those in the New World could not noticeably prevent job losses. American labour did, however, see a pro-union act signed by a reluctant President Hoover in 1932. This was the Norris—La Guardia Act which not only helped to pave the way for the extinction of the yellow dog contract but also made more difficult the use of legal injunctions against strikers, which had been so popular with employers during the 1920s. Although the tide of public and political sympathy was moving towards organised labour by 1932, during the worst years of the depression the ameliorative effect of the unions was slight.

How did people cope with the ravages of the depression? We have seen that the traditional net migratory flow from rural to urban areas was reversed, so that by 1932 there was actually a net migration from the town to the countryside (Chapter 5). In many cases these migrants were the sons and daughters of farmers who had never left the region; they returned to squat in order to escape from abandoned mines, closed lumber mills or the unemployment and bread lines in the city. Others migrated because of drought, and the movement out of the cotton belt, noticeable for decades, continued. Many of the migrants, or transients as they were commonly known, had a destination firmly in their minds; others wandered aimlessly as hobos, illegally riding trains, walking or hitch-hiking. Movement generally, as might be expected, was in a westerly direction with California as the desired destination for many. Those who remained searched anxiously for jobs within commuting distance of their homes, for most an unsuccessful and dispiriting task. Marriages were postponed, the married delayed parenthood; apart from economising on every item of expenditure there was little that the unemployed could do to lessen their plight. Once wages income ceased, savings were used up, insurance policies were cashed, possessions were pawned, and rent and mortgages went unpaid. Eviction for many families was inescapable — they moved in with friends or relatives or to cheaper accommodation. Fortunately, some landlords did not press for payment — perhaps the forest of 'for sale' signs, which indicated a very depressed property market, convinced them that allowing rents to accumulate was a sounder policy. In the autumn of 1931 over 100,000 American residents, 40 per cent of whom were native born, applied for 6,000 skilled jobs available in the Soviet Union. By that time the plight of the unemployed, with winter approaching, was desperate. To whom could they turn for help?

In the autumn of 1930 Herbert Hoover created the President's Emergency Committee for Employment (PECE) under the chairmanship of Colonel Arthur Woods. It is difficult to find anything positive to write about PECE; its role was one of encouraging state and local employment committees to raise funds so that they could look after their own jobless in the traditional American way. The committee made no attempt to gather much needed information on the extent of unemployment, nor had it any plans — even though its optimistic title emphasised employment — for job creation. In August 1931 PECE was replaced by a new body, the President's Organisation for Unemployment Relief (POUR) with Walter S. Gifford, president of the American Telephone and Telegraph Company, as its chairman. Although the name changed, the policies, or rather the lack of them, remained the same. Gifford, too, was an ardent believer in local responsibility; the state, city and county employment committees, run by people who understood the problems in their communities, could and should take care of their needy. The mission of POUR was to encourage grass roots charity; like its predecessor, it did not gather detailed information on the extent of the debilitating disease of unemployment which had seriously affected the nation. One could be forgiven for concluding that both PECE and POUR were an exercise in public relations rather than positive help for the jobless.

Both organisations reflected President Hoover's faith in voluntarism: the belief that, as in the past, people should take care of their own poor, using tax revenue and sums collected by private charities, but without help from the federal government. Intervention by Washington would serve only to sap initiative and, in the long run, would be more damaging than the crisis it was trying to solve. Of course, such views fitted neatly with Hoover's frequent public pronouncements that the economy was fundamentally sound, that recovery was already taking place, that no one had starved, that the people on breadlines were eating well and that the sidewalk apple seller, one of the most vivid symbols of the depression, merely demonstrated that selling apples was a profitable occupation. Hoover was not unconcerned or heartless: his record as a relief administrator during World War I had earned him international respect and admiration. Nor was he idle: the Hoover presidency was one of great activity. He did, however, find it difficult to convey his concern to the people at large and, because he lacked many of the skilful tricks which the career politician employed to elicit public support and sympathy, he became progressively identified with the depression. The poor sleeping on park benches covered themselves with newspapers dubbed 'Hoover blankets'; jack rabbits became 'Hoover hogs'; an empty pocket flapping in the breeze a 'Hoover flag' and the depressed, occupying shanty towns made out of packing cases and oil drums, lived in 'Hoovervilles'.

What Hoover wished to avoid was payment of dole: cash relief to the able-bodied unemployed. Dole was held to be a certain destroyer of character and self-respect. Indeed, during the 1920s American newspaper reports of Britain's system of unemployment benefit stressed its supposed ill effects on the working classes and the alarming lack of initiative which was the inevitable outcome of state handouts. As a result of this widespread feeling, local employment committees placed great stress upon work relief; certain tasks, often as basic as chopping wood, had to be performed before relief money was handed over. Hoover's aim was to keep the federal government out of relief and to urge state and local bodies to avoid dole payment; only the deserving poor, such as the aged, the infirm or mothers with dependent children should qualify for direct relief.

By the middle of 1932, however, locally funded relief and private charities were desperately short of funds. Distress had reached such levels that the federal government could no longer stand aloof from the problem. In July, Hoover signed the Emergency Relief and Construction Act which made available to the states, through the RFC, $300mn 'to be used in furnishing relief to needy and distressed people and in relieving the hardship resulting from unemployment'. These funds were allocated as loans, at 3 per cent interest, not as grants, though in 1934 payment was waived. It was made clear to the recipients that federal money was not to be regarded as a substitute for local funds but as a supplement to them. The money was forthcoming only when governors had certified that the tax revenue of the state and the sums raised by private charitable organisations were inadequate to meet relief needs. Moreover, in order to ensure that no state became dependent upon the federal government, the RFC disbursed only small sums to help with relief over a one- to three-month period. A further curb on the amount which could be obtained was the rule that no state could receive more than $45mn, which was 15 per cent of the total available. The money was gratefully received, but the small amounts distributed meant that the most severely affected states still faced serious relief financing problems. Residents in states run by inefficient political organisations were penalised, as applications for funds were either poorly presented or not presented at all. A further $332mn was available, also in the form of loans, for financing job-creating public works schemes.

Even though the help was extended in the form of loans, not grants, and the states themselves had to apply for and administer it, Romasco describes the Relief and Construction Acts, together with the creation of the RFC, as a marked departure from Hoover's philosophy of government. The President had been pushed further than he would have liked to go; perhaps this is one reason why, under his administration, federal agencies were so slow in spending on relief. It was Hoover's rigidity, his failure to see that voluntarism could not prevent the destitution which sprang from mass unemployment, and his inability to realise that this unique crisis required a change of direction, that lost Hoover the support of the electorate.

Hoover was not short of advice. As in any economic crisis, the variety of solutions proposed to the White House ranged from the absurd to the impossible. Even the middle ground, however, was a territory of confusion as economists who argued for extreme economy and no governmental intervention confronted those who proposed relatively expensive public works schemes (Barber, 1985). Gradually the support for orthodoxy waned and by late 1931 prominent voices were raised in favour of a planned economy. The Swope Plan, brainchild of Gerard Swope, president of General Electric, proposed the creation of trade associations in each industry. Membership would be compulsory; the aim was to co-ordinate production and consumption. The Chamber of Commerce had also lost confidence in the market place and called for a release from the uncertainty of competition. Hoover, as might be expected, was opposed to such initiatives, despite the evidence that many members of his natural constituency, which would include the business community, were beginning to appreciate the benefits of market sharing.

Distanced from the event by over half a century, it is difficult for us to comprehend the suffering endured by a sizeable segment of the American population during the Great Depression. It is worth recording at this juncture the desperation of the unemployed and their families, if for no other reason than that they, as voters, helped remove an incumbent President and thus change the direction of economic and social policy. It was these unfortunate people who had to rely upon their own dwindling resources and, when these were exhausted, upon public relief. Ordinary Americans who, before 1929, had been confident as to their future were turned into the unthinkable — paupers. Senators and Congressmen received letters from their constituents which spelled out with painful clarity the numb fear of petitioners who needed help; even the most hardened Capitol Hill legislator must, one hopes, have been moved.

The first task for the laid-off worker was to try to find another job. Data on accession rates — that is hiring — show that even in these hard times manufacturing firms were taking on workers, between 1930 and 1932, at similar rates to those of 1924, 1927 and 1928. This was, unfortunately, a solution for only a few because the rate at which workers were laid off after 1929 was considerably higher than it had been during the 1920s. A fortunate minority were able to find employment in the service sector; between 1929 and 1933 there was a noticeable increase in the number of very small retail stores in spite of the fact that the total number of retail outlets, of all sizes, decreased slightly. The number of eating places increased during the same period, though the value of sales and total employment declined; the same was true of drugstores. There was a striking growth in the number of second-hand stores and a proportionate rise in the numbers employed in them. The *Census of Business* (1933) records that 25 per cent of the service establishments and 22 per cent of the places of amusement which were operational in 1933 had come into existence after 1929. Examples given included: beauty parlours, hand (but not machine) laundries, shoe-shine parlours, radio repair shops, and upholstery and furniture repairers. Here we have examples of people moving into enterprises which required very little starting capital — often a home could be converted into a business while the family would provide cheap labour.

For the unemployed deprivation was real. Many schools felt compelled to provide breakfast for pupils who were showing signs of malnutrition; this service was extended to the weekend and even into vacations. Breadlines, queues of hungry people waiting for a hot meal, usually provided by church or by private charity, became commonplace. At a number of well-publicised Senate committee hearings witnesses told of children who were housebound because they had no shoes or clothing, of families existing on starvation diets, of the poor scavenging on refuse tips, of widespread poverty. The irony of the situation was not lost on the public; agriculture had a surplus of food so cheap that in some cases farmers did not think it worth harvesting, yet people were hungry. There were some isolated outbursts: farm protest, looting of foodshops, rent riots and hunger marches in the cities which often led to bloody encounters with the police. Perhaps the most famous protest of these years was made by a group of World War I veterans, some 10,000 in number, who descended upon Washington DC to demand immediate payment of a bonus given to them but not due to mature until 1945. Living in a Hooverville on Anacostia flats just outside the city, the Bonus Army waited patiently until they heard that Senate had voted down the bill which would have given them payment. Instead of dispersing, as Hoover had hoped, many of them stayed on and eventually the US Army was used, in a particularly shameful episode, to drive them from their primitive dwellings. Observers reported, however, that for the most part the unemployed seemed to display a sense of helplessness; they became withdrawn and, after repeated rejections, often ceased to look for work. Many blamed themselves for their misfortunes.

The problem of unemployment was not caused by men and women refusing to take jobs at the reduced wages which confronted them; it was the demand for labour which was deficient, not its supply. With a total loss of income, millions of Americans were eventually forced to ask for relief. The poor law which existed in 1930 bore a strong resemblance to the English Elizabethan system brought to the US by the colonists. It was a structure framed to deal with an expanding agricultural population whose experience of unemployment was expected to be brief. Relief was administered and financed by the locality: that is, the county, city, town or township. Before 1929 the aggregate sums paid for relief were rising; this was due to the fact that the population was ageing and, in addition, increasing provision was made for special groups such as the blind, veterans and mothers with dependent children, the deserving poor. The essence of the system was that each locality took care of its own destitute, and in times of emergency private charities stepped in to help out. Indeed, as soon as the depression began to bite, private charities sprang to the aid of the hard-pressed communities. The relief available was not generous and was only given to those with the appropriate residence requirements, who could prove a real need, sometimes after an insensitive and humiliating investigation into their financial circumstances. After the winter of 1930−1 it was clear that the depression was beyond the resouces of many private charities who were fast running out of money and had little prospect of raising more from private citizens or institutions whose income had fallen. Indeed, some private charities had gone into debt by borrowing against the following years' contributions. It was necessary, therefore, for the most hard-pressed communities to appeal to their state legislature for help.

In September 1931, New York, with the blessing of its Governor, Franklin Roosevelt, passed the State Unemployment Relief Act (known also as the Wicks Act) which distributed funds according to need. This pioneering move was soon followed by New Jersey, Rhode Island and several others; the sale of bonds, the imposition of new taxes or the diversion of existing tax revenue towards relief were the chief sources of funds. Intervention was vital to erase the threat of starvation but there were problems: in Pennsylvania, for example, legislation for relief was attacked on the grounds that it transgressed the state constitution and its implementation was delayed. Most counties or municipalities faced serious difficulties in raising money for relief since their tax base, heavily dependent upon property taxes, had been eroded; bankrupt businesses and out-of-work citizens did not pay taxes and the remainder were unwilling to see their fiscal burden increased. Some states were forbidden by their constitutions to go into deficit; borrowing was, of course, difficult, especially for those in greatest need, since they were also the greatest risk. The failure of local governments, private charities and states in the field of relief played a significant role in people's expectations of federal aid.

In an atmosphere of increasing anxiety, social workers, who were becoming a very powerful professional group, stressed the need for federal aid: without it, the unemployed could not be guaranteed even the minimum necessary for existence. There was, however, no clear precedent for intervention from Washington to aid the unemployed, though in the past help had been given to people who were the victims of natural disasters. In the spring of 1932 the federal government took its first tentative steps towards relief by giving surplus wheat to the Red Cross for distribution; a few months later more surplus wheat and raw cotton, by-products of the failed price stabilisation programme, were also distributed. Hoover was anxious not to involve the government directly in relief, firstly on philosophical grounds but also because he was trying to balance the budget and did not want additional government expenditure. However, the cost of federal relief was no longer seen as an obstacle by a growing number of people who felt that the key issue was the relief of suffering, not the balancing of books. The big breakthrough came with the Emergency Relief and Construction Act which gave a breathing space to big cities such as Detroit, Chicago, Philadelphia, and New York, where the relief problems were particularly acute. By 1932, if not before, it was clear that America's system of relief was inappropriate for a modern urban nation with an economy that could not be isolated from the vagaries of the trade cycle.

In 1928, Herbert Hoover, in a speech accepting his nomination for the Presidency, said:

We in America today are nearer to the final triumph over poverty than ever before in the history of the land. The poor-house is vanishing from among us. We have not reached that goal but . . . we shall soon, with the help of God, be in sight of the day when poverty will be banished from the nation.

These words, and his campaign slogan 'Two chickens in every pot and a car in every garage' could be accepted at the time as being part of the normal extravagance of political speechmaking. In 1932 the President and the people were crushed by events. Bankers, popular in 1929, were now derided; stock market speculators, admired in that year, were now despised; and the President who promised so much was swept aside by the political tide that brought Franklin Roosevelt to the White House.

Bibliography

The suffering of so many people during the early stages of the Great Depression, and the response of institutions to it, have attracted the attention of many authors. Some of the best accounts of life in those troubled times can be found in the works of C. Bird, D. Shannon, B. Sternsher, and S. Terkel. The disintegration of the established system of relief and the eventual intervention of the federal government is presented in J.C. Brown and in the more recent publication of J.T. Patterson.

Abbott, E. and Kiesling, K. (1935) 'Evictions during the Chicago rent moratorium established by the relief agencies, 1931–33', Social Science Review, Vol. IX.
Barber, W.J. (1985) From New Era to New Deal: Herbert Hoover, the Economists and American Economic Policy, 1921–1933, Cambridge University Press.
Beney, M. Ada (1936) Wages, Homes and Employment in the United States 1914–36, NICB, New York.
Bernstein, I. (1960) The Lean Years: A History of the American Worker 1920–33, Houghton Mifflin.
Bird, C. (1966) The Invisible Scar (New York, 1966) D. McKay.
Brookings Institution (1938) The Recovery Problem in the United States, Washington DC.
Brown, J.C. (1940) Public Relief 1929–1939, H. Holt & Co.
Brown, M. and Webb, J.N. (1941) Seven Stranded Coal Towns, W.P.A. Research Monograph XXIII, Washington DC.
Bruno, F.J. (1932) 'The treatment of the dependent unemployed in St Louis in the winter of 1931–2', South Western Social Science Quarterly, 13.
Chafe, W.H. (1969) 'Flint and the great depression', Michigan History Magazine, 53.
Daniels, R. (1971) The Bonus March: An Episode of the Great Depression, Greenwood Press.
Douglas, P.H. and Director, A. (1976) The Problem of Unemployment, Ayer Publishing. First published in 1931.

Ellis, E.R. (1970) *A Nation in Torment: The Great American Depression 1929–39*, Coward-McCann.

Freeman, H.H. (1932) 'How American cities are retrenching in time for depression', *National Municipal Review*, XXI, April.

Freeman, H.H. (1932) 'No one has starved', *Fortune*, VI, No. 3, September.

Garraty, J.A. (1978) *Unemployment in History*, Harper and Row.

Geddes, A. (1937) *Trends in Relief Expenditure, 1910–1935*, W.P.A. Research Monograph X, Washington DC.

Heleniak, R. (1969) 'Local reaction to the great depression in New Orleans, 1929–1933', *Louisiana History*, 10.

Hevener, J.W. (1978) *Which Side Are You On? The Harlem County Coal Miners, 1931–39*, University of Illinois Press.

Hoover, H. (1952) *Memoirs: The Great Depression, 1929–41*, Macmillan.

Hopkins, H.C. (1936) *Spending to Save: The Complete Story of Relief*, W.W. Norton.

McElvaine, R.S. (ed.) (1983) *Down and Out in the Great Depression: Letters from the Forgotten Man*, University of North Carolina Press.

Mitchell, B. (1947) *Depression Decade: From New Era through New Deal 1929–41*, Rinehart.

National Industrial Conference Board (1932) *Salary and Wage Policy in the Depression*, New York.

Norton, W.J. (1933) 'The relief crisis in Detroit', *Social Service Review*, VII, March.

Patterson, J.T. (1981) *America's Struggle Against Poverty 1900–1980*, Harvard University Press.

Piven, F.F. and Cloward, R.A. (1977) *Poor People's Movements: Why They Succeed, How They Fail*, Pantheon Books.

Ridley, C.E. and Nolting, O.F. (eds) (1935) *What the Depression has Done to Cities*, International City Managers Association, Chicago.

Romasco, A.U. (1975) *The Poverty of Abundance: Hoover, the Nation, the Depression*, Oxford University Press.

Rosen, E.A. (1977) *Hoover, Roosevelt and the Brains Trust: From Depression to New Deal*, Columbia University Press.

Schwartz, J.A. (1970) *The Interregnum of Despair: Hoover, Congress and the Depression*, University of Illinois Press.

Shannon, D. (ed.) (1960) *The Great Depression*, Englewood Cliffs.

Shover, J.L. (1965) 'Cornbelt rebellion', *The Farmers' Holiday Association*, University of Illinois Press.

Sternsher, B. (ed.) (1970) *Hitting Home: The Great Depression in Town and County*, Quadrangle Books.

Terkel, S. (1970) *Hard Times: An Oral History of the Great Depression*, Avon.

Walker, W. (1931) 'Distress in a southern Illinois county', *The Social Service Review*, 5, December.

Williams, F.M. *et al.* (1934) 'Changes in the cost of living of federal employees in the District of Columbia from 1928–1933', *Monthly Labour Review*, 39, July.

Wilson, J.H. (1975) *Herbert Hoover: Forgotten Progressive*, Little, Brown.

9

Is There an Explanation for 1929−33?

It is far easier to describe the crisis which devastated the American economy between 1929 and 1933 than to explain why it occurred. In part the problems are those normal to historical studies: controlled experiments cannot be performed and, moreover, the available data are often imperfect, with the result that majority verdicts rather than unanimity prevail. A further complication is that economic theorists differ fundamentally in their interpretation of major events.

The schools of thought which dominate the debate on the Great Depression can, very loosely, be grouped into two camps: Keynesians and monetarists. Keynesian analysis puts forward the view that unemployment is determined by the level of national income which, in turn, depends upon the aggregate demand for goods and services in the economy. Investment is the most volatile component of aggregate demand, and full employment is not possible if the volume of investment is too low. Keynes believed that the private sector of the economy had no self-correcting mechanism to guide it towards full employment; when idle resources existed, therefore, a counter-cyclical policy in the form of tax cuts or increased government spending was required to achieve recovery. In this model money plays a relatively passive role and is viewed as being incapable of regenerating the economy during a severe depression such as occurred during the 1930s.

Monetarists, on the other hand, believe that disturbances in the monetary sector are a primary cause of instability. The contraction in income, output and employment between 1929 and 1933, therefore, was influenced totally, or mainly, by changes in the money supply. According to this theory, monetary increase or decrease determines whether or not income, and also employment, rises or falls. Unlike the Keynesians, monetarists believe that the private economy has a tendency towards full employment and that a principal cause of instability is government intervention. What they seek to demonstrate is that government policy was instrumental in causing the depression, a fact which considerably weakens the case advanced for state intervention in economic matters.

This is necessarily a crude outline of two very sophisticated theories. To some

149

degree they are capable of reconciliation for, as R.J. Gordon (1981) shows, many economists happily combine elements of Keynesian and monetary theory. Those who keep fairly rigidly to these opposite camps, however, have very different ways of viewing the same problem. This division is illustrated by Temin (1981), a leading non-monetarist, who remarks of the monetarist Schwartz:

> Schwartz and I do not seem to have any common ground on which to discuss our historical stories. How can we talk about the historical facts when we perceive them so differently? How can we test hypotheses unless we agree on the mechanisms by which monetary forces affect aggreagte demand? ... [as] Schwartz and I are not terribly unusual supporters of our respective macro economic viewpoints, can the issue of the causes of the Great Depression be debated fruitfully at all? (Temin, 1981, p. 122)

To the reader who might be filled with despair one can offer the comforting thought that since so many eminent experts disagree, the scope for independent judgement, if logically pursued, is considerable.

In order to make an analysis of 1929−33 easier, we can divide it into two. As we have seen, the depression gradually changed its character, becoming even more intense as it gathered momentum; a distinction can be made, therefore, between the period from the initial contraction in 1929 until the devaluation of sterling in September 1931, and the more acute crisis from that date until the inauguration of Roosevelt in March 1933. In addition, the international ramifications of this economic catastrophe must be examined.

The myriad of theories which had been advanced during the 1930s to explain the depression was sharply reduced once Keynesian economics was established as the prevailing orthodoxy during World War II. Keynesians concentrated upon the sharp decline in investment which followed the collapse of the 1928−9 boom, and which was especially noticeable in the construction and consumer durable sectors, particularly in housebuilding and automobiles. The crucial role which the construction and automobile industries played in the growing economy of the 1920s has already been stressed (Chapter 3). During the recessions of 1924 and 1927, for example, the economy was kept buoyant by substantial construction activity and by the willingness of consumers to buy durable goods. As a result, these relatively minor contractions did not develop into major depressions. The boom of 1928−9 was the outcome of very high levels of expenditure on consumer durables and, although house building had fallen from the peak which it had reached in 1926, total construction was, by historical standards, very high. Both these sectors declined after the middle of 1929 and R.A. Gordon (1961; 1974), Hansen (1941) and Wilson (1942) advanced the thesis that there was nothing to prop up the economy once this occurred, unlike previous downturns; recession, therefore, soon turned to depression. As the economy collapsed, investors became increasingly pessimistic and their expectations of future profit were rapidly revised downwards. Deflation coupled with uncertainty was a powerful force, persuading people to convert their investments into cash, which resulted in a strain on all financial institutions, especially banks, and set in motion a downward spiral

of contraction. Why did this collapse in investment occur? It is theoretically possible, of course, that a single cause might be responsible but, in fact, a multi-
causal explanation is more likely.

The construction industry during the late 1920s faced a twofold problem: a
growing surplus of accommodation caused by overbuilding in the mid-1920s, and
a reduction in the rate of family formation. As a result the demand for housing
was already in decline (Chapter 5). It is easy to see why housing was so seriously
affected once the depression took hold. House purchase necessitates a high level
of debt and requires the confidence of both lender and borrower that repayment
will be possible. Moreover, as unemployment mounted, falling rents and surplus
accommodation were apparent; both were a powerful deterrent to new building.
There are few who would doubt the importance of the decline in construction
in explaining the severity of the depression or, indeed, the sluggish recovery after
1933, though why the industry should have led the economy into recession in
mid-1929 is not clear. It is most likely that building, an industry already victim
to retarding forces, responded fairly rapidly to falling income. In other words,
it was a follower not a leader during the early stages of the depression.

As for consumer durables, the most important of which was the automobile,
the very high rate of expansion in 1928 and early 1929 could not be sustained.
The market for automobiles was approaching a state of saturation and at some
point sales of new vehicles would become relatively difficult. Moreover, the
capacity of the industry was too great for even the peak output of 1929. A further
difficulty facing the consumer durable sector was that consumption was depressed by an increasingly unfavourable distribution of income. As the benefits of
1920s productivity gains went disproportionately to the small number of the rich,
the propensity to save was raised, and expenditure on consumer durables, and
other goods, was checked. This thesis has been given extra force by C.F. Holt
whose calculations on the distribution of income are shown in Table 9.1. If Holt's
findings are correct, they show that the bulk of the income generated during the
1920s went to a very small proportion of the total population. The richest 1 per
cent saw their real per capita income grow by 63 per cent between 1923 and 1929,
while the vast majority, the lower 93 per cent, experienced a contraction of 4
per cent over the same period. During the expansion which occurred between
1927 and 1929, the richest 1 per cent experienced a growth of 8 per cent in their
real per capita income while the rise for the lower 93 per cent was a more modest
2 per cent. Although Holt's findings have been challenged by Smiley (1983),
it is clear that the 1920s did witness a growing maldistribution of income in favour
of the wealthy.

Interesting and important as they are, Holt's estimates do not tell us why the
economy turned down in 1929 in particular. We need to look more closely to
see if the catalyst for the very severe decline in industrial production in the second
half of that year can be identified. Did the rise and fall of the stock market, for
example, play a major role? Wall Street crashed some months after the economy
had reached its 1929 peak and once share values tumbled, their owners suffered

Table 9.1 Disposable Income Per Capita, 1925–9 (figures in constant 1929 $)

	1925	1926	1927	1928	1929	1923–9 % change
Entire non-farm population	761	769	775	807	825	9
Top 1%	12,719	12,606	13,563	15,666	15,721	63
2–7%	2,498	2,490	2,522	2,674	2,700	23
Lower 93%	521	531	525	527	544	−4
Entire farm population	280	270	278	280	295	21

Source: C.F. Holt, 'Who benefitted from the prosperity of the twenties'?, *Explorations in Economic History*, 14 (1977).

a reduction in wealth which restricted their spending power. Furthermore, just prior to the crash, consumers had built up their indebtedness at a time of economic confidence and rising expectations but, once their asset holdings became less valuable, spending had to be restricted (Mishkin, 1978). This holds true for the entire period 1929–33 and since the really pronounced fall in share prices came after 1930, perhaps this linkage of the stock market to depression is more important as an explanation of the depression's longevity rather than its start. What effect the declining stock market had upon the public's faith in financial institutions as a whole is impossible to calculate. It is, however, reasonable to assume that the stock market did not sap confidence, to any great degree, until late 1930.

Field (1984) suggests that Wall Street played a significant role in the 1929 downturn because the high interest rates which were introduced by the Federal Reserve to curb speculation had an adverse effect upon the economy. These high rates were especially harmful to construction and to automobiles which, of course, required consumers to go into debt. Kindleberger (1984) believes the stock market influenced the economy by putting pressure on credit; banks, for example, cut down on their loans because they feared a collapse in the market and wanted extra liquidity to enable them to cope with it. All these are valid points; the role of debt is of particular importance throughout the period 1929 to 1933. When the depression began, the level of debt was relatively high for both businesses and consumers and it increased dramatically in real terms as prices fell.

Kindleberger argues that both the Keynesian and monetarist approaches are too insular in that they ignore international events. He places special emphasis on the sharp fall in wholesale prices which occurred throughout the world in late 1929, a phenomenon especially marked in commodities imported into the US. The cause, according to Kindleberger, was the shortage of credit which meant that goods which could not be sold were dumped onto markets, thus depressing prices. The price falls spread bankruptcy and bank failure, and increased real debt. Even when interest rates fell in 1930, the surpluses evident in all commodities were sufficient to ensure that what Kindleberger calls 'structural deflation' would continue.

1929, therefore, was a year when a variety of deflationary forces hit an economy that was not strong enough to withstand them. The distribution of income, the state of the housing market, the movement of the automobile industry towards saturation, falling prices, depression in agriculture, distress selling in the financial sector and high interest rates are among the adverse circumstances which we have isolated. It is impossible to say which of them was the most important. Indeed, Temin's candid statement that the depression began 'due to some combination of events that cannot be disentangled' has great appeal.

Temin (1976) added a new dimension to the debate on the origins of the depression by claiming that the decline in income and prices evident before the financial crisis of 1931 was caused by an unusually heavy drop in consumption. He attributed part of this to the stock market crash; another and more significant part to the fall in agricultural income. Even when aggregated, however, these two events could not totally account for the change. Temin, nevertheless, identified this inexplicable lack of consumption, which depressed demand and undermined business confidence, as an explanation for the continuing downward slide during 1930. Temin's thesis has, however, been undermined by Mayer (1978a) who demonstrates that similar contractions had occurred in years other than 1930, but were not accompanied by a severe depression.

The period from the Wall Street crash to the beginning of the European currency crisis in the middle of 1931 was one during which consumers bought less and businesses invested less. As unemployment rose and profits disappeared, expenditure fell. Falling prices made businessmen apprehensive as to the future; fewer people wanted to borrow and fewer banks wished to lend, and those already in debt found that its burden was increasing in real terms. Nevertheless, until the autumn of 1931 the US experienced a severe contraction in its economy but not a remarkable one; the worst was yet to come.

There is not doubt that there was a dramatic fall in investment once the depression began to bite. The problem is this: did this decline bring about a contraction in income, or did the fall in income lead to the decline in investment? Keynesians, of course, believe that the first of these relationships was true: the decline in investment is the key. We should note, in this context, that the Keynesians paid little attention to the Hawley–Smoot tariff increase of 1930 and felt that monetary policy was of little or no significance.

Keynesian dominance received a sharp jolt with the publication of Milton Friedman and Anna Schwartz's *A Monetary History of the United States 1867–1960* (1963), in which they asserted that the cause of the depression's severity was the decline in the nation's stock of money, which fell by one-third between 1929 and 1933. This monetary contraction was caused largely by bank failures, usually resulting from the inept policies pursued by the Federal Reserve, which have been described in Chapter 6. Monetarists believe that money changes explain income changes; Keynesians, on the other hand, assert that the fall in the quantity of money is a function of a decline in income. Put simply the issue is: does money influence income, or does income influence money? It has not yet been possible to test this relationship empirically in a way which satisfies a wide spectrum of opinion. Strongly expressed monetarist views, which have become widely accepted in the United States, can be found in Cagan (1965), Darby (1976) and Schwartz (1969; 1981). By way of contrast the reader is invited to read the vigorous onslaught on monetarism made by Kaldor (1970), and Temin's more comprehensive debate on the monetarist causes of the great depression.

Friedman had argued that fluctuations in the economy were casued by changes in the monetary sector long before Karl Brunner introduced the term 'monetarism' in 1968. Support for monetarism grew partly because of Freidman's skilful advocacy, but also because increasing numbers of economists became disillusioned with the failure of Keynesian economics to resolve the twin threats of inflation and unemployment; many economists and politicians swiftly seized upon monetarism as the means to solve these problems, which were becoming serious by the 1970s. The belief was that stable money growth at a level low enough to ensure that there was minimal inflation, plus an eradication of budget deficits were vital prerequisites for economic success.

Monetarists have, however, been faced with a number of theoretical problems which many of those implementing Friedmanite programmes have chosen to ignore. For example, there is the complex issue of defining money and measuring the money supply, a difficulty which was particularly evident during the period of monetarism in Britain after 1979. Any deficiencies or imprecision in the definition of money, however, mean that its links with changes in income and output cannot be demonstrated satisfactorily. More fundamentally, we could ask why a change in the supply of money should affect employment and output? If the money supply falls why is the result not simply a fall in prices, leaving the real economy unchanged? Nevertheless, in spite of these and other difficulties, the monetarist interpretation of the onset and the severity of the depression is widely accepted by economists and often presented without criticism in text books.

The gist of the monetarist case is that the restrictive policy pursued by the Federal Reserve in 1928–9, designed to slow down stock market speculation, had the effect, through higher interest rates and a reduction in the rate of monetary growth, of bringing the economic boom to an end. From that point the economy was driven to its trough by five shocks, one of which was the Wall Street crash; the others were episodes of banking panic. According to Friedman and Schwartz, the dramatic change in the character of the depression came in October 1930 with the first bank crisis. At this point an ordinary depression changed into the great depression. Stirrings of revival which were stifled by the bank failures of March 1931 and the winter of 1931–2, were finally extinguished by the banking debâcle which preceded Roosevelt's inauguration.

The principal effect of the spasms of bank failure, according to monetarists, is that they brought about a rapid decline in the total quantity of money, which fell by approximately one-third between 1929 and 1933. As a result of the reduced amount of money in the economy, aggregate demand collapsed, as did real output. The economy underwent a painful period of readjustment as it adapted to the now smaller stock of money. Thus we can see that this thesis assigns to monetary forces a central role in any explanation of shifts in aggregate demand. Moreover, for Friedman and Schwartz, the villain of the piece is the Federal Reserve which could, as we have seen in Chapter 6, have prevented the fall in the money supply by vigorous open market operations. Such actions would have enlarged bank reserves and given the banks the ability to withstand runs; as a result, the catastrophic decline in the quantity of money would have been prevented. Critics claim that, given the structure of US banking with its many small independent units, failures were inevitable. Nevertheless, Friedman and Schwartz believe that open market operations would have prevented a massive decline in the money stock and halted the disintegration of the economy in 1930. However, intead of pursuing expansionary policies as it had done in 1924 and 1927, the Reserve, for the most part, did quite the reverse.

The main source of instability was, therefore, intervention; the private economy, argue monetarists, is basically stable but this stability was destroyed by the ill-conceived actions of the Fed. Left to itself, claim Friedman and Schwartz, the banking system could have coped adequately with the crisis by refusing to convert deposits into cash, as it had done during times of panic before 1913. Instead the responsibility for ensuring bank stability was given to the Federal Reserve which failed in this task abysmally.

Some monetarists, especially Schwartz, write as if the debate over the role of money in the depression is now over and their battalions have been victorious. There is, however, still a great deal of disagreement amongst economists on the precise role of money, and we need to examine carefully the view that money explains all, or practically all, we need to know about the depression.

A central problem for all monetarists is the definition of the money supply and how changes in it should be presented. Friedman and Schwartz use two measures: firstly, M_1, which is defined as currency held by the public, plus current account deposits held in commercial banks, and secondly, M_2, which is currency held by the public, plus current and deposit accounts held in commercial banks. During 1928 and 1929 both M_1 and M_2 grew very slowly. Between 1929 and 1933, however, M_1 fell by 27 per cent and M_2 by 33 per cent.

Let us look, first of all, at the monetarist explanation for the downturn of 1929 which is based primarily on the reduction in the rate of growth of the money supply. Many economists are sceptical that this slow down in monetary growth could have brought about such a severe economic contraction. At most this was just one of the deflationary forces that helped translate prosperity into depression, and probably not the most prominent. The relatively high interest rates, which were a result of the Fed's attack on stock market speculation, did, however, play a destabilising role. Domestically, tight money hit the automobile and construction industries; internationally, foreign lending and commodity markets were dislocated. In this way Federal Reserve policies did affect the economy. Once the stock market crashed, however, interest rates fell, although they were pushed up again later in the depression, both in real terms as prices declined and nominally also, when the Fed periodically moved in to protect the dollar from speculation.

Further analysis reveals that although the nominal money supply fell after 1929, persistent price reductions meant that the real money supply continued to rise until 1931. Temin uses this point to back his claim that there is no evidence of monetary stringency between the Wall Street crash and Britain's abandonment of the gold standard in September 1931. He reinforces his assertion by pointing out that short-term interest rates were low; if money were in short supply, surely they should have risen? Although monetarists claim that neither interest rates nor real money changes are valid measures of monetary stringency, they have not been able to explain these movements convincingly to their critics. Temin has raised serious questions about the monetarist account of events up to September 1931; monetary factors alone cannot account for the course of the depression to that date. Indeed, non-monetary factors might be even more important than monetary during this period.

For the period after September 1931, when bank failures became more numerous and the collapse in the money supply extraordinarily severe, the monetarist case is much more powerful. Even a modern Keynesian would agree that such a large drop in the quantity of money was serious. As we have seen (Chapter 6), it was within the power of the Federal Reserve to pursue easy money policies which would have given the commercial banking system the ability to stem the flow of deposits. Instead, the policies which emerged were virtually tailor-made to destroy the banks and undermine the economy. As banks failed, apprehension spread and sources of credit were lost. The impact of bank failures in any economy is more destabliising than business bankruptcy because they alone can bring about a reduction in the money stock. A more vigorous monetary policy would certainly have made the depression less severe by shoring up the banks, providing more credit and improving the confidence of business, thus encouraging an increase in the demand for money. How do Temin and other non-monetarists view the contraction in the stock of money? They accept that it took place, but believe that it was caused by a falling demand for money, not a deficient supply. The collapse of profits meant that businesses borrowed less and could not repay their debts; the same was true of individuals whose incomes declined. The low rates of interest, bank failures, and the diminishing money stock are therefore a function of reduced income. This is the reverse of the monetarist case which argues a chain of causality from bank failures to the falling stock of money, which leads to a decline in aggregate demand.

We can also accept that after September 1931 there were strong non-monetarist influences on the economy. Increasing unemployment and collapsing agricultural income lowered effective demand: a natural consequence of the failure to sell goods was that business invested less and laid off more workers. A vicious downward spiral developed. Consumers bought only the essentials; falling prices did not encourage people to buy more as, in general, their aim was to wait until prices had hit rock bottom. Most importantly, the credit system collapsed; nominal interest rates were low but real rates very high so that borrowers faced a period of severe retrenchment. The federal government increased its expenditure on public works, but in 1932 adopted a fiscal policy which was deflationary. There were no built in stabilisers in the economy, no unemployment benefit to keep up the purchasing power of the workless, who had to live on their savings or charity. Nor was there any school of economists with a remedy for the crisis that was both politically and intellectually acceptable (Barber, 1985).

One interesting issue which deserves further research is the role of domestic debt in the depression. All manner of debts had increased during the 1920s: farm debt, urban mortgages, consumer and corporate debt rose to high levels. As the price level fell, indebtedness was raised substantially in real terms and obligations still had to be met, even though incomes and asset values had declined. During 1931 and 1932 banks put presure on customers to repay their loans and at the same time felt unable to give new credit. The effect of this dislocation in credit markets during 1930–3, which adversely affected households, farms and small firms by making loans expensive or difficult to obtain, seriously reduced aggregate demand (Bernanke, 1983). Debts were a major source of instability once the depression took hold (Hart, 1938; Lee, 1971; Minsky, 1984; Mishkin, 1978; Ratchford, 1946).

It would be a mistake to believe that all economists view the depression from a rigid monetarist/non-monetarist stance. Gordon and Wilcox, for example, have tried to amalgamate these two theories. They believe that both monetary and non-monetary forces determine the level of income, but consider that monetary forces were not powerful enough, before the middle of 1931, to explain the swift progress of the depression. In their analysis money plays a minor role up to that date; rather the most powerful forces pushing down the economy at the early stages were the falls in house building and in consumption expenditures. Gordon and Wilcox claim that the effect of the steady decline in construction from 1926 was disguised partly by a rise in non-residential building and also by buoyant consumption. In this analysis the stock market played a role in keeping consumption high during 1928 and most of 1929; as a result, the potential slump in construction was delayed. Once the stock market fell, housebuilding began its precipitous decline, and although the Hawley–Smoot tariff added to the contractionary pressure, Gordon and Wilcox see the collapse in construction as a key factor in an explanation of the depression's harshness. Both agree, however, that the monetary policy pursued by the Fed aggravated the depression and that a more expansionary policy would have made it less severe. This is especially true of events following the devaluation of sterling, and during the months of banking chaos before Roosevelt's inauguration, when economic recovery was checked by inept economic policies. Even during this period, however, non-monetary factors such as the low level of expectations on the part of investors and the tax increase of 1932 must be taken into account.

As might be expected, Gordon and Wilcox have themselves been criticised by those who believe that house building in particular declined as a result of falling incomes and did not itself bring about the reduction in income. In other words, house building was an endogenous, or dependent variable, not an exogenous variable. Their paper should be read, nevertheless, as an interesting attempt to bridge the gap between two academic extremes. Moreover, in a complex economy it is often difficult to judge what is, or what is not, an independent monetary or non-monetary action. For example, the tax increase of 1932, which is universally condemned, was instituted in order to bolster confidence in a dollar subject to speculation (Chapter 6). In other words, the tax increase was designed to support monetary policy (Lindert, 1987). Economic policy, therefore, cannot be as neatly divided into monetary and non-monetary categories as some writers assume. An analysis which considers all forces and tries to assess their impact at varying times during the depression has a great deal to commend it.

So far we have not considered the impact of the economic collapse in the United States upon the wider world or, indeed, the role of the international economy in intensifying America's depression. President Hoover believed that the slump which drove him from the White House originated in Europe; given the circumstances, this was a predictable conclusion. Kindleberger, in a more objective analysis, attempts to place America's depression in an international context. He eschews monetarism and sees the initial contraction in the US as brought about by a fall in house building, the deflationary force of which was worsened by the stock market crash. More importantly, the decline in US long-term lending, which was induced by the stock market boom, instituted an international depression. A world weakened by a high level of debts, as well as financial and structural problems, could not withstand the loss of the American capital on which it had come to depend. The falling prices of commodities and securities combined to make the banking systems of many nations highly suspect, and the European financial crisis of 1931 inevitable. As the crisis ricocheted round the world, the depression worsened because there was no international lender of last resort, no nation to act as an international central bank. Britain was too weak and the United States unwilling to fulfil this role. According to Kindleberger, the US could have rescued the international economy if it had lent counter-cyclically. This may well be true, but it is hard to see by what mechanism that desirable state of affairs could have been achieved.

A combination of events led to the US exporting the depression. The international slump began with the decline in long-term lending that took place during 1928–9 and the concomitant rise in interest rates. As the depression got underway, America rapidly reduced imports, seriously affecting the economies of primary producing countries (Fleisig, 1975). The Hawley–Smoot tariff, or rather the retaliation which it provoked, made things worse by reducing the level of international trade. The main point is that in each year after 1929 the supply of dollars reaching the rest of the world was less than was needed and far less than the recipient nations had come to expect during the late 1920s. This change of fortunes was serious for many nations whose economies, in 1929, were already precarious (Chapter 7). Germany, for example, was a debtor nation and needed a steady supply of dollars. The German economy had begun to move into recession in 1928; the reduction in the flow of dollars helped to translate this into a slump. In general, debtor nations faced the most serious problems once the depression began, especially as the vast majority were agricultural economies smitten by the collapse of primary product prices. Generalisations are, however, dangerous; two of the nations most affected by the slump were the leading borrower — Germany — and the leading lender — the United States. Both these advanced industrial nations, however, had large agricultural sectors which became particularly depressed and banking systems which were structurally weak and prone to collapse. It is no accident that the stability of Britain's banks and the insignificance of her agricultural sector protected her from the worst effects of the crisis.

Is there an explanation for 1919–33? Unfortunately not one which is acceptable to all. We can see, however, that the US economy which in 1929 seemed strong to contemporaries was, in fact, very vulnerable. Construction and automobiles, which formed the engine of growth during the 1920s, had come to the end of their period of expansion, while agriculture and the banking system combined to present a serious structural problem. Once the economy began its downward slide there was little to halt it. The policies pursued by the Federal Reserve made matters worse, and the federal government was trapped in a crisis over which it had no control. Hoover could have been politically more adept but it is difficult to see what he could have done to save the economy. The argument is really about the nature of the shock to the economic system. Was it monetary or non-monetary? Writings on the depression will continue to appear; the monetarist/non-monetarist controversy will continue. There is no substitute for reading some of the works in the bibliography attached to this chapter and reaching your own conclusion.

Bibliography

The crux of the debate on the causes and the severity of the depression during the Hoover years is contained in the books by K. Brunner (1981), M. Friedman and A.J. Schwartz, and P. Temin (1976). Many of the arguments advanced in these works are, however, highly technical. Readers who find difficulty with them could begin their further reading with R.A. Gordon (1974) and C.P. Kindleberger. Another text of value is that by W.J. Barber who presents details of the economic advice which was available to President Hoover.

Anderson, B.L. and Butkiewicz, J.L. (1980) 'Money, Spending and the Great Depression', *Southern Economic Journal*, 47.

Barber, C.L. (1978) 'On the origins of the great depression', *Southern Economic Journal*, 44.

Barber, W.J. (1985) *From New Era to New Deal: Herbert Hoover, the Economists and American Economic Policy, 1921—1933*, Cambridge University Press.

Bernanke, B.S. (1983) 'Non-monetary effects of the financial crisis in the propagation of the great depression', *American Economic Review*, 73.

Bolch, B.W. and Pilgrim, J.D. (1973) 'A reappraisal of some factors associated with fluctuations in the interwar period', *Southern Economic Journal*, 3.

Brunner, K. (ed.) (1981) *The Great Depression Revisited*, Martinus Nijhoff.

Brunner, K. and Meltzer, A.H. (1968) 'What did we learn from the monetary experience of the United States in the great depression?', *Canadian Journal of Economics*, 1.

Cagan, P. (1965) *Determinants and Effects of Changes in the Stock of Money 1875—1960*, NBER, New York.

Darby, M.R. (1976) *Macroeconomics*, McGraw-Hill.

Dorfman, N.J. (1968) 'The role of money in the investment boom of the twenties and the 1929 turning point', *Journal of Finance*, 23.

Fearon, P. (1979) *The Origins and Nature of the Great Slump 1929—32*, Macmillan.

Fleisig, H.W. (1975) *Long-Term Capital Flows and the Great Depression: The Role of the United States, 1927—33*, Arno Press.

Field, A.J. (1984) 'A new interpretation of the onset of the great depression', *The Journal of Economic History*, XLIV.

Friedman, M. and Schwartz, A.J. (1963) *A Monetary History of the United States 1867—1960*, NBER, New York.

Gandolfi, A.E. (1974) 'Stability of the demand for money during the great contraction — 1929—33', *Journal of Political Economy*, 82.

Gandolfi, A.E. and Lothian, J.R. (1977) Review of 'Did Monetary Forces Cause the Great Depression?', *Journal of Money, Credit and Banking*, 9.

Gordon, R.A. (1961) *Business Fluctuations*, Harper.

Gordon, R.A. (1974) *Economic Instability and Growth: The American Record*, Harper and Row.

Gordon, R.J. (1981) *Macroeconomics*, 2nd edn, Little, Brown.

Gordon, R.J. and Wilcox, J.A. (1981) 'Monetarist interpretations of the Great Depression: an evaluation and critique' in Brunner (ed.), *op. cit.*

Haberler, G. (1946) *Prosperity and Depression*, United Nations, New York.

Hansen, A. (1941) *Fiscal Policy and Business Cycles*, W.W. Norton.

Hart, A.G. (1938) *Debts and Recovery, 1929—37*, Twentieth Century Fund.

Hickman, B.G. (1973) 'What became of the building cycle?' in P. David and M. Reder (eds) *Nations and Households in Economic Growth: Essays in Honor of Moses Abramovitz*, Academic Press.

Hoover, H. (1952) *The Memoirs of Herbert Hoover: The Great Depression, 1929—1941*, Macmillan.

Kaldor, N. (1970) 'The new monetarism', *Lloyds Bank Review*, No. 97, July, pp. 1—18.

Kindleberger, C.P. (1973) *The World in Depression 1929—1939*, University of California Press.

Kindleberger, C.P. (1979) 'The international causes and consequences of the Great Crash', *Journal of Portfolio Management*, 6.

Kindleberger, C.P. (1984) *A Financial History of Western Europe*, Allen and Unwin.

Kirkwood, J.B. (1972) 'The Great Depression: A structural analysis', *Journal of Money, Credit and Banking*, 4.

Lee, M.W. (1971) *Macroeconomics: Fluctuations, Growth and Stability*, 5th edn, Irwin.

Lindert, P.H. (1981) 'Comments on "Understanding 1929—1933"', in K. Brunner, *op. cit.*

Mayer, T. (1978a) 'Consumption in the Great Depression', *Journal of Political Economy*, 86.

Mayer, T. (1978b) 'Money and the Great Depression: some reflections on Professor Temin's recent book', *Explorations in Economic History*, 14.

Meltzer, A.H. (1976) 'Monetary and other explanations of the start of the Great Depression', *Journal of Monetary economics*, 2.

Mercer, L.J. and Morgan, W.D. (1971–72) 'Alternative interpretations of market saturation: evaluation for the automobile market in the late twenties', *Explorations in Economic History*, 9.

Mercer, L.J. and Morgan, W.D. (1972) 'The American automobile industry: investment and demand, capacity and capacity utilisation, 1921–40', *Journal of Political Economy*, 80, November/December.

Minsky, H.P. (1984) 'Banking and industry between the two wars: the United States', *Journal of European Economic History*, 13, Fall.

Mishkin, F. (1978) 'The household balance sheet in the Great Depression', *Journal of Economic History*, 38.

Ratchford, B.U. (1941) *American State Debts*, Duke University Press.

Saint-Etienne, C. *The Great Depression 1929–1938: Lessons for the 1980s* (Stamford, 1984) Hoover Institution Press.

Schwartz, A.J. (1969) 'Why money matters', *Lloyds Bank Review*, No. 94, Oct.

Schwartz, A.J. (1981) 'Understanding 1929–33' in K. Brunner (ed.), *op. cit.*

Smiley, G. (1983) 'Did incomes for most of the population fall from 1923 through 1929?', *Journal of Economic History*, 43.

Temin, P. (1976) *Did Monetary Forces Cause the Great Depression?* W.W. Norton.

Temin, P. (1981) 'Notes on the causes of the Great Depression', in K. Brunner (ed.), *op. cit.*

Wilson, T. (1948) *Fluctuations in Income and Employment*, Macmillan.

Part III
The New Deal and World War II

10

The New Deal: An Introduction

When Franklin Delano Roosevelt took the oath of office on becoming President, public confidence in the American economy was at its nadir. The banking system was paralysed, agriculture and industry were in disarray, and the prospect of recovery was so distant that to many citizens the future appeared as bleak as the present. Morale was, not surprisingly, extremely low. There seemed little possibility that the collapse in the economy would be self-regulating. Intense debate amongst professional economists and business leaders showed that there was no unanimity as to how recovery could be achieved; just as there was a surfeit of agricultural produce, so there was of ideas. Congress, with a high proportion of new members, who had been swept to office on Roosevelt's coat tails, was bursting with theories for combating the crisis. There was a clear call, both from the legislature and the public, for a more dynamic approach to the nation's ills, and a greater degree of leadership than had been provided by Hoover.

The time was ripe for the federal government to embark upon a positive intervention in the economy if it wished to do so, though, as we have seen, the Hoover years had not been characterised by *laissez-faire*. Indeed Roosevelt, during the campaign of 1932, attacked Hoover not for inactivity, but for raising public expenditure, increasing state bureaucracy, and running the budget into deficit. FDR made no attempt to present himself to the nation as an economic radical in 1932 nor is there any evidence that such a stance would have increased his margin of victory. However, it is important to recognise the temper of the times in 1933. Businessmen and bankers were chastened and had lost much of the self-confidence which they had enjoyed during the halcyon days of the 1920s. Big business, which had been presented as the guarantor of prosperity in those years, stood accused as the harbinger of depression. Speculators, attacked by Roosevelt in his inaugural address, were now regarded as unclean, where previously they had aroused both envy and emulation. Public sympathy lay with the poverty stricken farmers, the unemployed and the homeless, not with those held to be responsible, if only in part, for hard times.

It is difficult for anyone whose economic experience is limited to the inflationary spiral which has been the lot of the world since the begining of World
War II to appreciate the unease over deflation prevalent in the early 1930s. The
price falls of the depression were not regarded universally as a bonus; on the
contrary, they were looked upon by many as the root cause of many ills including
farm misery, increasing real debts, unemployment, bank insolvency and low levels
of investment. One widespread but narrow view was that falling prices had come
about because of excess competition and production; the solution was to curtail
both. Others, under-consumptionists, felt that consumers did not have enough
income to buy all that the farm and the factory sent to market; they supported
plans for higher wages and a shorter working week. Though many sang the praises
of new or even rehashed economic theories, there were those, often in influential
positions, who still clung to the orthodoxies of the 1920s. Their priority was to
balance the federal budget, believing that with the deficit removed, improved confidence at home and abroad would create the right atmosphere for business to
embark upon a sustained recovery. Other upholders of orthodoxy stressed the
importance of the gold standard and yearned for Britain's return to it. Their voices
vied with those of the inflationists, the planners and others, to gain the President's ear in order to influence his decisions. Roosevelt was never short of advice.

The evidence of history was on the side of those who urged a greater degree
of federal intervention in economic and welfare policies. In the past, during periods
of crisis, in war or in peace, calls for government action had been loud. In the
1890s, for example, the Populist platform had called for an inflationary increase
in the money supply to raise the living standards of farmers. During World War
I federal agencies, in which businessmen played a crucial role, became an essential part of the drive to victory. Wartime parallels with the depression were
apparent with the establishment of the RFC, several of whose board members
had received their public service baptism in the War Industries Board of 1918.
Increasingly comparisons were drawn, even by Roosevelt, between the present
crisis and the war, when co-operation between business and government had produced such positive results (Leuchtenberg, 1964).

In the 1920s, manufacturing industry could be divided into two sectors. The
first, which was dominated by big business, practised oligopolistic competition.
In the machinery industries, petroleum, rubber, tobacco and automobiles, for
example, price competition was a thing of the past. Size and control of a large
share of the market were held to be great advantages in the expanding economy
of the 1920s and could still be an asset in the very changed conditions of 1929—33.
In many other industrial groupings, for example, furniture, leather, clothing, textiles and printing, the small firm dominated. In order to bring stability to an otherwise competitive industry many small businessmen had grouped themselves into
trade associations which became increasingly popular (Chapter 3). What many
businessmen and their organisations, such as the Chamber of Commerce or the
National Association of Manufacturers, wanted in 1933 was a reversal of the
savage deflation which they had suffered and a restoration of profits. They believed

that the way to accomplish this was a less rigorous interpretation of the anti-trust laws and the creation of industrial cartels which would operate in unison with government. Destructive price cutting would thus be brought to an end, a necessary prerequisite for recovery.

The business community ran a risk in involving itself with Washington as its public prestige was low and it was in no position to dictate to a government which had won such a resounding electoral victory. Furthermore, industrialists felt compelled to support moves which were designed to increase the powers of the President. Congress was a hotbed of radical ideas which so frightened the captains of industry that they, and their supporters, regarded Roosevelt by comparison as a symbol of common sense and stability. They hoped that he would use all the authority at his command to quash the more extreme proposals emanating from Capitol Hill.

Businessmen wanted to be in a position where they could play a part in formulating the recovery plans put forward by the new administration and oppose those which were perceived as being disadvantageous. They did not agree that the restoration of competition and the break-up of monopolies was the route to recovery. Indeed, many business leaders advocated the introduction of economic planning, which had acquired respectability during World War I, as a means of restoring normality. They dreaded the prospect of increased competition which they equated with further price falls and greater losses. It seemed preferable to accept planning and to build on the present industrial structure in an attempt to prevent future crises.

As Hawley (1966) shows, acceptance in principle of planning did not preclude arguments over what form it should take. One view was that business should be excluded from the planning process and that the task should be given to governmental agencies or non-business organisations. However, unlike many European countries, the US did not have a large, highly skilled bureaucracy to formulate and implement detailed planning policies. To some extent this deficiency was offset by the move to Washington of many of the best and the brightest from higher education and the social services, to become New Deal administrators. In the main, however, when the government wanted information to supplement its own inadequate data, or required additional administrative staff, industry was the only source available. For agriculture, unlike business, there was in the Department of Agriculture a relatively sophisticated bureaucratic machine which had strong links with both farmers and farm organisations. This may be one reason why agricultural policy was longer lasting than industrial policy (Skocpol and Finegold, 1982).

Business, therefore, was in a surprisingly strong political position in 1933. Its skills were in short supply and it was sufficiently well organised to be able to lobby effectively in favour of using trade associations as the basic structure for New Deal planning. In co-operating with government, industry could exploit Washington's lack of experience and easily outmanoeuvre other groups such as labour or consumers who collectively were very weak. Although Roosevelt would have had much popular support if he had attacked business, he needed its help for the implementation of New Deal planning and economic controls.

Roosevelt's campaign in 1932 had recognised the pressing problems facing the American people, but he had been vague as to how precisely he would cut the unemployment lines and raise farm prices. It may be that the electorate was so determined to depose Hoover that the superficiality of his opponent's programme was not a serious handicap. Roosevelt was a conservative: in 1933 he did not envisage a permanent role for government in the economy. He wanted to preserve American capitalism, not change it by advancing public ownership as a panacea. In fiscal matters he was instinctively cautious: he believed in a balanced budget and was a critic of the thesis that America could spend her way out of the depression. The new President had no knowledge of economics but he weighed up economic problems as a pragmatist rather than as an ideologue. His orthodoxy was tempered by the shrewd realisation that 'bold, persistent experimentation' was called for. Thus Roosevelt was attracted by the idea of moderate inflation, of a more equitable distribution of income, and even of the need for some planning, to give Americans the New Deal he had promised. He listened to the myriad of intellectuals and political leaders and extracted from their discourse — FDR was a listener rather than a reader and certainly no intellectual himself — that which appealed. However, he never wavered from his support for the private enterprise system (Friedel, 1973; Fusfeld, 1954).

One of Roosevelt's particular strengths was a marvellous speaking voice, in an age when the radio had come to play an important role in politics. His ability to convey compassion, concern, hope and courage was invaluable, in 1933, to his party and the people. The inaugural address of 4 March demonstrated FDR's deft use of language as it incorporated stirring phrases designed to make an immediate public impact. There was, however, little in his speech to indicate what action he proposed to cure the current economic ills. Shortly after the address, Roosevelt called Congress to convene in a special session on 9 March, and also began immediately to tackle the banking problem which was particularly serious (Chapter 6). A bank holiday closing all the country's banks was declared and the Secretary of the Treasury was told to produce emergency legislation for Congress to consider. Invoking the provision of the wartime Trading with the Enemy Act, the President also forbade the export of gold. Unable to draw upon their bank deposits, the public waited anxiously for the special session of Congress. It did not disappoint them; this was the famous 'hundred days' of the first Roosevelt administration.

The following is a list of the achievements of this 73rd Congress in its special sitting. Some of the measures taken are analysed in later chapters.

9 March   The Emergency Banking Act. It outlined plans to use the RFC to provide distressed banks with capital and also informed the public that solvent banks would reopen soon, after examination.

20 March   The Economy Act. A victory for budget balancers since it authorised a reduction in federal government expenditure by $500 m.

31 March   The establishment of the Civilian Conservation Corps (CCC), an
            agency which created conservation oriented public jobs, such as plant-
            ing trees and building dams, for young unemployed men, using the
            military as a model.

19 April   The gold standard was abandoned. A shock to financial conservatives,
            though it could be argued that the presidential embargo on the export
            of gold had, de facto, already released the US from its shackles.

12 May   The Federal Emergency Relief Act (FERA), which allocated federal
            money to the states for the purpose of relief but relied heavily upon
            state and local agencies for administration.

12 May   The Agricultural Adjustment Act (AAA), an attempt to raise farm
            prices by reducing planted acreage. Attached to this bill was the
            Thomas Amendment, which gave Roosevelt the power to increase
            the quantity of money.

12 May   The Emergency Farm Mortgage Act, which gave help to farmers in
            debt.

18 May   The Tennessee Valley Authority Act (TVA), which created a major
            public corporation whose function was to develop the region by
            building dams to provide electricity and control flooding, as well as
            by improving farm techniques and attracting industry.

27 May   The Truth-in-Securities Act, an early attempt to curb stock exchange
            abuses, many of which had been exposed by the Senate Banking Com-
            mittee's investigation of Wall Street.

5 June   The abrogation of the gold clause in public and private contracts. This
            denied creditors the right to press for repayment in gold dollars of
            the 'old weight and fineness'. The reduction of the gold content of
            the dollar in January 1934 would have resulted in a crippling blow
            to debtors if they had been obliged to settle their debts in gold at its
            old value.

13 June   The Home Owners Loan Act, which enabled householders to
            refinance their mortgages by using government agencies as creditors.

16 June   The National Industrial Recovery Act (NIRA), which was a massive
            exercise in governmental planning to achieve industrial recovery, in
            conjunction with a public works programme.

16 June   The Glass–Steagall Banking Act, which not only separated commer-
            cial from investment banking, but also provided for a limited insurance
            of bank deposits.

16 June   The Farm Credit Act, which brought order to the chaos which existed
            in agricultural credit.

16 June   The Railroad Co-ordination Act, which suspended the anti-trust laws
            for inter-state railroads and provided for the co-ordination of com-
            peting lines by a Federal Co-ordinator of Transportation.

The hundred days saw 15 major laws passed by Congress, urged on by the
President who had quickly taken the political initiative. This was an amazing,

hectic period in American history during which the hopes that the population once had for the future were rekindled. Anyone who doubted Roosevelt's dynamism and strength of purpose after the inaugural address had those doubts quickly cast aside. The President had made a dramatic impact and had shown courage as well as formidable political skill. His New Deal was beginning to take shape and the early reaction from the nation was one of enthusiastic support.

When we analyse the New Deal we will see that it is a very complex concept; the New Deal that was cut short by war in 1941 was very different from that of 1933. The shifts, the changes, the adjustments and the contradictions in Roosevelt's peacetime presidency mean that we cannot look at those years as a whole and hope to find a coherent economic strategy. The New Deal was constantly being adapted to meet new challenges, promote experimentation, accommodate powerful pressure groups, respond to new presidential advisors, take note of Supreme Court decisions and, of course, to jetison those parts seen to be ineffective. These changes can be interpreted as demonstrating that Roosevelt had a very open, flexible mind and was quite prepared to make fundamental changes in the thrust of his policy if it was necessary to do so. This is a charitable view. Critics claim that the variations show a shallow, devious, vacillating president who never thought through the implications of his legislation, but was motivated entirely by the desire to cling to power. Roosevelt had the capacity to inspire both deep affection in his admirers and great hostility in his enemies, which helps to explain the wide spectrum of vehement views on his presidency. It is true to say, however, and this will be a theme running through our analysis of the New Deal, that the legislation which comprised it must be seen as a response to political problems. It was an exercise in the art of politics, not economics (Romasco, 1983; Rosen, 1977).

An evaluation of Roosevelt's policies, therefore, presents some difficulty. Some have tried to divide his goals into three parts: reform, relief and recovery, a subdivision suggested by Roosevelt himself in one of his early 'fireside chats'. There is, however, a danger of considerable overlap in this approach as reform of the banking system, for example, was a vital prerequisite for recovery. Moreover, some of the agencies which the administration set up to aid the recovery programme, for example, the Public Works Administration, the Civil Works Administration, and the Works Progress Administration, had clear work relief functions. Important pieces of legislation such as the AAA and the TVA contained elements of reform, recovery and relief. Subdivision into the 'three Rs' is an interesting exercise, and a valuable teaching tool, but not a totally satisfactory way of analysing the New Deal.

Another way of giving these years some structure or form is to identify two or even three New Deals. The first, which lasted from 1933 to 1935, was much influenced by the ideas of Adolf Berle Jr, Raymond Moley and Rexford Tugwell, early Roosevelt advisors who formed the Brain Trust, an early presidential 'think tank'. The emphasis in these few years was on structural economic reform brought about by central planning. The main attack on the depression in the first New

Deal was launched with the implementation of the AAA and the National Recovery Administration (NRA). In 1935, however, changes occurred which led to a significant alteration in the style and even in the fundamental principles of economic policy. Schlesinger (1960) identifies 1935 as a watershed which marked the beginning of the second New Deal. This new strategy saw the emergence of a more competitive or capitalist society; a restoration of the competition which had been curbed under the first New Deal. Protection for the vulnerable from the possible dangers of this new anti-monopoly strategy was needed, and it was given. The formation of trade unions was made much easier by the passing of the Wagner Act (1935), so necessary for union growth after the Supreme Court had struck down the NIRA, and in that year the broad mass of the people were promised a welfare minimum by the *Social Security Act*.

The change of philosophy in 1935 was one of a return to the old American values and the reasons for it were varied. The fact that the Supreme Court had invalidated parts of the original legislation meant that there was an immediate need for something to replace it. Moreover, by 1934, the business community had become disenchanted with the administration's industrial strategy and had begun to attack it. For their part the New Dealers, seeing little advantage from co-operation with big business, moved from collaboration to offence; small business was now at the vanguard of the industrial revival which had been retarded by large corporations. A further spur for change came from the political armies which were gathering their forces to fight the New Deal both from the right and the left. The president was forced to take action in order to defuse their appeal. At the same time Roosevelt could see that some of the policies which had been put into practice had yielded disappointing returns and, therefore, fresh thoughts were needed to put before the electorate (Nash, 1979; Schlesinger, 1960). Perhaps, too, the 1933 New Deal had run out of steam and a new philosophy was the only way to reinvigorate it.

Leuchtenberg (1963) raises a voice of caution against the identification of too rigid a philosophical division in 1935. As he points out, much of the legislation which characterised the second New Deal, for example social security and utility regulation, had been under consideration for some time. Nash echoes several other scholars who feel that a division into two or three New Deals implies more order in Roosevelt's policies than there really was. Nevertheless, there was an intellectual readjustment around 1935 as new advisors such as Felix Frankfurter, Marriner Eccles and Lauchlin Currie took their places next to the President, ousting Moley, Tugwell and Berle. It is interesting to note that Roosevelt was quite able to cope with fresh minds and the change in emphasis which they heralded. The President's practice was invariably to take the theories which suited at the time and to discard them when they proved unattractive.

There was yet another change in the thrust of economic policy after the recession of 1937−8, which perhaps could be identified as a third New Deal. Roosevelt had been disturbed by the deficits which had been run since he assumed office, and by early 1937 resolved to cut public expenditure. His judgement that the economy was strong enough to withstand this move was faulty; as we will see in more detail later, the cutback in federal spending helped to bring about the serious recession of 1937−8. By the middle of 1938 Roosevelt was listening to economists who had absorbed Keynesian ideas. Although the President did not understand Keynesian economics, his gut reaction was that its prescription of more government spending to revitalise the economy was correct. Thus the deficit was now seen as a means by which the economy could be pulled from depression. In 1938 also, the Temporary National Economic Committee (TNEC) was established to investigate monopoly price fixing and restrictions on competition which, New Dealers convinced themselves, had helped bring about the contraction of 1937−8. Thus we see in the last few years of the New Deal a drive against monopoly capital and an acceptance of the economics of J.M. Keynes, a sharp contrast, indeed, with the policies of 1933. We will see, however, that New Deal rhetoric was not always accompanied by action and the changes in policy which have been outlined were often more apparent than real.

The New Deal was, as has been emphasised, a skilful political exercise with Roosevelt acting as a broker between various interest groups. Its success can be seen with his re-election in 1936 and in 1940; his fourth term, won in 1944, came after the New Deal had been laid to rest. It can be noted that his Republican opponents in 1940 and 1944 did not threaten to dismantle the New Deal, a sure sign of its popularity. Roosevelt clung to power even though levels of unemployment were very high — 14 per cent in 1941 — and although some key pieces of legislation probably retarded economic recovery. As we analyse economic policies it will be clear that many of the ideas and theories which appealed to Roosevelt can, with the benefit of hindsight, be seen as nonsense. Often, however, it is understandable nonsense. Economic policy, like politics, is the art of the possible. The President had many skilled advisors with widely differing views; he had to choose from what they had to offer. Decisions had to be made even though there were gross imperfections in the available data and, until the end of the 1930s, no economic theory which could help lessen the stranglehold of the depression. It is not surprising that political considerations dominated Roosevelt's actions.

In placing Roosevelt's New Deal policies in historical perspective, however, we will be emphasising their continuity with the past rather than viewing the post 1933 era as one of dramatic change. Far from being a revolution, the New Deal was part of the progressive tradition which long influenced the new Presdident's philosophy (Kirkendall, 1964).

The New Deal will be analysed under the following headings: agriculture, industry, monetary and fiscal policy, and relief. The 1930s, 'depression decade', was a time when the government struggled to get the economy back to the levels of prosperity experienced in the late 1920s and to use this as a firm basis for further sustained growth. The quicker this could be done the better, since the loss of goods and services that could have been produced if the economy had

Table 10.1 Index of Real Gross National Product (in constant dollars)

Year	Total	Per capita
1929	100	100
1933	69	67
1934	76	73
1935	83	80
1936	95	90
1937	100	94
1938	95	89
1939	103	96
1940	112	103
1941	130	118

Source: Calculated from *Historical Statistics of US, Colonial Times to 1970*, 2 vols (Washington DC, 1975).

been operating at full employment was enormous. The performance of the economy, in aggregate, is illustrated in Table 10.1 which shows that GNP at constant prices had fallen by over 30 per cent from its 1929 level by the time Roosevelt assumed office, just one indication of the magnitude of the task which he faced.

During the New Deal the economy recovered to peak in 1937, but then endured a brief, sharp recession. By 1940, however, the stimulating influence of the European war was clearly visible. Between 1933 and 1940 prices rose steadily but never regained their 1929 levels, interest rates remained extraordinarily low, and stock market prices had reached their 1931 level by 1937 but then fell steeply because of the recession. Unemployment, which stood at 24.9 per cent of the civilian labour force in 1933, fell to 14.3 per cent in 1937 but rose to 19 per cent during the following year; the New Deal never managed to emulate the unemployment levels of the late 1920s. Nevertheless, the expansion between 1933 and 1937 was extremely rapid, as the economy rebounded vigorously from the great depression. The decline in GNP which occurred between 1929 and 1933 had been made good by 1937 (Table 10.1). In the upswing of 1933–7, real GNP rose at around 9 per cent per annum; when the growing population is taken into account, however, real per capita GNP did not regain its 1920s peak until 1940.

Although rapid, the recovery was uneven; the expansion of non-durable goods was significantly greater than that of durables. Amongst the non-durables, textiles, alcoholic beverages, cigarettes and footwear had, by 1937, made significant gains over 1929 production. However, while the output of machinery and of iron and steel just failed to reach 1929 levels, the construction related industries of lumber, bricks and furniture fell far short of this target. Automobile output in early 1937 exceeded that of 1929 but suffered a severe contraction over the ensuing 12 months. Although the expansion from March 1933 to May 1937 was the longest period of cyclical growth to date, there was no euphoria over the state of the economy, especially as unemployment levels remained high.

The recession of 1937–8, which was unexpected and occurred before recovery was complete, adversely affected morale. It dealt a severe blow to New Deal policies and further depressed business confidence. Indeed, expectations were never sufficiently buoyant during this period to make possible the high levels of long-term investment which were essential if the damage done between 1929 and 1933 was to be fully repaired. Moreover, throughout this depression decade, retail sales remained below 1929 levels, company profits stayed relatively low, and the construction industry, so important during the 1920s, was unable to regain its vitality.

The action, intervention and experimentation which typified the New Deal may have helped the economy, but we must also consider the possibility that they may have hindered recovery or even have been neutral in their effect. There are many question marks hanging over virtually all the policies implemented by Roosevelt and his acolytes in their attempts to bring about full employment, rising incomes and prosperity to farming. Beginning with the agricultural sector, the New Deal policies will now be analysed to assess what part they played in the long march to recovery during the 1930s.

Bibliography

There is a voluminous literature on the New Deal but among the most valuable contributions to our understanding of this era are the works of E. Hawley (1966, 1975), R.S. Kirkendall, W.E. Leuchtenberg (1963, 1964), and A.U. Romasco.

Chandler Jr., A.D. (1977) *The Visible Hand: The Managerial Revolution in American Business*, Belknap Press.

Friedel, F. (1973) *Franklin D. Roosevelt: Launching the New Deal*, Little, Brown.

Fusfeld, D. (1954) *The Economic Thought of Franklin D. Roosevelt and the Origins of the New Deal*, Columbia University Press.

Hawley, E. (1966) *The New Deal and the Problem of Monopoly*, Princeton University Press.

Hawley, E. (1975) 'The New Deal and Business' in J. Braeman, *et al.* (eds) *The New Deal: The National Level*, Ohio State University Press.

Kirkendall, R.S. (1964) 'The Great Depression: another watershed in American history', in J. Braeman, *et al.*, (eds) *Change and Continuity in Twentieth Century America*, Ohio State University Press.

Leuchtenberg, W.E. (1963) *Franklin Roosevelt and the New Deal 1932–1940*, Harper.

Leuchtenberg, W.E. (1964) 'The New Deal and the analogue of war', in J. Braeman *et al.* (eds.), *op. cit.*

McCoy, D. (1973) *Coming of Age: The United States during the 1920s and 1930s*, Pelican Books.

Nash, G.D. (1979) *The Great Depression and World War II: Organising America 1933–45*, St. Martins Press.

Romasco, A.U. (1983) *The Politics of Recovery: Roosevelt's New Deal*, Oxford University Press.

Rosen, E.A. (1977) *Hoover, Roosevelt and the Brains Trust: From Depression to New Deal*, Columbia University Press.
Schlesinger Jr., A.M. (1959) *The Coming of the New Deal*, Houghton Mifflin.
Schlesinger Jr., A.M. (1960) *The Politics of Upheaval*, Houghton Mifflin.
Skocpol, T. and Finegold, K. (1982) 'State capacity and economic intervention in the early New Deal', *Political Science Quarterly*, 97.
Sternsher, B. (ed.) (1966) *New Deal Doctrines and Democracy*, Allyn and Bacon.

11

Agriculture and the New Deal

The farm problem in March 1933 was desperate. Agricultural prices had fallen much further than the cost of the goods which the farmer had to buy, debts had increased in real terms, foreclosure on mortgages had become common, supplies of credit had dried up as rural banks failed, and, in addition, land values had fallen. Farmers were hit by the high proportion of fixed costs in agriculture. Mortgages, taxes, and payments on equipment had to be met, but as three-quarters of the farm labour force were either farm operators or their families, cost saving redundancies were an option for very few. Moreover, the possibilities of escape to the city during the depression were limited; indeed, during this agricultural crisis, there was, paradoxically, a noticeable movement towards the countryside. Between 1930−5 the number of farms of less than 20 acres grew by 35 per cent, as people sought the comforting self-sufficiency of the smallholding. The farm population rose to an inter-war peak of just over 32 million in 1932 under the influence of a 'back to the land' movement; many of these were people who otherwise would have been an urban relief problem.

Unlike Britain, but like Germany and France, America had a relatively large agricultural sector. In addition, agriculture in the US exhibited great diversity, not merely in the range of foodstuffs and raw materials produced, but also in the size of farm. In 1929, for example, nearly half the nation's farms produced only 11 per cent of the agricultural goods traded. Many classified as farmers were part-time operators who had little to market once their family and livestock had been fed. Furthermore, some 45 per cent of American farms were operated by tenants; for cotton this proportion was far higher (Chapter 2). We see, therefore, an industry with a very large number of producers, where entry was relatively easy and where individuals were unable to influence total output. This explains why farm production and employment held firm in the depression. Business laid off workers and cut back on output; this option was not open to many farmers, as the labour employed was usually their families. As a result, output was maintained to cover fixed costs, but with a consequent fall in prices and land values.

The New Dealers regarded agriculture as a priority, believing that the depressed farm sector needed uplifting psychologically as well as economically. They felt that the economy as a whole would only recover when farm prosperity was achieved and that the agricultural sector would spearhead the industrial revival. Their reasoning was that farm prices had fallen fastest and could, therefore, with some encouragement, be expected to rise fastest. As 25 per cent of the population lived on farms, the growth in the income of such a substantial group would have positive repercussions on demand. Moreover, the reinvigoration of rural America (46 per cent of the population in 1930) would quickly follow increasing farm prosperity. There was a strong, sometimes romantic, attachment to the land in Roosevelt's philosophy; a belief that sturdy independent yeomen under threat should be protected from the chill blast of the market place. There was also a conviction that family farms should be protected as they were an intrinsic part of the American way of life. Their very existence was now under threat and federal help was essential to ensure their viability.

New Deal farm strategy looked to rising prices and the restoration of order in credit markets as the most immediate means of aiding farmers. In the longer term, the aim was also to create a balanced ecological system which would overcome longstanding problems which had become acute. This entailed the education of the rural population, persuading them not to deplete resources in the same cavalier manner as in pioneer days. As a result of instruction they could change their farming methods, for example by switching from wheat to pasture in order to combat dust storms. For the effective provision of cheap electricity, irrigation and flood control, massive investment would be required which only the federal government could provide. There was a widespread realisation that the most pressing problems could not be solved by individual farms or even by states. Some form of regional or national planning was vital to bring about the transformation of the depressed agricultural sector. The tremendous political advantage to be gained from holding the belligerent farmers to the New Deal platform was also clearly recognised.

The aim therefore was to raise farm prices until 100 per cent parity was reached; that is, farm purchasing power was to be raised to the relative position it had held between 1910 and 1914. This was to be done by persuading farmers to behave more like businessmen: output must be tailored to suit demand (Kirkendall, 1975; Saloutos, 1982). As many farmers were more akin to the self-employed than they were to companies, however, this analogy presented identity problems. Nevertheless, farm pressure groups, such as the American Farm Bureau Federation, which had become more influential during the 1920s, were anxious for federal government help in pushing up farm prices. Farm organisations vigorously advanced a whole range of ideas including monetary inflation, a mortgage moratorium and guaranteed costs of production schemes for governmental consideration. On the other hand, the prospect of a rise in farm prices was not welcomed by food processing companies, by some manufacturers whose raw materials would become more expensive, or by urban consumers.

The Agricultural Adjustment Act (1933)

The initial attack on the farm problem took the form of a piece of legislation, the sixth presented to Congress during Roosevelt's first hundred days. A very broad bill was drawn up, in the formulation of which spokesmen from several farm organisations had played a major role. Its breadth was necessary to accommodate the wide range of opinions on agricultural issues which existed in Congress. Deeply concerned about the mounting unrest in the countryside and recognising that prompt action was needed if agitation was to be curtailed, Congress passed the bill quickly.

The legislation came in three parts or titles (Baker *et al.*, 1963; Romasco, 1983). Title I set up the Agricultural Adjustment Act (AAA), with the aim of raising farm prices by persuading farmers to reduce the acreage devoted to certain 'basic' crops. Title II, the Emergency Farm Mortgage Act, was the first of a number of valuable government interventions to stabilise farm credit. Finally, Title III, the Thomas Amendment, gave the President wide-ranging powers to inflate the currency and bring about the price increases which its supporters felt would benefit the farm community. Roosevelt was an enthusiastic supporter of a number of inflationary experiments and hoped that they would boost farm income. The New Deal's largely unsuccessful attempts at recovery through monetary inflation will be discussed in Chapter 13.

The AAA went about its task of restoring 'parity' by trying to persuade farmers to reduce the acreage in basic crops, a scheme known as the domestic allotment plan. Note that the programme was voluntary; farmers did not have to join, but those who did would receive cash payments once they had agreed to conform. These cash payments were, of course, a powerful inducement to many farmers. Initially the total national desired maximum acreage for each crop was determined and this was divided into state subtotals. Participating farmers could then be allotted an acreage on the basis of their recent planting history. The total acreage was determined with regard to prices, stocks and a rough-and-ready estimate of future demand. Those crops singled out as 'basic' were wheat, cotton, field corn, rice and tobacco; hogs, milk and milk products were similarly treated. All were prone to surplus and the widespread view was that their output must be planned instead of being left to free choice. By the time the AAA came into effect, however, crops had already been planted so that a plough-up of part of the growing corn and tobacco crop was ordered, as was a selected slaughter of hogs. This was seen by farmers as a drastic but necessary move to reduce surpluses but it was met with great hostility by many Americans, especially those existing on meagre, relief-financed diets.

The AAA gave Henry A. Wallace, the Secretary of Agriculture, considerable powers. He was urged to encourage voluntary agreements between food processors and distributors so that marketing could be regulated. He was also empowered to eliminate unfair practices or excessive charges amongst distributors and processors by licensing them; in addition, he was closely involved in one of the most controversial elements of the AAA, the processing tax. The sums needed to pay the farmers to reduce acreage were provided not out of general revenue but by a special tax on food processors, which included, for example, meat packers, flour millers and those producing tinned foodstuffs. The rate for this tax, bitterly resented by those who paid it, was determined by the Secretary of Agriculture.

What we see in the AAA is a policy which strove for farm price increases, but did so indirectly by inducement to acreage reduction. It was also a voluntary scheme, though the Bankhead Cotton Control Act (1934) and the Kerr—Smith Tobacco Control Act (1934) introduced an element of compulsion. Farmers whose output of cotton and tobacco exceeded an established quota faced a punitive tax. Initially the AAA attempted to deal with overproduction in seven basic commodities; by 1935, however, this list had been extended to 15. The AAA was not perceived as a long-term solution to the agricultural problem, but as a means to overcome an immediate crisis, though it was clear, after a short while, that long-term government involvement was unavoidable. Nor was the AAA a very radical piece of legislation: it did not incorporate the more extreme demands made by farm organisations in 1933, using instead variations on a number of ideas such as McNary—Haugenism, which had been debated during the 1920s, and the domestic allotment plan, which had been pioneered by M.L. Wilson and others. The aim of the New Dealers was legislation which would enable private farming to survive and at the same time defuse the violent agitation of some farmers.

The New Dealers sympathised with the farmers' desire for increased prices, but there would be a lag before even an effective domestic allotment scheme had the desired effect. Farm debts, on the other hand, could be dealt with speedily. A large share of farm capital was invested in land and buildings, with the result that about 75 per cent of agricultural debt was in the form of long-term mortgages which many farmers could not repay. During the worst years of the depression, farm debts had risen in real terms and had increased as a proportion of the total value of real estate. Between 1930 and 1934, however, the absolute level of farm mortgage debt declined because of the transfer of many farms to creditors by means of foreclosure. The problem became so acute that many states passed laws forbidding such foreclosures (Chapter 5). Not all farms were in debt but even by 1935, 40 per cent of fully owner-operated farms were mortgaged. The Emergency Farm Mortgage Act made funds available for loans to farmers and also extended the activities of the federal land banks. The Farm Credit Act (1933) brought all federal agencies dealing with agricultural credit into one administratively neat unit. Under the FCA, the country was divided into 12 farm credit districts. In each there was a federal land bank which could make long-term loans, and also a variety of additional institutions which provided intermediate and short-term loans to both farmers and co-operatives (Johnson, 1940). As a direct result of federal government help, many thousands of farmers were able to refinance their outstanding debts at a time when commercial banks and life insurance companies were unable or unwilling to lend as freely as they had done during the 1920s. The refinancing of farm mortgages and the provision of cheap loans were a vital shot in the arm for agriculture.

The creation of the Commodity Credit Corporation (1933) was yet another way in which the farmer was assisted. The CCC (not to be confused with the Civilian Conservation Corps) had a twofold function: it enabled farmers to keep commodities off the market in anticipation of higher prices, and by lending to the farmer who was prepared to keep crops stored on his farm, it pumped more cash into the farm sector. CCC loans, financed by the RFC, were available, initially, to cotton and corn producers, but only if they had agreed to participate in the AAA domestic allotment scheme. The farmer borrowed, using his crop as collateral; if the price of his crop rose the farmer could repay the loan and the outstanding interest and recover his crop; if it did not, he could refuse to pay and the CCC took his crop. These advances became known as non-recourse loans because the government made no attempt, other than by taking possession of the crop, to enforce repayment of the principal and interest; furthermore, the CCC was prepared to lend again for the next year. It is important to note that the loan rate constituted a minimum price for the crop and therefore reduced the risk faced by some farmers, but it could lead to unmanageable surpluses for the CCC if output could not be held in check. In addition, the loan rate was subject to political pressure from powerful farm groups which naturally wished to raise it as high as possible. Moreover, when CCC prices exceeded the prevailing market price, both home and overseas sales declined and stocks increased; high loan rates encouraged farmers to maximise output.

New Deal credit provisions were probably of more importance to farmers than the crop reduction programmes of the AAA, and were certainly of greater benefit than the monetary experiments which were supposed to assist the agricultural community (Romasco, 1983). Credit is essential for the majority of farmers and its provision, at a relatively low cost, was welcomed, especially by commercial operators. Cheap credit enabled the owners of larger farms to purchase machinery, thus helping to raise agricultural productivity.

For some time it had been evident that poor farm practices, over many generations, had contributed to a progressive destruction of the soil. The problems of erosion were made more acute by the drought which gripped the Great Plains states. First noticeable in 1930, it had a devastating impact during 1934 and again in 1936, causing widespread distress in the affected region. New Dealers hoped that their policies of acreage reduction for soil-depleting crops, which included cotton, corn and tobacco, and the planting in their place of grasses and legumes, which were soil-conserving crops, would help curb erosion. In addition, the Civilian Conservation Corps used unemployed youths on a massive tree-planting project designed to conserve the soil.

We see, therefore, New Deal farm policy helping the farmer directly and indirectly: directly through domestic allotment payments and crop loans; indirectly by crop control which would lead to higher prices, by programmes to store surplus commodities which would lead to more stable prices, and finally by the reduction of soil erosion.

The Soil Conservation and Domestic Allotment Act (1936)

In January 1936, when the Supreme Court invalidated the AAA, it was deemed
essential to replace it with new legislation. The nature of the problem facing the
farmer had changed from the dark days of 1933. By 1936 the acute crisis in
agriculture had passed; the parity ratio (see Table 11.1) in 1936 reached 92, having risen from a 1932 low of 58, and debts were no longer such a burden. In
addition, droughts had lessened the threat of surpluses: indeed, drought, and the
attendant storms, or black blizzards, attracted much public concern. For
farmers whose crops shrivelled up and died the market price was irrelevant, as
they had nothing to sell and no means of paying their debts. These changed circumstances required an agricultural policy with a new emphasis.

Table 11.1 The Parity Ratio, 1933−41 (1910−14 = 100)

Prices received index (all farm products)		Prices paid index[a]	Parity ratio	Parity ratio including government payments
1929	148	162	92	—
1933	70	109	64	66
1934	90	120	75	80
1935	109	124	88	95
1936	114	124	92	95
1937	122	131	93	97
1938	97	124	78	83
1939	95	123	77	85
1940	100	124	81	88
1941	124	133	93	98

Note: (a) Index of prices paid by farmers for commodities and services, including interest, taxes and farm wage rates.

Sources: *Historical Statistics of US, Colonial Times to 1970*, 2 vols
(Washington DC, 1975); H.D. Guither, *Heritage of Plenty* (1972),
p. 174.

The Soil Conservation and Domestic Allotment Act (SCDAA) which replaced
the AAA had the stated aim of raising farm income to parity, but it recognised
that the individual crop emphasis of 1933−5 was inflexible. Taking account of
the drought, this legislation offered to pay farmers, on a voluntary basis, for planting fewer crops which would deplete the soil and more which would help to conserve it. Soil-depleting crops, of course, included those classified as 'basic' under
the AAA; it was hoped, therefore, that surpluses could be controlled while the

soil was conserved. As this policy was implemented regionally, it could be used to combat drought-induced dust storms and also produce more feed for livestock in the parched states. The farmers in the drought-affected states also qualified for additional federal aid, which included cattle and sheep purchase programmes and loans for freight charges and feedstuff costs. The legislation of 1936 was much influenced by the drought and was intended to correct the long established poor farming techniques which had contributed to it. The President had not, of course, lost sight of the primary aim of raising farm income — certainly not in an election year.

The Agricultural Adjustment Act (1938)

The droughts, however, concealed the underlying problem of overproduction, which came to the fore again in 1937 when the rains returned and ensured a bumper crop. At the same time, the economy plunged into the serious depression of 1937–8. These events adversely affected farm income and the parity ratio fell, in 1938 and 1939, to levels not much higher than those reached in 1934. New legislation was needed that would, on the one hand, take account of the possible effect of renewed drought on output, and, on the other, effectively control any surplus, always a reality if the weather was good, so that farm prices could be stabilised. The consumer, too, had to be protected, lest actions taken to control the surplus led to serious shortages and to unacceptably high prices. The Agricultural Adjustment Act (1938) was an attempt to achieve a balance between these potentially conflicting aims.

At the core of the AAA (1938) was the idea, advanced by Secretary Wallace, of the 'ever normal granary'. By this he meant that output should be regulated so that the excess, or carry over, at the end of each crop year would be 'normal', in the sense that there would be adequate supplies of produce but not a surplus which would depress prices. To achieve this end the AAA kept some old legislation, for example, CCC loans, and soil conservation plans, and it stressed the desire of government to assist farmers to raise their purchasing power as close to parity as was possible. In order to satisfy both the farmer and the consumer, the aim was balanced abundance. The non-recourse loans advanced by the CCC were necessary if the farmer was to hold any surplus off the market in years of plenty; indeed, systematic storage was an integral part of the 'ever normal granary'. At the other end of the scale, acreage allotments for cotton, corn, rice, tobacco and wheat were designed to keep prices buoyant. The non-recourse loans also played a vital role because they set minimum crop prices for co-operating farmers; theoretically, at least, the accumulation of surpluses could be prevented if a low loan rate were set. An additional tool to combat surpluses was available: if two-thirds of farmers growing the five basic crops voted in favour of marketing quotas, heavy taxes on sales in excess of quota would be imposed. Finally, wheat

growers saw the introduction of a crop insurance scheme, with the premium being paid in good years and the benefits received when crops were lost.

The AAA (1938) was in operation for only a short while before demand, influenced by war in Europe, began to rise steeply, forcing up the parity ratio to
105 in 1942. It is impossible to say how long farm incomes would have taken
to get back to 100 per cent parity without the stimulus of war. Hostilities also
provided an outlet for surplus commodities, stocks of which had risen to disturbing levels under the non-recourse loan scheme. The CCC was therefore saved
from sharing the fate of Hoover's Farm Board by rising overseas demand.

New Deal Agricultural Policy: An Evaluation

It is extremely difficult to evaluate the New Deal programmes for agriculture,
if for no other reason than that so many different agencies were involved, whose
separate contributions cannot be disaggregated. Consider, for example, not just
the AAA, the SCDAA and the CCC, but also FERA, RA, FSA, and the Rural
Electrification Administration (REA). All these agencies, and others, had an impact
upon the farm sector. The New Dealers were convinced that no plan for agriculture
could be effective without production controls, though the general view was that
this would be a short-run measure. It was too simple, however, to advise that
farmers should behave rather like businessmen and co-ordinate more closely output
with demand. Agriculture consisted of many different sorts of farms, on a variety of soils, in different climatic regions, producing diverse crops. Could millions
of these farmers operate like small businesses? Possibly the bigger commercial
operators could, but large numbers of very small farms could not. The existence
of agricultural diversity led to a disunity in demands; the small farmers often
wanted the government to adopt more radical programmes than did the larger
commercial producers. The latter group opposed schemes designed to assist
marginal operators; big farming, not surprisingly, did not support aid for the small
and inefficient. As the larger commercial farmers were, through their farm
organisations, politically powerful, they could, by effective lobbying, put pressure
on key Congressmen and Senators. They were thus able to mould much of the
New Deal farm legislation to suit their own ends; it was the big farmers and land
owners who gained most from the acreage reductions. For their part, New Dealers
were often divided in their views on what constituted a successful farm policy.
Was it just a matter of price and income, or should it include, for example, changes
in fundamental relationships such as those between landlord and tenant? There
was an understandable lack of cohesion in the aims of agricultural policy; differences concerning not only the ends of a farm strategy, but the means to achieve
it.

Difficulties were further compounded by America's position as an exporter of
farm products. The US had about 20 per cent of its working population in
agriculture during the 1930s, compared with about 25 per cent for France and

18 per cent for Germany. These European nations were not major exporters and chose to protect their farmers by raising tariff barriers intended to keep out cheap, competitive farm products. In the United States, measures instigated to increase domestic agricultural prices had potentially serious effects on exports at a time when surpluses of practically every foodstuff and raw material were readily available in international markets. A policy designed to raise domestic prices but still dispose of America's excess farm products overseas was clearly incompatible with the fixed exchange rates of the gold standard. Therefore, the devaluation of the dollar in 1933 and the abandonment of the gold standard were consistent with inflationary farm policies.

Farmers were particularly alert to changes in their relative purchasing power which they measured with reference to the parity ratio. It was simple, and politically attractive, for the New Dealers to espouse the cause of 100 per cent parity, a 'fair price' for farmers or a short hand for protecting the rural way of life. After all, what was the alternative? As the parity ratio existed it was natural that it should be used, but no detached observer could claim that the relationship between the prices paid by farmers and the prices received for farm products between 1910 and 1914 was a sensible guide for farm policy during the 1930s. Why should a price relationship that existed before World War I, when food prices were relatively high and urban wages relatively low, be the guiding light determining agricultural strategy?

There were, of course, advantages to be gained from raising agricultural purchasing power, which had been so desperately low in 1933. Farmers are consumers as well as producers, and an increase in their ability to buy manufactured goods would have had an expansionary impact upon the economy as a whole. However, the achievement of parity was made more difficult by the administration's industrial policies.

The first New Deal was attempting to engineer a recovery which, if successful, would make 100 per cent parity an increasingly elusive goal. The administration brought about a rise in manufacturing prices by implementing the National Recovery Act, while at the same time a variety of monetary measures was introduced in an attempt to bring about a general inflation. These policies inevitably raised the cost of the goods that the farmer had to buy; to achieve 100 per cent parity, therefore, farm prices would have had to rise by more than they actually did. Furthermore, a rapid inflation of food and raw material prices would not have been unreservedly advantageous for the economy as a whole as it struggled to recover. The disposable income of consumers would be cut, leaving them with less to spend on manufactured goods; workers would respond to rising prices by demanding additional wage increases; and the unemployed would be especially hit by expensive food, with implications for relief payments. Finally, industries using agricultural raw materials, for example cotton textiles, would be faced with an unacceptable rise in costs, which would adversely affect investment decisions. It may be, therefore, that the economy benefited from the failure of agricultural policy to reach parity though in attempting to bring about both industrial and farm recovery any government would have been faced with a difficult economic balancing act. In this context it is worth noting that the processing tax introduced with the 1933 AAA was regressive, and helped to retard recovery. Although this tax had benefits as a lucrative revenue earner, it was passed on in higher prices for food and clothing, thus curbing the spending power of consumers, especially those on relatively low incomes.

A look at the index of prices received for farm products (Table 11.1) shows a clear upward movement from 1933 to 1937; 1938 and 1939 were relatively poor years, but by 1941 this index had marginally exceeded its 1937 level. As it was the aim of the administration to raise farm prices, do these figures mean that agricultural policies were an unqualified success? Unfortunately, no such simple deduction can be made. Price rises were supposed to result from a reduction in output brought about by the use of acreage allotments. If we examine the average acreage planted, between 1931 and 1933, for corn, cotton, wheat and tobacco, and compare these figures with those for 1940−2, we find that there was a reduction for each crop. It was most marked for cotton (38 per cent), but the other commodities also show clear, although less pronounced, declines. However, it is not certain that all of the acreage reduction was induced by New Deal policy, as recurring droughts led to reduced acreages for several crops. We can assume, though, that most of the reduction was due to the adoption of acreage allotments. Reduced acreage, unfortunately, did not result in reduced output. Corn, wheat and tobacco all had a higher average output in the years 1940−2, with acreage allotments, than they had between 1931−3 without them. On the other hand, the production of cotton had declined 17 per cent by 1940−2, a significant fall, even though this figure was much influenced by a bumper crop in 1931 and an exceptionally poor one in 1941. Agricultural output as a whole fell substantially in 1934, then recovered to its 1933 level in 1937 (Table 11.2).

Schultz (1945) rightly deduces that, with the exception of cotton, acreage allotments had no substantial price and income effect. He explains how the allotment scheme failed by observing that, when reducing acreage, the farmer was careful to remove his least fertile acres from planting. Each farmer had a vested interest in growing as much as possible on his reduced acreage, and could achieve this aim by becoming more productive. More fertilizer, better seeds, and, where possible, machines, were employed to this end. It is ironic that at a time when agricultural labour was cheap and in excess, the number of tractors and combines on American farms increased. Some operators even financed their purchases of equipment from the payments they received for acreage reduction, and others found that cheap credit lowered the cost of mechanisation relative to that of labour. A consequence of the shift from work animals to machines was the conversion of pasture to cropland and an increase in foodstuffs. Furthermore, by instructing the farmer in soil conserving techniques, the Department of Agriculture ensured that once the land recovered, yields of any basic crops planted would be good. In short, while acreage reduction can cut output for a few years, as long as farmers are free to produce what they want, output will recover. Under such circumstances,

Table 11.2 Farm Income and Output

Year	FARM INCOME ($ MILLION)						OUTPUT Index of gross farm output 1929=100
	'Realised gross farm income '(a)	Cash receipts from marketing			Direct govt payments	CCC loans made	
		Total	Crops	Livestock			
1929	13,938	11,312	5,130	6,182	—	—	100.0
1932	6,405	4,748	1,996	2,752	—	—	98.1
1933	7,107	5,332	2,486	2,846	131	—	100.2
1934	8,568	6,357	3,021	3,336	446	260	88.1
1935	9,696	7,120	2,977	4,143	573	311	95.2
1936	10,756	8,391	3,649	4,742	278	29	92.6
1937	11,367	8,864	3,924	4,940	336	1	102.4
1938	10,149	7,723	3,200	4,523	446	280	106.7
1939	10,585	7,872	3,336	4,536	753	457	109.8
1940	11,059	8,382	3,469	4,913	723	308	112.2
1941	13,851	11,111	4,619	6,492	544	453	120.4

Note: (a) 'Realised gross farm income' represents total cash farm income and includes government payment to farmers under the various New Deal farm programmes.

Sources: *Historical Statistics of US, Colonial Times to 1970*, 2 vols (Washington DC, 1975); J. Kendrick, *Productivity Trends in the US* (NBER, Princeton University Press, 1961), Table B-11.

the key factor influencing output is the weather. Acreage control, therefore, did not solve the problems of low earnings and unstable income in agriculture.

The domestic allotment programme was, of course, oriented to output, not to price, but the CCC, whose original function was to control fluctuations in price, came to discharge an additional price function. This was to maintain the price of some crops at levels that were higher than those established in the free market. The inevitable result of this policy, as output could not be controlled, was the growth of surpluses. A simple solution would have been to lower the loan rate, but this was difficult to do as the political clamour to keep the rate high, or indeed force it higher, was intense. These were the voices to which Roosevelt listened. The CCC, therefore, along with the drought, played an important role in raising and stabilising farm prices after 1934.

Price rises, however, were not without costs, as they affected exports of farm produce. Total exports rose from their 1932–3 trough until checked by the recession of 1937–8, though virtually all this increase came from a rise in non-agricultural sales. Raw cotton exports, so long dominant in overseas trade, fell away as prices rose; the same was true of wheat and corn exports, though the drought was instrumental in transforming the United States into a net importer of these commodities during the mid-1930s. Europe had always been the principal destination for US agricultural exports, but, during the 1930s, high tariff barriers, a shortage of dollars, relatively low national incomes, cheaper supplies, bilateral trade agreements, and moves towards self-sufficiency were especially damaging to American trade. Of major exports, only tobacco, the demand for which was relatively inelastic, remained stable. Agricultural exports, measured by value, had been declining absolutely and relatively for some time; the 1930s stagnation was not so out of line with past experience that it can be blamed entirely on New Deal policies. Indeed, looking at the inter-war years as a whole, apart from a brief rise in 1924 and 1925, the trend of US agricultural exports was downward. The export problem proved to be an intractable one during a decade in which international trade was stagnant. As a result, agricultural exports, which had been 47 per cent of total exports in the years 1922−4, fell to 25 per cent of the total figure during the years 1937−9 inclusive.

The attempts to encourage a revival in the agricultural sector during the New Deal were often misguided and sometimes contradictory. There were, of course, a number of benefits which led to an improvement in the quality of farm life: government intervention to reform farm credit was an obvious one, as was the provision of a minimum price for some crops. A wiser and more systematic use of water resources, for which the federal government was responsible, led to increased flood control, cheaper energy and the development of irrigation, all of which were substantial long-term gains. The attempts to improve farming techniques and to curb soil erosion had made some headway by 1940, but given the scale of the problem there was still a great deal to do. Moreover, drought was intermittent; when it disappeared, so did much of the incentive for change. Thanks to New Deal-inspired improvements, however, American farmers were able to increase output impressively during World War II.

The acreage allotment scheme, though it did not in the end fulfil its aim of reducing output, did give participating farmers a much needed cash injection, as did the CCC loans (see Table 11.2). There can be little doubt that these measures were instrumental not only in raising the morale of farmers, but also in attracting a considerable amount of political support for Roosevelt in rural areas. Farm income did rise steeply from the deep trough of 1932, but not to the level of 100 per cent parity which was the aim. As the farmer's disposable income rose, he and his family were able to pay their taxes and spend more on non-farm goods, which helped the economy as a whole to expand faster. Farmers are spenders as well as producers. The forces which increased farm income, however, had their origins in a wide variety of stimuli which included drought and non-farm recovery, as well as New Deal policies. That is not to say that government payment to farmers was unimportant, as a glance at Tables 11.1 and 11.2 will show. In 1939 government payments amounted to nearly 10 per cent of total farm income and were of especial importance to cotton, corn and wheat growers.

The farm strategy must be seen as part of a general package designed to bring about economic recovery. Roosevelt, campaigning in 1932, called farm relief 'the fundamental issue in this campaign'. Nevertheless, there can be little doubt that it was a mistake to assign to agriculture such a prominent role in the plan to revitalise the economy, because this sector was not powerful enough to discharge that function. There was a big difference between agriculture sharing in a general recovery, and leading it. In assessing the economic impact of the New Deal agricultural programmes, therefore, we can note a high level of criticism. In a lengthy analysis of the first AAA, published by the Brookings Institution (Nourse *et al.*, 1937) the authors delivered a split decision. Two of the three were not convinced that farm policy aided total recovery at all. The conclusion from Benedict's (1953) study is even more critical. Policies designed to increase food and raw material prices are not the best basis for economic recovery for a nation with a farm population of some 30 million, many of them marginal operators, out of a total population of approximately 130 million. As Romasco (1983) points out, however, for Roosevelt the farm problem was also a political problem, and the policies that have been analysed are best understood as responses to political rather than to purely economic or social pressures.

Many of the criticisms directed at New Deal farm policies stem from the fact that they were not designed to eradicate rural poverty. Many tenants and most farm labourers benefited little from the domestic allotment programmes, which were constructed to help commercial operators on relatively large holdings. Small-scale farmers found it much more difficult than large farmers to reduce acreage, and tenants were frequently denied the payments for acreage reduction which were pocketed by their landlords. Attempts to enable tenants to share in the financial rewards of the domestic allotment scheme were thwarted by landlords, who rid themselves of their renters and farmed their newly consolidated land using recently purchased machinery. As Fite (1984) has pointed out, New Deal programmes encouraged southern farmers to mechanise. Price supports provided a relatively stable income and cheap government credit made it advantageous for them to substitute capital for cheap local labour. As a result the demand for share-croppers and tenants declined, as land owners preferred wage labour. The number of share-croppers, both white and black, had increased during the 1920s but declined in the 1930s. The number of black share-croppers had fallen from the 1930 level of 393,000 to 299,000 by 1940; for whites the reduction was even greater, from 383,000 to 242,000. Mechanisation also meant fewer jobs for agricultural labourers.

We have seen that the benefits of the New Deal to farmers tended to favour owners of commercial enterprises rather than renters, croppers or small-scale operators. It is, however, essential to realise that without the support of the land-owners and commercial farmers no agricultural programme would have worked. The crux of the matter was that US agriculture was cursed with too many farms and too many people. Moreover, where farm income was lowest and farms least productive, the population was growing fastest: for example in the southern Appalachian mountains and in the cotton belt, where population was another surplus crop. Farms, with only one-quarter of the nation's population, had over one-third of the children but only one-tenth of the national income. Clearly, for a sustained increase in farm income to take place, there had to be a movement

Table 11.3 Farm Population and Migration, 1933–41 (000s)

	No. of persons on farms 1 January	Migration to farms	Migration from farms	Net migration from farms
1929	30,220	1,698	2,120	−422
1933	32,033	1,544	1,219	+325
1934	31,945	951	1,433	−482
1935	31,301	783	1,198	−415
1936	31,377	825	1,467	−642
1937	30,906	719	1,409	−690
1938	30,620	872	1,401	−529
1939	30,480	823	1,243	−420
1940	30,269	819	1,402	−583
1941	29,988	696	1,329	−633

Source: *Historical Statistics of US, Colonial Times to 1957* (Washington DC, 1961), Series C76–78.

of surplus rural population to the cities. Migration from farms to urban areas during the 1930s was not as high as it had been during the 1920s (Chapter 2). The result, as Table 11.3 shows, was that the farm population in 1940 was about the same as in 1929; migration had therefore rid rural America of its population increase, but had not made any significant inroad into the surplus. Given the relatively high levels of urban unemployment which existed as late as 1941, it is not surprising that the cities were not as powerful a magnet as they had been during the 1920s. In spite of low farm incomes farmers stayed put; indeed, at a time of desperately low farm prices in 1933, there was a net movement from urban areas towards farms. What governs the level of rural urban migration is not farm prices, nor income, but the availability of jobs off the farm. This is clearly illustrated by the migratory flows during World War II. In those years farm prosperity rose, but in spite of this change in fortune there was a massive movement of people away from farms to industrial jobs. Even though farm income rose faster than non-farm income, the differentials between them were so great that, especially for the marginal farmer, industrial wages were still much higher. If migration to cities could have proceeded more rapidly during the 1930s it would have had a significant effect upon rural poverty, but the failure of the economy to create more urban jobs held back this movement. This demonstrates, if nothing else does, that industrial progress is the key to agricultural good fortune and not, as the New Dealers believed, vice versa.

Any analysis of New Deal farm policies has to take into account the difficulties encountered by policy makers. Indeed, one might ask what alternatives were there to the strategy adopted? Public ownership of the agricultural sector was surely not feasible, and even if it had been could have offered no guarantee of success.

To leave the farmers at the mercy of free market forces would have led to even more anguish. The problems of agriculture have to be seen in the context of the economy as a whole. A too vigorous increase in farm prices would have had a deleterious effect upon urban consumers and upon business, which in the long run would have rebounded on the farmer. A policy of maintaining farm income directly, rather than by supporting prices, would have been expensive and would have aroused opposition not only from urban Americans but also from commercial farmers, who had no desire to see the marginal operator kept on the land.

On the other hand, agricultural policy often tried to pursue conflicting aims. One strand of the farm strategy desired, and achieved, a better use of key resources such as production, credit and marketing. Another strand sought, through government payments, a higher income for the farmer. Yet some of the steps taken, for example through soil conservation, to improve the allocation of resources, led to a higher agricultural output and, ultimately, to lower farm income. Conversely, policies implemented to achieve a higher farm income sometimes led to a misallocation of resources. Improving agricultural efficiency and giving the farmers a higher income were separate issues which were misguidedly treated as one (Schultz, 1945). An important device to raise farm income, the non-recourse loan, was potentially dangerous since the high level of stocks that this scheme encouraged could, in the future, depress agricultural income if, as with Hoover's Farm Board, they were placed on the market. The key to this problem was the failure to control output through acreage reduction. Domestic allotments had a further disadvantage in the eyes of those who wanted to help the poorest of those on the land: the farmers who found it most worthwhile to reduce acreage were not necessarily those on low incomes, hence the benefits from government payments were not evenly distributed. These benefits did, however, make the life of farmers producing 'basic' crops far more tolerable than would have been possible under Hoover's voluntarism.

Dispossessed tenants faced the dismal prospect of seasonal agricultural work, topped up by relief. Many of these homeless dispossessed took to the roads to join other migrants. Although they were romantically dubbed 'depression pioneers' by some New Dealers, they were transients, following the harvest or heading for cities or, like those immortalised in John Steinbeck's *Grapes of Wrath*, for California. The New Deal, however, was not responsible for all tenant displacement. Indeed, it could be argued that without governmental attempts to raise cotton prices particularly, the efflux would have been even more pronounced.

It is easy to be too critical of the New Deal's failure to make significant inroads into rural poverty. Little was known of the extent of destitution in the countryside until the investigations instigated, in many cases, by the New Dealers themselves. The magnitude of the problem was a surprise to those who fondly imagined that abject misery was the preserve of urban Americans. One of the first programmes to attack rural poverty came with the establishment in 1934, inside the FERA, of a Rural Rehabilitation Division. The following year its duties were taken over by the newly formed Resettlement Administration which combined a policy of rehabilitation with one of resettlement. To help with the former, needy families were given loans or grants to enable them to re-establish themselves as self-supporting farmers. The resettlement programme recognised that farm families living on submarginal land should be moved from it, and their abandoned plots converted to public parks or forests. Such families could then be relocated in new, planned settlements, 'greenbelt communities', which would attract other needy people, for example from mining areas. Industries would develop inside each of the new communities and those living there would enjoy the benefits of good, relatively cheap, housing and jobs. These radical resettlement programmes — an attempt to attack the causes of poverty — were few in number, and the scheme did not last long. In 1937 the Farm Security Administration replaced the RA, and its emphasis was on rehabilitation rather than resettlement. The problem with programmes to help poor farm families was that they had no effective political support, as those who might have gained from them were poorly organised. Those who opposed them, however, especially the organisations representing commercial farmers, were able to mount a vigorous opposition and ensure that the sum of money spent to assist marginal operators was minimal (Kirkendall, 1975; Saloutos, 1982). Moreover, the radical nature of the attempts at resettlement upset conservative, pro-agri-business forces and they were able to halt this modest attempt to alleviate rural poverty. Most important of all, the extent of the problem was so great that programmes such as those mentioned would not have had more than a marginal impact even if conservative agricultural opposition had not been present. Thus the New Dealers were unable to make any changes in the structure of agriculture, and the problem of farm poverty was still acute in 1941. The rural poor did benefit, of course, from the public works schemes established by the Public Works Administration (PWA), the Civilian Conservation Corps and the National Youth Administration, but not all those without work could find employment on these projects (Chapter 14).

All rural Americans, however, gained from the spread of electricity during the 1930s, which transformed life on many farms. Rural electrification had little appeal for private utility companies which found the dense urban market a far more profitable proposition. It was clear that the spread of low cost electric power to the countryside would only come if the federal government were to take the initiative. It did so, in 1935, with the establishment of the Rural Electrification Administration. By providing loans, especially to non-profit, rural co-operatives, electrification spread; less than 11 per cent of farms were electrified in 1935, but by 1940 the figure had risen to 25 per cent, and the expansion had only just begun. Not only were more rural Americans able to enjoy consumer durables such as irons, radios, washing machines, refrigerators and the like, but also many time-consuming farm chores were made more tolerable with the use of electric powered machinery and lighting. The advent of electricity on the farm was welcomed as enthusiastically as was the automobile during the 1920s, and there were few, if any, New Deal initiatives more popular than the REA.

Lest we are too dismissive of the New Deal's farm policy, it is worth noting that many of the problems which we have identified did not disappear after 1945. The surpluses generated by Commodity Credit Corporation loans were disturbingly high during the 1960s but were reduced by the extensive overseas aid programmes of that decade. During the early 1970s poor harvests, at a time when stocks had been lowered, combined with sales of grain to the Soviet Union, led to an increase in farm income and a rise in farm prices. By the early 1980s, however, surpluses appeared once more, especially in the Midwest, and distress sales of family farms again became common, while large agri-business enterprises survived. Some farmers claim that the problems facing many small operators in the mid-1980s are as acute as those of the 1930s. Government attempts, over half a century, to stabilise farm income have still not found the ideal solution. It is no surprise, therefore, that the New Dealers, in the space of a few years, did not produce a perfectly satisfactory farm package.

In spite of the formidable problems and the restraints, the new Dealers had moved towards a more effective farm policy by 1938. During this morale-boosting journey, cash payments to farmers and intervention to provide a solution to the debt crisis meant that families could stay on the land until non-farm jobs became available for them during World War II. The depression showed that the federal government had a continuing role to play in farm policy and the New Deal did not shirk this responsibility, though some might argue that having intervened, the government would never be able to deny farmers support in the future. While the results in terms of aiding economic recovery and helping the rural poor are open to criticism, given the complexity of the problems it is hard to envisage acceptable strategies that would have been more effective.

Bibliography

One of the best brief accounts of agriculture under the New Deal is by R.S. Kirkendall (1975) which can be supplemented by the more detailed work of M.R. Benedict. Regional studies are especially important in any analysis of Roosevelt's farm programmes. A.J. Badger's investigation of tobacco in North Carolina and that of G.C. Fite on the cotton South are both first-rate studies of their chosen area. Finally, the economic, political and social aspects of farm policy have been skilfully woven together by A.U. Romasco.

Badger, A.J. (1980) *Prosperity Road: The New Deal, Tobacco, and North Carolina*, University of North Carolina Press.

Baker, G.L., *et al.* (1963) *Century of Service: The First 100 Years of the United States Department of Agriculture*, US Dept. of Agriculture, Washington DC.

Benedict, M.R. (1953) *Farm Policies of the United States 1790–1950*, Twentieth-Century Fund, New York.

Brown, D.C. (1980) *Electricity for Rural America: The Fight for the REA*, Greenwood Press.

Conrad, D.E. (1965) *The Forgotten Farmers: The Story of Share Croppers in the New Deal*, University of Illinois Press.

Fite, G.C. (1954) *George N. Peck and the Fight for Farm Parity*, University of Oklahoma Press.

Fite, G.C. (1984) *Cotton Fields No More: Southern Agriculture, 1868–1980*, University Press of Kentucky.

Fligstein, N. (1981) *Going North: Migration of Blacks and Whites from the South, 1900–1950*, Academic Press.

Holley, D. (1975) *Uncle Sam's Farmers: The New Deal Communities in the Lower Mississippi Valley*, University of Illinois Press.

Johnson, E.L. (1940) 'Agricultural Credit', *Yearbook of Agriculture*, Dept of Agriculture, Washington DC.

Kirkendall, R.S. (1975) 'The New Deal and agriculture' in J. Braeman *et al.*, *The New Deal: The National Level*, Ohio State University Press.

Kirkendall, R.S. (1966) *Social Scientists and Farm Politics in the Age of Roosevelt*, University of Missouri Press.

Lary, H.B. (1943) *The United States in the World Economy*, US Dept of Commerce, Washington DC.

Lowitt, R. (1984) *The New Deal and the West*, Indiana University Press.

Mertz, P.E. (1978) *The New Deal and Southern Rural Poverty*, Louisiana State University Press.

Nourse, E.G. *et al.* (1937) *Three Years of the Agricultural Adjustment Administration*, Brookings Institution, Washington DC.

Perkins, V.L. (1969) *Crisis in Agriculture: the Agricultural Adjustment Administration and the New Deal*, University of California Press.

Richards, H.I. (1936) *Cotton and the AAA*, Brookings Institution, Washington DC.

Romasco, A.U. (1983) *The Politics of Recovery: Roosevelt's New Deal*, Oxford University Press.

Saloutos, T. (1982) *The American Farmer and the New Deal*, University of Iowa Press.

Saloutos, T. and Hicks, J.D. (1951) *Agricultural Discontent in the Middle West, 1900–1939*, University of Wisconsin Press.

Sanderson, D. (1972) *Research Memorandum in Rural Life in the Depression*, Ayer Publications. First published in 1937.

Schultz, T.W. (1945) *Agriculture in an Unstable Economy*, McGraw-Hill.

Shorer, J.C. (1965) *Cornbelt Rebellion: The Farmers Holiday Association*, University of Illinois Press.

Vance, R.B. (1971) *All These People: The Nation's Human Resources in the South*, Russell and Russell. First published in 1945.

Whatley, W.C. (1983) 'Labor for the picking: the New Deal in the South', *Journal of Economic History*, 43.

12

The New Deal and the
Search for Industrial Recovery

Although the central thrust of New Deal recovery policy emphasised the growth in agricultural income which would be brought about by the AAA, industry was not ignored. Of all the pressure groups which lobbied the President, the best organised was business (Himmelberg, 1976). After years of bankruptcies and losses, businessmen wanted a strategy which would ensure a rapid return to profitability. Trade associations, which had expanded during the 1920s, seemed to them an ideal base on which to programme an equation of output and demand. These associations had already brought about a considerable degree of inter-industry co-operation: financial and production information, for example, had been pooled, and jointly financed advertising campaigns run. An expansion of this co-operation, it was argued, could reduce the deflationary effects of competition.

Amongst those experts advising Roosevelt, a split emerged between those, such as Rexford Tugwell, who advocated economic planning on a national basis and others who felt that it should be confined to individual industries. Tugwell believed that if planning was to stabilise production, employment and prices, it had to embrace all industries: only then could the waste inherent in the capitalist system, and exposed by the depression, be eradicated. To many this smacked of excessive central control or even socialism. An emphasis on planning for individual industries seemed more in line with past experience; after all, such an approach was a normal part of the operations of large corporations. Moreover, the wartime experience of business and government, to which many now looked as a model, had shown the necessity for industrial planning. During the darkest years of the depression, planning had considerable intellectual appeal (Kidd, 1985) but it was seen by the majority as a device to smooth out the imperfections of capitalism, not to replace it.

Organised labour was willing to play a part with the government in the rejuvenation of the economy. Already woefully weak during the 1920s, it had been battered by the depression. Membership fell from 3.4 million in 1929 to under three million in 1933, as the bastions of unionism — coalmining, construction and transport — were especially hard hit. The loss of revenue placed an enormous strain on local unions, many of which were not noted for honesty or administrative efficiency. Most of the few strikes which did take place were aimed at preventing wage cuts or dismissals, but they achieved only limited success. The shock of the depression was sufficient incentive for the American Federation of Labor to cast off its traditional support for voluntarism and, in 1932, to approve the introduction of unemployment insurance. In addition, the AFL pressed the case for a shorter working week — 30 hours — with no reduction in pay. The election of 1932 was an occasion when the urban masses, employed and unemployed, voted for Roosevelt in overwhelming numbers. They looked to him for a solution to the problems of unemployment and relief. Organised labour found widespread support for the view that higher wages would create more demand in the economy and that a reduction in hours worked would create more jobs. Indeed, in Congress there was enthusiasm both for the introduction of legislation that would restrict the working week to 30 hours, and for relatively costly public works schemes.

The National Industrial Recovery Act: 1933–5

Roosevelt was opposed to the 30-hour bill and was not a supporter of extensive government work creation projects. He was determined that when a strategy for industrial recovery was formulated he, not Congress, would be in control. Any legislation, however, would have to reconcile the conflicts of the various interest groups. In order to achieve his objective a vague, all-embracing measure, the National Industrial Recovery Act (NIRA), which suspended the anti-trust laws for two years, was signed by the President on 16 June 1933. Rather like the AAA, the NIRA had something for everybody. Business pressure groups such as the Chamber of Commerce and the National Association of Manufacturers applauded the NIRA, as did many prominent captains of industry, believing that this new law would give them relief from the competitive system to which they paid lip service. However, while minimum prices were set under the Act, as a *quid pro quo*, business had to accept minimum wages and maximum hours for their employees and the right of labour to bargain collectively. Planners, at least those who supported the NIRA's application to individual industries, were pleased, believing that the increased purchasing power of labour and the redistribution of income which would result from the legislation would lead to rapid recovery, and public opinion was very favourable. However, although co-operative control of the economy by business, labour and government acting in consort was encouraged, the Act was based upon a number of political trade-offs, not upon a coherent economic strategy, other than one to raise prices. Most important for Roosevelt was that with the passing of the NIRA, the initiative for industrial recovery passed to him, for this law gave the President enormous discretionary powers.

The NIRA had two principal titles. The first created the National Recovery Administration (NRA) which was not located in the Department of Commerce, as some had expected, but was a new agency with General Hugh Johnson at its head. With the anti-trust laws suspended, the NRA encouraged committees representing management, the public and labour to draw up codes of fair competition for each industry, so that prices, output and employment could be planned. These groups, which represented a cross-section of the community, were intended to act as checks and balances to prevent the dominance of any sectional interest. Codes were drawn up under the supervision of a federal administrator and when formulated were sent to the President for his approval or rejection. If Roosevelt approved a code it became legally binding on all members of an industry, whether or not they had signed the NRA agreement.

The weakness in the tripartite structure lay with the representatives of labour and the consumers, both of whom were poorly organised. Trade associations took the lead in drawing up the codes, and the administration of each was undertaken by a committee comprising members of the industry concerned and an NRA official. The NRA administrators were forced to rely heavily on industry, partly because there were so many codes that an army of bureaucrats would have been required to oversee them; indeed, NRA officials were frequently drawn from the business community. A further problem was that data on each industry were scarce and often could only be supplied by companies themselves or by trade associations. Business, therefore, was in an extremely advantageous position (Chapter 10). The NRA relied on industry to ensure the smooth running of each code, assuming that labour would protest if abuses occurred.

Each code was supposed to ensure that unfair competition, for example price cutting and other trade practices now considered illicit, was stopped. It would be wrong to assume that all industries were united concerning what should take priority within the confines of each code. Some wanted to ensure that no manufacturers could sell goods below cost, others attached most importance to output control, while a further group demanded that any new investment should be limited. These, and other views, led to codes with diverse or even contradictory aims. Note the use of the adjective 'fair' in the codes; a comforting, soothing word but very difficult to define. It did, however, satisfy many doubters who had no wish to see competition abolished altogether. Instead, industry was to operate within a new set of rules which would ensure acceptable standards and still avoid the evils inherent in monopolistic practices. Competition was therefore permissible within the bounds of these 'Queensberry Rules'; bare knuckle conflict, however, would be a thing of the past.

Similarly, labour was rewarded with 'fair', that is, minimum, wages and 'fair', that is, maximum, hours of work. Furthermore, under Section 7a of the NRA, employees were given the right to organize and to bargain collectively through representatives of their own choosing; no worker was to be required to join a company union as a condition of employment. The sentiments expressed in Section 7a owed a great deal to the World War I War Labor Board and to the 1932

Norris—La Guardia Act. Industry disliked Section 7a and attempted to steer labour towards employee representation plans or company unions; in this it was relatively successful. A further important reform introduced by the codes was the elimination of child labour, which was welcomed both by those who had been campaigning against this abuse of the young for decades and by those who regarded juvenile workers as cheap competition for adults.

General Johnson, who had served previously as a liaison between the Army and the War Industries Board, was an energetic campaigner for the NRA. He persuaded, bullied or cajoled industries to establish a code authority and, as a sign of their support, to display the Blue Eagle which was the emblem of the NRA. His aim was that consumers should buy only those goods which sported a Blue Eagle emblem. The code-making machinery for entire industries was laborious and time-consuming. The President's Re-employment Act simplified matters by enabling individual businessmen to show support for the NRA by agreeing to abide by its key policies. Such was the pressure on firms to display the Blue Eagle that, by the spring of 1935, approximately 95 per cent of all industrial workers had been covered by 546 basic and 185 supplementary codes. By that time, however, many, including those who had been enthusiastic supporters of the original NIRA legislation, were convinced that the NRA was a dismal failure.

Industry and labour had hoped to benefit in different ways from the NRA. Business wanted stability, increased profits, a restriction on competition, and a halt to overproduction and to the downward spiral of wages and prices. Labour wanted growth in employment and a shift of income towards workers whose spending would promote recovery. Organised labour also hoped for increased membership. Higher wages would obviously raise business costs but the New Dealers hoped that industry would be able to absorb some of these costs and that, as a result, the increase in prices would not be as great as the increase in wages. In short, extra sales would lead to lower unit costs and eventually to more jobs and even more sales; if, however, prices rose in advance of wages, this optimistic scenario would be doomed. New Dealers recognised that this was a possibility, but they hoped that it would not become a reality. Indeed, the high wage philosophy had widespread support.

The government looked to the NRA to perform an important psychological function by assuring the public that the administration had an economic policy and that Washington and the White House had taken the initiative. It gave the business community, whose expectations were at an exceptionally low level, hope that the curse of low prices and low profits which they had endured for several years would be lifted. An increase in business optimism was an essential prerequisite for recovery. In a wider sense too, the NRA was intended to provide for a change in mood with its encouragement for consumers and producers to unite under the Blue Eagle banner.

Title II of the NIRA set up the Public Works Administration (PWA), the aim of which was to create government-funded jobs; $3.3 bn was provided for this purpose. Public works could attack unemployment directly and the wages paid would increase total purchasing power, to everyone's benefit. The PWA and the NRA should have been regarded as integral parts of the New Deal's recovery strategy. Unfortunately, however, these two agencies were kept separate and Harold Ickes became head of the PWA. In sharp contrast to Johnson, Ickes was extremely cautious. Scrupulously honest, he spent public money very slowly, at a time when speed and generosity were essential. Construction, the most depressed of all industries, needed a massive cash injection to finance many small projects; major public works, which Ickes felt gave best value for money, took time to plan before men could be put to work. Large numbers of jobs should have been created immediately but, while the NRA moved ahead with full speed, the PWA was disappointingly slow in discharging its important task. Roosevelt, however, made no attempt to urge Ickes to greater haste. The President, as we have observed, had only limited faith in the regenerative powers of public works. Nevertheless, although the PWA was regarded by Roosevelt as an emergency measure, it outlasted the NRA by several years.

The NRA was declared unconstitutional by the Supreme Court in May 1935. In announcing this decision the Justices did Roosevelt a great favour, because by that time it was evident that the NRA had not fulfilled the expectations of its proponents and had few remaining supporters. Certainly, the performance of the economy during the two years of the NRA was far from satisfactory. The vigorous recovery that had begun in March 1933, before the establishment of the NRA, had not been sustained. Indeed, industrial production, which rose rapidly after March as manufacturers anticipated price increases, declined from a summer peak. It was not until late 1934 that industrial output began the sustained increase which terminated in 1937 (Figure 12.1). Compared with the rapid growth in real output which followed the 1920–1 depression, the performance of the economy during the NRA period was very disappointing. Manufacturing employment also rose sharply in the spring of 1933 but by the end of the year progress had ground to a halt. From that time until May 1935 there was little reduction in the number of jobless and, as a result, unemployment amongst manufacturing workers was about 15 per cent above its 1929 level. Although there was expansion in the consumer goods sector, where automobiles and cotton goods performed well, construction and the capital goods industries failed to grow rapidly. During the NRA period, company wage bills rose faster than did employment, and those in full-time work saw their real incomes increase, as earnings rose faster than the cost of living. Unfortunately for the unemployed, as more work became available, those on short-time working increased their hours and, as a result, the number of new jobs was restricted. Furthermore, there is the possibility — which we will examine later — that the rise in wages acted as a barrier to job creation. In short, the NRA was more successful in raising prices and wages than it was in increasing output and employment.

Economic progress under the NRA was erratic, and certainly not sufficient to prevent those who always opposed it from gaining converts to their cause. Business, especially big business, had secured enormous advantages under the Act, as the code authorities were controlled by trade associations in which the

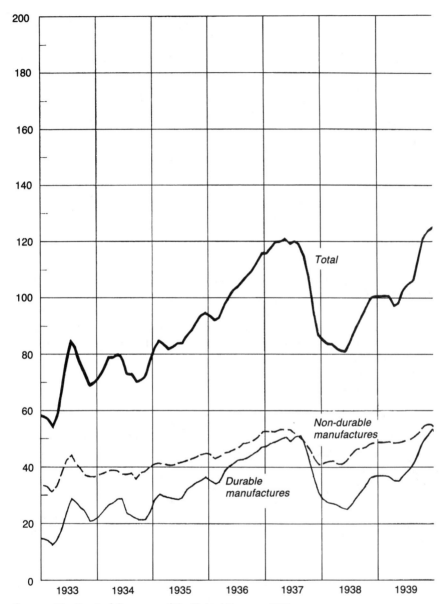

Source: The Board of Governors of the Federal Reserve, 1942.

Figure 12.1 Index of Industrial Production (1935−9 = 100)

politically powerful corporations were dominant. They faced little effective opposition from labour or consumer representatives (Bellush, 1975). Yet even business, by 1935, opposed the NRA. We have seen that in 1933 the view that competition was an obstacle to recovery was widely held. Once the atmosphere of crisis passed, and the promised recovery failed to materialise, the toleration of monopolistic practices and New Deal bureaucracy waned. The anti-monopoly tradition in the US was very powerful; it had been suppressed in 1933 because of the unusual conditions of that time but, when recovery was not sustained, it soon resurfaced, proclaiming the virtues of competition. As time went on business became convinced that the New Deal itself was a powerful deterrent to recovery and was apprehensive that its regulatory features, which had been accepted in an emergency, might become permanent. The devaluation of the dollar, the departure from the gold standard, concessions to organized labour and the work relief schemes were all attacked. The deficit and anything which would enlarge it, such as proposals for social insurance, was opposed on the grounds that it would lead to higher taxes, to uncontrollable inflation and to too much power for central government and for corrupt politicians. Business wanted a balanced budget but, of course, if Roosevelt had agreed to a significant reduction in public expenditure many of his New Deal programmes would have had to be reduced or abandoned.

The war model of recovery (outlined in Chapter 10), initially so attractive to both industry and government, was not a recipe for fighting the depression. War-time pressures in controlling a buoyant economy were not the same as those confronting a government trying to pull the economy out of a serious recession. Moreover, the NRA was particularly ill equipped to deal with the pressing problems facing industry in 1933. As Romasco observes, although the word recovery was used in the title of the NRA, its policy was not based on any carefully constructed theory. In spite of all the rhetoric, there was no overall plan for the economy other than inflation. As a result of the lack of clarity and direction, what emerged was a series of complex, disjointed, often contradictory initiatives. For example, industries using the same type of labour did not operate under the same wage and hour agreements, so that hours of work and minimum wages for truck drivers would be different if they transported coal, sand or gravel. Plants operating under several codes found themselves working with contradictory wage and hour agreements. As far as industry was concerned, the prime purpose of the codes was to raise prices. To hope that industry would not embark upon such a course was clearly unrealistic. To believe that industry, labour and government would form a partnership when industry was, relatively, so strong is a further indication that the broad sweep of NIRA objectives paid little heed to reality. By 1935, the NRA had few friends and there was widespread disillusionment with economic planning.

Labour proved no match for business because the latter controlled the administration of the codes (Bellush, 1975). Although Section 7a made the formation of trade unions easier (Roos, 1971), many companies challenged this part of the NRA. Henry Ford, for example, refused to co-operate with the NRA because he disliked its labour provisions. Other companies reactivated company unions or employee representation with such success that between 1933 and 1935 company unions grew faster than trade unions (Bernstein, 1969; Derber, 1964). Nevertheless, trade unions did grow, especially in centres such as bituminous coalmining and garment making, where there was a nucleus of committed organizers.

There was a new climate of enthusiasm amongst workers, whose expectations of advancing living standards and confidence in the expertise of their employers had been destroyed by the depression. Moreover, the public hostility towards unions, evident during the 1920s, now became muted and even changed to sympathy for workers who wanted more purchasing power and more control over their working conditions. The big advance in union membership, however, did not begin until 1935.

The complexities of the codes led to increasing frustration for both businessmen and labour. Wages in particular — where occupational, regional and, in the South, racial differentials existed — were an administrative minefield. High-wage companies encouraged legislation which raised the costs of their competitors; high-wage regions were anxious to see their differentials with low-wage areas narrowed. The New Dealers made the mistake, not confined to the NRA, of believing that if prices and wages rose, purchasing power would be boosted and so would the economy. In their analysis of the depression they confused cause and effect: low prices were the result of the depression, not its cause, and price increases were not necessary to rejuvenate the economy. Additional government spending, without all the regulations designed to foster inflation, would have increased aggregate demand and made a much more positive contribution to recovery.

In a particularly critical work, Weinstein (1980) has subjected the NRA to close analysis and has attempted to quantify its impact. He claims that the inflation induced by the codes had a harmful macro-economic impact, because the expansionary effect of a vigorous growth in the money supply between 1933 and 1935 was nullified by price increases. The monetary growth was not caused by the codes nor indeed was it the result of any deliberate policy. It stemmed, in the main, from a sizeable inflow of gold into the US, the reasons for which are given in Chapter 13. The codes, on the other hand, did raise prices by increasing wages and also by giving increased monopoly power to industry. During the NRA period, Weinstein calculates that the codes were responsible for an annual increase in wages of 26 per cent and an annual increase in prices of 14 per cent. The price rises were sufficient to ensure that the real money supply did not increase at all during these years; the stimulus to employment and output that should have sprung from an expanding money supply was therefore lost.

Labour thus experienced both gains and losses. In spite of heavy unemployment and inflation, to contemporaries a curious combination, real wages increased. The restriction on hours of work spread employment to more people and the imposition of minimum wages led to a narrowing of pay differentials between skilled and unskilled, between employees in high-pay and low-pay industries, and between men and women. There was, therefore, some redistribution of income towards the low-paid. Real wages, however, are of value only to the employed, and the high rates of pay, especially for unskilled workers, perhaps priced many of them out of jobs; employers were keen to economise on labour as its cost rose relatively steeply.

To eradicate unemployment a vigorous sustained recovery, such as that which occurred after 1920−1, was needed. The failure of the economy to grow rapidly from a similar low point in 1933 was not entirely due to NRA codes; other aspects of the New Deal were attacked by business and other commentators, if not with equal vehemence. The overall effect of the NRA, however, was to ensure that there were fewer jobs and a lower output in 1935 than one would have expected in the absence of codes.

The NRA experiment turned out to be confusing and misguided. As Hawley in his classic study of monopoly points out, New Deal policy towards business was economically illogical but politically popular. The American people wanted an economic system that was stable, provided full employment and gave the consumer a wide range of choice at competitive prices. But they were also suspicious of central direction, monopoly power and the eclipse of the small business. Although it was widely accepted in 1933 that competition was harmful, the public was happier with the concept of 'fair' competition than it would have been with monopoly. The NRA, therefore, was both against competition and for it. It was not an exercise in national planning but one of piecemeal arrangements where pressure groups, already powerful, tried to increase their control. Much of the contradiction and complexity of the NRA, however, sprang from the fact that Americans yearned for the simplicity of a bygone age when the 'little man' seemed dominant but, at the same time, wanted the benefits of big business. The imposition of monopoly and the total eradication of competition were politically unacceptable.

Once the Supreme Court had struck down this New Deal initiative for industrial recovery, Roosevelt faced the problem of what should replace the NRA. The second New Deal, which began in 1935, saw a re-emergence of faith in competition; trust busting was to replace planning. Business, of course, wanted to retain exemption from the anti-trust laws but jettison the rest of the NRA. However, the new advisors surrounding Roosevelt were advocates of market forces and as business became publicly disenchanted with the New Deal, the President moved to denounce the corporations as 'economic royalists'. Business hostility to practically all of the New Deal soured relationships with Roosevelt and ended the brief era of co-operation with government. The era of industrial planning, such as it was, also ended. When the AAA was declared unconstitutional there was a rush to produce new legislation for farmers; no similar attempt was made to replace the NRA.

The Supreme Court decision invalidating the NRA had removed Section 7a, leaving organised labour in an extremely vulnerable position. The second New Deal sought to limit the potential disadvantages of this new competitive society by social reform. One of the most striking of these reforms was the 1935 National Labor Relations Act (NLRA) or, as it was more popularly known, the Wagner Act. Roosevelt was little interested in labour issues and the initiative for this legislation was taken by Senator Robert Wagner of New York. Wagner had been disappointed by the ease with which industry had been able to thwart the spirit of Section 7a and he persuaded Senate to support legislation that was deliberately pro labour. His argument was that if legislation did not favour labour, when business resorted to the courts in its battles against unions, the courts would interpret even-handed legislation in a way that would favour employers (Fleming, 1957).

The Wagner Act, therefore, was not merely an extension of Section 7a. It sought, for example, to restrain employers from coercion but did not legislate against such action by workers; it also permitted the closed shop. With this legislation company unions were outlawed, representatives of the majority of the workforce were empowered to speak for them all and employers were obliged to bargain collectively with the chosen representatives of their workers. To supervise the working of the NLRA, and to interpret its provisions, a national Labor Relations Board (NLRB) was established. Most employers were horrified, but were confident that the NLRA would be declared unconstitutional. However, in 1937 the Supreme Court upheld the Act.

One surprising feature of the 1930s is the rapid growth of trade unions during a period of heavy unemployment. This expansion would not have been possible without pro-labour legislation. We should not ignore, however, in any study of labour's advance, the role of vigorous personalities such as John L. Lewis and Sidney Hillman, or the determination and militancy of the rank and file. In 1935 the American Federation of Labor (AFL) split and a number of unions left to form the Committee for Industrial Organization (CIO), whose aim was to unionise the mass-production industries, which had been ignored by the more craft-conscious AFL. The AFL responded to this challenge by stirring from its slumber and organising in hotels and restaurants and even by competing for members with the CIO in mass-production industries. Many bitter strikes were fought against employers in automobiles, rubber and steel (Edwards, 1981). Success was such that in 1940 union membership was around the nine million mark, a significant improvement on the three million of 1933. Some workers gained from the Fair Labor Standards Act (1938) which forbade the use of child labour in inter-state commerce and, in addition, imposed maximum hours and minimum wages which affected some 12 million workers.

The labour legislation here briefly outlined illustrates one aspect of the New Deal's fight against big business, as well as its concern with social reform. It is difficult to calculate the macro-economic effect of trade union expansion during the 1930s. There is no doubt, however, that business oppposed the Wagner Act so violently that investment decisions, and therefore job creation, might well have been adversely affected.

Wages and Unemployment

One interesting feature of the period of recovery after 1933 is the behaviour of wages. Table 12.1 shows how quickly hourly earnings in manufacturing industry rose during the first two years of the New Deal, when they were influenced by the NRA. However, even after the NRA was declared unconstitutional, hourly

Table 12.1 Earnings and Hours, 1929–41

Year	Manufacturing industry			Real earnings, non-farm employees (1914 dollars)	
	Average hourly earnings	Average weekly hours	Average weekly earnings	After deduction for unemployment	When employed
1929	$0.56	44.2	$24.76	$855	$898
1933	0.44	38.1	16.65	561	882
1934	0.53	34.6	18.20	592	860
1935	0.54	36.6	19.91	623	874
1936	0.55	39.2	21.56	675	888
1937	0.62	38.6	23.82	749	937
1938	0.62	35.6	22.07	680	927
1939	0.63	37.7	23.64	743	937
1940	0.66	38.1	24.96	798	998
1941	0.73	40.6	29.48	909	1,066

Source: Manufacturing hours and earnings: *Historical Statistics of US, Colonial Times to 1970*, 2 vols (Washington DC, 1975) Series D802, 803, 804; real earnings, non-farm employees: S. Lebergott, *Manpower in Economic Growth 1964*, Table A-17.

wage rates did not fall and by 1937 were in excess of 1929 levels. Moreover, rates were not depressed during the serious recession of 1937–8 and moved upwards as the economy recovered. This pattern was repeated in non-manufacturing industry. We can also note the reduction in the length of the working week which was, on average, substantially lower at the end of the decade than it had been in 1929. As a result, average weekly earnings did not reach pre-depression levels until 1940.

To concentrate upon weekly earnings, however, could be seriously misleading; we must also take into account the incidence of unemployment and any movements in the price level. The final two columns in Table 12.1 are an attempt to allow for changes in these variables. A cost of living index for urban dwellers would show that although prices rose from the very low levels reached in 1933, even at the end of the decade the cost of goods purchased by consumers was considerably below pre-depression levels. As a result, the real earnings of fully employed workers were, after 1937, higher than they had been in 1929. At the cyclical peak in 1937, however, some seven or eight million Americans were still unemployed. If allowances are made for this high figure, annual real earnings did not overtake 1929 levels until the war-induced increases of 1941. We can see that fully employed workers experienced rising living stadnards during the New Deal, which was an era of substantial increases in wages even though unemployment was high. The reasons for the rise in hourly earnings include the minimum rates established under the NRA, the growth of trade union powers and perhaps a belief, shared by some businessmen, that high wage rates were beneficial to the economy and should not be cut, even after the demise of the NRA. While many workers benefited from wage increases, however, it may be that these relatively high payments prevented more of the unemployed from being drawn into the workforce. At lower rates of pay, so this argument goes, additional labour might have been employed and, as a result, misery lessened for millions.

Wright (1986) points out that the effect of the NRA minimum wage policy was greatest in the South, the nation's low-wage region; its implementation led to the narrowing of differentials between the South and the rest of the country. Southern wages remained relatively high even after 1935, when they were influenced by a number of factors including the level of relief payments set by the Works Progress Administration. The most direct impact which the government had on southern wages, however, came with the passage of the Fair Labor Standards Act in 1938 which, to the joy of northern manufacturers, raised southern rates. Manufacturers in the South were unable to mount an effective political campaign against minimum wages which, in any case, attracted great support from those who thought they would benefit from them. Moreover, there was a general feeling that the region's wages were far too low for a decent basic standard of living and should be raised for that reason alone.

Minimum wages, however, had serious implications for southern labour, as they led to increased mechanisation and fewer jobs. Inevitably blacks suffered as the cost of unskilled workers was kept high, and a disproportionate number found themselves seeking relief. Wright emphasises the role of wage regulation as a root cause of the failure of industrial employment to show a net growth between 1929 and 1939.

The relationship between employment and wage rates is a tricky one. The manufacturer, when making investment decisions, has to consider not just the real wages of employees, but the cost of employing labour after allowing for any rise in producers' prices and any increase in output per person. As Figure 12.2 shows, most states suffered a loss of manufacturing jobs between 1929 and 1939, but amongst those which made gains were North Carolina, Georgia, Virginia and Tennessee and other border or southern states. We could agree with Wright that the expansion of industrial jobs in the South would have been greater without minimum wage legislation, but it is a mistake to view the region as stagnant during this period.

Table 12.2 illustrates the pattern of employment and unemployment during the depression decade. The increase which took place in the labour force is immediately noticeable. This expansion was not caused by immigration, which was extraordinarily low in the 1930s; it was a rise in the proportion of the native-born population of working age which provided the extra hands that the economy was unable to use. By 1937 there were practically as many Americans employed as there had been during 1929, when the unemployment rate was only 3.2 per cent. The recession of 1937−8 checked the rise in employment, but in 1940 there were

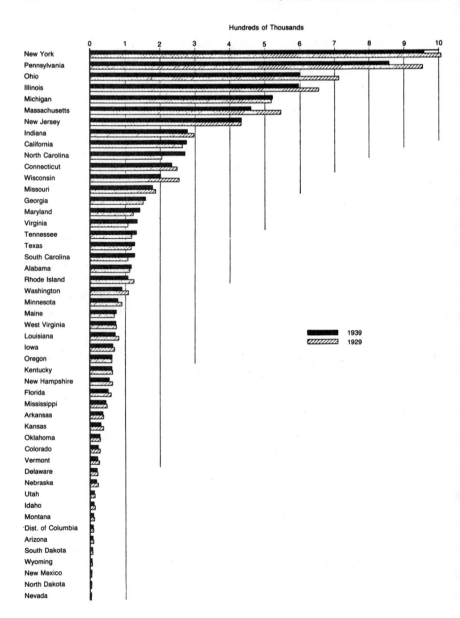

Source: US Census of Manufacturers, 1939.

Figure 12.2 Wage Earners (average for the year) Engaged in Manufacturing, by States, 1939 and 1929

Table 12.2 Employment and Unemployment, 1929–41

Year	Civilian labour force	IN EMPLOYMENT			UNEMPLOYMENT	
		Total (millions)	Farm (millions)	Non-farm (millions)	Lebergott (%)	Darby (%)
1929	47.7	46.2	10.5	35.7	3.2	3.2
1933	50.9	38.0	10.0	28.0	25.2	20.6
1934	51.7	40.3	10.0	30.3	22.0	16.0
1935	52.3	41.7	10.1	31.6	20.3	14.2
1936	53.0	44.0	10.1	33.9	17.0	10.0
1937	53.8	46.1	10.0	36.1	14.3	9.1
1938	54.5	44.1	9.8	34.3	19.1	12.5
1939	55.2	45.7	9.7	36.0	17.2	11.3
1940	55.6	47.5	9.5	38.0	14.6	9.5
1941	55.9	50.4	9.1	41.3	9.9	6.0

Source: Cols 1–5: *Historical Statistics of US, Colonial Times to 1970*, 2 vols (Washington DC, 1975), Series D4, 5, 6, 7, 9; M. Darby, 'Three and a half million US employees have been mislaid', *Journal of Political Economy*, 84 (1976).

two million more Americans working in the non-farm sector than in 1929. Unfortunately, over eight million Americans, or 14.6 per cent of the labour force, were still unemployed in that year. The problem after 1933 was that an insufficient number of jobs was created to provide work for a rapidly growing labour force; without these increasing numbers the problem of unemployment would not have been so acute. This observation, of course, would have been of little comfort to the millions who could not find the employment which they so desperately wanted.

Recently, Darby (1976) has examined the unemployment estimates for the 1930s. Many scholars have been perplexed by the failure of unemployment to fall close to its natural rate at a time of rapid increase in nominal wages. The natural rate of unemployment can be defined as that rate which, given the structure of the economy, cannot be reduced without serious inflation. Darby's estimates, shown in Table 12.2, are lower than Lebergott's because he classifies all workers on federal emergency relief projects as employed, not unemployed. Darby's calculations show that unemployment was coming down rapidly and that the natural rate, which he suggests was about 5 per cent, would have been reached in 1938 but for the recession of that year. This thesis, of course, depends not only on the acceptance of the natural rate hypothesis for the 1930s but also on the assertion that the millions on relief work could have obtained alternative regular employment. The Darby paper has been effectively attacked by Gordon (1976), and by Kesselman and Savin (1978). Among their criticisms is that the Lebergott estimates, from which Darby subtracts relief workers, actually understate the extent of unemployment. These calculations do not include the large numbers of part-time workers (nearly 10 per cent of the labour force in 1937); moreover, if one were to calculate unemployment as a percentage of non-farm employees (21.3 per cent in 1937) instead of the civilian labour force, as above, the Darby estimates would be much inflated. Although the Darby figures are more compatible with post-1945 calculations than the Lebergott series, the latter is preferable for the estimation of the number of jobs which the private sector needed to create in order to eliminate the need for New Deal work relief (Smiley, 1983).

Investment and the New Deal

The key to the elimination of unemployment during the 1930s was a rapid expansion in investment. Perhaps the New Deal's greatest failure lay in its inability to generate the revival in private investment that would have led to greater output and more jobs. The principal components of private investment are given in Table 12.3; they describe the familiar pattern of expansion to 1937, followed by rapid growth once recovery from that recession got underway. Even in 1937, however, total investment was significantly less than that achieved during the late 1920s and did not even reach 1929 levels in real terms until 1940. In particular, residential construction, so important in the recovery of the British and Swedish economies, remained depressed in spite of the very low rates of interest which prevailed. The decline in the rate of population growth, restricted immigration and migration and the reluctance to borrow for house purchase in spite of low prices, combined to depress the demand for housing. Thus construction, a major employer and consumer of raw materials, and a vital component of the engine of growth during the 1920s, lay dormant for much of the 1930s.

Table 12.3 Gross Private Domestic Investment, 1929–41 ($ b.)

Year	Gross private new construction	Producers' durable equipment	Total gross private domestic investment
1929	8.9	5.6	16.2
1933	1.5	1.5	1.4
1934	1.9	2.2	3.3
1935	2.4	2.9	6.4
1936	3.3	4.0	8.5
1937	4.4	4.9	11.8
1938	3.9	3.5	6.5
1939	4.9	4.0	9.3
1940	5.7	5.3	13.1
1941	6.9	6.6	17.9

Source: J.A. Swanson and J.H. Williamson. 'Estimates of national product and income for the United States economy', *Explorations in Economic History*, 10 (1972–3), Table A-2.

The recovery in producer durables, which include industrial machinery and office and transport equipment, was relatively more satisfactory. Even so, it was not until 1941 that the 1929 figure was surpassed. American industry did not invest, during the 1930s, at the same high rate as during the preceding decade. Indeed, the New Deal era saw a much greater expansion in consumption than in investment. One result of this relatively low rate of investment was that capital equipment was ageing rapidly. A survey taken in 1935 concluded that 65 per cent of the nation's metalworking equipment was over ten years old: in 1925 the figure had been 44 per cent and in 1930, 48 per cent. Ageing capital had an effect upon productivity, which grew only modestly during the 1930s. But when industrial production did rise sharply, for example in 1933 and 1936–7, sales failed to keep pace with production. The problem seemed to be one of demand for goods, not the supply of them.

Why was there a reluctance on the part of business to increase investment to the extent necessary for full employment levels of real income and output to be reached? This was a period when rates of interest were very low and when aggregate corporate profits rose steadily, although even in 1937 they were some 30 per cent lower than they had been during the late 1920s. The period 1933–7 was one of easy credit but, in spite of this, bank lending to business remained depressed. Moreover, the stock market, even with its new reforming regulations, was not able to regain the attraction it had once enjoyed, and new security issues were few. One cannot escape the conclusion that capital was not in short supply. Business was, however, reluctant to borrow in order to undertake long-term investment.

There is no doubt that business had been badly frightened by the liquidation of 1929–33 and lacked confidence in the future. The investment which had taken place during the late 1920s had been so extensive that many companies concluded that they could produce all that they could sell, with their existing capital equipment. Perhaps, too, there was a lack of investment opportunities; no equivalent emerged to the automobile industry, or utilities, or housing, which had played such a dominant role in the twenties boom. Alvin Hansen (1938), a prominent contemporary economist, raised the spectre of secular stagnation. He argued that in the late nineteenth century, demographic growth and the opening up of new territories, at home and overseas, played a vital part in economic expansion. The other important stimulus was technology. By the 1930s, however, population growth and territorial expansion had come to a halt, while technology had entered a partial eclipse, brought about by the maturity of the automobile and of the railroads. In any case, technology by itself could not make up for the serious retardation in the two other variables; therefore, as a result, investment was low and the economy was forced into stagnation. Hansen was right to identify declining population growth as a serious disincentive to investment, though his secular stagnation thesis rapidly became unacceptable when the economy expanded during and after World War II.

The atmosphere during the 1930s, therefore, was not conducive to long-term investment growth. The business community, however, would have added a further dimension to any debate on the problem, citing their most popular bogey, the New Deal. While Roosevelt's policies had initially attracted the enthusiasm of industry and had helped raise confidence from the very depths, disenchantment had quickly set in. The deficit, the most identifiable cost of the New Deal programme, was tolerated in the first few years of his administration but was progressively identified with unsound finance and all the evils that were supposed to flow from it. In addition, New Deal policy was seen by some as an undesirable shift of power to Washington, by others as an unacceptable growth in bureaucracy, and by all as a compromise with organised labour. Specific New Deal measures came under attack; the regulation of capital markets and the TVA are just two examples. Tax increases angered business and were seen as a logical result of the deficit. In 1935, for example, corporate income tax and excess profits tax were raised and the financing of the Social Security Act increased employers' tax burdens. In 1936, a tax on undistributed profits added to business anguish. All these factors, argued industrialists, helped to undermine business confidence and, therefore, to depress investment.

The inconsistency of the federal government was certainly not designed to overcome this problem. We have seen the New Deal move from support of planning and quasi-monopoly, between 1933 and 1935, to enthusiasm for competition and opposition to big business after that date. The 1933–5 period was, of course, one of compromise. As things turned out, there was no national planning, and the imposition of monopoly was tempered by the concept of 'fair competition'. The second New Deal era witnessed similar adjustments to take account of political pressure. For example, Congress passed the Robinson–Patman Act (1936) and the Miller–Tydings Act (1937), which attempted to protect small retail stores from their larger rivals. This was not consistent with a move towards more competition. Beginning in 1935, New Dealers, responding in kind to mounting corporate hostility, began a vociferous attack on 'big business', which was especially marked after the 1937–8 recession. The President needed a scapegoat for the 'Roosevelt depression', which had arrived as an unwelcome guest after four years of the New Deal, and the major corporations provided it. The Temporary National Economic Committee (TNEC) was set up to investigate and to expose the levels of monopoly price fixing which the New Dealers were convinced had led to the collapse of 1937–8. The shifts in government policy, and the bitterness of the exchanges between business and Roosevelt were not likely to encourage an expansion in investment.

The irony of the situation is that in its relationships with industry, the New Deal bark was always more pronounced than its bite. Moreover, as Hawley (1966) has shown, the anti-monopoly posture of the second New Deal was pursued with no more vigour than was the monopoly policy under the NRA. The reasons for this are clear. The public, whilst showing a distaste for big business, also recognised that its benefits could not be ignored: cheap automobiles, refrigerators and radios could not be manufactured in small workshops. Nowhere was this more clearly shown than in wartime, when big business was again embraced by the federal government. An order for one thousand aeroplanes or tanks cannot be given to one thousand small companies. What emerged from the New Deal was a policy towards business that was economically illogical but politically successful, because it reflected the ambivalence of the US population. People entertained romantic notions about the 'little man', but at the same time wanted the real benefits of big business. The rhetoric for and against monopoly failed to change the structure of American industry; business morale, on the other hand, was not helped in the long run by the words or the deeds. The business community, however, had no agreed strategy for ending the depression and their most popular prescription, the balanced budget, was a recipe for continuing economic misery, not vigorous economic expansion.

During the late 1920s, manufacturing industry had played a major role in the economy. Within this sector none was more dominant than the automobile industry, the performance of which illustrates some of the general observations made in this chapter. The motor vehicle industry recovered rapidly from the depths of the depression; the fall in the number of vehicles produced between 1929 and 1934 and their increasing age were powerful stimulants. By 1937 the average number of wage earners in the industry and its total wage bill had just exceeded the 1929 peak. Automobile producers had responded to the backlog of business and in four years had clawed back to pre-depression heights. Unfortunately, the 1937−8 recession was a shattering blow: sales fell by approximately 50 per cent and there were extensive lay-offs amongst the workforce.

Motor vehicle production, therefore, illustrates the savagery of the 1937−8 depression, which held back full recovery for several years. It shows also that because of, or despite, the New Deal a major manufacturing industry did achieve substantial growth in output and employment. In aggregate, the physical output of manufacturing industries was about the same in 1937 as it had been in 1929. Within this broad category, however, some industries grew and others contracted. The fastest growth of output in this period was experienced by refrigerators and rayon (over 200 per cent), followed by glass, tin cans, canned fruit and vegetables, washing machines and radios (40 to 60 per cent). Half of all manufacturing industries experienced a decline in output. Among the most seriously affected were locomotives, and the construction-related cement, planing mill products and lumber mill products. Rayon and refrigerators were more limited in potential growth than automobiles and could never have the same impact upon the rest of the economy (Fabricant, 1940).

The advances and declines in individual manufacturing industry had an effect upon the distribution of employment. Fabricant's estimates show that between 1929 and 1937 the declining industries lost 600,000 jobs, while those which prospered increased employment by 800,000, a slightly larger net gain than the figure shown in Table 12.4. Geographically, regions which saw the greatest increase in jobs were the southern and border states, and California. The old centres of manufacturing were less fortunate and were also hit far more seriously by the depression of 1937−8 (Figure 12.3).

The manufacturing sector could not, by itself, bring about full employment

Table 12.4 Distribution of Employed Labour Force (000s)

	Total	Mining	Construction	Manufacturing	Transport and public utilities	Wholesale and retail	Finance, real estate and insurance services	Total government
1929	31.3	1.10	1.50	10.7	3.9	6.1	1.5	3.4	3.1
1933	23.7	0.74	0.81	7.4	2.7	4.8	1.3	2.9	3.2
1934	26.0	0.88	0.86	8.1	2.8	5.3	1.3	3.1	3.5
1935	27.1	0.90	0.91	9.1	2.8	5.4	1.3	3.1	3.5
1936	29.1	0.94	1.10	9.8	3.0	5.8	1.4	3.3	3.7
1937	31.0	1.10	1.10	10.8	3.1	6.3	1.4	3.5	3.8
1938	29.2	0.90	1.10	9.4	2.9	6.2	1.4	3.5	3.9
1939	30.6	0.85	1.20	10.3	2.9	6.4	1.5	3.5	4.0
1940	32.4	0.93	1.30	11.0	3.0	6.8	1.5	3.7	4.2
1941	36.6	0.95	1.80	13.2	3.3	7.2	1.6	3.9	4.7

Source: *Historical Statistics of US, Colonial Times to 1970*, 2 vols (Washington DC, 1975), Series D127–39.

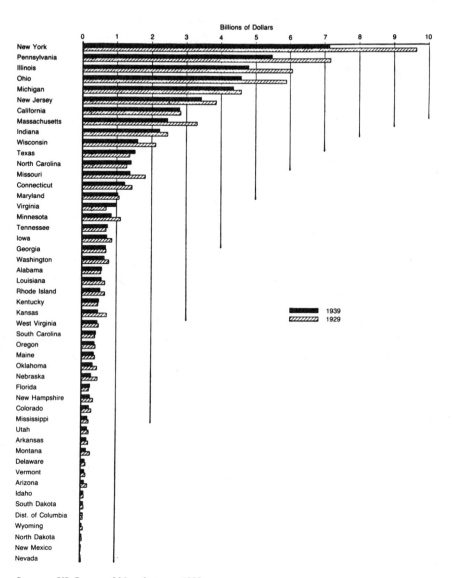

Source: US Census of Manufactures, 1939.

Figure 12.3   Value of Manufactured Products by States, 1939 and 1929

in the economy. During the 1920s we saw that the numbers of employed in manufacturing remained constant, while the expanding labour force found jobs elsewhere. Table 12.4 shows the distribution of the employed labour force during the 1930s. These figures refer only to paid employees in the non-farm sector and do not include proprietors, the self-employed or unpaid family workers. They are, therefore, not necessarily comparable with other labour force data. Nevertheless, it is apparent that there was very little increase in paid employment in the manufacturing sector between 1929 and 1937. Furthermore, transport and public utilities lost 800,000 jobs, construction 400,000 and finance, real estate and insurance 100,000. The service sector, which had been instrumental in creating jobs during the 1920s, offered little help to the unemployed during the 1930s. Government employment at federal, state and local level provided the biggest expansion in paid employment during the depression decade.

It must be concluded that New Deal policies directed towards industrial recovery were not a success. It is understandable that there was a demand for legislation, given the desperate circumstances of early 1933. It is natural, too, that the codes of the NRA should have been viewed as a solution to these ills. Business morale was at rock bottom and the NRA, by utilising existing trade associations, could rely on the support of many corporate leaders. The attraction of involving labour and consumers in co-operation with employers to work together towards a common goal was obvious. The psychology of federal intervention seemed sound. Moreover, the electorate wanted action — perhaps any action — to remedy the crisis. However, there was no unanimity amongst economists about what should be done and no theory which provided a clear escape route from the depression.

Economic policy, once chosen, waas difficult to implement because of imperfections in the available data and a lack of administrative experience at government level. The task of restoring the battered economy was formidable; the entire country was prostrate, not just a part of it. Although the NRA now seems a bizarre experiment, it was attractive to many contemporaries and not so far removed from the experience of business as to be denounced as dangerous radicalism.

The chief failing of the non-agricultural sector was its inability to raise investment to the level required for full employment. Part of the explanation for this failure lay in the conditions of the time: the real or imagined shortage of investment opportunities. Another part, of course, was the adverse influence of early New Deal programmes on output and prices and on the business psyche. Roosevelt and his advisors imagined that the economic problems facing industry were primarily structural — hence the emphasis on policies such as minimum wages, maximum hours, monopoly and, finally, competition. In other words, the New Dealers concentrated on micro-economic policy, as one might expect given the nature of economic theory at the time. But it was macro-economics, which focuses attention on the determination of total employment, output and the price level by positing the determination of national income through aggregate demand and aggregate supply, which was important. What was required was an increase in aggregate demand until full employment was achieved, not policies such as those of the NRA.

The US economy had a high degree of under-utilised capacity, and the idle resource which most effectively resisted New Deal assaults was unemployment. The most direct remedy was fiscal expansion: the use of a large budget deficit to bring about a sharp rise in aggregate demand which, in turn, would lead to a rapidly growing national income. Government spending, however, was not directed towards this desirable end.

Bibliography

The classic work on the New Deal and the structure of the economy is by E.W. Hawley, but both B. Bellush and R.F. Himmelberg have made important contributions to our understanding of the NRA experiment. I. Bernstein (1969) has produced a highly readable account of the volatile labour struggles of this era, and A.U. Romasco not only analyses Roosevelt's industrial strategy but also places it within the framework of the New Deal as a whole.

Bellush, B. (1975) *The Failure of the NRA*, W.W. Norton.
Bernstein, I. (1950) *The New Deal Collective Bargaining Policy*, University of California Press.
Bernstein, I. (1969) *Turbulent Years: A History of the American Worker, 1933–41*, Houghton Mifflin.
Brody, D. (1980) *Workers in Industrial America*, Oxford University Press.
Chandler, L.V. (1970) *America's Greatest Depression, 1929–1941*, Harper and Row.
Clawson, M. (1981) *New Deal Planning: The National Resources Planning Board*, Johns Hopkins University Press.
Collins, R. (1981) *The Business Response to Keynes, 1929–1964*, Columbia University Press.
Derber, M. (1975) 'The New Deal and Labor' in J. Braeman *et al.*, *The New Deal: The National Level*, Ohio State University Press.
Edwards, P.K. (1981) *Strikes in the United States, 1881–1974*, Oxford University Press.
Fabricant, S. (1940) *The Output of Manufacturing Industries, 1899–1937*, NBER, New York.
Fine, S. (1963) *The Automobile under the Blue Eagle*, University of Michigan Press.
Fleming, R.W. (1957) 'The significance of the Wagner Act', in M. Derber and E. Young (eds) *Labor and the New Deal*, University of Wisconsin Press.
Friedlander, P. (1975) *The Emergence of a UAW Local, 1936–39: A Study in Class and Culture*, University of Pittsburgh Press.
Galambos, L. (1966) *Competition and Cooperation*, Johns Hopkins University Press.
Galenson, W. (1960) *The CIO Challenge to the AFL: A History of the American Labor Movement, 1935–1941*, Harvard University Press.
Gordon, R.J. (1976) 'Recent developments in the theory of inflation and unemployment', *Journal of Monetary Economics*, 2.
Hansen, A. (1938) 'Economic progress and a declining population growth', *American Economic Review*, 29.
Hawley, E.W. (1966) *The New Deal and the Problem of Monopoly*, Princeton University Press.
Himmelberg, R.F. (1976) *The Origins of the National Recovery: Administration, Business, Government and the Trade Association Issue 1921–33*, Fordham University Press.
Johnson, J.P. (1979) *The Politics of Soft Coal: The Bituminous Industry from World War I Through the New Deal*, University of Illinois Press.
Kelly, A.H., Harrison, W.A. and Belz,H. (1983) *The American Constitution: Its Origins and Development*, 6th edn, W.W. Norton.
Kesselman, J.R. and Savin, N.E. (1978) 'Three-and-a-half million workers were never lost', *Economic Inquiry*, 16.

Kidd, S. (1985) 'National Planning' in S.W. Baskerville and R. Willett (eds) *Nothing Else to Fear: New Perspectives on America in the Thirties*, Manchester University Press.

Lewis, H.G. (1963) *Unionism and Relative Wage rates in the United States*, University of Chicago Press.

Lucas, R.E. and Rapping, L.A. (1972) 'Unemployment in the Great Depression: is there a full explanation?', *Journal of Political Economy*, 80.

Lyon, L.S. *et al.* (1935) *The National Recovery Administration: An Analysis and Appraisal*, Brooking Institution, Washington DC.

Marshall, F.R. (1967) *Labor in the South*, Harvard University Press.

McQuaid, K. (1982) *Big Business and Presidential Power: From FDR to Reagan*, Morrow.

Potter, J. (1974) *The American Economy between the World Wars*, Macmillan.

Romasco, A.U. (1983) *The Politics of Recovery*, Oxford University Press.

Roos, C.F. (1971) *NRA Economic Planning*, Da Capo Press. First published in 1937.

Smiley, G. (1983) 'Recent unemployment estimates for the 1920s and 1930s', *Journal of Economic History*, 43.

Weinstein, M.M. (1980) *Recovery and Redistribution under the NIRA*, North Holland Publishing Co.

Woytinksky, W.S. *et al.* (1953) *Employment and Wages in the United States*, Twentieth-Century Fund, New York.

Wright, G. (1986) *Old South, New South: Revolutions on the Southern Economy Since the Civil War*, Basic Books.

13

Banking, Money and the Deficit under the New Deal

When Roosevelt came to office the financial sector, paralysed with fear, had virtually ceased to function. Hoover held his succesor responsible for the chaos, which had progressively worsened during the 'lame duck' period as public fears about the policies of the new Democrat administration assumed paranoic proportions. However accurate Hoover was in apportioning blame, it was Roosevelt who had to face these unprecedented problems and take immediate action.

His first priority was to restore confidence in the ramshackle banking system. Other financial institutions, however, including the stock market, were in an almost equally parlous state; government intervention would be necessary before normal operations could be resumed. There was great public hostility towards the 'money changers', on which most politicians sought to capitalise. Investigation into banking and stock market operations revealed some dishonesty and frequent manipulation of the system by the rich and powerful (Pecora, 1939). It appeared that the small investor had suffered disproportionately while several large-scale speculators had successfully managed to inflate their gains and to minimise their losses. The result was a widespread demand for regulation to ensure less deviousness and greater stability in financial markets.

There was, too, the pressing problem of debt. Business debts had become an intolerable burden; private mortgages which could not be serviced affected both borrowers and lenders. Mortgage, life insurance, and investment companies were in deep distress. There was a demand for low-cost credit which the market could not provide. Most people, however, were convinced that the only short-term solution to the debt problem was inflation. Congress contained vociferous inflationists of every hue: more silver currency, more bank notes, indeed almost any device to raise prices to the levels which had prevailed during the late 1920s had its supporters, the chief exception being the use of extensive budgetary deficits. The demand for price increases was especially strong from the rural states, although how a general inflation would restore all prices to their pre-depression levels after their vastly differing falls, was never satisfactorily explained.

Serious inflationists could see that the rules imposed by the gold standard

217

restricted domestic policy. Noting the relative success of the British economy since the devaluation of sterling in September 1931, they called for a reduction in the external value of the dollar and the abandonment of the gold standard. Orthodoxy, however, was still strong, and a significant number of advisors close to the President hoped to persuade him to stay on gold. In the short term at least, Roosevelt felt that he had to satisfy those in the financially conservative camp. He had campaigned, in 1932, on a sound money platform and on many occasions had sworn his oath on the altar of the balanced budget. His aim was to bring about inflation and to finance his New Deal programme within such a framework — a totally unrealistic objective.

Shortly after his inauguration Roosevelt was able to delight the budget balancers with the Economy Act. This legislation, which came into effect on 30 March 1933, proposed not only severe cuts in the remuneration of federal employees but also a reduction in payments to veterans and their families. The economies would save $500 m.; it is illustrative of Roosevelt's powers of political persuasion that the bill was passed by a Congress bent on inflation. The President had made a genuflection towards orthodox finance: it was fortunate for the economy that his dedication to that cause was not greater.

Bank Stabilisation

The most pressing problem in March 1933 was presented by the banks; for the background to this crisis see Chapter 6. By the time of Roosevelt's inauguration the governors of most states had closed their banks, and in the remainder depositors faced restrictions on withdrawals. FDR's first presidential act was to close all the nation's banks from 6 March until 9 March, when new legislation aimed at solving the crisis would be presented to Congress. With this banking holiday in force, no bank could pay out to depositors or, indeed, transact any business without the permission of the Secretary of the Treasury. The Emergency Banking Act, which became law on 9 March, gave the President powers to supervise the reopening of the banks to ensure that depositors would be safeguarded. Banks could not be opened immediately, since they needed examination in order to assess their overall position; the banking holiday was therefore extended. Meanwhile, Congress amended the RFC Act to enable that agency to invest in the capital of commercial banks. It is important to recognise the crucial role played by the RFC in the regulation of America's distressed credit and banking system under the New Deal. The lending powers and scope for intervention of the RFC were considerably widened, enabling it to make a far greater impact than was possible under Hoover.

A hasty investigation of each bank was undertaken to see if it was sound enough to reopen. In this context the banks were divided into four categories. First, there were those, numbering about 50 per cent of the total, which were judged so secure that they could reopen immediately. Secondly, 25 per cent would be allowed to reopen once the banking holiday had been terminated, but depositors would face limitations on withdrawals. A third group contained those institutions which required help to reorganise before opening and finally, nearly 1,000 banks — roughly 5 per cent of the total — were liquidated.

Life without banking services was a unique experience for Americans. In the majority of states, bank holidays had been in force when Roosevelt became President; people had, therefore, been without banks for some time. Many faced acute problems because of the shortage of cash. Firms and municipalities printed scrip to pay their employees or even minted tokens for the same purpose. Individuals were forced to resort to barter, or to the use of Canadian dollars or Mexican pesos or any substitute for American currency. Many, of course, had hoards of cash which they had previously removed from the banking system and were therefore able to avoid such inconvenicnces (Ballantine, 1948; Manchester, 1960). A few small communities did not see the resumption of banking services until some time after the holiday ended: they had to wait until their vulnerable bank was declared safe. Nevertheless, the public bore the disruption with good heart, seeing that the benefits of the holiday far outweighed its cost.

On 12 March, Roosevelt, in the first of his 'fireside chats', spoke to the nation on the radio and assured the public that when the banks reopened they would be safe. On the following day, Federal Reserve banks reopened and with them sound commercial banks in the 12 Federal Reserve cities. The next day saw sound banks opening in the 250 cities which had clearing houses, followed by others as they were declared fit to resume business (Jones, 1951; Kennedy, 1973; Upham and Lamke, 1934). The exercise was a remarkable success. Depositors had listened to the President, believed him, and in large numbers returned their savings to the banking sector; this was in spite of the fact that the examination of each bank had been undertaken in haste and many assessments made on a rule of thumb basis.

The action taken under the Emergency Banking Act was not sufficient to guarantee long-term stability to a banking system which, because of its structure, was prone to instability. A more thorough reform came with the Glass—Steagall Banking Act of 16 June 1933. This legislation owed its existence to the Senate Committee on Banking and Currency and therefore cannot be regarded as a New Deal initiative. With its passage, all foreign transactions of the Federal Reserve System came under the control of the Federal Reserve Board. The growing power of the Reserve Board can be seen in its stipulation that member banks had to keep it informed about the character and amount of all loans and investments. The Act also forbade the payment of interest on demand (that is, current account) deposits by member banks, and the Reserve Board was given the power to set a maximum rate of interest that could be paid on time (that is, savings account) deposits. These measures reflected the view that the payment of competitive interest rates during the 1920s had forced many banks into dangerous speculation. Another supposed advantage of the ban on interest payment on demand deposits was that it might prevent the concentration in New York City of bank balances which could be used for security speculation and lead, instead, to a more equitable distribution of reserves. This regulation of interest payments was not a radical departure from past practice, as several states had imposed such a restriction on their banks during the 1920s.

During the 1920s also, many large commercial banks had moved into the security business and behaved rather like investment banks, underwriting and selling securities; investigations had revealed unethical practices by prominent bankers trading in this way. More important, however, was the acquisition of securities by banks, which were paid for by the use of deposit funds which were themselves payable on demand, a process fraught with danger. The Banking Act separated commercial from investment banking; commercial banks were henceforth forbidden to underwrite issues or deal in securities other than those issued by state or local governments.

The most important ingredient in the search for banking stability was the introduction of a deposit insurance scheme, which was incorporated in the Banking Act initially as a temporary measure. As we have seen, even in good times a unit banking system has to live with failures. A scheme which guarantees the safety of deposits must increase the public confidence and make failures less likely. In the past, several states had introduced deposit insurance schemes (White, 1981) but all had failed in the face of declining agricultural prices or deep depression. An alternative to some form of deposit insurance, in 1933, would have been a nationalised banking system or the imposition, from the centre, of widespread branch banking. Neither possibility was seriously pursued. The 1933 legislation did provide national banks with the same branching opportunities as state chartered banks, but this encouraged only a very slow growth of branching. The loyalty to unit banking was strong and the possibility of imposing a radical change upon the banking structure was remote. The compromise was deposit insurance; with it unit banking could survive (Golembe, 1960).

Deposit insurance owed little to the New Deal. Roosevelt was initially hostile to the idea, as were many of the bigger banks which resented the payment of relatively large sums to the insurance fund in order to protect their smaller, weaker brethren. Eventually, the federal government accepted the political pressure in favour of deposit insurance against bank failure, and a new agency, the Federal Deposit Insurance Corporation (FDIC), was established to administer the scheme: it has remained in operation to this day, and similar deposit institutions have risen for other types of financial intermediaries.

All the banks which were members of the Federal Reserve were required to join FDIC; others who applied could be admitted if, after an examination, the FDIC was satisfied that the bank was sound. The pressure on banks to join the scheme was strong and by the summer of 1934, some six months after commencement, about 97 per cent of all commercial branch deposits were covered by the FDIC. From this date there was a dramatic fall in bank failures, as is evident from Table 6.1.

The effect of deposit insurance on the commercial banking sector was far reaching. The regular inspection by the FDIC which was required for membership raised banking standards. Most early schemes had failed because too many participating banks were improperly run and potentially insolvent; now, however, with weaker institutions excluded, the insurance scheme was on firmer ground. Even bank liquidation could be handled smoothly with no loss to depositors, for under such circumstances, deposits were paid promptly by the FDIC. Where feasible, the Corporation always did its best to ensure that a distressed bank was merged with a sound bank. If a merger was not possible, rather than leave a district with no banking services, a new national bank was opened. Bank failure has a more dramatic effect upon the local economy than business failure and the institution of deposit insurance was essential in the struggle to minimise insolvency. Even in the 1980s the FDIC is still important to depositors. During 1984 the Corporation listed 540 problem banks; many were small institutions with weak agricultural loans but others were larger, nationally chartered banks. With over 40 bank failures per year during the mid-1980s many Americans were grateful for FDIC cover.

Although the Banking Act 1933 did not emerge from a New Deal initiative, its successor, the Banking Act 1935, was drafted on the President's orders. The Act was adopted after extensive Congressional hearings (H.M. Burns, 1974) and a driving force behind this regulation was Marriner Eccles, whom Roosevelt had appointed as governor of the Federal Reserve Board in 1934. The 1935 Act began by drawing up a permanent plan for deposit insurance and raised the limit for deposit cover from $2,500 to $5,000. The Federal Reserve Board was reconstituted as the Board of Governors of the Federal Reserve Systsem, with the majority of its members being political appointees. More important was the increase in the powers given to the Board. From 1935 the Board had mandatory authority to set the rediscount rate, to change member bank reserve requirements and to regulate loans on securities. The Federal Open Market Committee, which had been established in 1933, was scrapped and a new body, with the same name, but a different membership, replaced it. This Committee had complete control over open market operations for the entire banking system. No reserve bank could pursue an independent course of open market operations nor could it decline to obey policy instructions from the Committee. The power of the Federal Reserve System over monetary policy was centralised and strengthened, as was the power of government over the System. The 1935 Act did not, however, make membership of the Federal Reserve compulsory for all banks.

What were the effects of banking legislation during the New Deal period? The RFC played a crucial role in rescuing many banks and financial intermediaries. To some extent banking standards were raised by FDIC inspection and supervision or, to put this point another way, entry into banking became more difficult. Because of Federal Reserve controls on interest payment on deposits, competition between banks was restricted. Friedman has pointed out that, since the establishment of FDIC, a collapse of the US banking system, such as occurred between 1929 and 1933, and its attendant monetary contraction, is hard to visualise. In recent times, he argues, the danger has come instead from inflationary increases in the stock of money. Furthermore, because of these Acts, there was a shift in power from the regional Federal Reserve banks to the Board in

Washington DC which is illustrated by the establishment of the Open Market Committee in 1935. Friedman also perceives a shift in power from the Federal Reserve System to the Treasury Department: that is, a movement from the monetary to the fiscal authorities. It can be argued that in the longer term regulations such as those governing the payment of interest on deposits (Regulation Q) have weakened the banking sector. As market interest rates rose above the rates imposed by regulation, other financial institutions grew to fill the gap left by the limitations imposed on the banking system. There is now a strong movement to bring about deregulation and to restore competition in American banking. Americans should not forget, however, that it was regulation which gave banking much needed stability during the 1930s and thereafter.

Wall Street

One institution ripe for regulation in 1933 was the stock exchange. There was a popular belief that the crash of October 1929 was instrumental in starting the depression, and that much of the subsequent decline in security prices could be laid at the door of unscrupulous market operators. As the investigations into stock market practices led to sensational revelations, the press was able to feed on the moral indignation of the population. Misleading information in prospectuses, favoured buyers being given inside information, large holders of stock manipulating prices and prominent bankers buying stock with bank funds were some of the practices which raised the ire of even those who had never bought a share. The public supported moves to root out speculation but not to restrict reasonable investment. We have seen that some of the commercial banking legislation reflected this concern and was designed to make such speculation more difficult. As a first step, more openness and honesty were required from issuers of securities under the Truth-in-Securities Act. In 1934 the Securities Exchange Act created the Securities Exchange Commission (SEC), another New Deal regulatory agency, with Joseph P. Kennedy as its first chairman. Under this legislation, prior to a new issue being placed before the public, the SEC had to be satisfied that full and accurate information was available; in addition, regular information about each corporation had to be filed with the SEC prior to publication. This was an attempt to eradicate the most obvious dishonest practices and, given the determination of early chairmen, it was effective in so doing. The publicity given to insider trading scandals in 1986, however, shows that the possibility of malpractice still remains. A further check on speculation was the Federal Reserve Board's power to set margin requirements, that is, the amount of credit which can be extended on securities. These Fed regulations were used to limit the extension of credit for the buying and carrying of securities.

The New Deal reform of the securities industry aroused great hostility from the financial and business community. Nevertheless, although Roosevelt was quick to denounce the 'money changers', even if he had wanted to it would have been difficult to take draconian action and at the same time restore confidence in the market. The legislation which emerged was very limited, it did not lead to any dramatic organisational changes and the SEC was always strongly in favour of private business (Benston, 1975; Parrish, 1970). Benston even suggests that the disclosure of information forced upon corporations had no measurable positive effect and therefore must be considered irrelevant. Again we see that the colourful language which accompanied New Deal action was more flamboyant than the policies which were finally implemented. What is clear, however, is that in spite of the public cleansing of Wall Street, the stock market did not play a key role in the economy during the New Deal period. For example, total new security issues, which had reached $11.5 bn in 1929, rose to a New Deal peak of $6.2 bn in 1936. Table 13.1 shows not only how stock prices tumbled from the dizzy heights of 1929 but also how restrained was the recovery until 1937. The market was unable to capture the hearts and pockets of those Americans who had invested in it so heavily during the late 1920s.

Table 13.1 Index of Common Stock Prices (1935−9 = 100)

Year	Total	Industrial	Railroad	Public utility
1929	201	171	391	274
1932	51	42	70	92
1933	67	60	101	91
1934	77	73	110	81
1935	83	82	90	84
1936	118	115	137	122
1937	118	118	130	110
1938	88	90	70	86
1939	94	95	75	99
1940	88	88	71	96
1941	80	80	71	81

Source: Board of Governors of Federal Reserve System, *Banking and Monetary Statistics, 1914−1941*, Table 133, p. 479.

The Problem of Debt

Banking and stock exchange legislation was an important part of the New Deal reform programme. It did not, however, resolve some crucial financial issues which were pressing in 1933. One of these was the level of debt, which we have isolated as being a major factor contributing to the depression. When Roosevelt took office there were millions of debtors: individuals, farmers, companies, even states and local governments. They could not service loans which had been taken out when times were good and which increased, in real terms, with deflation.

Their problems did not make life easy for creditors, for the assets used as collateral in taking out loans had suffered a serious contraction in value. Take, for example, savings and loan associations which, on the eve of the depression, held nearly a quarter of all outstanding non-farm residential mortgages. As savers withdrew their funds, as banks holding the cash reserve of savings associations failed, and as mortgages were foreclosed, these institutions found themselves making a forced investment in property which was falling in value and virtually unsaleable. Thus, the non-bank institutions which provided a vital link between savers and borrowers needed stabilising (Krooss and Blyn, 1971).

The federal government performed a valuable service to agriculture in lessening the burden of farm debt; it seemed proper that the non-farm sector should also have its misery reduced. In particular, there was great resentment felt by those who had lost, or might lose, their homes because of their inability to make mortgage repayments. A newly created agency, the Home Owners Loan Corporation (HOLC) ensured that, between mid-1933 and mid-1936, when it ceased to function, one out of every five mortgaged dwellings received aid. The HOLC enabled mortgages to be rewritten so that they could be repaid over a long term at relatively low interest rates. This helped to pull the property market from the depths of depression and at the same time raised the morale of many property owners who had faced the possibility of eviction.

Another example of federal intervention in urban mortgage finance was provided by the Federal Home Loan Bank system, which was established in 1932. The 12 Federal Home Loan Banks lent to savings and loan associations, mutual savings banks and insurance companies in order to improve the provision of long-term loans for home ownership. The Federal Saving and Loan Insurance Corporation (FSLIC), established in 1934, helped protect depositors in these institutions in much the same way that the FDIC insured bank deposits. Finally, the Federal Housing Administration (FHA), created in 1934, gave insurance protection to private lending institutions which provided long-term mortgages. Thus the federal government, which before the depression did not play any role in mortgage finance, quickly assumed a commanding position under the New Deal. However, in spite of this federal help to both mortgage holders and to the suppliers of mortgage credit, the construction industry remained disappointingly sluggish during the 1930s, even though a high proportion of Americans lived in inadequate housing. Nevertheless, without such help, the housing market would have been in even deeper distress, as would many home owners and lending institutions.

In our analysis of business during the depression we stressed the role of investment and pointed out that its failure to expand held down output and employment. Table 13.2 charts the progress of private and public debt during the period 1929 to 1941. It shows clearly that aggregate private debt fell sharply to 1933 and from that point there was no marked increase until 1941. Of all the categories identified, only consumer debt rose to levels comparable with the 1920s. This is consistent with the observation made in the preceding chapter; the New Deal saw a rise in consumption expenditures but private capital expenditures lagged

Table 13.2 Net Public and Private Debt, by Major Sectors, 1929–41 (in billions of dollars, as of end of year)

Year	Total	Public			Private									
		Total	Federal	State and local	Total	Corporate			Individual and non-corporate					
						Total	Long-term	Short-term	Total	Farm		Non-farm mortgage	Other non-farm	
										Production	Mortgage		Commercial and financial	Consumer
1929	191.9	30.1	16.5	13.6	161.8	88.9	47.3	41.6	72.9	2.6	9.6	31.2	22.4	7.1
1930	192.3	31.2	16.5	14.7	161.1	89.3	51.1	38.2	71.8	2.4	9.4	32.0	21.6	6.4
1931	182.9	34.5	18.5	16.0	148.4	83.5	50.3	33.2	64.9	2.0	9.1	30.9	17.6	5.3
1932	175.0	37.9	21.3	16.6	137.1	80.0	49.2	30.8	57.1	1.6	8.5	29.0	14.0	4.0
1933	168.5	40.6	24.3	16.3	127.9	76.9	47.9	29.0	51.0	1.4	7.7	26.3	11.7	3.9
1934	171.6	46.3	30.4	15.9	125.3	75.5	44.5	30.9	49.8	1.3	7.6	25.5	11.2	4.2
1935	175.0	50.5	34.4	16.1	124.5	74.8	43.6	31.2	49.7	1.5	7.4	24.7	10.8	5.2
1936	180.6	53.9	37.7	16.2	126.7	76.1	42.5	33.5	50.6	1.4	7.2	24.4	11.2	6.4
1937	182.2	55.3	39.2	16.1	126.9	75.8	43.5	32.3	51.1	1.6	7.0	24.3	11.3	6.9
1938	179.9	56.6	40.5	16.1	123.3	73.3	44.8	28.5	50.0	2.2	6.8	24.5	10.1	6.4
1939	183.3	59.0	42.6	16.4	124.3	73.5	44.4	29.2	50.8	2.2	6.6	25.0	9.8	7.2
1940	189.8	61.2	44.8	16.4	128.6	75.6	43.7	31.9	53.0	2.6	6.5	26.1	9.5	8.3
1941	211.4	72.4	56.8	16.1	139.0	83.4	43.6	39.8	55.6	2.9	6.4	27.1	10.0	9.2

Source: *Historical Statistics of US, Colonial Times to 1970*, 2 vols (Washington DC, 1975), Series X393–409.

behind. Throughout this period interest rates were, by historical standards, exceptionally low, demonstrating that the supply of loanable funds was plentiful but the demand for them far from strong. In sharp contrast, we can note the rapid increase in federal government debt, a direct result of the budget deficit which was financed by borrowing. In other words, in order to fund the deficit the Treasury issued new government securities, the bulk of which were purchased by the commercial banking system and by non-bank institutions. The federal government's need for credit grew, while that of business, mortgage holders and agriculture shrank.

Monetary Policy

The New Deal reformed the American financial system but its monetary policy was, in the words of Friedman and Schwartz, 'hesitant and almost entirely passive'. As a result, monetary policy played only a minor role in influencing the economy during this period. Of course, by 1933, there was a great deal of disillusionment concerning the efficacy of monetary policy which had, in the eyes of contemporaries, failed to halt the disastrous collapse of 1929—33. Given these views, it is not surprising that few looked to an expansionary monetary policy as a route to prompt recovery. Moreover, considering the conditions of the time — very low interest rates and timidity on the part of both borrowers and lenders — even a more vigorous monetary policy would have had only a limited impact upon the economy during the early years of the New Deal. Fiscal policy, energetically pursued, could have resolved the problem of under-utilised capital and labour resources in the 1930s more rapidly than monetary policy. Monetary policy can, however, play an important supportive role to fiscal policy by keeping interest rates low and thus enabling the deficit to be financed cheaply.

New Deal monetary policy brought about great changes in the monetary standard of the United States. The aims were simple: to raise prices to pre-depression levels and to maintain them once they had risen. It was felt that the vast majority of the population would gain from inflation, especially farmers and any others in debt. The means to this end can be seen in the government's gold policies. Early in the New Deal, gold holdings were nationalised and the export of gold and gold certificates was forbidden, ending the international convertibility of the dollar into gold. Gold clauses in contracts were cancelled and the use of gold coins and gold hoarding was forbidden.

Meanwhile, Roosevelt was given, by the Thomas Amendment which was attached to the AAA, extraordinary powers to inflate the economy. He could ask the Federal Reserve Board to purchase up to $3 bn in government securities in order to increase credit through open market operations and could also authorise the Treasury to issue $3 bn in banknotes (greenbacks). Further powers enabled him to reduce the gold content of the dollar by as much as 50 per cent, to establish bi-metalism and to accept payment in silver from foreign debtors. The President was not obliged to use all or any of these devices; indeed, he never did issue greenbacks. As Chandler (1970) observes, however, the Thomas Amendment showed the authority of the government over the Federal Reserve. If, for example, the Fed refused to buy securities, the President could easily expand credit by using the Thomas Amendment and the Fed was very conscious of the inflationary forces which he could unleash.

Monetary actions, however, were dominated by gold and silver. Roosevelt was intellectually imprisoned by the ideas of an economist, Professor George F. Warren, who claimed, erroneously, that if the price of gold rose, then domestic price levels would increase, almost immediately, by the same amount. Accordingly, the government set about raising the price of gold by instructing the RFC to purchase increasing amounts at high prices. The dollar price of gold was steadily increased or, to put this another way, there was a decline in the gold value of the dollar. With the Gold Reserve Act of January 1934, Roosevelt fixed the price of gold at $35 an ounce, which meant that the gold value of the new dollar was approximately 59 per cent of the old. There is no evidence that the new price of gold had been arrived at by any careful analysis but the Gold Reserve Act did give the President the authority to change that price in the future if he wished. The revaluation of the nation's gold stock resulted in an enormous profit which went to the Treasury and was used to found an Exchange Stabilization Fund.

Alterations in the price of gold obviously had implications for the foreign exchange value of the dollar. In March 1933 the dollar was clearly out of line with those many currencies that had been devalued during the depression. As a result, American exports were relatively expensive in foreign markets and imports relatively cheap. Devaluation of the dollar would increase demands for exports, helping among others, the farmer, and at the same time would encourage the production of import substitutes. This, of course, implies that no retaliatory action would be taken against the United States which was, in itself, an argument for moderating US devaluation. New Dealers saw an additional advantage in raising the dollar price of gold, since the value of the dollar in terms of foreign currencies would automatically fall. Roosevelt was a keen advocate of devaluation and the decline in the value of the dollar on the foreign exchanges, which began as soon as he came to power, accelerated with the gold purchase programme. However, we should note that Britain was forced off gold in 1931 because her reserves were insufficient to combat the heavy speculation against sterling. The US, in sharp contrast, had a large gold reserve and could have withstood any speculative pressure on the dollar for some time. Devaluation not only helped American exports but it was essential too because New Deal measures to raise domestic prices would have made exports even more uncompetitive if the exchange rate had remained unchanged.

Since the United States had embarked upon a course of currency depreciation as a means of raising prices, Roosevelt had no option but to tell the World Monetary and Economic Conference meeting in London in June 1933, that the US could not co-operate with other nations in an attempt at foreign exchange stabilisation. The President was correct in his judgement that domestic recovery should have priority. In any case, the possibility that the participating nations would have been able to reach agreement on a programme for exchange stabilisation, when so many had differing views, was remote. Nevertheless, the devaluation of the dollar and the gold purchases placed enormous pressure upon those countries, such as France and Belgium, which had never devalued their currencies and had stayed loyal to the gold standard. Their economic situation grew more parlous and eventually they too were obliged to devalue.

A further result of the gold strategy was a massive inflow of bullion into the United States. The value of the nation's gold stock was $8.2 bn in 1934, but by 1941 it had risen to $22.7 bn; the vast bulk of this growth came from an increase in imports. International political and economic uncertainty, especially in Europe, plus a growing confidence in the dollar, persuaded foreigners that it was safer to send their gold to the US than to keep it in their own countries.

Not only did the New Deal embark on a gold purchase policy, it also attempted a similar exercise for silver. By 1932 silver prices had fallen to extremely low levels and the silver mining states were anxious to see this trend reversed. Many farmers and senators from the southern and, especially, western states wanted inflation and supported moves to introduce silver coinage in order to generate price rises. Roosevelt yielded to these pressures, and in late 1933, the government began to purchase the entire domestic production of silver at an artificially high price. In June 1934 the Silver Purchase Act stipulated that the treasury would buy silver at home and abroad until the monetary value of silver stocks equalled one third of the value of gold stocks, or until the market price of silver rose to the level of its monetary value. The silver purchase programme, however, had litte effect domestically other than as a massive subsidy to the silver industry (Brennan, 1969). Abroad, it had a severe deflationary impact on nations, such as China, whose monetary system was based upon a silver standard, just as the gold policy had put similar pressure on gold standard countries.

The period after 1933 stands in marked constrast to the 1920s when we consider capital flows. During the 1920s, funds had left the US for overseas destinations, attracted by relatively high interest rates. After 1933 there were very few new overseas issues and, in spite of relatively low interest rates, funds flowed into the United States. It is worth noting that the dollar had been devalued in 1933 even though America's balance of payments was in surplus; that surplus remained strong throughout the 1930s. Fear of war and currency depreciation abroad were powerful forces: low interest rates, labour unrest, persistent deficits, and the pursuit of inflationary policies did not dent the growing world-wide confidence in the dollar.

Nor were American citizens to be persuaded to lend overseas. The Johnson Act (1934) had outlawed lending to those countries which had defaulted on American loans, and since this included virtually all 1920s borrowers, outlets were limited. It was not, however, this legislation which reduced American capital flows to a trickle. It was the losses incurred after 1930, the fear that repayment of loans would be difficult for many borrowers, and general uncertainty, which persuaded US citizens to keep their savings at home. Unfortunately, the refusal of Americans to lend long-term funds abroad, while understandable, had a serious retarding effect upon international economic recovery. At the same time, it is clear that US domestic economic policies under Roosevelt were not in any way hindered by balance of payment constraints nor by pressure on the dollar, as they had been during Hoover's presidency.

We have already characterised New Deal monetary policy between 1933 and 1937 as passive. It is true that during these years the money stock rose by about 50 per cent, an extremely rapid increase, but this growth was brought about by the gold influx, not by vigorous open market action. Nor were relatively low interest rates a result of Federal Reserve policies. Indeed, although the Fed thought that it was pursuing an easy money policy because its discount rate was low by historical standards, the rate was actually high in relation to prevailing short-term market rates which were, of course, extraordinarily low. As a result, banks found borrowing from the Federal Reserve relatively expensive and, therefore, had an incentive to accumulate reserves. In fact, the growth in bank reserves between 1934 and 1937 — a result of the gold inflow and the silver purchase programme — was rapid; reserves were soon far in excess of legal requirements. The banks could have used these funds to expand loans but the demand for funds was relatively low, they were reluctant to undertake risky or illiquid lending, and, furthermore, they also welcomed the security which their reserves gave against deposit withdrawals. The banking system, therefore, did not increase the money supply or credit to the extent that its reserve position entitled it to.

Nevertheless, by 1936, the Federal Reserve was disturbed by the inflationary potential that it perceived in the excess reserves. As the economy had been growing for four years and as wholesale prices had risen during this period by 50 per cent, the Fed decided that the time was ripe for intervention to prevent any possible future uncontrollable expansion of credit. The Fed did not intend to bring the current economic expansion to a halt but, tragically, its actions added to the contractionary impact of the administration's deflationary fiscal policy.

The Federal Reserve chose to remove the inflationary threat by raising reserve requirements, which it did in two stages, beginning in August 1936. Simultaneously, the Treasury began to sterilise increases in the gold stock. In other words, the growing stock of gold was prevented from increasing bank reserves, an action which reduced potential credit expansion. The aim was merely to shrink the excess reserves, but bank credit and the money supply faltered and began to decline, while interest rates started to increase. Banks reacted to the assault on their reserve position by curtailing lending and selling investments in order to maintain liquidity. While monetary policy became less expansive, so too did fiscal policy. Tax revenues increased and federal expenditure was cut in an attempt to balance the budget. Fiscal and monetary retrenchment together were responsible for the short but very sharp recession of 1937—8, which reduced industrial production by over 30 per cent and added more than 2.5 million to the already high unemployment total. The 1937−8 contraction was a self-inflicted wound which acted as a severe check to the economic recovery. In the spring of 1938, however, expansive fiscal and monetary measures helped pull the economy up so that it could take advantage of the growing demands brought about by the impending war.

Monetary policy did not generate the recovery in the American economy after 1933. In part this was because a vigorous monetary policy was never attempted, in part because monetary policy, by itself, was incapable of achieving full employment. In spite of all the inflationary powers given to Roosevelt, the price level in 1941 was still below that of the late 1920s. Moreover, precisely how much of the post-1933 inflation was due to monetary policy is difficult to calculate, since so many of the various New Deal programmes were designed to raise prices. It appears that Roosevelt was prepared to embark upon inflationary policies but was not able to embrace them with sustained enthusiasm. The price increases after 1933 were sufficient to remove much of the political pressure imposed upon him by inflationists but stopped short of bringing new troubles from those who feared the onset of hyper-inflation.

Fiscal Policy

Table 13.3, which illustrates the state of the federal budget during the 1930s, shows that New Deal expenditure rose until 1936, then dropped sharply to a low point in 1938 before rising again. As taxation increased, federal revenue also rose, reaching a peak in 1938 but falling in 1939. Expenditures were always in

Table 13.3 The Federal Budget, 1931−39

Year	Receipts	Expenditures ($ billions)	Deficit	Deficit as % of GNP	Deficit as % of federal expenditures
1931	3.1	3.6	−0.5	0.6	13.8
1932	1.9	4.7	−2.8	4.8	59.6
1933	2.0	4.6	−2.6	4.6	56.5
1934	3.0	6.6	−3.6	5.5	54.5
1935	3.7	6.5	−2.8	3.7	43.0
1936	4.0	8.4	−4.4	5.3	52.4
1937	5.0	7.7	−2.7	3.0	35.1
1938	5.6	6.8	−1.2	1.4	17.6
1939	5.0	8.8	−3.8	4.2	43.2

Source: *Historical Statistics of US, Colonial Times to 1970*, 2 vols (Washington DC, 1975), Series Y335−7.

excess of receipts, which aroused great controversy. The business community, especially, was much exercised by the deficit, which the government was unable or unwilling to eradicate. At a time of mass unemployment, created by a lack of aggregate demand, we would expect the government to have stimulated demand by running a deficit; this could have been achieved by a combination of tax reduction and increased expenditure. On superficial examination, therefore, budgetary policy seems to have been sound. However, as unemployment was still high in 1940 and a serious recession jolted the economy in 1937–8, fiscal policy could not be counted an unqualified success. What was the rationale behind the persistent deficits and large tax increases at a time of heavy unemployment?

In spite of the deficits, Roosevelt must be seen as a fiscal conservative. He believed that the economic problems which confronted him were structural, and could only be solved by policies which, for example, made the distribution of income more equitable or implemented planning agreements. Governmental spending could not be used as a direct attack upon the structural problem nor could it do more than create a few additional jobs in the short run. We have already seen the President's lack of faith in large-scale public works projects. He did not believe, at least until 1938, that the deficit could be used as an economic tool in the struggle to attain full employment. If he had seen the deficit as the key to economic revival between 1933 and 1936, Roosevelt would not have made such efforts to erase it. The deficit, therefore, was not planned; it was simply a result of the cost of the New Deal programmes and the payment of veterans' bonuses, to which Roosevelt objected, being in excess of revenue. Indeed, because full employment did not materialise, expenditure on relief remained higher than he had anticipated and the balanced budget that he desired eluded him. On the other hand, as much as he disliked the deficit, the President was not willing to scrap large parts of his cherished New Deal so that expenditure and revenue could be brought into balance.

If the size of the deficit did not govern the level of expenditure and receipts, then what did? As Leff (1984) shows, Roosevelt had two tax systems: one to raise revenue; the other a symbolic showpiece used to satisfy the President's ideology and to flail those who roused his ire. Taxation, especially between 1933 and 1935, hit the poor disproportionately hard, as indirect taxes on consumables such as tobacco and alcohol were increased. This is not consistent with the declared policy of countering a lack of consumption in the economy. From 1935, Roosevelt, having abandoned his attempt at co-operation with business, embarked upon a 'soak the rich' programme in which achievement fell a long way short of rhetoric. As an exercise in income redistribution it was not a success but the new taxes and the fierce language frightened the business community, with adverse effects upon investment. The ratio of federal taxes to GNP rose from 3.5 per cent in 1929 to 7.5 per cent in 1937; the increased taxes reduced both disposable income and the expansionary effect of fiscal policy. Taxation policy had little to do with recovery — indeed, it could well have retarded it.

New Deal expenditure, too, owed much to the political pressure which competing groups could exert. The level and the direction of funding was not dictated by the aim of maximising economic performance or even equitably distributing relief. Instead it was a response to widespread concern about the conservation of natural resources, a desire to alleviate suffering and to influence voting both in Senate and in the electorate at large. Perhaps the reason why the South, the poorest region in the US, received relatively little in per capita expenditure compared with some of the more affluent western states was that the South was firmly in the Democrat camp; other states needed convincing of the merits of the New Deal (Reading, 1973; Wright, 1974). We should remember, however, that both the per capita cost of living and income in the South was low. Moreover, blacks in the South who did benefit from the New Deal could not respond by voting, as they were not enfranchised.

After the 1936 election, Roosevelt, responding to widespread criticism of the deficit, cut expenditure and raised taxes; new taxes to finance the social security programme were especially regressive. This fiscal retrenchment coincided with growing monetary stringency: the result was the 1937−8 'Roosevelt depression' which caught everyone by surprise. Business felt that the New Deal had brought about the slump by excessive taxation; the remedy, according to business leaders, was lower taxes which would lead to economic growth and, ultimately, more tax revenue. Like all political leaders through the ages, Roosevelt received conflicting advice as the depression worsened. The suggestions included a move to a balanced budget at all costs, as deficits had not worked; a return to NRA type planning; a vigorous attack upon monopolies; full co-operation with business. Finally, one group urged greater government spending on the grounds that the deficit had been too small (Stein, 1969). As the President pondered the options, he received several messages from Keynes urging him to undertake more spending. By the spring of 1938 Roosevelt had decided that recovery from the recession could only be achieved by the implementation of a new spending programme and a reversal of restrictive Treasury and Federal Reserve monetary policy.

Why Roosevelt chose the spending option is not clear. It is true that by 1938 several advisors who could be called Keynesians, or who had independently reached a similar position on the efficacy of government spending, had the President's ear. Moreover, with the publication of his *General Theory of Employment Interest and Money* in 1936, Keynes had provided an intellectual justification for deficits, though not one which immediately convinced all economists. It is more likely, however, that FDR was swayed by political considerations: the impossibility of balancing the budget while at the same time preserving the New Deal, which had become so important, politically, at the state and local levels. A bureaucracy had grown which depended for its existence on federal expenditure; many sectors of the economy still clamoured for, and needed, state aid. Since the political and administrative machinery now existed to absorb large increases in government spending, it seemed practical to use it. Public expenditure from 1938 can be described as Keynesian, albeit of a limited nature, since it was spending specifically with recovery in mind. Roosevelt, however, was not totally committed to the strategy of recovery via a deficit and still clung to the structural argument which had been part of his intellectual baggage for so long.

For much of the New Deal period fiscal policy was erratic and misdirected. It was essential for government expenditure to increase in order to offset the massive reduction in business and consumer spending which had taken place after 1929. Consumer spending would have received a boost which would, in turn, have persuaded businessmen to invest more. Spending did rise under the New Deal, of course, and between 1933 and 1936 recovery was stimulated. Expenditure, however, was relatively low between 1933 and 1935 although much more expansionary in 1936; after this a reduction helped precipitate the recession of 1937–8.

The result of increasing federal expenditure was deficits which disturbed many contemporaries who considered them excessive, persistent and unjustifiable. There was no way of demonstrating that deficits benefited the economy, and tax rates were raised and new taxes introduced, therefore, in an attempt to ensure that they did not become even larger. Raising taxes, however, reduced the expansionary effects of the budget.

The size of the deficit, in fact, is a poor guide to the expansionary nature of fiscal policy. A deficit can be the result of increasing unemployment which reduces the number of tax payers, and hence tax revenue, rather than of a deliberate policy of increased expenditure or tax reduction. If we want to compare the effect of fiscal policy over a number of years we must take into account any alteration in the level of employment. The full employment deficit calculates the annual deficit, assuming that the economy is operating at full employment. Using this important analytical tool, E. Cary Brown found that federal fiscal policy between 1933 and 1939 was less expansionary during 1933, 1937, 1938 and 1939 than it was under Hoover in 1931. Furthermore, the states and local authorities were even more concerned about budget deficits than the federal government; they ran budget surpluses which helped erode the expansionary effects of federal expenditure. If all units of government are aggregated, Brown found that fiscal policy was more expansionary in 1931 than in any other year during the 1930s. Pepper's analysis of the federal budget is also depressing; he demonstrates that fiscal policy in 1933, 1937, 1938 and 1939 was no more expansionary than it had been in 1929 under Hoover. The deficits which had caused Roosevelt such anguish were simply not big enough to stimulate the economy to full employment.

Contemporaries did not, of course, consider the full employment budget; they looked at the ordinary deficit. Although we can see, with the benefit of hindsight, that more spending and lower taxes were needed to bring about a vigorous economic revival, we must remember that massive deficits would have been required to match the decline which had taken place in consumer and business spending. Such deficits would not become acceptable until World War II. Fiscal policy was not used as a device for economic recovery. During the first New Deal, the restrictive and inflationary policies introduced by the AAA and the NIRA

led the assault on the stricken economy. A large deficit would have been a far
more effective way of reducing the numbers of the unemployed and harnessing
other under-utilised resources. New Deal expenditures, nevertheless, did assist
recovery; without them the situation would have been a good deal worse.

Bibliography

A more extensive treatment of New Deal banking reforms than has been possible in this
chapter can be found in H.M. Burns. Both L.V. Chandler and M. Friedman and A.J.
Schwartz also devote attention to banking legislation and, in addition, offer a critique on
monetary policy. The evolution of Roosevelt's fiscal policy has been authoritatively trac-
ed by M.H. Leff and by H. Stein.

Ballantine, A.A. (1948) 'When all the banks closed', *Harvard Business Review*, XXVI,
    March.
Benston, G.J. (1973) 'Required disclosure and the stock market: an evaluation of the
    Securities Act of 1934', *American Economic Review*, 63.
Brennan, J.A. (1969) *Silver and the First New Deal*, University of Nevada Press.
Brown, E.C. (1956) 'Fiscal policies in the thirties: a reappraisal', *American Economic
    Review*, December.
Burns, H.M. (1974) *The American Banking Community and New Deal Banking Reforms
    1933–35*, Greenwood Press.
Burns, J.M. (1956) *Roosevelt: The Lion and the Fox*, Harcourt Brace.
Chandler, L.V. (1971) *American Monetary Policy 1928–1941*, Harper and Row.
Copeland, M.A. (1961) *Trends in Government Financing*, NBER, Princeton.
Eccles, M.S. (1951) *Beckoning Frontiers: Public and Personal Recollections*, Knopf.
Friedman, M. (1980) 'The changing character of financial markets', in M. Feldstein (ed.)
    The American Economy in Transition, University of Chicago Press.
Friedman, M. and Schwartz, A.J. (1963) *A Monetary History of the United States,
    1867–1960*, NBER, Princeton.
Golembe, C.H. (1960) 'The deposit insurance legislation of 1933: an examination of its
    antecedents and its purposes', *Political Science Quarterly*, 75, June.
Jones, J.H. (1951) *Fifty Billion Dollars: My Thirteen Years with the RFC (1933–1945)*,
    Macmillan.
Krooss, H.E. and Blyn, M.R. (1971) *A History of Financial Intermediaries*, Random House.
Leff, M.H. (1984) *The Limits of Symbolic Reform: The New Deal and Taxation,
    1933–1939*, Cambridge University Press.
Lekachman, R. (1966) *The Age of Keynes*, Random House.
Manchester, W. (1960) 'The Great Bank Holiday', *Holiday*, 27, February.
Nash, G.D. (1979) *The Great Depression and World War II: Organising America
    1933–45*, St. Martins Press.
Parrish, M.E. (1970) *Securities Regulation and the New Deal*, Yale University Press.
Pecora, F. (1939) *Wall Street under Oath: The Story of Our Modern Money Changers*,
    Simon and Schuster.
Peppers, L. (1972–73) 'Full employment surplus analysis and structural change: the 1930s',
    Explorations in Economic History, 10.
Reading, D.D. (1973) 'New Deal Activity and the States, 1933–39', *Journal of Economic
    History*, 33.
Stein, H. (1969) *The Fiscal Revolution in America*, University of Chicago Press.

Sweezy, A. (1972) 'The Keynesians and government policy, 1933–1939', *American Economic Review, Papers and Proceedings*, LXII.

Upham, C.B. and Lamke, E. (1934) *Closed and Distressed Banks: A Study in Public Administration*, Brookings Institution, Washington DC.

White, E.N. (1981) 'State sponsored insurance of bank deposits in the United States, 1907–1929', *Journal of Economic History*, XLI.

Wright, G. (1974) 'The political economy of New Deal spending: an econometric analysis', *Review of Economics and Statistics*, 56.

14

The New Deal: Relief, Security and Survival

By March 1933 the distress caused by mass unemployment, the inadequacies of voluntary relief organisations and the farm crisis was acute. Under Hoover, the federal government had intervened, albeit on a small scale, in an attempt to lessen suffering. The RFC lent to the states for relief purposes and stocks of surplus wheat and cotton, accumulated by the Federal Farm Board, were given to the Red Cross for distribution to the needy. Far more was needed, however, as the local system of poor relief was in a state of collapse; there was a widespread demand for federal intervention on a large scale. This was provided, in 1933, by the Federal Emergency Relief Administration (FERA) which, under the leadership of Harry Hopkins, aimed to provide an adequate system of relief for those in need and to boost economic recovery by increasing purchasing power. FERA funds were allocated to the states as grants not loans and, initially, $500 mn was made available for distribution.

The Federal Emergency Relief Administration: 1933–5

Five hundred million dollars was a relatively small sum but Roosevelt was confident that the relief problem would not persist for more than a few years. Moreover, a commitment to a long-term relief programme would have indicated a lack of faith in New Deal recovery measures. Federal grants to the states were not a new concept but the magnitude of the relief problem, and the need for a response to it, was without precedent. The destitute were not evenly spread across the country and precise information on numbers was lacking. Furthermore, not only did urban and rural poverty require different approaches, but the administrative difficulties posed by policies which needed immediate implementation were formidable. An October 1933 Census revealed that 10 per cent of the population were dependent upon unemployment relief; the states of New York, Pennsylvania, Ohio and Illinois together had one-third of the nation's relief population. Although most of the unemployed were unskilled, a considerable number of skilled workers and professionals were also jobless. Not surprisingly, blacks were relatively harder hit than whites.

The easiest way of dealing with the problem would have been to give deserving cases direct cash relief. Roosevelt and his advisors were, however, opposed to dole payments which, they felt, lowered lthe morale of the recipient and led to an erosion of work skills. Although the FERA dealt with both employables and non-employables, where possible it hoped that the former would be provided with work relief; it looked to the states to set up useful public works schemes which would give employment to a variety of people. Once these schemes were approved, funds were forthcoming, but each state was expected to make a contribution towards relief, according to its financial strength. Washington was anxious to ensure that federal money was used honestly and that minimum relief standards were imposed. Thus the states were asked to set a 'fair rate of pay' for the work performed and not to discriminate against applicants on grounds of race, religion, colour, non-citizenship or political affiliation. Work projects had to be justified and provide jobs similar to those in private industry; 'works test' tasks such as chopping wood were discouraged. Finally, professional accounting methods were to be used, a sharp contrast to the casual nature of relief financing in many counties.

The task of the FERA was to distribute relief funds equitably between the states, which used existing institutions, the Emergency Relief Administrations operating at county level, to channel relief to those who needed it. Local people therefore determined who was and who was not eligible for assistance. Power remained with the states and their political subdivisions; there were no federal work projects but there were new federal rules which Washington attempted to enforce.

The aid given to each family or individual under the FERA was designed to ensure that the needy maintained minimum living standards and did not endure physical suffering. It was recognised that there were great differences in costs and living standards between urban and rural areas, and a scale was drawn up by each local relief agency based upon the budgetary deficiency principle. This required an estimate of the weekly needs of an individual or a family, and an estimate of weekly income, which included wages or other cash income, returns from the sale of farm or garden produce and all other resources including savings. The difference between requirement and income, the budgetary deficiency, was provided by the local agency, which kept a regular watch on recipients and monitored any change in financial circumstances. No one could be given, or could earn in work relief, more than the budgetary allotment. Therefore, work relief projects, which had pay scales similar to private industry, strictly limited the hours which could be worked each week so that there was no incentive for a worker to stay on relief if private employment became available.

The organisation of work relief projects during 1933 seemed, to the federal government, disappointingly slow. Not only was the FERA moving cautiously but the PWA, which had been established by the NIRA to create jobs in heavy industry, was making little headway in their provision. As the economic boom which had greeted Roosevelt's inauguration faltered in the autumn, a serious unemployment problem loomed for the winter of 1933—4. To combat this crisis, a new agency, the Civil Works Administration (CWA), was created in November 1933 with the aim of providing, almost immediately, jobs for four million workers. Half the CWA labour force comprised people taken from the relief rolls, the remainder were self-sustaining unemployed: employables without jobs but not on relief. With great rapidity those on work relief under the FERA were transferred to the CWA, leaving the former agency with the task of giving direct relief to unemployables. Most of the many CWA work projects were sponsored by states or by localities, with only a small number originating from federal agencies. In contrast to FERA, however, the CWA was operated directly as a federal pro-gramme; CWA workers were paid by federal cheques and federal CWA offices were set up in each state to exercise administrative control. Wages were not paid according to the budgetary deficiency principle but followed PWA practice of variations for the type of work performed, reflecting relative skills in each of three different geographic zones. Although maximum weekly hours of employ-ment were prescribed, earnings were higher than under the FERA.

By January 1934 the CWA had over four million people employed on the largest work relief programme of the depression (see Figures 14.1 and 14.2); its workers built or repaired roads and public buildings and laid out parks. The CWA was, however, relatively expensive and aroused the resentment of those not on relief but unable to obtain relatively well paid CWA employment. Roosevelt looked upon the CWA as a temporary rather than a long-term measure and the agency was run down after the spring of 1934, but not before it had accomplished many worthwhile projects, provided much needed relief and enabled many to gain experi-ence in the administration of work relief. About $950 mn was spent on CWA projects, of which $860 mn came from the federal government; the remainder was provided by the states and by local sponsors. Total earnings paid under the programme amounted to $718 mn, which gave some buoyancy to a depressed economy.

As CWA activities drew to a close, the FERA began a new operation, which was known as the Emergency Work Relief Program. As before, grants were given to the states for use in both direct and work relief projects, though the agency stressed that wherever possible, work rather than direct relief should be provided for employables. The work carried out was similar to the projects instituted by the CWA: about a quarter of the expenditure went on highways and roads, while public buildings were also constructed or repaired. The majority of those employed were unskilled workers but a serious attempt was made to find places for the white-collar and professional unemployed. The budgetary deficiency principle was retained and the hours of work were restricted to those necessary for workers to earn their calculated budgetary allowance. This work programme reached its employment peak during January 1935, when 2.5 million were engaged. Even in June 1935 the FERA provided relief jobs for two million, but by the end of the year this figure had been reduced to 60,000, as the WPA began to monopolise work relief.

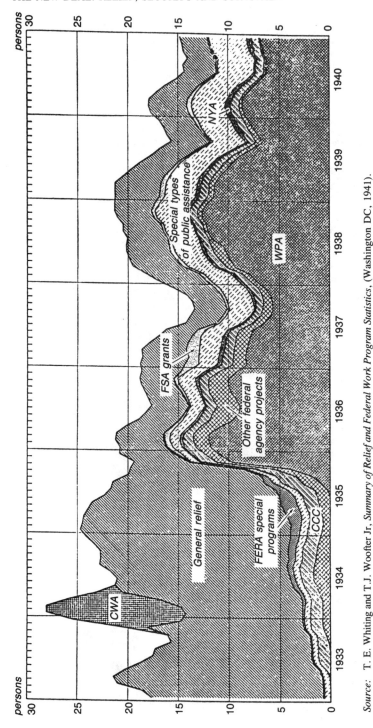

Source: T. E. Whiting and T.J. Woofter Jr, *Summary of Relief and Federal Work Program Statistics*, (Washington DC, 1941).

Figure 14.1 Persons Benefiting from Employment on Federal Work Programmes and Public Relief, by Programme, January 1933–December 1940

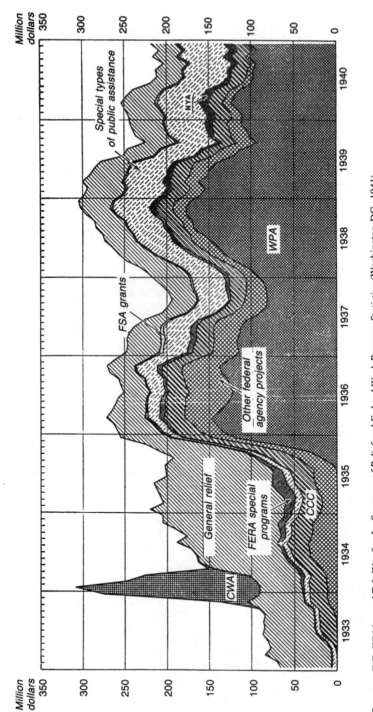

Source: T.E. Whiting and T.J. Woofter Jr, *Summary of Relief and Federal Work Program Statistics* (Washington DC, 1941).

Figure 14.2 Amount of Earnings of Persons Employed on Federal Work Programmes and Payments for Public Relief, by Programme, January 1933–December 1940.

In spite of the emphasis on work relief under the FERA, direct relief was given to more than 50 per cent of all cases on relief rolls. Thus, in January 1935, 2.8 million were on direct relief, some 300,000 more than the number on work relief. Indeed, the total cost of relief programmes for the three years that the FERA was in operation came to $4.1 bn; of this, $1.5 bn was spent on work relief, $2.0 bn on direct relief and the residue funded a number of special programmes which will be discussed shortly. Many employables, therefore, did receive direct relief in spite of Roosevelt's determination to avoid dole payments. The reasons for the high level of direct relief included: shortage of local funds for projects, shortages of skilled or supervisory workers, the inefficiency of some units of local government, the need to avoid competition with private enterprise and, of course, the sheer impracticality of employing so many jobless on work projects (Burns and Williams, 1941). Direct relief, therefore, continued to be of importance under the FERA.

In order to cater for special needs, five emergency relief programmes were developed by the FERA. Two of these were educationally oriented. First, the emergency education programme took qualified teachers off the relief rolls (44,000 by March 1935) and paid them to help eradicate illiteracy and teach a wide range of topics, including general education for adults and vocational training. Secondly, the college student aid programme was designed to give part-time employment to college students who could not afford to continue their education. Equally important was the aim of reducing the flow of young people onto the labour market. The students worked under the direction of their educational institution in a variety of mainly white-collar jobs where they did not displace other employees. Their rate of pay was at least 30 cents per hour and no one could work more than 30 hours in any week. From October 1934 to May 1935 an average of more than 100,000 young people each month were helped by this programme which was discontinued in June 1935, though a similar exercise was conducted by the National Youth Administration (NYA) in subsequent years.

The third programme which depended heavily on federal finance was designed to assist inter-state transients. These unfortunates did not have the residence qualifications necessary to obtain poor relief in the states where they became destitute and they aroused a great deal of resentment in hard-pressed communities when relief was requested. States did not want to help transients and clung to the doctrine of local responsibility for relief, although that was clearly inappropriate. A Transient Division of the FERA, the first ever national programme for needy non-residents, was established to encourage states to set up relief centres or work camps where medical care, food, shelter and clothing were available; the able-bodied obtained 30 hours of relief work per week, often contributing to the building and maintenance of their camps. They also worked on soil conservation, reforestation and pest control, as well as general construction work. During 1933—5,200,000 families or 700,000 individuals were helped, figures which demonstrated a serious social problem, but the Transient Division was wound up in 1935 with the FERA itself.

The two remaining special programmes were directed towards rural America.

Uneconomic farms, the loss of non-agricultural jobs, mechanisation, no security of tenure, lack of skills, low savings, drought and population pressure combined to account for rural misery. Farmers, with 9 per cent of the nation's income, had 30 per cent of the nation's children; they had inferior education and health facilities, as well as grossly inadequate housing. In addition, the droughts of 1934 and 1936 had affected 10 per cent of the land area of the US. There was much need in rural America and the FERA gave help, with the distribution of farm surpluses to relief families through the Federal Surplus Relief Corporation (FSRC). Its aims were to improve the standard of relief by gifts of surplus meat, cereals and fruit and, at the same time, to raise farm prices. Surplus cotton was used for work relief projects making clothing, towels and bedding. The FSRC did encounter difficulties: the storage and distribution of perishable foodstuffs was one, as was the fear of competition from retailers who had customers on relief and objected to the free gifts of food to those who might otherwise purchase it. Between 1933 and 1935, $2.7 mn worth of surplus goods were distributed before this agency became the Federal Surplus Commodity Corporation (FSCC).

The second special FERA initiative to combat rural misery was the rural rehabilitation programme. This recognised that rural destitution was different from urban unemployment and could not be resolved by the same treatment. Moreover, there were groups of people, for example those whose farms had been foreclosed or whose crops had failed, for whom the AAA was of little help (see Chapter 11). There was also the notion, part practical, part romantic, that the small family farm was wholesome and must be preserved; to achieve this end the traditional rural—urban migration should be reduced. Rural rehabilitation was designed to help the farmer to be self-supporting either on his own farm or on new good land if necessary. Under this scheme farmers were given help in the form of credit for restocking, buying equipment or moving to more fertile land. In July 1935 these activities were transferred to the Resettlement Administration but in the month prior to this move, some 200,000 farm families obtained rehabilitation loans, while over 360,000 were repaying loans they had already received. Loans, however, are helpful only to those who can demonstrate an ability to repay, a category which does not include the destitute.

In relation to the scale of the problem, the FERA special programmes made little practical impact. In 1935, 2.5 million rural families (some ten million people) were dependent on some form of relief; it was general relief from the FERA which was of paramount importance. The special programmes accounted for only 5 per cent of FERA expenditure and benefited few people, as Figures 14.1 and 14.2 demonstrate.

A new agency, the Civilian Conservation Corps (CCC), separate from the FERA, had been established in 1933. Its aim was to relieve distress amongst young men and war veterans by sending them to work in camps, restoring depleted natural resources. State welfare agencies selected CCC enrolees, with preference given to those whose families were receiving or were eligible for relief. They were required to surrender to their dependants the bulk of their $30 per month allowance. Valuable work was accomplished, which included the building of minor roads and bridges, the erection of telephone lines and the planting of several million trees. The number of enrolled personnel in the CCC averaged 300,000 during the summer months of 1933, reached 480,000 during the autumn months of 1935 and even averaged over 270,000 each month during 1940.

The year 1935 marks a watershed in the development of the American welfare state. The FERA, founded in a year of crisis with the aim of getting money to the states quickly, was retired as the main vehicle for relief. It had been introduced as a temporary programme but it was clear that after two years the relief problem had not evaporated as expected. This is scarcely surprising. In February 1934, FERA, CWA and CCC together gave aid to eight million households or some 22 per cent of the population. Only a remarkable economic recovery would have reduced relief to such minuscule proportions that it could be handed back entirely to the states and localities. The federal government was forced to stay in relief but wanted to work out a new, permanent system of co-operation with the states.

What had the FERA accomplished? It had channelled relief to the needy in larger amounts than ever before. The average monthly relief benefits for each case rose from $14 in January 1933 to $28 in January 1935. Differentials in payments between states were, however, great; this average encompassed benefits as high as $42 in Massachusetts and as low as $11 in South Carolina. FERA officials gained valuable experience — learning by doing — in the administration of relief and in the organisation of work programmes. However, to obtain relief each recipient had to be destitute — no income, no savings, insurance policies cashed in — and was forced to submit to a degrading means test in order to establish need. Although relief payments increased under the FERA, they were never generous. The average sums awarded monthly to each family were equivalent only to the weekly pre-depression wage of a fully employed industrial worker. One of the reasons for this is that the FERA was starved of funds (Hopkins, 1972; Patterson, 1987). Roosevelt was never a supporter of substantial relief payments, being on the one hand sensitive to objections from the taxpayers and on the other disturbed by the risk of inducing permanent dependency.

Nor did the states and local authorities wish to spend more on relief. Between 1933 and 1935 relief expenditure amounted to $4.1 bn; of this, 71 per cent came from federal funds. The power of the state and local relief administration inevitably allowed political favouritism and racial prejudice a fair degree of latitude. In addition, sheer incompetence often held back the development of work relief projects. By 1935 Roosevelt was determined that the federal government should 'quit this business of relief', by which he meant dole payments to needy unemployables. Local effort should aid these unfortunates while the federal government could monopolise work relief. Other deserving groups — dependent children, the needy blind and the aged — could also rely on some federal aid but only in conjunction with state action.

The Works Progress Administration and Social Security: 1935—41

As Patterson (1981) notes, the structural changes in the American welfare system during 1935 had four parts. First, general relief for unemployables was to be funded by the states and localities alone. Inevitably, the definition of an 'unemployable' created difficulties which were not merely semantic for those denied relief, especially as it was in the interests of local agencies to declare as many employable as possible. This was not the only problem which faced those who administered general relief policies. What was to be done for those able-bodied unemployed who could not get work on relief jobs? What about migrants who, as we have seen, were assisted by the FERA? Furthermore, it soon became clear that the estimates accepted by Roosevelt of the numbers of general relief claimants were far too modest.

The second part of the new welfare system was work relief for destitute employables for whom the federal government, believing unemployment to be a national problem, was prepared to take responsibility. The FERA system of grants to states was replaced by a new body, the Works Progress Administration (WPA), which operated, like the CWA before it, as a federal agency. All WPA officials were federal appointees. In addition, the budgetary deficiency system of payment was scrapped. Roosevelt's expectation was a system of work relief over which the federal government would have greater influence than it had under the FERA. The states and the localities still, however, played an important role after 1935. Local relief agencies determined which of their needy should be sent to the WPA, where they would be further assessed before being placed on a project. The vast majority of the WPA projects were initiated by cities, towns or counties and local sponsors paid nearly 30 per cent of their cost. What we see, therefore, is a different relationship between the federal government and the political subdivisions under the WPA, not total central control.

The third part of the welfare package was social insurance. The Social Security Act (1935), which together with the Wagner Act formed the most basic New Deal reform legislation, provided for old-age pensions and unemployment compensation. It is important that these two provisions should not be considered as relief or welfare. They were not payments for the destitute but for people who had contributed to an insurance scheme. The old-age benefit system was financed by taxes on both employers and employees in equal amounts. Contributors who reached 65 years of age were eligible for pensions which were first paid in 1940. The pension was not a flat rate given to all recipients; the sum awarded depended upon contributions, which were based upon the earnings of the worker. High pay resulted in a relatively high pension. Not all citizens were given the opportunity of joining the scheme, as certain occupational groups, for example domestic servants and agricultural workers, were excluded.

Unemployment compensation was financed by a federal tax on employers, but these payments could be credited to an approved state fund. In response to this incentive, all 48 states adopted unemployment pension schemes. The aim was to provide weekly payments to eligible workers who were laid off, but for a limited number of weeks only, at a rate which was dependent upon, but less than, the regular wage. When benefits were exhausted the unemployed had to seek work relief or, failing that, general relief. Like old-age assistance, there were exclusions: workers in small firms, domestic servants and farm workers were amongst those denied the opportunity to participate.

The fourth component was categorical public assistance for the blind and the elderly who were in need, and also for dependent children. The Social Security Act enticed states to set up programmes for these groups by enabling the federal government to give grants proportional to the amounts made available by the states. Such federal money was forthcoming only if minimum standards of categorical assistance were adopted over an entire state. By 1940, 41 states had instituted federally approved schemes which gave assistance to the needy blind; the same number gave aid to needy children and all 48 states helped needy persons over 65 years of age.

None of the schemes was ideal. Some attracted criticism from the conservative right, which felt that they would inevitably sap initiative. More coherent criticism came from a wider spectrum of interest groups which viewed the reforms as both too cautious and inadequate. General relief, which passed entirely to the states and local authorities, suffered a relapse. There were great variations in how general relief cases were treated after 1935 but a governing principle was often to minimise expenditure. Thus transients, who had been helped by the FERA, were declared as employable by the states but as unemployable by the federal government. As states increased residency requirements for relief, the 'depression pioneers' encountered few local agencies prepared to help them. In some states the system of poor relief slipped back to the old charity days of the 'work test'. Surplus commodities could be the main or only form of relief, and certain groups such as Hispanics, blacks or aliens were faced with discrimination or exclusion. Often, the amount of relief given was determined not by need but by the availability of local finance. Many states did not organise relief in a professional manner nor raise the appropriate tax revenue to fund it. In particular, there was a great difference between the large northern industrial states, with their relatively generous relief payments and sensible use of professional administrators and social workers, and most southern states — the poorest in the country — which saw little need for such a bureaucracy (Brown, 1940).

The New Deal failed to resolve, perhaps even to comprehend, the problem of general relief. In the first place, those eligible were far in excess of the number anticipated. Furthermore, although general relief was supposed to be confined to unemployables, it had to be extended to those who failed to get work relief, to those whose work relief wage was insufficient to support a large family, and even to those in private employment whose income was too low for survival. From January 1936 to December 1940, $2.2 bn was spent on general relief but the sums awarded were often grossly inadequate and many deserving cases received no assistance at all.

Public Works, Unemployment and the New Deal

The linchpin of the New Deal's relief strategy from 1935 was public works (Bremer, 1975–6). The PWA continued, with an emphasis on heavy construction, but the most important agency was the WPA, whose chief administrator was Hopkins. Work relief schemes had a long history, even by 1935 (Sautter, 1986), so their implementation was not radical. The advantages seemed clear: maintenance of skills, the provision of income, an uplift in morale, and an end product useful to the community. These benefits were a compensation for the additional cost of work relief over dole payments.

During times of unemployment, work relief programmes always have a popular following — the 1980s are no exception to this rule. There are, however, a number of problems in any public works programme which make its adoption as a weapon against unemployment far from straightforward. There are conflicting issues which have to be resolved, often by compromise, quite apart from the simple practical difficulties of finding suitable projects for millions of unemployed which can be implemented rapidly. The paper by Kesselman is an excellent guide to these conflicts, some of which will be examined now.

Leaving aside the question of whether or not dole payments are morally degrading, work relief supporters would point to their skill retention and work habit advantages. To obtain these benefits, a work programme should employ people on a wide range of jobs and also train them to acquire new skills. The vast bulk of WPA employment was, however, for unskilled workers on construction projects. This was of no help to the unemployed production-line worker or the clerk, nor to the estate agent or cobbler. Nor were there any attempts to encourage workers to increase their skills or to acquire new ones, even though this would have made them more attractive to private employers. For the majority, the WPA was not an exercise in skill preservation, nor could skilled workers performing unskilled construction tasks have found the experience morally uplifting. However, those experiencing long-term unemployment could well lose the work habit and, after some years, become unemployable. Work projects gave many in this category the opportunity to substitute activity for idleness, to their long-term benefit. The New Deal did make some imaginative efforts to provide jobs for those with special talents: the Federal Theatre brought entertainment to the people; the Federal Writers' Project employed talented writers to compile local guide books and a variety of excellent historical studies; WPA artists painted murals on public buildings, and the Federal Music Project gave a helping hand to young composers. These were small-scale but courageous attempts to mitigate serious unemployment in the arts, yet they aroused the wrath of many commentators.

The skill issue is closely related to another question: what kind of projects should be undertaken? The New Dealers were anxious to avoid the accusation of being in competition with private business; work relief projects, therefore, were only authorised if they would not have been undertaken by private industry, and generally were activities which did not produce output for sale (Hopkins, 1972). Public works such as roads, bridges, sanitation improvements, municipal swimming pools, public buildings and so on were the dominant activity. These were, in the main, absorbers of unskilled labour. Manufacturing enterprises were ignored, even though this might well have been the best use of available labour and would have resulted in a more useful, though contentious, end product. The TVA, for example, aroused furious reaction when, as a public corporation, it not only generated electricity, controlled floods, prevented soil erosion and created jobs, but also produced nitrogen fertilizers which were sold to the public. The fear of a collision with private enterprise prevented the development of a massive public housing drive. House building would have created many varied jobs in this particularly depressed industry and in the many trades linked to it. Large-scale slum clearance and rehousing would have fallen within the orbit of the PWA but even if that agency had made a serious attempt to do so, it would have been unable to overcome the vested interests which opposed federally financed housing. At the end of the decade, thanks to Senator Wagner, some moves had been made in this direction, but this was a crusade which never caught the imagination of Roosevelt and little had been accomplished by the outbreak of war.

How is the labour to be chosen for public works? Which of the unemployed but employable (often a difficult distinction) should be eligible for work relief? Should only those on the relief rolls be considered or could those not on relief or even those with jobs be considered? To be eligible for WPA work an applicant had to be an unemployed employable over the age of 18, who was either in receipt of relief or entitled to it. An investigation, usually by the state relief agency, was a necessary prerequisite to determine eligibility. Exceptionally, those not in need might be hired for administrative, supervisory or skilled jobs when it was not possible to find suitably qualified persons on the relief rolls. A further restriction prevented more than one member of a family from obtaining WPA employment, with the work usually being given to the head of the family. This rule provided an incentive for sons and daughters to leave home in order to set up separate households and even to marry, since married applicants were often given preference by the WPA. It is important to remember, however, that eligibility for the WPA did not guarantee a relief job. Indeed, after 1935, work relief programmes gave employment only to between one quarter and one third of the estimated unemployed (Burns and Williams, 1941). To have provided work relief for every applicant would have involved higher levels of public expenditure than Roosevelt felt was justified. When public expenditure was cut, relief jobs declined: between January and August 1937, WPA jobs were reduced by 50 per cent, as a result of the budget balancing exercise which helped to precipitate the 1937–8 recession (Figure 14.2). The shortfall in work relief inevitably put pressure on general relief and also gave local relief administrators great power in the selection of work relief applicants.

As we have seen in the previous chapter, it was concern over the federal deficit which led Roosevelt to raise taxes and thus diminish the expansionary effects of

New Deal spending. This concern also ensured that the WPA was under-funded and that it could never give work to all the able-bodied unemployed. By the same token, the great boost to consumer spending that was supposed to derive from the WPA never materialised.

One of the thorniest issues in public works is the rate at which labour should be paid. Should wages be linked to some index of need, for example the size of the worker's family? Should they be relatively low in order to maximise the numbers who can be employed and also to encourage workers to move to private jobs whenever they become available? Low relief wages, on the other hand, may lead to labour unrest in private industry if workers believe that they could give their employers an incentive to reduce their wages to a similar level. Furthermore, relief wages, if pitched too low, will conflict with the stated aim of bolstering worker morale (Burns and Kerr, 1937, 1941; Howard, 1973).

The WPA tried to take account of differing opinions on earnings. In order to create a new wage structure it dispensed with the FERA budgetary deficiency system, which had led to time consuming investigations about income levels and also to varied hours of work. WPA workers received a 'monthly security wage' which varied according to three criteria: the level of skill required for the job, the geographic region, and the degree of urbanisation of the county in which the worker lived. A maximum of 140 hours of work each month was laid down which, of course, put a ceiling upon earnings. In 1936, however, Congress accepted that the WPA should pay the prevailing hourly wage rate. This amounted to retaining the monthly security concept but adjusting the hours of work to take account of the new hourly rates. The result was that the length of the working week differed for various groups of WPA workers, leading to the same sort of difficulties as had occurred under the budgetary deficiency system. On building sites, for example, bricklayers worked fewer hours than hod carriers who in turn worked fewer than labourers to achieve the WPA weekly wage. In 1939 the prevailing wage concept was abandoned in favour of a standard monthly work load of 130 hours, with a flexible wage rate which reflected variations in the local cost of living.

On average, WPA wages were higher than under the FERA, though there were wide differentials between the wages earned by a skilled urban northerner and an unskilled rural southerner. The very low rate for rural dwellers was partly compensated for by the fact that the WPA paid cash on a regular basis to Americans who were used to payment in kind, as well as giving continuity of employment and relatively short hours. On the other hand, poor rural families were often large, and the WPA rule of limiting employment to only one family member not only discriminated against women but also put WPA recipients at the mercy of local relief. Many WPA workers, therefore, had the greatest possible incentive to find private jobs. Nevertheless, some analysts believe that WPA employment was sufficiently lucrative to pull workers away from the lowest paid private jobs. Indeed, there were complaints from many who found it difficult to hire domestic or casual farm labour at the very low rates of pay which had previously been acceptable to them. To many New Dealers this merely demonstrated that private sector wages were too low and should be raised for both social and economic reasons. Whether work relief wages were so high that private employers in, for example, manufacturing or construction could not afford to employ more labour is possible but defies quantification. It was certainly a scenario which the New Dealers hoped to avoid.

The results of the work relief programmes — roads, sewage plants, airports, public swimming pools and so on — are still used and valued by the American people. Few would deny that the output of the WPA was useful but a calculation of the benefits derived from the work programme is far from easy. Many contemporaries were scathing in their criticism of the WPA, denouncing its poor organisation, bad commercial practices and idle labour force. Critics felt that the costs of the work projects outweighed the benefits and that, as a result, taxpayers' money was being wasted. Many WPA programmes were an easy target for a hostile press and for the growing numbers of vociferous opponents which the New Deal generated.

At first glance we can agree with those who were sceptical of the WPA: if some of the criteria for measuring efficiency in private business are used in a similar way for public projects, contrasts emerge. Take, for example, the quality of labour in the private and public sectors. When high pay private jobs expanded, the best workers gravitated to them, causing a decline in the quality of labour in the public works sector. The faster the turnover of the relief labour force, the happier were WPA officials, but a rapidly changing workforce is not a highly efficient one. Efficiency was further reduced because minimal standards were used when persons were certified fit for work on public projects. As a result, projects had a disproportionate number of elderly, disabled, juveniles and other marginal employees. There are strong social grounds for employing these groups but in this conflict between relief and work efficiency, labour productivity will be adversely affected. All projects needed a mix of labour, including managerial and skilled; these were often difficult to hire at WPA rates and the most likely to leave. A shortage of supervisory staff made executive organisation of work and workers a perpetual problem. In order to maximise employment, many WPA projects, unlike the PWA, minimised capital inputs — picks and shovels were used instead of machinery. This further lowered the productivity of the workforce.

The popular stories of WPA men standing idle, leaning on shovels, were, when not simply the exaggeration which accompanied disapproval, the result of a relatively low quality, poorly equipped workforce. Work could not be planned as efficiently as in private industry. Men engaged in physically arduous labour needed rest, especially working outdoors, and the shortage of basic equipment, such as lorries, made continuity of operation impossible. The aim of the WPA was to create jobs quickly. The PWA was far more particular in choosing projects which had a clear economic value, and which needed long-term planning, costly raw materials and expensive capital equipment. But the PWA was not an agency which could put the unemployed to work quickly and cheaply.

Should those on work relief be classified as employed or unemployed? We raised this issue in Chapter 12 and came to the conclusion that they were unemployed. We can now reinforce that view by appreciating that with the restrictions on hours worked and on earnings, with the mounting public cynicism about their worth and the clear understanding that agencies such as the WPA were a holding operation until private sector jobs could be secured, the workers themselves could scarcely have failed to regard themselves as unemployed. On the other hand, many who 'worked for the government' were deeply grateful to the New Deal for lifting the despair of idleness.

The WPA was not the only federal work agency but it was by far the largest after 1935. For example, in June 1939 over 2.5 million workers received WPA wages, a quarter of a million were employed on PWA projects, and just over 200,000 were enrolled in the CCC. There were, of course, fluctuations in WPA numbers which are illustrated in Figures 14.1 and 14.2. Looking at the average number employed on a half-yearly basis the peak was 3.2 million in December 1938, whereas during the previous December only 1.6 million were employed. By the middle of 1942 the WPA had built or improved 644,000 miles of roads, 122,760 bridges and viaducts, 38,800 schools, 8,000 parks, 2,290,000 sanitary privies and 23,700 miles of sewers. Before it was phased out in 1943, $11.4 bn had been spent, a not inconsiderable sum. Perhaps this agency more than the others fell between the two stools of relief and work. As Patterson states, the answer to the relief problem was a system of universal income maintenance which was far too radical to gain widespread support.

A rapid expansion of employment, however, required a recovery in the economy, the key to which was an increased level of federal deficit and the rise in consumption which would have followed in its wake. Greater expenditure on all forms of relief, including more varied public works projects, coupled with a reduction in taxation was the remedy. As we have seen in the previous chapter, however, the level of public spending required to bring about a full recovery was so large that it was politically impossible to implement, at least in peacetime, even if there had been widespread approval for it amongst economists. Nevertheless, between January 1933 and December 1940 the aggregate payments to recipients under various public relief and federal work programmes amounted to $21.1 bn (Figure 14.2). The earnings from federal work programmes were 60 per cent of the total. The federal government, therefore, spent large sums on relief and many of the shortcomings of its efforts were due to the magnitude of the problem facing Roosevelt when he took office.

Social Security

The other component parts of the 1935 welfare reform can also be criticised. The old-age pension provision was a response in part to the increase, both absolute and relative, of elderly people in the population, which accelerated between 1920 and 1930 because of the sharp decline in the birth rate. There was a also a recognition that the elderly had particular employment problems, that many had no income and that others had lost their savings during the worst years of the depression. With the growth of urbanisation and the advent of smaller families, the possibility of children caring for aged parents was reduced. An added dimension, however, was that the elderly were becoming a powerful pressure group. Dr Francis Townsend's *Old Age Revolving Pensions Plan*, which he proposed in 1934, sought to alleviate the economic distress faced by the elderly and to add considerably to the level of demand in the economy by giving all citizens over the age of 60 years $200 each month; the recipients would have to promise not to work and to spend all the money in the month in which they received it. Not surprisingly, the Townsend Plan was very popular with the over-60s, and by 1935 its founder had over three million disciples. The old-age pension scheme that emerged with the Social Security Act undermined Townsend's political support before the election of 1936.

The old-age pension scheme, and indeed that for unemployment insurance, was very conservative. They were financed rather like private schemes, with most contributions coming from the private sector and the role of the federal government minimised, a move designed to mute right-wing criticism. We have noted that there were exclusions — agricultural workers, domestic servants, workers in small businesses and migrants — from the insurance schemes, which denied many of the poorest the opportunity to benefit from them. These groups of people did not have steady jobs (indeed the unemployed gained nothing from these schemes) so were less able to make regular contributions; moreover, their employers were hostile to paying their share, especially as so many in these categories were black. We should note too that the taxes levied to build up the Social Security fund were both regressive and deflationary. They fell disproportionately upon the less well off and took purchasing power away from consumers at the very time when New Dealers were attempting to expand consumption.

The categorical public assistance programme gave minimal support to groups desperately in need; however, there were no national standards and benefits varied widely from state to state. In the most fiscally tightfisted, claimants got little; in others, groups such as blacks, single-parent families or migrants could expect nothing. We should not regard the welfare state which was introduced in 1935 as a radical departure from past practice nor as the birth of decent welfare payments to deserving cases. 1935 is a watershed because legislation was passed which introduced permanent federal aid for welfare; once this had happened, the federal presence could only lead to improved standards. One major New Deal omission was that the medical lobby was able to defeat plans for health insurance, to the long-term disadvantage of the poor and chronically sick.

Additional Federal Programmes

After 1935 the CCC and the PWA continued to operate. They were joined by the National Youth Administration (NYA) which was established in 1935 and took over the student work programme initiated by the FERA, extending it to high school students. In addition, the NYA administered a scheme which provided part-time employment and work experience for young people, mostly between the ages of 18 and 24, who did not attend school but were without sufficient income to meet their basic needs.

Finally, the Farm Security Administration, which was originally the Resettlement Administration, was created in July 1935. It continued the rural rehabilitation schemes already in progress, giving loans to tenants whose land was judged potentially capable of supporting a family. The agricultural problem was not one of unemployment; the farm family had work to do but needed loans for seed purchase or for equipment and also technical instruction before their farm could be viable. Rehabilitation loans by 1943 amounted to nearly $870 mn or just over $25 for every member of the 1940 farm population.

Where there was evidence of great deprivation, often caused by natural disasters such as flood or drought, rural rehabilitation grants were available for necessities such as food and clothing. Over $150 mn had been distributed by 1943, which amounted to $5 per head of the 1940 farm population. The FSA also tried to assist migratory farm workers by establishing camps for them. The resettlement projects were an exercise in community planning, inaugurated by the RA and taken over by the FSA. The plan was to move half a million families from submarginal land to rural communities and to build 50 new towns. The programme, which aroused great hostility, in the end relocated only 4,000 families and built three 'greenbelt towns' near the cities of Washington, Milwaukee and Cincinnati.

Chapter 11 analysed many of the problems encountered by farmers in need, but without strong political clout. Those who gained most from New Deal agricultural programmes were the land owners and large-scale farmers. Attempts to aid tenants and other small-scale operators were doomed to failure, partly because of the enormous scale of the problem but also because Congress would never provide the extensive funding required for programmes which at best would lead to more farm competition and at worst could be denounced as socialism. Moreover, though we should not exaggerate this, some New Deal policies led to the displacement of tenants, especially in the South, throwing them onto the labour market at a time of minimum job opportunity. Even the benefits of old age pensions and unemployment payments, established by the Social Security Act, were denied to most rural dwellers.

Another way in which many rural poor were disadvantaged was by the skewed distribution of WPA funds. The South had the heaviest concentration of poverty in the country, yet the states which exceeded the annual average per capita WPA expenditure were either those most heavily industrialised or, if rural, in the West or the North. Between 1936 and 1940, not one southern state did better than average using this measure and most did a good deal worse. Work relief would have been particularly valuable in raising southern income but it would not, of course, have removed the original causes of much of the poverty.

Rural relief problems were formidable and it would be foolish to minimise their scale and to ignore the political realities which prevented the widespread adoption of radical solutions. Moreover, the extent of rural poverty was not recognised until the investigations of the New Dealers lifted the stone of ignorance. We need to remember too, as outlined in Chapter 11, that farm policies, especially those which restored the credit system and helped to check soil erosion gave much needed relief to many rural families.

Amongst the poorest of the rural poor were America's blacks, most of whom were tenant farmers or share-croppers. They not only obtained limited benefits from the AAA programmes but also found it more difficult than whites to get relief jobs or adequate direct relief. Even if they were successful in joining New Deal programmes they found that CCC camps were racially segregated and that the NRA followed the prevailing southern custom of paying blacks lower wages than whites for doing the same standard of work. Although the New Deal made these and other compromises with racism and although Roosevelt, fearful of antagonising powerful southern senators, would not fully commit himself to a federal law to abolish lynching, blacks did feel that they gained from the New Deal. For the first time many southern blacks found themselves actually eligible to receive relief, albeit segregated. A demonstration of their support for Roosevelt's economic and social measures came in the 1936 election, when those blacks who were enfranchised began to switch their traditional allegiance from the Republican Party to the Democrats. Black Americans, however, had to wait until World War II put such great pressures upon the economy that they could more easily move into the economic domain of whites and lay the foundation stones for the post-war civil rights movement.

It would be wrong to assume that the depression left the entire American population in a state of paralysis. Many tried to avoid the necessity of relief by migrating. Although the farm population increased during the 1930s, the number living on farms was the same in 1940 as it had been in 1929. Thus farm people still moved to urban areas, but not on such a scale as they had done during the twenties or were to do during World War II. These migrants were joined by others, usually unemployed urbanites who were searching for jobs. Many on the move were relatively well educated compared with those on relief, had smaller families and a clear destination in mind. They were not aimless wanderers but were moving to areas where they had personal contacts or where they hoped letters of introduction would help them to secure employment. Others found new occupations more in keeping with hard times. By 1939 the number of cafes and restaurants was greater than in 1929, so was the number of second-hand stores, petrol stations, beauty parlours and, of course, with the ending of prohibition, liquor stores. The increase in the number of jobs created by this expansion was but a very small compensation for those lost.

By the outbreak of war in Europe, relief was still important to millions of Americans (see Figures 14.1 and 14.2) because unemployment was still high and underemployment, especially in rural areas, was widespread. The New Deal had introduced marked changes in relief policy, involving the federal government, permanently, in a variety of programmes which helped the destitute and, through the Social Security system, established an embryo welfare state. Although aspects of these relief policies are open to criticism, they were a serious attempt on the part of a concerned central government to mitigate the worst effects of the depression. Moreover, having involved itself in social policy, Washington would find disengagement from this new obligation impossible. Many of the problems that we have outlined, however, stem from a failure to bring about an economic recovery sufficient to achieve full employment levels. Jobs, not relief, were what the public wanted. The New Deal, unfortunately, could provide neither private jobs for all nor work relief for all.

The relief-related expenditures, did, however, make a significant contribution to recovery, even though they were limited because of the government's fear of adding to the budget deficit. From the beginning of 1932 to the end of 1940, federal work and public relief average annual expenditures amounted to $2.6 bn. By this means personal disposal income was raised and aggregate demand increased. The relative size of this outlay can be seen by comparing it with the annual average budget deficit, which between 1933 and 1939 was $3.0 bn. Moreover, as Copeland points out, a comparison of relief expenditure and income decline must make allowances for the fact that the purchasing power of the dollar was one-fifth higher during the 1930s than in 1929. Without these programmes the level of economic activity would have been far lower than it was. Thus New Deal relief expenditures were not only important in mitigating the effects of acute social distress but also made a more significant contribution to economic recovery than did the NIRA or the domestic allotment scheme of the AAA.

Bibliography

A thorough account of New Deal relief initiatives can be found in the contemporary publications of J.C. Brown and A.E. Burns and E.A. Williams. A valuable addition to these is the excellent study of American poverty by J.T. Patterson. R. Lowitt and M. Beasley have edited the reports made by Lorena Hickok as she travelled through the most affected states during the mid-1930s. They provide a vivid account of the deprivation that she witnessed. The section in this chapter on public works owes a great deal to J.R. Kesselman's fascinating paper on this subject.

Bakke, E.W. (1940) *The Unemployed Worker: A Study in the Task of Making a Living Without a Job*, Yale University Press.
Berkowitz, E. and McQuaid, K. (1980) *Creating the Welfare State: The Political Economy of Twentieth Century Reform*, Praeger.
Blumberg, B. (1979) *The New Deal and the Unemployed: The View from New York City*, Bucknall University Press.
Bremer, W.W. (1975–76) 'Along the "American Way": the New Deal's work relief programs for the unemployed', *The Journal of American History*, 62.
Brown, J.C. (1940) *Public Relief, 1929–1939*, H. Holt and Co.
Burns, A.E. and Kerr, P. (1937) 'Survey of work-relief wage policies', *American Economic Review*, 27.

Burns, A.E. and Kerr, P. (1941) 'Recent changes in work-relief wage policy', *American Economic Review*, 31.

Burns, A.E. and Williams, E.A. (1941) *Federal Work, Security and Relief Programs*, WPA Research Monograph XXIV, Washington DC.

Clark, J.G., Katzman, D.M., McKinzie, R.D. and Wilson, T.A. (1977) *Three Generations in Twentieth Century Ameria: Family, Community and Nation*, Dorsay.

Copeland, M.A. (1961) *Trends in Government Financing*, NBER, Princeton.

Ehrenreich, J.H. (1985) *The Altruistic Imagination: A History of Social Work and Social Policy in the United States*, Cornell University Press.

Gill, C. (1973) *Wasted Manpower*, Da Capo Press, New York. First published 1939.

Hirshfield, D.S. (1970) *The Lost Reform: The Campaign for Compulsory Health Insurance in the United States from 1932–1943*, Harvard University Press.

Hopkins, H.C. (1972) *Spending to Save: The Complete Story of Relief*, W.W. Norton.

Howard, D.S. (1973) *The WPA and Federal Relief Policy*, Da Capo Press, New York. First published in 1943.

Kesselman, J.R. (1978) 'Work relief programs in the Great Depression' in J.L. Palmer (ed.) *Creating Jobs: Public Employment Programs and Wage Subsidies*, Brookings Institution, Washington DC.

Lowitt, R. and Beasley, M. (1981) *One Third of a Nation: Lorena Hickok Reports on the Great Depression*, University of Illinois Press.

Lynd, R.S. and M.L. (1937) *Middletown in Transition: A Study in Cultural Conflicts*, Harcourt Brace.

Lubove, R. (1968) *The Struggle for Social Security 1900–1935*, Harvard University Press.

Macmahon, A.W., Millett, J.D. and Ogden, G. (1941) *The Administration of Federal Work Relief*, University of Chicago Press.

McCoy, D.R. (1958) *Angry Voices: Left of Centre Politics in the New Deal Era*, University Press of Kansas.

McWilliams, C. (1942) *Ill Fare the Land Migrants and Migratory Labor in the United States*, Little, Brown.

Mertz, P.E. (1978) *New Deal Policy and Southern Rural Poverty*, Louisiana State University Press.

Nelson, L.J. (1983) 'Welfare capitalism on a Mississippi plantation in the Great Depression', *Agricultural History*, 57.

Patterson, J.T. (1981) *America's Struggle Against Poverty 1900–1980*, Harvard University Press.

Salmond, J.A. (1967) *The Civilian Conservation Corps, 1933–1942: A New Deal Case Study*, University of North Carolina Press.

Sautter, U. (1986) 'Government and employment: the use of public works before the New Deal', *The Journal of American History*, 73.

Schwartz, B.F. (1984) *The Civil Works Administration, 1933–1934: The Business of Emergency Employment in the New Deal*, Princeton University Press.

Sitkoff, H. (1978) *A New Deal for Blacks: The Emergence of Civil Rights as a National Issue*, Oxford University Press.

Stein, W.J. (1973) *California and the Dust Bowl Migration*, Greenwood Press.

Terkel, S. (1970) *Hard Times: An Oral History of the Great Depression*, Avon.

Webb, D.N. (1935) *The Transient Unemployed*, WPA Research Monograph III, Washington DC.

Webb, J.N. and Brown, M. (1938) *Migrant Families*, WPA Research Monograph XVIII, Washington DC.

Witte, E.E. (1962) *The Development of the Social Security Act*, University of Wisconsin Press.

Wolters, R. (1970) *Negroes and the Great Depression*, Greenwood Press.

15

The New Deal: A Conclusion

The New Deal began with Roosevelt's 'first hundred days' and ended, if legislation is used as a yardstick, in 1938 with the Fair Labor Standards Act. Alternatively, one might place the end in 1939 or 1940, as events in Europe and the Pacific began to change the concerns of the administration. As Roosevelt himself observed 'Dr New Deal' had to be replaced by 'Dr Win-the-War'. As we have seen, the New Deal was not an exercise in applied economics but in political economy during which policy adjustments were frequently made to accommodate powerful pressure groups. By 1938 the President and his disciples were facing mounting hostility. The New Deal had always attracted vociferous opposition: communists and socialists denounced it, as did radicals and conservative organisations, such as the American Liberty League. The formidable political skill of the President had enabled him to occupy the middle ground and thus limit the attack from both the right and the left, sometimes by stealing their thunder. The 1938 elections, however, saw great Republican gains; together with conservative Democrats they strangled further reform.

By 1938 the New Deal was on the defensive. Unemployment was still high and had been made worse by the recession of 1937–8: few, therefore, had any confidence in the administration's recovery policies. Many in rural America opposed the pro-labour Wagner Act and were sceptical of urban-oriented work relief policies, though they were happy to take for themselves what the New Deal had to offer. In 1938, too, the paralysis which had existed in March 1933 seemed distant and Congress was not inclined to give Roosevelt the freedom of action which he had enjoyed during his first years of office. The President was becoming preoccupied with foreign affairs and the impending war in Europe would inevitably be a dominant issue in the election of 1940, in which Roosevelt ran for an unprecedented third term. His victory effectively blocked much of the conservative attack upon the New Deal and assured the future of key reforming policies. However, even before the US entered the war in December 1941, the emergency public assistance and federal work programmes were becoming redundant. By late 1943 the FSA, the CCC, the NYA and the WPA had been discontinued, though there was a fond hope on the part of the most ardent New Deal supporters that programmes had merely been suspended and might be revived after the war.

The aim of the New Deal had been recovery, and the restoration of order and stability to the US economy and to society. Fiscal policy was not used to this end, nor was monetary policy seen as the guarantor of full employment. Instead, the New Deal stressed structural issues: planning, a shorter working week, minimum wages, the distribution of income, retirement at 65, more schooling for young people, price supports for agriculture, and the growth of organised labour. New Dealers debated whether there should be more or less competition and whether big or small business should be favoured. The federal government became a regulator, or supervisor, responsible for stabilising the economy and playing, it hoped, the major role in transforming the nation's economic and social structure.

Eschewing vigorous monetary and fiscal policy in favour of structural reform was not the way to rapid recovery. Moreover, some of the most important attempts at structural change achieved nothing positive. The structure of industry, for example, had not been changed by 1940. The distribution of income, on the other hand, had been modified; about 5 per cent of the population received 30 per cent of the nation's total family income in 1929, but only 24 per cent in 1941. However, this decline may be partly illusion, a tribute to the ability of the rich to disguise their income at a time of increasing taxation. In any case, if a squeezing of the rich did take place, it may well have been a consequence of the stock market collapse of 1929 and its aftermath, rather than of New Deal policies. Income distribution figures show that middle income groups, not the poor, benefited from any change. New Deal largesse was, to a great extent, governed by the effectiveness of those who clamoured for aid; those not organised got less, as when large-scale agriculture was rewarded more heavily than small. The federal government was a 'broker state' which distributed benefits, but did not distribute them evenly. The New Deal, therefore, provided every incentive for supplicants to organise into effective lobbies.

We have stressed two factors in our analysis of the New Deal. First, it operated within the framework of a capitalist system in which Roosevelt had an unshakeable faith. For critics to denounce the New Deal as communist, socialist, or even fascist, is nonsense. Institutions remained in private hands even when there was a strong case, as with banking, for a state takeover. Secondly, the New Deal was not a radical departure from past practice. As Hughes shows, Roosevelt's policies were firmly in line with American tradition. Many of the banking reforms and the wrong-headed monetary experiments, for example, had their roots in late nineteenth-century Populism. A master at judging what was acceptable to the majority of the American people, Roosevelt was not an ideologue nor a reforming zealot.

This is not to deny that the New Deal did bring about change in both the short and the long run. After 1933 the federal government assumed a new importance. Previously Washington had been remote from the lives of many Americans but by 1940 the federal government played a key role in relief, in welfare, and in stabilising the economy. New Deal relief was given to approximately one third of the country's workers; households and farms benefited from federal credit initiatives and youngsters in education received help from Washington.

Any evaluation of the New Deal must take stock of the state of the nation in March 1933. The business and banking communities were stricken with fear; the public, too, were close to despair. If Roosevelt had failed to raise morale and had not shown such a commanding presence, the economic collapse could have been complete. The restoration of hope must be amongst the President's greatest triumphs, concomitant with the salvation of America's financial system. Although much of what followed can be dismissed as contradictory, or inimical to private investment, and therefore inhibiting recovery, there is much to praise and even to admire. The special programmes, for example those relating to the arts or to rural rehabilitation, were motivated by compassion. The attempt to correct generations of environmental neglect and the founding of a more equitable system of welfare benefited many millions in the long run. Federal involvement in relief was essential to relieve suffering. Criticism of New Deal economic policy can be made with the benefit of hindsight, but Roosevelt could not have implemented the macro-economic measures needed to stimulate the economy, since economists had not formulated a theory which demonstrated what should be done.

Could New Deal reforms prevent another Great Depression? A repeat of 1929–33, with its price falls and widespread bank failures, is unlikely because the banking and financial structure is now much more secure. Indeed, since the introduction of FDIC, the control of inflation has been a more pressing problem than fear of deflation. This does not mean that the US economy is immune from serious depression, but that the combination of events which occurred after 1929 is unlikely to be seen again. We should note, however, that events during the 1980s show disturbing similarities to the 1920s. Agriculture is in deep crisis, with many farmers unable to repay loans and unable to secure new ones as land values have fallen. Their misfortune has put pressure on the banking system, though the effects of failure have, so far, been contained by the FDIC. A general fall in real estate values, which is not inconceivable, could put such great pressure on so many banks that the FDIC, if left to its own resources, could not cope.

Another potentially destabilising circumstance is that many US banks have lent heavily to oil-producing countries which, since the collapse in oil prices, have been unable to repay their debts. The possibility of major defaults is real. Indeed, by the spring of 1987, Brazil, Ecuador, Peru and Bolivia were among seven Latin American countries who had suspended interest payments on their foreign debt. All had borrowed heavily from the US. At home, consumer, business and government debt is at record levels. Indeed, the level of debt is so high that it has been suggested that it could perform a role similar to that of the stock market in 1929 and lead ultimately to the destruction of the financial system (Thurow, 1986). However, one feature of the current US economy which does not replicate the 1920s is the existence of an enormous budget deficit.

In marked contrast to the inter-war years, the US, in 1985, officially became a net debtor, dependent upon capital inflows to finance its domestic and its external deficits. The federal budget deficit has pushed US interest rates to relatively high levels, making US government and corporate bonds particularly attractive to foreigners. Thus, the world's wealthiest nation emerges as the major international debtor. In a curious twist of fate, the US has become dependent upon imports of capital, the diminution of which could lead to a liquidity crisis.

Another American problem, evident since 1973, is the poor productivity performance of the economy. As competitiveness has declined, import penetration has increased and living standards have stagnated. Average hourly earnings boomed during the 1950s and the 1960s, but since 1973 families have been forced to rely upon higher levels of debt and the employment of married women to maintain consumption levels. As in Britain, there is no way of raising productivity sharply in the short run. Many economists, however, in searching for a scapegoat, have come to the conclusion that amongst the inhibitors of productivity advance are controls on industry, many of which are products of a New Deal mentality. The current clamour for deregulation comes from those who argue that if legislation to regulate industry was appropriate in a decade of deflation, such as the 1930s, it is now counter-productive. Only by severing these controls can industry and commerce respond to market forces and in so doing become more efficient.

After almost half a century, the New Deal still occasions vigorous debate. It also, periodically, attracts support from politicians who wish to be identified with Roosevelt's charisma and compassion but conveniently forget that the greatest failure of the New Deal was its inability to cure unemployment. World War II finally erased the last traces of the Great Depression, and the performance of the economy during these crucial years, dealt with in the next chapter, stands as a fascinating story in its own right.

Bibliography

G.D. Nash has written an excellent overview of this period. J.R.T. Hughes (1977) shows that much of the thirties legislation which aroused such controversy was not a radical departure from past experience. As J.W. Duncan and W.C. Shelton demonstrate, New Deal demands increased both the quantity and the quality of the statistical information collected by the government.

Duncan, J.W. and Shelton, W.C. (1978) *Revolution in United States Government Statistics 1926–1976*, Bureau of the Census, Washington DC.
Graham Jr., O.L. (1976) *Toward a Planned Society: From Roosevelt to Nixon*, Oxford University Press.
Hughes, J.R.T. (1977) *The Governmental Habit: Economic Controls from Colonial Times to the Present*, Basic Books.
Hughes, J.R.T. (1979) 'Roots of regulation: the New Deal' in G.M. Walton (ed.) *Regulatory Change in an Atmosphere of Crisis: Current Implications of the Roosevelt Years*, Academic Press.

Krooss, H.E. (1970) *Executive Opinion: What Business Leaders Said and Thought on Economic Issues, 1920s–1960s*, Doubleday.

Leuchtenberg, W.E. (1983) *In The Shadow of FDR: From Harry Truman to Ronald Reagan*, Cornell University Press.

McCoy, D.R. (1972) *Coming of Age: The United States during the 1920s and 1930s*, Pelican Books.

Nash, G.D. (1979) *The Great Depression and World War II: Organising America 1933–45*, St Martins Press.

Patterson, J.T. (1967) *Congressional Conservatism and The New Deal: The Growth of the Conservative Coalition in Congress, 1933–1939*, University Press of Kentucky.

Thurow, L.C. (1986) 'Yes, the 1920s and '30s Can Come Again', *International Herald Tribune*, 24 January.

Wolfkskill, G. (1962) *The Revolt of the Conservatives: A History of the American Liberty League*, Houghton Mifflin.

16

World War II:
The End of the Depression

This chapter is not intended to give a detailed picture of economic and social change between 1939 and 1945. Those who require a more thorough account of America at war can consult the bibliography which concludes this book. What follows is an outline of the transition from the depression to the prosperity which the New Deal had been unable to achieve. The level of federal expenditure necessary to secure full employment proved, in the end, acceptable only within a framework of war. The millions of new urban jobs which the war generated gave many farmers the opportunity to flee from a life of persistent poverty and debt, while those who remained on the land became a good deal richer. High profits quickly restored business morale. Direct government investment, unthinkable during the 1930s, was welcomed rather than opposed as usurping the role of private enterprise. Roosevelt, who had been elected President for a fourth time in November 1944, died the following April with victory in Europe and in the Pacific assured. At war's end, great victories in the economic struggle had been won. But would Roosevelt's successor, and the American people, muster the economic wisdom and political will to prevent the revival of endemic poverty, structural dislocations and depression?

From New Deal to Pearl Harbor

The New Deal had run out of steam before Hitler's blitzkrieg attack on Poland in 1939. By 1938 Roosevelt's political stock had fallen appreciably from the peak reached with his victory over Alf Landon in 1936. The President's plans to transform the Supreme Court, which had invalidated elements of the New Deal, were viewed by many as an unseemly challenge to a revered institution. Moreover, the recession which began in 1937 discredited his economic strategy, demoralised many supporters and ensured substantial gains for the Republican Party in the midterm election of 1938. During this election, Roosevelt had campaigned vigorously against a number of prominent southern Democrats, whose reactionary conservatism he wished to replace by more liberal candidates. The intervention was counter-productive, and those he opposed returned to Washington even more implacably opposed to the New Deal.

In Congress, conservative Democrats, many of them from the South, allied with Republicans to frustrate reformist legislation. By 1938 many politicians and a large part of the electorate wanted a respite from the 'bold persistent experimentation' which had been so appealing in 1933. Furthermore, the President was becoming preoccupied with foreign affairs in Europe, Latin America and Asia, and domestic issues became progressively less important to him. As the storm clouds gathered over Europe, Roosevelt was obliged to gather new political allies who, he felt, would only support the administration's foreign policy aims if its domestic liberalism was tempered. The New Deal, therefore, was halted by a solid conservative attack at a time when its champion's attention was diverted by international problems.

The American people were determined not to be drawn into any new overseas conflict. Disillusionment with World War I, widespread during the 1920s, was given an additional stimulus by the Nye Committee. Its hearings, during 1935–6, gave credence to the popular view that the only groups to gain from this war had been big bankers and big business. Such sentiments were readily accepted by a public which despised banks and was deeply distrustful of large corporations. Congress attempted to ensure that the US would never again become ensnared in other nations' wars by passing a number of Neutrality Acts. While campaigning for re-election in 1936, Roosevelt had identified himself with the popular isolationist sentiments. Privately, although he supported attempts to appease Hitler during the Munich crisis of 1938, the President was deeply concerned about the rise of Nazism. Once war broke out in September 1939 he informed the American people that, though they were obliged to be neutral in deed, their thoughts, like his, should be with the Allied powers.

The outbreak of war led to the emergence of vociferous pressure groups urging, on the one hand, help for the Allies and, on the other, strict non-intervention. As the Nazi blitzkrieg machine remorselessly crushed enemies and neutrals alike, US public opinion swung towards sympathy for Britain. In the presidential election of 1940, fortunately, foreign affairs were kept out of the campaign. Wendell Wilkie, Roosevelt's Republican opponent, was not an isolationist; he favoured helping Britain and was highly critical of the lack of military preparedness in the US. By maintaining a low profile, Roosevelt was again victorious. The gains which Wilkie made among farmers and in small towns in the Midwest were swamped by the votes of the urban masses. Blacks and whites in the cities clung to the man who had given them the New Deal; Roosevelt was swept back to the White House for an unprecedented third term.

Even if the US did not become a participant, the war in Europe was bound to affect her economy. In 1940 America was in a position to respond quickly to the demands for foodstuffs, raw materials and armaments. The agricultural sector had large stocks of grains and of cotton, which had been purchased by the Commodity Credit Corporation. The spread of farm machinery, the introduction of better seeds, the dissemination of disease control techniques and the increased vitality of the land brought about by New Deal conservation measures had given the farm sector the ability to produce more. Indeed, although the multitude of New Deal farm programmes were designed to curb output, farms could more easily increase rather than reduce production.

As unemployment was still high, there was ample labour for industrial expansion, especially if the rural unemployed migrated to factory work. Moreover, the workforce was better educated and more adaptable than it had been between 1914 and 1918. The administrative experience gained in World War I and by the New Deal agencies provided the US with a reservoir of expertise, which could be drawn upon in a national emergency. In addition, the depression had necessitated systematic data collection, a service which could be expanded if required. Finally, the recession of 1937–8 had led to a growing acceptance of Keynesian ideas, which would prove invaluable in managing a war economy.

On the debit side, it is clear that as investment had been low during the 1930s, industry's stock of capital equipment was relatively old. A combination of increased business confidence and rising profits was needed to induce firms to invest. But big business and the New Deal administration were at daggers drawn. The attack on the evils of monopoly by the Temporary National Economic Committee was interpreted by the business community as a hostile act. If the US economy were placed on a war footing, relations with business, especially big business, would have to be repaired. The US did not have a large standing army and, with defence expenditure at less than 2 per cent of GNP in 1939, the military was quite unprepared for a major war.

Roosevelt had to use all his political skill to manoeuvre the US closer to a war which he probably felt was inevitable, without leaving himself open to the accusation that increased defence activity was, in reality, preparation for intervention. In late 1939, however, the Neutrality Acts were amended to permit belligerent nations to purchase US goods, if they paid cash and could provide their own transport. As the Allies controlled the Atlantic, they could now acquire much needed military supplies. There was, however, a restriction on Britain's ability to pay, as her gold and dollar reserves were limited.

In 1940, when France fell, it became increasingly clear that Britain could not survive without direct US aid. War loans had been discredited during the 1920s but a donation of products vital to the British war effort would provoke isolationist opposition. Roosevelt, therefore, decided to lend goods rather than money, and pressed for the Lend Lease Act, which was passed by Congress in March 1941. This Act gave the President the power to sell, transfer, lease or lend defence equipment to any country whose defence was considered essential to that of the US. Initially, $7 bn was appropriated by Congress for Lend Lease, but a total of $50 bn was finally spent, the major part going to Britain. Eventually, 38 countries received Lend Lease even though many, not directly involved in the fighting, had a supply of dollars sufficient to pay for goods in cash. The advantage of Lend

Lease to them was that they were able to purchase commodities which, because of war restrictions, would have been unavailable even to cash purchasers (Mikesel, 1952). In other words, Lend Lease was most important as a procurement mechanism.

Britain had to pay for most of the goods she received from the US in 1941, as Lend Lease took time to become fully operational, and not until 1943 did deliveries under this scheme exceed supplies paid for in cash. The result was that Britain's net asset position in the US contracted by $16 bn during World War II. Furthermore, as it turned out, goods received under Lend Lease after V-J Day were chargeable. During the war years, in exchange for Lend Lease goods, Britain provided facilities and supplies for US military personnel in Great Britain and also supplied materials and labour for military projects in Great Britain and the Empire.

Although Lend Lease was a vital lifeline for Britain, there were some drawbacks. To ensure that Britain did not become a subsidised industrial rival, the US Congress insisted that no Lend Lease goods could be used for the production of exports. In addition, governments eligible for Lend Lease had no entitlement to goods; they could only make requests. If the US felt that a country could afford to purchase, it would be required to do so. Britain, therefore, faced a continual drain on her gold and dollar reserves during the war and emerged from it in a particularly vulnerable position. No such pressure was placed upon the Soviet Union, the second largest recipient of Lend Lease.

The demands of war from both home and overseas stimulated the US economy. Expanding civilian consumption, domestic military requirements and the needs of the Allied powers all competed for key resources. Clearly, some administrative organisation was required to ensure that scarce raw materials could be conserved and allocated to high priority users and to decide what should happen if rising private consumption conflicted with the need for additional military output. Between 1939 and 1941, a number of defence agencies were created in an attempt to rationalise competing demands without alarming those who did not want America to become embroiled in war.

In November 1939, the War Resources Board (WRB) was established, comprising a number of leading businessmen under the chairmanship of E. R. Stettinus of the US Steel Corporation. Stettinus wanted to co-ordinate military production under a single authority which would have strong links with big business. This was politically unacceptable to Roosevelt and the WRB was scrapped in November 1939. For several months no further attempt was made to set up a regulatory agency, but in May 1940 the Office of Emergency Management (OEM) was created. Within the framework of OEM, the National Defense Advisory Commission (NDAC) operated, staffed with representatives of business, organised labour, government and the universities, several of whom had worked in World War I and New Deal agencies. During its short existence, NDAC took positive steps to improve data collection, to institute controls on profits on war contracts and to rationalise priorities. Vatter believes that the NDAC laid the foundations on which other agencies could be built. In August 1940, the Defense Plant Corporation was founded as a subsidiary of the RFC, its *raison d'être* to accelerate the expansion of industrial capacity.

1941 saw a number of organisational changes. His presidential victory in 1940, and the swing of public opinion towards Britain, had strengthened Roosevelt's hand. In January 1941 the Office for Production Management (OPM) was established to replace NDAC, under the joint leadership of W.S. Knudsen, an executive of General Motors, and S. Hillman, head of the Amalgamated Clothing Workers trade union. One of the duties of the OPM was to decide which defence materials were needed and how they could best be produced. Continuing shortages of raw materials led to the creation of the Supply Priorities and Allocation Board (SPAB), with Donald Nelson of Sears Roebuck at its head. SPAB established priorities and controlled raw materials. Once policies had been decided they could be implemented by OPM (US Bureau of the Budget, 1946).

Production for the mobilisation effort was poorly co-ordinated before Pearl Harbor. Fortunately, because there was so much slack in the economy and because war expenditure was relatively low, disturbing strains were not noticeable until late 1941. However, Roosevelt failed to control a wasteful rivalry between the many defence agencies and the armed services. In large part, this was because rapid adoption of a centralised system of war purchasing would have aroused hostility. Moreover, the conflict between the various competing groups gave more power to the final arbiter, Roosevelt. To sum up, before the Japanese attacked Pearl Harbor on 7 December 1941, America was on the way to creating a war economy. By the last quarter of 1941 military spending was 16 per cent of GNP, and between 1939 and 1941 the federal deficit had doubled. Conscription was introduced in 1940; by late 1941 the use of certain raw materials was curtailed, restrictions on civilian consumption were imposed, and several war agencies had been established.

A key problem for the rearming nation was that war expenditure led to more jobs, higher income and, inevitably, a rise in consumer expenditure. It was difficult to persuade firms to leave the expanding civilian market and tool up for a war which might never materialise. Automobile factory sales had reached 3.9 million in 1937, fell to 2.0 million in 1938, but rose to 3.7 million in 1940, a figure which was maintained during the following year. It is hardly surprising that the automobile companies refused to convert passenger car assembly lines to military use. Total raw steel production rose from 67 million short tons in 1940 to 86 million short tons in 1942; the steel companies, however, refused to expand capacity because they feared a collapse in military orders. Even though business was tempted by costs-plus-fixed-fee defence contracts and tax concessions, the private market was too attractive to abandon.

Between 1939 and 1941 real GNP rose by 20 per cent and expenditure on consumer durables increased by 23 per cent in real terms. Firms responded to this expansion by increasing investment; gross private domestic investment rose steadily from $9.6 bn in 1939, to $13.1 bn in 1940 and to $17.9 bn in 1941, with the latter figure actually exceeding the peak which had been established in 1929. Unemployment fell from 14.6 per cent of the civilian labour force in 1940 to 9.9 per cent in the following year; although some distance from full employment, this was the lowest figure since 1930. The average weekly earnings of production workers in the manufacture of durable goods increased from $26.19 in 1939 to $33.56 in 1941. Many Americans could now afford to buy goods which they had been denied for years, and industry was happily satisfying that demand. The resulting conflict between civilian and military pressures could not be allowed to continue.

The Farmer at War

In wartime the role of the agricultural sector was to provide food and raw materials for America and her allies. Within this broad remit the farm sector had to remedy specific shortages; for example, the Japanese advance through south-east Asia cut off vital imports (sugar, oil and fruit) which had to be replaced. Agricultural output is difficult to increase or to reorientate in a short period. There were especial problems in co-ordinating and mobilising millions of small farmers who were

Table 16.1 Agricultural Change During World War II

	1940	1941	1942	1943	1944	1945
Farm population (mn)	30.5	30.1	28.9	26.2	24.8	24.4
Net change of farm population through migration (000)	−788	−1,587	−3,145	−1,740	−748	671
Per capita personal income of farm population from all sources ($)	249	335	487	629	671	705
Index of average value of farm real estate per acre (1967 = 100)	21	21	23	25	28	31
Total outstanding farm mortgage debt ($bn)	6.6	6.5	6.4	6.0	5.4	4.9
Parity ratio (1910−14 = 100)	81	93	105	113	108	109
Index of total farm output (1967 = 100)	60	62	69	68	70	69

Source: Historical Statistics of US, Colonial Times to 1970, 2 vols (Washington DC, 1975), Series K1, 3, 16, 261, 361, 353, 414.

reluctant to plant new crops unless the government underwrote a large part of the risk. For some years the government had been struggling to implement a policy designed to restrict output, not to raise it; a reversal was not possible immediately, particularly at a time when stocks of farm produce were plentiful and when all concerned were anxious to avoid a boom and bust similar to that induced by World War I. Farmers were particularly keen to obtain guarantees from the government that a serious slump would not result from increased output (US Bureau of the Budget, 1946). A further problem was that agricultural policy cannot exist in isolation from the rest of the economy: a balance had to be achieved between the high prices necessary to stimulate output and excessive farm price increases, which would lead to spiralling industrial costs and compensatory wage demands from consumers.

During World War II, total farm output increased by approximately 17 per cent, with the fastest rate of growth occurring betweenn 1942 and 1944 (Table 16.1). Compared with the situation in World War I, when agricultural output was stagnant, the farm sector exhibited great flexibility, though some farmers did use scarce resources to grow surplus or low priority crops. During these years the US farmer produced 50 per cent more food annually than in 1917–18, whilst employing 10 per cent fewer workers. This was achieved without substantially increasing the acreage for basic crops. One should not, of course, lay too much emphasis on comparisons with 1917–18, two relatively poor crop years. Nevertheless, agricultural performance between 1939 and 1945 was far more satisfactory than in World War I.

In 1939, with a two-year supply of wheat, corn and cotton, the farm sector was swamped with surpluses. By 1940 the shortage of storage space was so acute in wheat-growing regions that old school buildings and even churches were utilised. Steel containers were placed at railroad sidings to store the corn crop. The 'ever normal granary' had produced such plenty that the Commodity Credit Corporation seemed about to suffer the same fate as had the Federal Farm Board in 1931 (Schultz, 1945). In spite of great efforts to contain it, the volume of agricultural output in 1940 was 10 per cent greater than in 1933 and 16 per cent above the level of 1918.

Initially, farmers were despondent at the prospect of a war which they expected to destroy trade, and the collapse of agricultural exports in 1941 seemed to confirm that prognosis. Nevertheless, farmers and agricultural administrators found it difficult to shake off their depression mentality, and wanted to avoid a further expansion of stocks which would have an adverse effect upon prices when the war was over. There was, therefore, a reluctance to increase the acreage devoted to food and feed crops in the early stages of the war. Thus 86 million acres of corn were harvested in 1940, and only 87 million acres in 1942, rising to 94 million acres in 1944. For wheat, the acreage harvested was 53 million in 1940, 50 million in 1942, 51 million in 1943, and 60 million in 1944. This sluggish response came in spite of the fact that the price of corn and wheat practically doubled between 1939 and 1943, though farmers could complain that shortages of labour and fuel blunted their reaction to market forces.

Because of the great surpluses of grains which could be used as animal feed and war-induced changes in land use, the production of livestock increased more than that of crops during the war years. Pasture land increased by just over 20 per cent at the expense of crop land. As a result, meat production rose by over 50 per cent, with pork the leading product; poultry and dairy products were not far behind. These output levels were far in excess of the increases achieved during 1914—18 when feedstuffs were scarce. In 1940 they were not only plentiful but could also be supplemented by imports from Canada. Not until 1944 was the supply of feedstuffs significantly reduced, and farmers responded by increasing acreage. During the war, the civilian per capita consumption of dairy produce (excluding butter), meat and poultry products, pulses, vegetables and grain products increased markedly. Consumer expenditure on foods produced on US farms rose from $14 bn in 1940, to $24 bn in 1945 as the public, unable to purchase consumer goods because of rationing, used their newfound affluence to extend their diet. By late 1942, however, shortages of meat, fats, dairy produce and canned foods were apparent. Even though food production was susbstantially above the 1935—9 average, consumer demand was too high to be fully satisfied. Moreover, the armed forces, whose per capita consumption was far greater than that of the civilian population, and America's allies had a claim to a substantial proportion of agricultural output.

In sharp contrast to the pattern of grain production, there was a large increase in the output of oil-bearing crops. It was essential, once the Japanese had cut off US supplies in the Pacific, to produce import substitutes. The acreage devoted to soy beans and to flax seed doubled; cotton seed and peanuts were also important sources of vegetable oil. While Schultz sees the expansion of oil-bearing crops as one of the outstanding achievements of agriculture during the war, Benedict, on the other hand, finds their performance disappointing, as output fell so far short of the targets set.

Nearly half the rise in farm output during the war was due to an increase in yields. Here improved farming techniques played a major part, including the use of better seeds, higher levels of expenditure on fertilisers, and an increased knowledge of disease and pest control. The advice given to farmers by the State Agricultural Extension Services and the elimination of many wasteful practices under New Deal soil conservation programmes also proved valuable. Just as important was the unusually favourable weather during the war years. Had the droughts of the 1930s reappeared, serious agricultural bottlenecks would have resulted (Wilcox, 1947). A further weapon in the armoury to increase output was the production targets, which were introduced in early 1942. Their adoption ensured greater flexibility as domestic and foreign demand changed. The incentive to cultivate crops in short supply could be increased by means of price supports; in this way, for example, the production of oils and fats was stimulated.

The Farm Labour Force

Growing labour shortages gave farmers the incentive to mechanise, and rising income gave them the means to do so. The number of tractors and other mechanical equipment which minimised the need for seasonal labour increased rapidly between 1939 and 1943, but was then restricted as farm machinery was rationed. Increasing affluence enabled farms in regions which had witnessed great deprivation during the 1930s to embrace technology and improve labour productivity. The numbers of horses and mules declined, releasing for other uses land which had been set aside to provide feed for them. The spread of electricity into rural areas, made possible by the New Deal's Rural Electrification Administration, enabled farmers to use their labour more efficiently by, for example, introducing milking machinery. However, the bigger farms run by commercially oriented operators were best able to seize the opportunities which the war provided. They were the most likely to increase mechanisation and had the skills to implement new farming techniques. Even in 1945, fewer than half US farms possessed a tractor; war demand presented greater opportunities to the large farmer than the small.

Between 1939 and 1945, about five million people left farms for the armed forces or non-agricultural jobs (Table 16.1). The farm population, which was 23.6 per cent of the total population in the former year, was only 17.5 per cent in the latter. Rural America surrendered many of its disguised unemployed, particularly those from the Great Plains states, which had been devastated by drought, and the subsistence holdings of the South East. Their destinations were the centres of shipbuilding, munitions and aircraft manufacture, mostly located in the states of California, Washington and Michigan. Urban centres such as Los Angeles, San Francisco, Detroit, Norfolk (Va.) and Mobile (Ala.) swelled with migrants. Blacks left their dismal croppers cottages and moved not only to those metropolitan centres which had been a magnet for over two decades, but also to the Pacific coast. The exodus of labourers and share-croppers from the South was the main cause of the 22 per cent contraction in that region's farm population (Wright, 1986). The most marginal farmers were the first to give up their unequal struggle with the land.

The reduction in the number of tenant farmers (2.4 million in 1940; 1.9 million in 1945) helped to transform parts of the countryside. Tenancy had been declining since 1930 but the war greatly accelerated this trend; as a corollary, the number of fully and partially owned farms increased, as some tenants were able to purchase the land which they farmed. The 6.4 million farms in existence in 1939, however, had been reduced to 5.9 million by 1945. The migrations enabled farmers to consolidate holdings into bigger units — the war saw fewer farms of larger average size, as small tenant plots were amalgamated and farmed with the help of machinery.

During the war, 730,000 family workers and over 600,000 hired workers left agriculture; by 1941 signs of an emerging labour shortage were evident, which soon affected wages. On average, daily rates for hired workers (without accommodation) rose from $1.55 in 1939 to $4.35 in 1945. Wage rates rose fastest on the Pacific coast and on the Great Plains where feed and livestock production was most intense. In order to contain competitive wage bidding, agricultural wages were controlled, initially in 1942, and during the following year more rigorously, by the War Food Administrator. However, rates had to be high enough to retain sufficient labour.

As we have seen, one response to labour shortages was greater mechanisation. Another was dilution; juveniles, the elderly and females played an increasing role in agriculture. Farm labour worked longer hours and was used with increasing care, and Congress, by granting selective exemptions from military conscription, prevented a further reduction in the workforce. In addition, foreign workers were recruited by the government from Mexico and the Caribbean to join prisoners of war in providing extra farm hands. By adding new workers to the labour force, by working longer hours, but above all by increasing productivity, American farmers overcame the difficulties presented by a shrinking agricultural population. The wartime increase in productivity meant that the number of persons 'fed' by a single farm worker rose from 10.7 in 1940 to 14.6 in 1945.

The Distribution of Foodstuffs

Initially, no urgent need was felt for new government regulation. It was believed that additional output would naturally follow the rising prices which would be brought about by increased demand. General price increases, unfortunately, have some disadvantages. They encourage farmers to produce commodities which may not be required for the war effort, for example short staple cotton, and also lead to the erosion of urban real wages. Alternatively, farmers can be stimulated to produce particular crops via price supports, for which there was a long history in the United States. The War Food Administration had guaranteed the price of hogs and wheat in 1917, the Federal Farm Board had attempted to prop up prices in 1931 and the Commodity Credit Corporation had put a floor on the price of several crops in 1933. The high prices which prevailed for basic crops forced the Department of Agriculture to establish high loan rates and price supports in its attempt to persuade farmers to shift to substitute crops which were held to be of greater importance to the war effort.

In 1941, when the country became conscious of the rising cost of living, it was evident that some controls were necessary. However, skilfully pressured by the farm lobby, Congress accepted that price controls should not be placed upon any agricultural commodity until it reached 110 per cent of parity. Such a generous commitment could not be maintained if the growing inflation was to be restrained. Roosevelt wanted agricultural prices to be kept at 100 per cent of parity, which farm interests were reluctant to concede. Agreement was eventually reached in late 1942; as a reward for complying with Roosevelt's request, farmers were granted tighter wage controls and the promise that price supports would be continued for two years after the war. With a guarantee of a price floor, the spectre of the post-1918 boom and collapse was erased and increased output could be pursued with more confidence. In spite of Roosevelt's efforts, however, prices continued to exceed 100 per cent parity. Farm pressure groups were successful in their determination to maintain a price system, the parity ratio, which had as its basis price relationships which prevailed in 1910–14. Parity was not an effective guide for farm policy during World War II.

To stabilise rising consumer prices, the government decided to pay subsidies on key commodities. The farm organisations opposed subsidy payments because they believed that consumers could afford to pay higher prices; furthermore, if consumers became used to high prices in war they would probably pay them in peace. Nevertheless, in spite of these objections, the government maintained subsidies as an essential part of its anti-inflation programme. In May 1943, the retail prices of lamb, mutton, pork, veal, coffee and butter were reduced by about 10 per cent. To maintain output at these lower prices a subsidy was paid to food processors. By the end of the war $500 mn had been spent subsidising meat, and over $400 mn on dairy produce.

In war, government has the task of seeing that food and raw materials are distributed according to centrally determined priorities. As consumers, with rising incomes, competed for food products on which there were price controls, it became clear that the introduction of rationing was unavoidable, though there was a conflict between the OPA and the Department of Agriculture as to where the responsibility should lie. Three key agencies emerged to oversee allocation: the Combined Food Board handled priorities for Lend Lease recipients, the Office of Price Administration (OPA) was in charge of rationing and price control, and overall responsibility for the distribution of foodstuffs was given, in 1943, to the War Food Administration (WFA). Of course, many other wartime agencies were involved.

The WFA was depression minded, fearing the accumulation of surpluses. Consequently, its distribution of stocks was relatively unrestrained. The OPA urged a more conservative stock policy but, fortunately, bumper crops during the war and, most important, during the post-war years, prevented the crisis which a harvest failure would have precipitated. Rationing was masterminded by the OPA which distributed supplies made available by the WFA. Sugar and coffee, both imports, were rationed, as were processed foods and meat. US rationing was not as rigorous nor as systematically organised as in Britain, but in both countries the public saw that it was an equitable means of distributing food. In spite of rationing, per capita food consumption in the US increased. The diet of the average American during the war was far more varied than the monotonous, though healthy, fare consumed in Britain. Per capita meat consumption in the US was 134 lbs before the war and reached a wartime peak of 162 lbs in 1944; the figures for Britain were 132 lbs and 115 lbs. Such plentiful domestic food supplies were the result of the WFA's generosity, which became even more pronounced in 1944—5, and of the farmers' shift to livestock production.

Rising Farm Living Standards

World War II had a dramatic effect upon the farm and the farmer. A declining farm population and rising agricultural prices led to a rapid increase in both per capita income and the parity ratio (Table 16.1). The fastest rate of growth occurred between 1939 and 1943; thereafter, subsidies modified price increases. The parity ratio reached 105 in 1942, its highest level since 1919, and rose to a wartime peak of 113 in the following year (Table 16.1), but the 1917 peak of 120 was never achieved in World War II. Farmers benefited enormously from the war; farm income rose faster than non-farm income, although we should remember that this increase was from the exceptionally low levels of the late 1930s. Farm workers also experienced a sharp increase in wages. The differentials between farm and non-farm incomes were narrowed but, in 1946, the average per capita income of farm dwellers from all sources was only 60 per cent of that of non-farm people.

High farm prices led to rising land values, just as they had between 1915 and 1920. The reaction of farmers to the land boom in World War II was, however, different. During World War I there had been a frantic scramble to buy land and, as a result, mortgage indebtedness rose. Between 1939 and 1945, however, mortgage indebtedness fell from $6.6 bn to $4.9 bn (Table 16.1). Perhaps farmers had learned a lesson from the collapse in land values during the 1920s, or perhaps they heeded the warnings of banks and government agencies not to engage in land speculation (Wilcox, 1947). Many, of course, were in a position to pay cash for land, especially as the opportunity to purchase consumer durables was curtailed by rationing. Whatever restraint was uppermost in their minds, the result was that farmers were in an excellent financial position in 1945. High levels of savings meant that rural banks were awash with deposits.

The war helped generate a revolution on the land which had been beyond the scope of the New Deal. The provision of large numbers of non-farm jobs, sustained high prices, the use of new techniques, the reduction of stocks of grain, the adoption of machinery and a decline in the numbers of rural poor were the beginnings of a radical transformation in agriculture. Farmers hoped that the disasters of the 1920s, which had spelled ruin for many, could be avoided in the post-war world, and they looked to the government, which had become deeply involved in the agricultural sector during the Depression, to be equally enmeshed after 1945.

The Economy after Pearl Harbor

After 7 December 1941, the US strove to mobilise resources with all possible speed, in order to win a total victory. Government spending reached new heights, company profits soared and monopolistic collusion went unchecked, as the energies of the New Dealers were directed towards the war. Expenditure on the armed forces, which had risen from \$1.3 bn in 1939 to \$6.26 bn in 1941, underwent an even more dramatic expansion: \$22.9 bn in 1942, \$63.4 bn in 1943, \$75.9 bn in 1944 and \$80.5 bn in 1945. The financial commitment to the services went far beyond that of 1917–18. Indeed, these sums made New Deal spending seem paltry by comparison. Total expenditure on the WPA was only \$9 bn between 1935 and 1945. The \$50 bn which was spent on Lend Lease was almost equal to total federal expenditure between 1933 and 1939. The New Deal's critics had constantly accused the government of undermining the economy with its profligacy; expenditure on the war, however, proved acceptable to all shades of political opinion.

The transformation of the economy is clearly visible in Table 16.2, which shows that real GNP rose by 70 per cent between 1939 and 1945. Industrial production grew steadily from the summer of 1938 and especially rapidly from the spring of 1940. America's entry into the war gave the economy an additional boost. Over \$100 bn worth of war contracts were placed in the first half of 1942, though the largely unco-ordinated scramble for resources encouraged much waste. Up to Deember 1942, over 70 per cent of all war contracts had been awarded to the hundred largest organisations; the industrial capacity of small businesses was therefore under-utilised. Wartime expansion reached its peak in 1943 after which point the rate of growth in GNP lessened. By then, however, public opinion had come to accept that government expenditure could bring about the economic revival which had been so elusive during the 1930s.

Table 16.2 Wartime GNP: Total and Per Capita in Current and 1958 Prices

	Current prices		1958 prices	
	Total ($bn)	Per capita ($)	Total ($bn)	Per capita ($)
1929	103	847	204	1671
1933	56	442	142	1126
1939	91	691	209	1598
1940	100	754	227	1720
1941	125	934	264	1977
1942	158	1171	298	2208
1943	192	1401	337	2465
1944	210	1518	361	2611
1945	212	1515	355	2538

Source: *Historical Statistics of US, Colonial Times to 1970*, 2 vols (Washington DC, 1975), Series F1–4.

Total output expanded impressively during the war, with the manufacturing sector to the fore (the manufacturing labour force rose from 11 million in 1940 to 17.3 million in 1944). Durable manufactures, which had begun a sustained expansion in 1940, reached a peak in the winter of 1943−4 (Figure 16.1). By 1943 the production of machinery had risen by over 300 per cent since 1939, transport equipment by 600 per cent, and non-ferrous metals by 100 per cent. Between 1941 and 1945, 300,000 aircraft were produced, 51 million tons of merchant shipping and 8.5 million tons of naval shipping. By 1944 war production was approximately twice as great as that of Germany, Italy and Japan combined, and provided 60 per cent of combat munitions for the Allies. American business had, with encouragement from the government, devoted its formidable energies to the war effort. Automobile manufacturers turned their talent to aeroplane manufacture. The Ford Motor Company constructed at Willow Run, a small community near Detroit, a massive airplane plant which, at its peak, produced one giant bomber each hour. The aircraft industry, which had been about the sixtieth largest industry in the US on the eve of the war, was the tenth largest by 1944. As a consequence of the reorientation of production, new passenger automobile sales were practically zero in 1943 and 1944, and rose to only 70,000 in 1945. At the end of the war, therefore, there was a pent-up demand for the automobile manufacturers to satisfy. Shipbuilding, too, was a wartime priority. Fortunately, the US had begun an emergency ship construction programme before Pearl Harbor; this was of considerable benefit once hostilities commenced and speedy construction was essential. In the early stages of the war it was decided that the US would concentrate on merchant marine shipping and the British on naval vessels. America's solution to the shipping crisis was to mass produce ships of a simple design — Liberty ships — which permitted the maximum use of prefabrication and sub-assembly. Welding replaced riveting in order to save labour and increase productivity. In 1941 the average time taken to construct a Liberty ship was 355 days; by late 1942 this had been reduced to 56 days, and one yard actually completed a vessel in two weeks.

The emphasis on durable goods explains why the rise in manufacturing output was so much larger than the expansion in GNP. Non-durable manufactures, however, also expanded. In spite of wartime pressures, the output of textiles and alcoholic beverages rose by 50 per cent and processed foodstuffs by 40 per cent between 1939 and 1945. Much of the increased war demand, therefore, was met by expanding total production rather than by diverting civilian resources to the war effort.

The government played a leading role in the mobilisation of resources, and, of necessity, relations with the business community were repaired. This was not the time to wage a crusade for radical reform, but for using the existing structure to maximum effect. If monopolistic practices helped pave the way for victory, they were permissible. Industrialists, for their part, realised the power of government to keep the economy, and therefore profits, buoyant. As in World War I, 'dollar-a-year men', usually from the large corporations, moved into positions

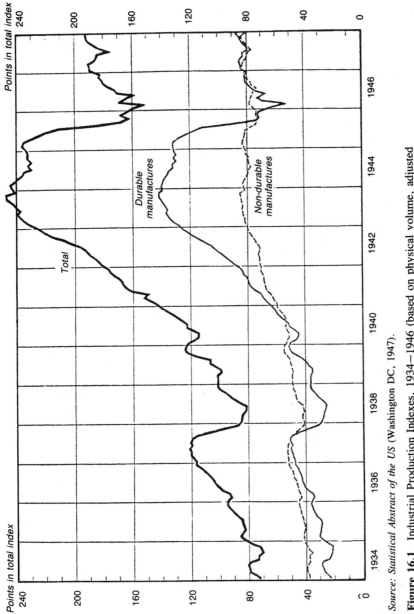

Source: Statistical Abstract of the US (Washington DC, 1947).

Figure 16.1 Industrial Production Indexes, 1934–1946 (based on physical volume, adjusted for seasonal variation, 1935–9 average for total=100)

of managerial authority in Washington. They naturally brought with them an unshakeable belief in the efficiency of big business and were able to strike up a close relationship with the military, who preferred to deal with a few large corporations rather than with many small firms. Big business benefited particularly from the war; 30 private firms received approximately half of all war contracts and most of the subcontracting was between large companies. Small business was often forced to concentrate on civilian production, where labour and raw materials were in short supply.

In order to give the war effort a greater sense of urgency, Roosevelt created the War Production Board in January 1942, with Donald Nelson as its chairman. Its task was to act as both catalyst and supervisor in the drive for more production. By the middle of 1942, the manufacture of motor cars was forbidden as was house building, and the use of scarce materials in the manufacture of consumer goods was restricted. The WPB also controlled the allocation of raw materials to firms working on war contracts. Manufacturers were enticed into accepting war work by tax incentives and guaranteed profits. Corporate profits, after tax, rose from $5.6 bn in 1939 to a wartime peak of $11.2 bn in 1944.

The WPB failed to display dynamism and was, moreover, prone to internal squabbles which Nelson was unable to resolve. The President, therefore, created the Office of War Mobilization (May 1943) under the chairmanship of James F. Byrnes, with wide-ranging powers to act as an arbiter between competing military and civilian demands. For the first time, there was an agency which could co-ordinate the needs of both military and civilian organisations. The OWM did not face the challenge of raising output; that had already been accomplished. It soon, however, had to deal with the problem of selective reconversion to civilian output, as a surplus was apparent in some branches of armament production by late 1943.

The agencies which were established to instil a sense of direction and urgency into the war effort were not an unqualified success. In both industry and agriculture, despite the recent experience in World War I, organisations were slow to evolve, seemed incapable of resolving differences between themselves, the military, business and the New Dealers, and lacked a strong central authority to impose priorities. Roosevelt was partly to blame for this. He liked competition between a number of agencies rather than one which was clearly dominant. Fortunately, output rose impressively, even though the bodies designed to stimulate and control it were often prey to conflict.

Between 1940 and the end of the war, manufacturing industry spent $11.4 bn on new plant and equipment, a higher level of expenditure than for the whole of the 1930s. The government, on the other hand, spent $16 bn through the Defense Plant Corporation, a subsidiary of the RFC, creating new capital for private industry; a further $1.7 bn went to establish additional capacity for the government itself. The largest part of new capacity, therefore, from which poured forth the hugely increased volume of manufacturing output, was the result of public funding (R.J. Gordon, 1969). This was essential, as private business was either reluctant to invest in new types of industrial plant or was so determined to pursue narrow sectional interests that serious bottlenecks occurred in essential supplies. The government built synthetic rubber plants which, by 1944, accounted for nearly 90 per cent of all rubber consumed. At the outbreak of war there was only one US manufacturer of aluminium, a metal essential for aircraft production. The government ensured that supplies would be sufficient by creating new manufacturers. Federal money poured into shipyards, ammunition plants and into the Manhattan Project, which developed the atomic bomb. Government investment, therefore, was vital to those industries which were under the greatest pressure during the war (J.H. Jones, 1951). Certain of these war plants were taken over by private business at extremely favourable rates after 1945.

There were great political pressures on the administration, which sought to influence the location and the types of war plant. Industrial growth during these years had a profound impact on regions previously lacking a non-agricultural base. The South, whose politicians had scorned federal funding during the 1930s, fought for government money (Wright, 1986). This region was the recipient of military training camps, shipyards, ordnance factories, transportation and chemical plants, and new petroleum plants (Tindall, 1967). New investment in the poorest region of the US laid the foundation for an expansion of relatively high-pay, non-farm jobs in the post-war period. War, therefore, economically transformed the economy of the South by enabling millions of southerners to migrate and by sparking an industrial revolution which would have been impossible in peacetime.

In most cases, the government was industry's only customer and was prepared not only to fund generously but also, through the Office of Scientific Research and Development (1941), to co-ordinate the efforts of scientists. The big corporations and the universities were best equipped to handle sophisticated research and development in a range of fields which included electronics and jet propulsion. Strong links were forged between business and the armed forces, which later became identified as the 'military—industrial complex'.

During the New Deal, government expenditure had been confined to roads, dams and other civil engineering projects. During the war, these limitations no longer applied and Washington was able to spend billions of dollars building up the manufacturing sector and even operating some plants itself. Though business liked to see war production as a triumph of free enterprise, the role of government investment was crucial. So much so, in fact, that federal guidance of the economy during the post-war years was viewed, even by businessmen, as a route, and perhaps as the only route, to economic stability.

The Labour Force

The expansion of the armed forces was a major priority for the government. From 1.6 million in 1941, the numbers enlisted rose to 11.4 million at the end of the war. During this period, therefore, an additional ten million men and women had to be selected, trained and sent to Europe or the Pacific. This rapid increase in forces personnel, however, did not bring about a commensurate decline in the labour force (Table 16.3). The employed non-farm workforce rose from 41.3 million in 1941 to a peak of 45.4 million in 1943; by 1945 it was 44.2 million. It was as essential to have workers in the factories and the fields as in the theatre of war. Indiscriminate conscription would have left key industries desperately short of labour and the forces short of weapons. The expansion of the civilian labour force during the war does, however, require an explanation.

Table 16.3   The Labour Force during World War II ('000 persons 14 years and over)

	Total labour force	Armed forces	Civilian labour force	Employed		Unemployed	
				Farm	Non-farm	% of civilian labour force	% of non-farm
1940	56,180	540	55,640	9,540	37,980	14.6	21.3
1941	57,530	1,620	55,910	9,100	41,250	9.9	14.4
1942	60,380	3,970	56,410	9,250	44,500	4.7	6.8
1943	64,560	9,020	55,540	9,080	45,390	1.9	2.7
1944	66,040	11,410	54,630	8,950	45,010	1.2	1.7
1945	65,290	11,430	53,860	8,580	44,240	1.9	2.7

Source: Historical Statistics of US, Colonial Times to 1970, 2 vols (Washington DC, 1975), Series D1–10.

Initially, there were millions of unemployed to be absorbed by the expanding economy; by 1942, full employment had been reached and during the remaining years of the war the unemployable dominated the jobless total. Job creation, brought about by high levels of government expenditure, had finally triumphed over the cancer of unemployment. The absorption of the unemployed into the ranks of the employed, however, does not explain the growth in the total number at work. Some of the rise occurred because of a natural growth in the population of working age, but more important was the emergence of hidden, or disguised, reserves of labour to fill the expanding jobs. People who previously did not want to work, or those who had felt that searching for jobs was pointless, given their scarcity, became available for employment. Those whom employers would not hire in times of plenty (for example, the disabled) were placed on the pay roll. In other words, the labour force participation rate changed. Workers beyond retirement age, young people below conscription age, and, especially, women entered the labour force in large numbers. So many, in fact, wanted to work that the depressingly high unemployment figures of the 1930s appear a gross underestimate.

The manufacturing workforce increased by about 60 per cent during the war, but during the same period industrial production doubled. Labour was used with greater efficiency, as management was able to offer extensive overtime and introduce a shift system which would not have been tolerated by workers in peacetime. The introduction of new capital equipment plus a greater emphasis upon training and efficiency, often in response to shortages of workers with particular skills, enabled labour productivity to increase by 25 per cent. It was the intelligent use of labour rather than its quantity which helped to explain the rise in war production. High productivity not only ensured a high volume of output, but also cheaper output during a time of inflation.

Industry also benefited from a redistribution of the labour force. Migration removed millions from subsistence agriculture and other low-pay jobs. Not all moved over long distances. Many of those who gravitated to the new plants faced gross overcrowding, deteriorating public health and hostility from the local population. Migration led to racial clashes, in places to which blacks and Mexicans moved. Indeed, blacks experienced great difficulty in securing jobs in the expanding defence industries. In response to a threat by black leaders to organise a march on Washington, in the summer of 1941, to publicise their grievances, Roosevelt issued an Executive Order prohibiting discrimination and set up the Fair Employment Practices Committee. It attempted, with only very modest success, to ensure equal opportunity in hiring on government contracted work. Inter-state migration between 1941 and 1945 was, on average, double that of 1920–40. This, plus a virtual cessation of house building, led to a backlog of demand which the construction industry began to satisfy after 1945.

World War II, like its predecessor, encouraged women to join the ranks of the waged. From 13.8 million in 1940, the female labour force rose to 18.4 million in 1944; the most marked increase was in the number of married women (from five million to 8.4 million). The bulk of wartime job expansion occurred in manufacturing industry and women were able to move into shipyards, heavy engineering and aircraft manfacture, as well as the more traditional clerical employment. The majority of migrants were women and it is possible that this movement helped to destabilise further families who were already split by the conscription of a husband or father. As in 1918, most women surrendered, not always willingly, their lucrative war jobs to returning veterans.

Workers were drawn to defence-related industries by high wage levels. The average weekly earnings of a durable goods production worker rose rapidly ($28.07 in 1940; $51.38 in 1944). Other industries also showed large increases; bituminous coal (from $23.74 to $49.32) and construction workers (from $31.70 to $52.18) are typical examples. These were high weekly earnings, at a time of regular employment with frequent overtime; annual earnings were, therefore, also high. Wages increased faster than the consumer price index, although, as we shall see later, this index has serious deficiencies which render real wage calculations difficult. Families with more than one wage earner often had incomes which would have been beyond their wildest dreams during the depression. The poor were especially able to make significant gains and the distribution of income became more equitable.

Both world wars led to a sharp rise in trade union membership. Between 1941 and 1945 total membership rose from 10.5 million to 14.8 million, continuing the strong upward trend evident since 1935. Unions were helped by the 'maintenance of membership' policy adopted by the War Labor Board. Under this system, every new worker hired in a plant with a union contract became a member automatically, unless he contracted out within 15 days. The union leaders had accepted a no-strike agreement with Roosevelt during the war but, inevitably, there were strikes as militants flexed their muscles against their employers and absent union officials. Although wildcat strikes attracted great publicity, output as a whole was little affected by industrial disputes. The power of unions, and their spokesmen, during the war was, however, insignificant compared with that of business (Koistinen, 1973).

The performance of the civilian labour force during the war was exceptionally good; labour shortages were never as acute as those of raw materials and transportation equipment. To achieve a small increase in the size of the labour force at a time when ten million active people were removed for military service was an achievement which surprised many contemporaries. Industry coped well with the influx of workers, many of whom had no industrial experience, by organising training programmes, and helping with accommodation, nurseries, schools and the other services which new arrivals needed. The labour supply, however, was not strained to breaking point. There were still large numbers of underemployed in rural America and the participation rate of women was far below that of Britain where, of course, they were conscripted. Perhaps the ample supply of labour can be offered as an explanation as to why manpower planning was so slow to develop and was never implemented with much conviction.

The Attempt to Control Inflation

As incomes increased far faster than the supply of the goods which consumers wanted, inflation was evident even before America entered the war. Since 1933 the government had been trying to raise prices; by 1941 they had reached their 1929 level and continued to rise, threatening to make war contracts progressively more expensive. Increased taxation and the growth of personal savings (from $6.9 bn in 1939 to a peak of $39.3 bn in 1944) played a part in limiting inflation, but the government also took a direct role in curbing price increases. By controls on prices and wages, by the payment of subsidies and by the introduction of rationing, the advance of inflation was checked between 1942 and V-J Day (Figure 16.2). Price rises during World War II were much more effectively contained than in World War I.

Early in 1942, the OPA was given the power to set maximum prices, but could not control food prices until they had reached 110 per cent of parity. These selective price controls were ineffective, especially as food prices were a key ingredient in the cost of living index. In April, therefore, the OPA issued the General Maximum Price Regulation (known as General Max) which, with a few exceptions,

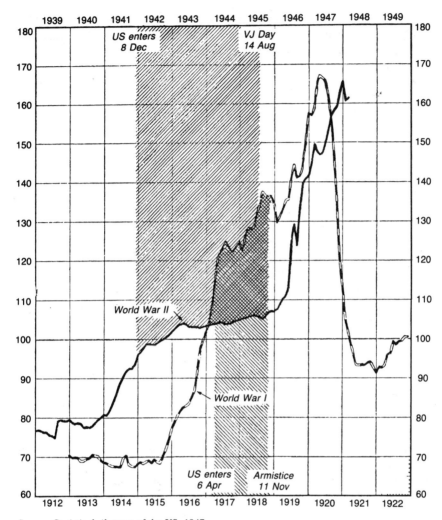

Source: *Statistical Abstract of the US*, 1947.

Figure 16.2 Wholesale Prices in Two World Wars (1926 = 100)

froze prices at March 1942 levels. This too was ineffective, partly because it did not include farm prices or wages. Even after the establishment of the Office of Economic Stabilization (October 1942), which had the power to control both wages and farm prices, inflation continued. In April 1943, Roosevelt issued a 'hold the line' order which directed war agencies to restrict wage and price increases which would inflate the consumer price index. In order to moderate wage claims, subsidy payments were used to lessen price rises; these, however, were expensive and contributed to the already increasing public debt.

Wage control posed serious problems. With labour in short supply, and costs of production guaranteed by government contracts, there was little to check the rising wage bill. Controls on wage rises would lead to a reduction in labour turnover and the creation of a more stable workforce, which would be more receptive to training. The War Labor Board, which had repersentatives from business, labour and the general public, was given responsibility for wage moderation. In July 1942 the WLB instituted the 'Little Steel' formula, which stated that a 15 per cent rise in hourly wage rates was permissible to cover the rise in the cost of living between 1 January 1941 and 1 May 1942. If workers had already received a pay increase they were entitled to less than 15 per cent, but those who had been particularly disadvantaged by the cost of living rises could be entitled to more.

The 'Little Steel' formula did not control the wage explosion. It referred only to hourly wage rates; earnings continued to rise because of overtime and incentive payments. Workers were also able to negotiate substantial fringe benefits, such as holidays with pay and pensions payable after 1945. In this way, particular industries could still attract labour. As the government had never instituted an effective policy for the direction of manpower, a freeze on earnings would have led to serious bottlenecks in the labour market. Roosevelt's 'hold the line' order was more effective in controlling wage rates, but they still increased and at a faster rate than prices.

The government was obliged to promise excess profits taxes, prices controls and subsidies in order to persuade labour to surrender its collective bargaining rights. Rationing, however, was essential once price controls were introduced, since consumers could afford to buy far more than the civilian output currently being produced. Without rationing, lengthy queues and an extensive black market would have developed. In spite of great administrative difficulties (nearly 130 million ration books were issued in 1942), certificates or stamps were required for purchases of butter, coffee, sugar, shoes and petrol. Petrol rationing had the great advantage of reducing the consumption of rubber (tyres), a scarce commodity. The day after V-J Day petrol rationing was discontinued and, by the end of 1945, only sugar was still rationed. This can be contrasted with the experience of Britain where rationing, already draconian, was extended after 1945. Rationing in the US was seen as irksome but fair; the alternative would have been a free for all, resulting in a massive waste of labour as workers searched for goods to buy.

The stability of the consumer price index between 1942 and 1945 is remarkable, even more so if compared with that of World War I (Figure 16.2). Although it had been argued that a tight monetary policy would have been equally successful in controlling inflation and would have secured additional benefits in increased output and employment (Evans, 1982), in general the price controls are considered a great success (Galbraith, 1952, 1981; Vatter, 1985). It would, however, be foolish to take the published wholesale price index at its face value. There were hidden price increases which the index cannot measure. Deterioration in quality, the elimination of discounts, the discontinuation of special services, short measures, new charges for deliveries, high black market prices and even corruption were a cost to consumers which was not calculated. (Beckhart, 1972; Rockoff, 1978). The war price index is misleading, and as a result real wages are inflated, making comparison between war and non-war periods impossible. Nevertheless, we should not underestimate the effectiveness of price controls. Inflation was far lower with the controls than it would have been without them, and prices rose steeply when controls were removed in 1946. The administration's inflation policy was, therefore, successful.

Financing the Arsenal of Democracy

Between 1941 and 1945, the total expenditure of the federal government amounted to $317 bn; as revenue was only $147 bn there was a cumulative deficit of $170 bn (Table 16.4). The Treasury, therefore, was forced to borrow large sums of money from the public and the banking system. A key factor in the Treasury's strategy was its resolve that interest rates should not rise above their current low levels. Such low rates were considered advantageous, as they had been in 1917−18, because they would enable the deficit to be financed cheaply. A further similarity with World War I occurred when the Federal Reserve became subordinate to the Treasury, which took the initiative in monetary policy during the war.

Table 16.4   Federal Government Finances, 1939−45 ($ bn; years ending June 30)

	Receipts	Expenditures	Surplus or deficit (−)	Total gross federal debt
1939	6.6	9.4	−2.9	48.2
1940	6.9	9.6	−2.7	50.7
1941	9.2	14.0	−4.8	57.5
1942	15.1	34.5	−19.4	79.2
1943	25.1	78.9	−53.8	142.6
1944	47.8	94.0	−46.1	204.1
1945	50.2	95.2	−45.0	260.1

Source: Historical Statistics of US, Colonial Times to 1970, 2 vols (Washington DC, 1975), Series Y339−42.

The Fed supported the Treasury by purchasing or selling, as required, all government securities at officially agreed prices and yields. As a result, not only were interest rates pegged but government bonds became highly liquid. The Treasury felt that the demand for securities would be increased by the ease with which they could be bought or sold, rather than by high interest rates. Low interest rates, once chosen, had to be maintained; the introduction of higher rates would have reduced the price of earlier issues and, in addition, would have created uncertainty amongst investors. If potential bond purchasers became convinced that interest rates were about to rise, they would not buy until the increase materialised.

In order to finance the colossal deficit, seven War Loans and one Victory Loan were floated. Federal Reserve Banks and commercial banks purchased these war bonds, but the Treasury was particularly successful also in encouraging their acquisition by individuals. Securities were marketed in a variety of forms to attract the small investor. Massive publicity campaigns, redolent of World War I, which harnessed the flair of Madison Avenue and the persuasive powers of cinema and sporting personalities, were used to tap the nation's reservoirs of patriotism. The public responded by spending some of their ample savings on bonds.

A potential danger of this easy money policy was that private borrowers might seize the opportunity of obtaining cheap credit for the purchase of consumer goods. A variety of factors, however, restrained the growth of private credit. The Federal Reserve exercised credit control by raising the minimum sum required for down payments; in addition, commercial banks were exhorted not to lend for such purposes. More importantly, rationing restricted the amount of consumer goods on the market and the growth of personal savings was so rapid that if such goods did become available they could be bought without credit (Chandler, 1953).

The real danger stemmed from the fact that the wartime easy money policy was highly inflationary. As a result of its adoption, the money supply rose by approximately 150 per cent during the war, outstripping both the rise in GNP and in wholesale prices. The price controls previously analysed were, therefore, essential in restricting the growth of consumer prices to 25 per cent of money supply expansion. The low interest rate strategy had the undoubted advantage that, at the end of the war, the federal debt could be serviced at far lower interest charges than those prevailing after 1918. As Trescott (1960) observes, however, a higher interest rate would have encouraged the public to hold more securities and less cash; it would also have reduced the growth of the money supply and, therefore, of inflationary pressure. The authorities had not absorbed all the financial lessons which were to be learned from World War I.

A large gap between expenditure and receipts is a feature of any war economy: the rise of public debt was a natural consequence of the understandable inability of the government to meet all war expenditure with tax revenue. Between 1941 and 1945, 46 per cent of federal expenditure was provided by taxation. This figure, although greater than the 33 per cent achieved during World War I, was below the proportion raised in taxes by both Canada and Britain. Why was the amount not higher? Any war administration has an incentive to raise as much tax revenue as possible, since the demand for finance is virtually inexhaustible. High taxation reduces the level of debt, while at the same time money taken from consumers in taxes helps to moderate inflationary pressures.

There are, however, both economic and political restraints on the amount of taxation which a government can impose. Very high levels of personal taxes can act both as a disincentive to work and as a cause of resentment. Moreover, in a democracy, extraordinarily punitive tax increases can be difficult to impose, even during a war, as electoral considerations can never be totally ignored. High taxes on company profits can lead to waste and inefficiency, the cost of which can be offset against tax bills. Raising corporate taxes does not have the same impact on consumer demand as raising income tax, although, in the interests of equity, the level of war profits must be kept in bounds by the use of fiscal penalties. In the final analysis, the amount of tax revenue raised and the speed and efficiency with which this can be done, depends upon the tax structure.

After the 1937−8 recession, several New Deal economists were converted to Keynesian economics. Although few in number, they occupied positions of influence, and when war demands first imposed a strain upon the economy they advised against tax increases until full employment had been reached (B.L. Jones, 1972). Congress also played a part in keeping the tax burden relatively low, especially in the early stages of the war; a cautious respect for the wishes of their constituents kept taxes below the levels requested by the administration. Once the US entered the war, the need for higher revenues quickly became apparent. In 1943, the pay-as-you-earn system was introduced for personal taxes. This was an important change, because it enabled the government not only to collect more revenue, but also to acquire it before inflation had reduced its value. PAYE eliminated the lag between public expenditure and tax collection; it also increased the possibility of removing purchasing power from consumers by ensuring that increases in tax rates would have an immediate effect (Stein, 1969). The revenue from individual income taxes rose from $6.4 bn in 1943 to $18.4 bn in 1945.

The next most important contribution to total federal receipts came from company taxes, which increased from $9.6 bn in 1943 to $16.4 bn in 1945. These two sources provided the government with over 70 per cent of its revenue in 1945. One of the most striking effects of the war, therefore, was the growth of direct taxation, which had accounted for only about 40 per cent of government revenue during the late 1930s. Millions of Americans had the new experience of paying income tax, and the number of individual income tax returns rose from 3.9 mn in 1939 to 42.7 mn in 1945. The broadening of the tax base had the further advantage of providing the federal government with the possibility of maintaining higher levels of public expenditure after 1945.

It is accepted that fiscal policy in World War II was a distinct improvement on that of World War I, but still disappointing. Personal taxation should have been higher in order to reduce the Treasury's dependence on the banking system to finance the war. Increased personal taxes, as we have seen, would also have resulted in lower inflation. Congress, however, showed no enthusiasm for such a policy and never fully understood the disinflationary benefits of raising income taxes (Studenski and Krooss, 1952).

The experience of full employment in World War II led not only to a universal acceptance of its desirability, but also to a conviction that it could be achieved in peace. As Stein (1969) observes, full employment had given new hope to millions of people and high profits to business. In 1944, Thomas Dewey, the Republican presidential candidate, had no doubt that the maintenance of full employment would be a priority for his administration, were he elected. Congress and most professional economists were convinced that fiscal policy would be the guarantor of future stability. Monetary policy was virtually disregarded as a useful economic tool, having failed, in the eyes of many, to cure the Depression. A majority believed that fiscal policy had demonstrated great powers during the war and with an extended tax base could be used either to stimulate or curb demand.

A wide variety of individuals with previously differing ideologies had become Keynesians. They had witnessed a massive rise in government spending which had created more jobs and called forth a phenomenal rise in output. This new euphoria was translated into legislative action. In 1946, Congress passed the Employment Act, which, although disappointing to many liberals because of the lack of the adjective 'full' in its title, was a revolutionary step for the US (Hughes, 1977). The federal government was obliged to manage, or fine tune, the economy so that the horrors of mass unemployment would never return. Thus government now had a permanent role to play in economic management, a role for which there was widespread political consensus.

America in 1945

In 1945 the American people were far wealthier than they had been in 1939. High wage jobs had been created to which millions had migrated. Many families had for years enjoyed not only the luxury of more than one wage earner, but also many hours of overtime. Some particularly disadvantaged groups had made significant economic gains. Blacks, for example, were more numerous in cities, in manufacturing jobs and in trade unions than they were before the war began. World War II, like World War I, had brought about a more equitable distribution of income. Indeed, for the period covered by this book, only war seemed able to achieve this desirable end. In spite of the euphoria, however, there was a fear that full employment might be a transitory phenomenon. Would there be sufficient jobs for the millions of men and women who were shortly to be demobilised?

The transition to civilian life for veterans was made easier by the passage of the GI Bill of Rights (1944) which gave them the opportunity, which many gratefully seized, of subsidised higher education. For others, unemployment benefit enabled job search to proceed at a relatively leisurely pace. Depression levels of unemployment did not return. In spite of the fact that the labour force continued to expand, the average annual rate of unemployment to 1970 was about 5 per cent. War had led to tremendous upheaval. Migrants welcomed the high incomes which they were able to earn, although many had to endure appalling living conditions in their new environment. Blacks, America's most numerous minority group, made advances. Even though the armed forces were still segregated at the end of the war, those who had been sent overseas became aware of cultures where the level of racial discrimination was far lower than in the US. Indeed, America had waged war against an evil, racist regime; it took little imagination to see that a war should now be waged against racism at home. Many blacks who had remained in civilian life had been freed from the shackles of share-cropping and had moved to big cities; many more would follow in the post-war decades.

Blacks and whites enjoyed increased living standards. They had, however, been denied for some years the consumer goods which they desired. As rationing was rapidly discarded, the public prepared for a major spending spree on consumer durables. Americans had not forgotten the depression but believed that the government was now in a much more powerful position to dictate to the economy, rather than vice versa.

The war had demonstrated the formidable productive power of the economy. We should, however, put this in perspective. As Vatter (1985) shows, the growth of industrial production between 1941 and 1944 was not much better than that achieved between 1921 and 1924. Nevertheless, business was able to satisfy the pent-up demands of the population, and in addition could pass on to consumers some of the benefits of wartime research and development. Big business emerged from the war with added strength (as did large-scale agriculture and big trade unions) and having gained a new respect from the public. Its war record was good; the identification with the depression was forgotten. The close links between big business, the military and the government which were forged in war remained strong in peace. Industry was keen to portray the triumphs of the war as a natural result of private enterprise, thus conveniently forgetting that much of the new industrial capacity and the productive initiatives stemmed from government intervention.

The US did not withdraw from world affairs after 1945, but became militarily and economically interventionist. The armed forces remained relatively strong in peace; they did not wither away as they had done during the 1920s. The research and development necessary to equip the military with ever more sophisticated weaponry was carried out by big corporations and universities, with the government as paymaster. Military spending had created economic prosperity in many parts of the US, not least the South. Senators and Congressmen were anxious to ensure that such expenditure continued after the war and an expanding military industrial complex became a prominent feature of the post-war economy.

In this context it is important to remember just how powerful, relatively and absolutely, was the US economy in 1945. Germany and Japan lay in ruins; Italy and France were in economic disarray. Even Britain, who had not been invaded, faced serious problems of readjustment to a peacetime economy. America was the major source of the raw materials, manufactured goods and foodstuffs which all nations required; none, however, had sufficient dollars to purchase in any quantity. US aid was vital for Europe in 1945, though a systematic plan did not emerge until Secretary of State George Marshall outlined the Marshall Plan in 1947.

Federal intervention in the economy did not begin with the New Deal but there is no doubt that it intensified during that period. The war also gave the government a higher profile, which it maintained after 1945. Not only were New Deal obligations continued, for example in social security and in farm price supports, but people increasingly looked to Washington for economic guidance. The rest of the world also looked to Washington for leadership in the United Nations, for support in setting up the International Monetary Fund, and for Marshall Aid. The federal government's new international role and its determination to fine tune the domestic economy contrast sharply with the attitudes of the 1920s.

Bibliography

A. Millward has written an excellent history of the global impact of hostilities which enables the reader to put the changes in the US economy into international perspective. Concentrating on the United States, the comprehensive volume published by the US Bureau of the Budget, and the more recent study by H.G. Vatter, provide sufficient information for a detailed understanding of the war economy. Any analysis of agriculture during this period relies heavily on W.W. Wilcox. The intricacies of war finance are expertly outlined in P. Studenski and H.E. Krooss; H. Stein is the best guide to fiscal policy. Two first-rate regional studies, by G.D. Nash on the West and by G. Wright on the South, are essential reading for any one interested in the power of war to generate change. Finally, J.M. Blum, G. Perrett, and R. Polenberg serve as admirable introductions to the social transformation which took place within the United States between 1941 and 1945.

Anderson, K. (1981) *Wartime Women: Sex Roles, Family Relations and the Status of Women during World War II*, Greenwood Press.
Bailey, S.K. (1950) *Congress Makes a Law: The Story behind the Unemployment Act of 1946*, Columbia University Press.
Beckhart, B.H. (1972) *The Federal Reserve System*, American Institute of Banking.
Benedict, M.R. (1953) *Farm Policies of the United States 1790–1950*, Twentieth Century Fund.
Bernstein, B. (1966) 'The automobile industry and the coming of the Second World War', *South Western Social Science Quarterly*, 47.
Blum, J.M. (1976) *V Was For Victory*, Harcourt Brace Jovanovic.
Brody, D. (1975) 'The New Deal and World War II', in J. Braeman, *et al.*, *The New Deal: The National Level*, Ohio State University Press.
Brogan, H. (1985) *Longman History of the United States of America*, Longman.
Carr, L.J. and Stermer, J.E. (1952) *Willow Run: A Study of Industrialisation and Cultural Inadequacy*, Harper.
Chafe, W. (1970) *The American Woman: Her Changing Social, Economic and Political Roles 1920–1970*, Oxford University Press.
Chandler, L.V. (1951) *Inflation in the United States 1940–48*, Harper.
Chandler, L.V. (1953) *The Economics of Money and Banking*, Harper.
Clive, A. (1979) *State of War: Michigan in World War II*, University of Michigan Press.
Collins, R.M. (1981) *The Business Response to Keynes 1929–1964*, Columbia University Press.

Evans, P. (1982) 'The effects of general price controls in the United States during World War II', *Journal of Political Economy*, 90.

Fairchild, B. and Grossman, J. (1987) *The Army and Industrial Manpower*, Greenwood Press. First published in 1959.

Flynn, G.Q. (1979) *The Mess in Washington: Manpower Mobilization in World War II*, Greenwood Press.

Freeman, J. (1978) 'Delivering the goods: industrial unionism during World War II', *Labor History*, 19.

Galbraith, J.K. (1952) *A Theory of Price Control*, Harvard University Press.

Galbraith, J.K. (1981) *A Life in Our Times*, Houghton Mifflin.

Gordon, R.J. (1969) '$45 billion of US private investment has been mislaid', *American Economic Review*, 59.

Harris, H.J. (1982) *The Right to Manage: Industrial Relations Policies of American Business in the 1940s*, University of Wisconsin Press.

Hughes, J.R.T. (1977) *The Government Habit: Economic Controls from Colonial Times to the Present*, Basic Books.

Janeway, E. (1951) *Struggle for Survival: A Chronicle of Economic Mobilization in World War II*, Yale University Press.

Jones, B.L. (1972) 'The role of Keynesians in wartime policy and postwar planning, 1940–1946', *American Economic Review*, LXII, May.

Jones, J.H. (1951) *Fifty Billion Dollars: My Thirteen Years with the RFC*, Macmillan.

Jungk, R. (1958) *Brighter than a Thousand Suns: The Moral and Political History of the Atomic Scientists*, Harcourt Brace.

Koistinen, P.A.C. (1973) 'Mobilizing the World War II economy: labor and the industrial military alliance', *Pacific Historical Review*, 42.

Lichtenstein, N. (1982) *Labor's War at Home: The CIO in World War II*, Cambridge University Press.

Lingeman, R.R. (1970) *Don't You Know There's a War On?*, Putnam.

Long, C.D. (1944) *The Labor Force in Wartime America*, NBER, New York.

Long, C.D. (1958) *The Labor Force under Changing Income and Employment*, Princeton University Press.

Mikesell, R.F. (1952) *United States Economic Policy and International Relations*, McGraw-Hill.

Milward, A. (1977) *War, Economy and Society 1939–1945*, Allan Lane.

Nash, G.D. (1985) *The American West Transformed: The Impact of the Second World War*, University of Indiana Press.

Nelson, D. (1946) *The Arsenal of Democracy: The Story of American War Production*, Harcourt Brace.

Perrett, G. (1973) *Days of Sadness, Years of Triumph: The American People 1939–45*, Coward, McCann and Geoghegan.

Polenberg, R. (ed.) (1968) *America at War: The Home Front, 1941–1945*, Prentice-Hall.

Polenberg, R. (1972) *War and Society: The United States 1941–1945*, Lippincott.

Polenberg, R. (1980) *One Nation Divisible: Class, Race, and Ethnicity in the United States since 1938*, Viking Press.

Ransom, R.L. (1982) 'In search of security: the growth of government spending in the United States, 1902–1970', in R.L. Ransom et al., (eds) *Explorations in the New Economic History: Essays in Honor of Douglas C. North*, Academic Press.

Rockoff, H. (1978) 'Indirect price increases and real wages during World War II', *Explorations in Economic History*, 15, October.

Schultz, T.W. (1945) *Agriculture in an Unstable Economy*, McGraw-Hill.

Shepherd, G.S. (1947) *Agricultural Price and Income Policy*, The Iowa State College Press.

Stein, H. (1969) *The Fiscal Revolution in America*, University of Chicago Press.

Studenski, P. and Krooss, H.E. (1952) *Financial History of the United States*, McGraw-Hill.
Tindall, G.B. (1967) *The Emergence of the New South, 1913–1945*, Louisiana State University Press.
Trescott, B. (1960) *Money, Banking and Economic Welfare*, McGraw-Hill.
US Bureau of the Budget (1946) *The United States at War: Development and Administration of the War Program by the Federal Government*, Washington DC.
Vatter, H.G. (1985) *The US Economy in World War II*, Columbia University Press.
Wilcox, W.W. (1947) *The Farm in the Second World War*, The Iowa State College Press.
Wright, G. (1986) *Old South, New South: Revolutions in the Southern Economy since the Civil War*, Basic Books.

Index